# RECORDS

*—of the—*

# TOWN *of* PLYMOUTH

**PUBLISHED BY ORDER OF THE TOWN**

VOLUME 1

1636 TO 1705

*Wm. T. Davis, et al.*

HERITAGE BOOKS
2010

# HERITAGE BOOKS
*AN IMPRINT OF HERITAGE BOOKS, INC.*

**Books, CDs, and more—Worldwide**

For our listing of thousands of titles see our website
at
www.HeritageBooks.com

A Facsimile Reprint
Published 2010 by
HERITAGE BOOKS, INC.
Publishing Division
100 Railroad Ave. #104
Westminster, Maryland 21157

Originally published
Plymouth:
Avery & Doten, Book and Job Printers
1889

— Publisher's Notice —

In reprints such as this, it is often not possible to remove blemishes from the original. We feel the contents of this book warrant its reissue despite these blemishes and hope you will agree and read it with pleasure.

International Standard Book Numbers
Paperbound: 978-1-55613-181-3
Clothbound: 978-0-7884-8564-0

# PREFACE.

At the annual meeting of the Town of Plymouth held on the seventh of March, 1887, it was voted, on motion of Arthur Lord, "that a committee of three be appointed by the Moderator to consider the expediency of printing and publishing the whole, or any part, of the Town Records as a part of the history of the Town, and report at the adjourned meeting, with an estimate of the expense."

The committee, consisting of Arthur Lord, Charles G. Davis, and William W. Brewster, presented at the adjourned meeting, held on the 4th of April, the following report:

"The committee appointed under Article 16 of the warrant relating to the printing and publishing of the Town Records as a part of the history of the town, submit the following report:

The records of the proceedings of the town, from the date of the earliest record to the year 1828 are contained in four volumes, which are numbered and dated as follows: Vol. 1, 1660; vol. 2, 1660 to 1710; vol. 3, 1716 to 1795; vol. 4, 1795 to 1828.

The dates above given do not accurately cover the periods included in the several volumes. These volumes contain the record of all the formal action of the town, which it would be expedient, in the opinion of the committee, for the town to publish. These embrace the records of the town meetings, the laying out of highways, the grants of land by the town, and cover the important periods of local history, the union of the colonies, the various French and Indian wars, the Revolution, the war of 1812, and the interesting action of the town in relation to the Embargo, and contain much of national and public, as well as local interest, which has never been published in permanent form.

The first volume, which in the lapse of years has become somewhat illegible and worn, was copied under a vote of the town in 1824, by Rossiter Cotton, and that copy in 1860 was compared with the original and corrected by Daniel J. Robbins, under the direction of the Selectmen, in compliance with a vote of the town. A copy of volume 2 of the records was made by Daniel J. Robbins in 1860, under a vote of the town, and these copies, with the certificates of the copyists, are deposited for safe keeping in the Registry of Deeds.

With the aid of these copies it is believed that an accurate transcript of the records could be made for publication. The importance of their publication will be readily admitted. Within the past few years many other towns, notably Braintree, Dedham and Groton, have caused to be published their early records, and the wider interest in the Plymouth records affords a much stronger argument than exists in those towns for their publication.

The committee have considered mainly the question of expense, believing that the only opposition to the publication of the town records would arise on that ground. From estimates which have been submitted to them by responsible printers here and in Boston, it is believed that the expense of the publication of an edition of one thousand copies of one volume of about three hundred pages, which would include all the records in the first volume of town records and part of the second would be about one thousand dollars. This would include all the records to a date subsequent to 1700.

The committee are assured that an edition of that size could be readily disposed of at a price which would repay to the town all money by it expended in its publication; so that all the burden the town would assume would be the granting of the use of the money necessary until the edition was sold.

Believing that under this view of the matter the town would

PREFACE. VII

gladly incur the slight expenditure to insure the publication of its early records, they recommend the adoption of the vote submitted herewith.

They make no recommendation as to the publication of the remaining volumes at this time, believing that their publication can await that of this first volume, and that then the town will willingly vote to continue their publication, if experience shall show that the opinion of the committee as to their probable cost to the town was correct."

In accordance with the above recommendation of the committee it was voted "that a committee of five, of whom the Moderator shall be one, be appointed by the chair with authority to print or publish, at a cost not exceeding one thousand dollars, so much of the town records as a part of the history of the town as they shall deem expedient, and that the Selectmen be authorized to borrow a sum of money not exceeding such amount as may be required to carry out this vote."

The committee as appointed by the chair consisted of the Moderator Wm. T. Davis, Arthur Lord, Charles G. Davis, Wm. W. Brewster and Thomas B. Drew. The editorial management of the publication was placed by the committee in the hands of the chairman, whose introductory chapter will further explain its character and scope.

The present volume of three hundred and thirty-six pages includes the first volume of town records, and ninety-eight pages of the second, closing with the record of the town meeting held May 21st, 1705.

It is the hope of the committee that sufficient interest will be excited by the volume to secure a continuance of the work of publication.

Wm. T. Davis,
Arthur Lord,
Charles G. Davis,
Wm. W. Brewster,
Thomas B. Drew,
*Committee of Publication.*

Plymouth, Nov. 15th, 1889.

# INTRODUCTION.

The records of Plymouth, exclusive of the records of births, deaths and marriages, are contained in nine volumes, the first covering the period from 1636 to 1692; the second from 1692 to 1716; the third from 1716 to 1795; the fourth from 1795 to 1828; the fifth from 1828 to 1854; the sixth from 1854 to 1866; the seventh from 1866 to 1878; the eighth from 1878 to 1887, and the ninth from 1887 to the present time.

These records have been kept by Nathaniel Sowther from 1636 to April, 1645; by Nathaniel Morton from March, 1647, to June, 1685; by Thomas Faunce from July, 1685, to May, 1723; by John Dyer from March, 1723-4, to March, 1732-3; by Gershom Foster from March, 1732-3, to March, 1733-4; by John Dyer again from March, 1733-4, to March, 1739-40; by Edward Winslow from March, 1739-40, to January, 1741-2; by Samuel Bartlett from January, 1741-2, to March, 1766; by John Cotton from March, 1766, to March, 1767; by Ephraim Spooner from March, 1767, to April, 1818; by Thomas Drew from April, 1818. to March, 1840; by Timothy Berry from March, 1840, to March, 1852; by Leander Lovell from March, 1852, to March, 1878, and from March, 1878, to the present time by Curtis Davie, the present Town Clerk.

Nathaniel Sowther was chosen Clerk of the Colony Court on the third of January, 1636-7, in obedience to a law passed probably November 15, 1636. Before that time the Plymouth Colony records were kept by the different Governors, William Bradford, Edward Winslow and Thomas Prence, and are in their handwriting. At the time of the passage of the above law another law was passed providing "that every man's marke of his cattle be brought to the towne book where he lives and that no man give the same but shall alter any other brought by him and put his owne upon them."

There was no Town Clerk at the time of the passage of this law, and Mr. Sowther, as clerk of the Colony Court, opened a "town

## INTRODUCTION.

book" and made the entries relating to marks of cattle to be found on the opening pages of this volume.

These entries, which are not dated, must have been made between November 15th, 1636, the date of the passage of the law and the last day of March, 1637, the date of the succeeding entry. Not only was there no Town Clerk at that date, but it is difficult to define the exact point of time when Plymouth became a town. It was never incorporated, nor ever by any act of colonial legislation created into a municipality. Its first recognition by the General Court as a town was in an order passed on the 28th of October, 1633, "that the chiefe governm$^t$ be tyed to the towne of Plymouth and that the Gov$^r$ for the time being be tyed there to keepe his residence & dwelling, and there also to hold such Courts as concern the whole."

The bounds of the town were not fixed by law until the second day of November, 1640, when it was ordered by the Court of Assistants : "Whereas by the act of the General Court held the third of March in the sixteenth year of his said Majestie's now reign (1639–40) the Governor & Assistants were authorized to set the bounds of the several townships it is enacted and concluded by the Court that the bounds of Plymouth township shall extend southwards to the bounds of Sandwich township and northward to the little brook falling into Black Water from the commons left to Duxbury and the neighborhood thereabouts and westward eight miles up into the lands from any part of the bay or sea; always provided that the bounds shall extend so far up into the woodlands as to include the South Meadows toward Agawam lately discovered and the convenient uplands thereabouts."

For the want of a more certain date the 28th of October, 1633, when the order was passed by the Court of Assistants making the town of Plymouth the seat of the colonial government, may be properly considered the true period of the birth of the town as distinct from the Colony of New Plymouth. The town records were not begun, however, until three years later, when, as has been stated, Nathaniel Sowther, the Clerk of the Colonial Court, entered the marks of cattle in obedience to the requirements of law. The two clauses on the second page of this volume relating to the cattle of Nathaniel and John Morton, and dated 1653, are not parts of the original record, having been interlined by Nathaniel Morton at that date, after he became Clerk of the Colonial Court and assumed the functions of Town Clerk.

## INTRODUCTION. XI

Of Nathaniel Sowther little is known. He appeared in Plymouth in 1635, and was made a freeman on the 4th of October in that year. He was chosen Clerk of the Colonial Court, as above stated, on the third of January, 1636-7, and was succeeded by Nathaniel Morton in 1647. In 1638 he bought of Lieut. Wm. Holmes a house lot where the northerly row of tombs now stands on burial hill, and there lived until his removal to Boston, about the year 1649. He died in 1655, leaving no male descendants. By a first wife, Alice, who died in 1651, he had two daughters; Hannah, who married Wm. Hanbury, and Mary, who married Joseph Starr. In 1655 he married a second wife, widow Sarah Hill. It has been thought by some that his name Sowther was identical with that of Southworth, but in the records he invariably spelled it either Sowther or Souther, while the name of Southworth, which he had frequent occasion to write, he always spelled either Southworth or Southwood. It is a little singular that the pronunciation of Southworth at the present day as a christian name is almost always in accordance with the Southwood spelling which disappeared from the records at a very early day.

There was no provision of law for a Town Clerk during Mr. Sowther's term of service, and he continued to keep the town records as the Clerk of the Colony. The only requirement touching the subject was contained in an order passed by the General Court on the third of March, 1645-6, "that the Clarke or some one in every towne do keepe a register of the day and yeare of every marryage byrth and buriall & to have 3$^d$ a peece for his paynes." This order did not specifically require the appointment of a Town Clerk, and as long as the records were kept by the Clerk of the Colony in distinct town books, the demands of the order were satisfied.

The last entry made by Mr. Sowther bears the date of April 8, 1645, and the first entry of his successor, Nathaniel Morton, that of March 4, 1647. The last entry made by Mr. Sowther in the Colonial Court records bears date July 7, 1646, and the first made by Mr. Morton that of December 7, 1647. The gap in the Colonial records is filled chiefly by the handwriting of Wm. Bradford, then Governor, one single entry having been made apparently by the same unknown hand which fills the gap in the town records.

No record exists of the precise time when Nathaniel Morton was appointed Clerk of the Colonial Court. It is only known that he entered his first record of the proceedings of the Court on the 7th

## INTRODUCTION.

of December, 1647, and his first record of the town on the 4th of the following March. The office held by him and Mr. Sowther was that of "clarke" until March 5, 1667-8, at which date he for the first time signed his name as secretary. Like his predecessor, he kept the town records in his capacity as Colonial Clarke or Secretary until the 4th of August, 1679, when, as appears from the record on page 160 of this volume, he "was sworne Clarke of the Towne of Plymouth for this present yeer."

Mr. Morton is known not only as the Secretary of Plymouth Colony, but as the author of "New England's Memorial" published in 1669. He was born in 1613, and came to Plymouth in the Ann with his father, George Morton, in 1623. He married in 1635 Lydia Cooper, and one of his children, Remember Morton, married in 1657 Abraham Jackson, the ancestor of a family which has always been prominent in the Old Colony. He lived for many years on the estate now occupied by Frederick L. Holmes, adjoining Hob's Hole Brook, but in the latter part of his life until his death he occupied a house which stood on the easterly side of Market Street, immediately above the estate of Mrs. John B. Atwood. His last entry in the town records is dated May 18th, 1685, and he died on the 28th of the following month.

Thomas Faunce was chosen Town Clerk July 6, 1685, and his first entry was the record of the meeting at which he was chosen. He served until May 13th, 1723, at which date his last entry was made. He was born in 1647, and notwithstanding he was an old man at the date of his retirement, he lived until the 27th of February, 1745, after he had entered his ninety-ninth year. He was the son of John Faunce, who came in the Ann in 1623, and he married in 1672 Jean, daughter of William Nelson. His mother was Patience Morton, a sister of Secretary Morton, his predecessor in office. He was the last ruling elder of the First Church, having succeeded Elder Thomas Cushman, who died on the 10th of December, 1691. During the closing years of his life Mr. Faunce lived in Chiltonville, on the southwesterly side of the old Manomet Road, a little north of the Eel River Bridge. As his term of service as Clerk extended beyond the period covered by this volume, a reference to his successors will be reserved for future publications of the records.

This volume is largely devoted to grants of land by the town and the bounding out of lands granted by the Colonial Court. Such records are somewhat dry in their details, but they disclose the methods, most interesting to the antiquary and historian, by which the foundation of our land titles was originally laid. The grants of lands by the Colony Court began before the town had secured any possessory rights, and the grants or sales made by the town did not cease until the present century had opened.

Until the spring of 1624 the tillage lands of Plymouth were used in common. At that time, as Bradford says, the Pilgrims "began now highly to prize corn as more precious than silver, and those that had some to spare began to trade one with another for small things, by the quart, pottle and peck; for money they had none, and if any had corn was preferred before it. That they might therefore increase their tillage to better advantage, they made suit to the Governor to have some portion of land given them for continuance, and not by yearly lot, for by that means that which the more industrious had brought into good culture (by such pains) one year, came to leave it the next and often another might enjoy it; so as the dressing of their lands were the more sleighted over and to less profit; which, being well considered, their request was granted."

In compliance with the above request, one acre of land was given to each person. Sixty-nine acres were given to those who came in the Mayflower, including twenty-nine acres between the town brook and Fremont Street, east of Sandwich Street, sixteen on Watson's Hill, five between the Burial Hill and Murdock's Pond, and nineteen between Court Street and the harbor, bounded on the north by the Railroad Park.

Thirty-three acres were given to those who came in the Fortune in 1621, including six acres immediately north of the Railroad Park, eight immediately north of the second or Woolen Mill Brook, and nineteen between the first, or Shaw's Brook, and the Second Brook.

Ninety-five acres were granted to those who came in the Ann and the Little James in 1623, including forty-five acres lying north of the Second Brook and extending across the Third, or Cold Spring Brook, and fifty acres lying on both sides of Hob's Hole Brook, and along the shore farther south.

These lands, including one hundred and ninety-seven acres within a territory not more than two and a half miles long, and a quarter of a mile wide, were doubtless the old cleared corn lands of the Indians. Their grants are recorded in the Plymouth Colony Records.

## INTRODUCTION.

The second division of lands also recorded in the Plymouth Colony Records was made January 3, 1627, when each free holder received twenty acres.

Up to the year 1651 the Colony granted and laid out to Freemen in different parts of the town lots varying in size from five to one hundred acres. Plymouth, at that time, included Plympton, Kingston, Carver, and a part of Halifax. Jones' River Meadows lying in what are now Kingston and Plympton, were granted to eight men in 1640. In the same year the South Meadows were granted to eighteen men, and Dotie's Meadows to five men. All these grants are recorded in the Colony Records. The bounding out of many of these grants was subsequently made by the Town Surveyors and recorded in the Town Records.

The Winnatucksett Meadows, the Monponsett Meadows, the Punckatesett lands in what is now Tiverton, and lands in Freetown, which belonged to the town, were granted by the town, and their bounds are entered in the Town Records. Indeed, all the lands included within the original limits of Plymouth are granted and bounded out in either the Colony, Town or Proprietors' Records except a small part of Halifax, the bounds of which are recorded in the Pembroke and Middleboro records, and are a part of the major's and twenty-six men's purchase added to Halifax, and a small part of Carver, which the Proprietors of the South Purchase of Middleboro laid out by mistake within the bounds of Plymouth, and are bounded out in the records of the South Purchase of Middleboro.

On the 9th of February, 1701-2, a lot of thirty acres was granted by the town to every proprietor or freeman, and on the 16th of the following month it was voted that all the lands not disposed of within a tract a mile and a half square, should be held by the town, and all the unallotted lands outside of that tract should be granted to the freemen of the town. The boundaries of the mile and a half may be found in a foot note on the 296th page.

Before the consummation, however, of this grant to the proprietors the town voted on the twenty-fourth of May, 1703, that all the common land described on page 314 should be devoted to a sheep pasture, but after the failure of this enterprise the lands were disposed of, as stated in the foot note on the above mentioned page.

The proprietors, under the above grant, two hundred and one

## INTRODUCTION.    XV

in number, organized, with the choice of Thomas Faunce as clerk, on the 26th of December, 1704, and on the 3d of the following January each proprietor received a twenty acre lot, and soon after a sixty acre lot. After the incorporation of the town of Plympton, on the 4th of June, 1707, the proprietors took the name of the Plymouth and Plympton Proprietors, and after the cedar swamps which had been previously surveyed by order of the town by Jacob Tompson had been divided in thirty-nine lots among the members, all the remaining lands, including more than thirty thousand acres, except a few strips and gores were laid out in ten great lots and also divided.

The successors of Thomas Faunce as Clerk of the Proprietors were Samuel Bartlett, chosen May 25, 1747; John Cotton, chosen April 6, 1767, and Rossiter Cotton, chosen March 31, 1790, soon after which date the affairs of the proprietors were closed. Their records contained in two volumes are deposited with the records of the town.

The land within the mile and a half tract was disposed of by the town at various times a few lots at the base of Burial Hill, on School Street, as late as the year 1810. The only lots remaining unsold, so far as the editor knows, are Training Green, Cole's Hill, Burial Hill, a part of Court Square, once called the "great gutter," a triangle of land at the foot of Middle Street, in the rear of the old Bramhall store, a strip twelve feet wide at the junction of Sandwich and Water Streets, a lot on School Street, two lots on South Street and the South Pond Road, ninety-four acres of woodland at New Guinea, on both sides of the Kingston line, Town Dock, and a hundred acres of woodland at Manomet Ponds, given by the Proprietors to the town for the benefit of the Indians.

In the preparation of his work for the press the editor has made a transcript of the original records, following closely their punctuation, orthography and use of capital letters. In some instances words have been supplied by the copies above mentioned where their illegibility or loss has occurred since the copies were made. In all other instances lost words are indicated by stars.

The numbers enclosed in square brackets show the numbers of the corresponding pages in the original records.

It will be observed that in some instances entries have not been made in chronological order. One of these will be found on the 26th page, another on page 208, others on pages 214, 215, 216, 218 and 329, and in various other places in the volume. These irregularities are to be accounted for in various ways. The original first volume of records was at some time in such a dilapidated condition that its leaves were separated and pasted at their inner edges on blank sheets of paper and rebound. In the arrangement of these sheets many of these irregularities occurred. It is evident also that there were loose papers in the town archives thought worthy of preservation which were inserted in the volume at the time it was rebound, without regard to their dates. In some instances these sheets were probably copied and entered wherever in any part of the original volume there was sufficient blank space.

It must be remembered in connection with the dates of various entries that until 1752 the year began in England and its colonies on the 25th of March, and that double dates were often applied to all days between the 1st of January, and the 24th of March, inclusive. Thus an entry made on the 10th of February, 1750, old style, would be 1751, new style, and would be dated 10th of February, 1750–1.

In conclusion, the editor trusts that the work on which he has bestowed much careful labor will meet the approval of both the committee of which he is a member and of the town whom he serves.

W. T. D.

# PLYMOUTH RECORDS.

(NOTE.—A law was passed by the Colony Court, November 15, 1636, "That every mans marke of his Cattle be brought to the towne book where he lives and that no man give the same but shall alter any other brought by him and put his owne upon them.")

[1.] * Bartlet a peece cut out of the right eare before and * out of the left eare behind.

* Church [1]cropt on both eares and a slitt in the downewarde.
* Little a slit in the further eare.
* Higgens a peece cut out behind in the right eare a slitt cut in the same place.

Edmund Chandler a slit cutt in the neather side of the left eare under the eare.

Steephen Tracy a slitt under each eare.

Richard Sparrow the top of the right eare cut of and two notches cut out of each side hether eare.

Mr John Weekes a swallow tayle cut out on the left eare.

William Pontuss swallow cropt upon the * and a snip cut out upon the outside of the right eare.

[2.] * * * * * * * *

Mris ffuller a half cut out behind the right eare.

Christopher Waddesworth a swallow forke * * and a sn'p not cut out.

Georg Soale a peece cut out like a + of the under side of the right eare downewarde.

Josias Cooke a half round cut out upon * and a peece cut out round upon the back side of * .

Experience Michell cutt with this mark △ *.

John Tilden cutt with this mark ± in the right *.

* Alden a peece like a long round cut * *.

[2] John Dunhame two scotches upon the right eare *.

John Cooke the yonger a peece cutt out from the top * of the eare almost upon the outside of the right eare.

---

[1] Sliced off at the top.
[2] This line is erased in the records by lines drawn through it.

ffrancis Cooke a hole in the left eare and a slit in the right eare downe the middest of the eare.

[3.] Mr Thomas Prence three marks in the outer side of the eare thus

Leiftennant Willm Holmes foure marks in the fore side of the far eare thus

Jonathan Brewster a crop upon the nar eare and * of fur eare cutt of.

1653. Nathaniell Morton the markes of his mare two holes in each eare her naturall markes of a black couller * tending to an iron gray being whit on the * the topp of her head downward and for his other cattle an hole in each eare.

Nehemiah Smyth a slit into the middest of the left eare the under peece cutt forth toward the root.

Steven Bryants marke a slit in the le_t eare on the topp of the eare.

Thos: Popes marke the topp croped of the farr eare and out of the same eare on the right side.

Mr Atwood cropt upon the left eare and a hole in the other.

Abigaill Clarke a halfe moone on the right eare.

Mr Browne a round hole in the nar eare and on the right eare * * on both sides thus (o).

1653. John Mortons marke a peece cut out of the neare eare and a snipp kutt of the same eare my Mare coulte a starr of white in the forehead and two hinde feete white the horse coulte * and a tipp of white on the Nose and for cattell the Marke aforesaide.

John Wood a hollow cut out on the top of right yeare.

Giles Rickett the top of the left yeare cutt of and a slit upon the same yeare.

[4.] Leiftennant Southworth the marke of his Cattle is a cropp on the left eare.

John Dunhame senior the marke of his Cattle is a croch on the left eare.

[5.] The last day of March 1637.

It is concluded upon at a Townes meeting that Nicholas [1] shall repaire the Hering ware and draw and divide the Hering this yeare and shall have foure and fourty bushells of Indian corne for his paynes but the Town shall pay him for the boards used about the repaire thereof. And it is agreed also that * shall bring the corne to his house which shalbe due for * of hering as he hath by the last day of January upon * that he that shall make default herein shall pay a fourth more and shall pay the officer for distraining for *

William Nelson is hyred to keep the cowes this yeare at the same wages he had the last year wich is 50 bushells of Indian corne and is to keep them untill the middle of November next.

[7.] Mr Prence Gov<sup>r</sup>.

At a meeting of the Townesmen of New Plymouth held at the Govnors the XVIth day of July 1638 all the Inhabitants from Jones River to the Eele River being * thereunto To consider of the disposition of the stock given (by Mr James Shurley of [2] London merchant) to the poore of Plymouth who had playnely declared by severall letters in his owne hand writing that his intent therein was * wholly to the poore of the Town of New Plymouth * wordes of the said lres recorded it doth most playnely appear. And whereas there was some difference how farr the Town of New Plymouth doth now pperly extend because some have extended the same as farr as betwixt the said Rivers in regard the constablery and liberties of the said Towne extend themselves so farr yet after much agitation and allegations made It was concluded that the Inhabitants of the said Towne of New Plymouth dwelling betwixt the houses of Willm Pontus and John [3] Dunham on the south and the outside of the new streete on the north side have power to order and dispose of the said stock of cowes so given as aforesaid And have thereupon nominated and appointed Thomas Prence gent Gov<sup>r</sup>. Willm Bradford and Ed-

---

[1] Probably Nicholas Snow.

[2] In March, 1623-4, Edward Winslow returned from England in the Charity, bringing with him the first cattle introduced into the Colony, and a letter from James Shurley, one of the merchant adventurers, presenting a heifer as a gift, with its increase, for the benefit of the poor of the town.

[3] The house of Wm Pontus was near the farm of Thomas O. Jackson and the house of John Dunham was near what is now called the Poor-house pond The New Streete was what is now called North Street.

ward Winslow gent and Assistants of the Gov'nt, Stephen * [1] John Done and Thomas Willet gent and John Dunhame * to have the power and authoritie for there foure next years to put forth and dispose the said stock of cowes to * the Inhabitants of the poore of the sd Towne of Plymouth as shalbe thought fitt to ptake therein, and by such * in their Judg$^{nt}$ and discretion shalbe thought meete and according to the mind of the Donor in his fores'd letters declared And also by way of curtesye to supply the wants of some others wch doe inhabite wthin the liberties of said Towne if they shall thinke fitt.

[9.] 26th July 1638.

The stock at this tyme was thus disposed.

John Shawe—foure shares } in the pyde cowe [2]
ffrancis Billington sixe shares } wch was Goodman
M$^{rs}$ Hodgkinson two shares } Shawes.

Mr John Holmes sixe shares } in the browne back
Mr Thomas Hill foure shares } cowe was at Georg
Ralph Wallen two shares } Soules.

Josuah Pratt foure shares } in the black heiffer
Thom Atkinson foure shares } wch was Henry
Samuell Eddy foure shares } Howlande.

Mr Raph Smith six shares } In the Red cow wch
Natha$^{ll}$ Sowther six shares } was Mr Smyths.

Mr Hellot six shares } In the browne back cowe
Thom Lettice six shares } wch came from Henry Howland.

There remayned more to the stock at the same tyme
Two steers in goodman Dunhams hands.
One red steere in goodman Shawes hands.
One browne steere in Mr Smyths hands and a bull calf.
One bull calfe in Georg Soules hand.
One cowe calf wch came from Henry Howland.
One old cowe in goodman Dunhams hands.
In money due to the stock £4 10s.

The cow calfe was put to Goodman Dunhame for as long as the farm cowes are and a yeare longer upon the same conditions that the cows are.

---

[1] Probably Stephen Bryant.

[2] Pyde for pied meaning spotted or speckled.

[10.] At a Townes meeting held the VIth day of February
This order was 1638 Mr Thomas Prence Govnor
agreed upon to Richard Willis
stand this year is hyred to keepe the Townes cattell for fifty
March 17th 1639. Bushels of Indian corne and is to keepe them
from the first of Aprill to the middest of November following weh must be paid by eich
man according to the number of his cattle
pportionally and according to the tyme they
are kept by him. But if the want but a month or
VI weeks of the whole tyme then they are to
pay as if they had remayned the whole tyme
and if any do refuse to pay because his cattle
went not with the heard; yet notwithstanding
he is to pay his pportion as if they had beene
hearded with the rest.

It is also agreed upon that onely the milch cows and working beasts shalbe kept about the Towne * and the rest to be remooved from the Towne in May and he that doth not remoove his other cattle then to forfeit tenn shillings a peece for every beast remayneing here.

It is likewise agreed upon that none shall suffer any calves to goe without a keeper upon penalty of five * a peece to be forfeited to the Townes use except they to be kept in enclosed grounds.

It is ordered also that none shall suffer any goates to goe without a keeper upon penalty to forfeit five shillings a peece for every default to the townes use.

It is ordered likewise that the Milner shall observe such order in stoping and loosening of the water as shalbe given by the overseers of the hering ware.

John Dunhame and Willm Pontus doe undertake to peure the hering ware repaired and drawne and what they agree for with any that shall doe the worke shalbe payd by the whole Towne according to eich in pporcon of shares.

[12.] It is lastly agreed upon That if any shall refuse or neglect to make theire fence about theire gardens betwixt his neighbour and himself whereby any losse or detryment doth accrue to his neighbour upon warning thereof given hee that hath the damnage shall cause the said fence to be made and thother to pay him what he shall disburse aboute it and if he refuse to pay it then his goods to be distrayned for it.

At a Townes meeting held the xix March 1639,

It is ordered and agreed upon That Thomas Atkins and John Wood shall repaire the hering ware this yeare and shall draw and deliver the herings to eich man according to his shares due to them and shall have ii$^s$ p thousand for their paynes of the Towne and after the same rate of the country for those the shalbe allowed to eate and for bayte and to be payd either in money or corne at Harvest at such rate as it doth then passe at from man to man.

It is also agreed upon that whosoever shall take any herings either above or below the ware after the ware is sett or shall robb the ware shall forfaite five for one.

[13.] At a Townes meeting the xvflth December 1640

The ffreemen wthin the Towne do genally consent That [1] Mr Chauncey shall have the place that he desireth to be graunted unto him if no way can be found for his staying at Plymouth but if any do goe wth him that should have lands elswhere and take them up there then there shalbe a ratable pporcon abated of the land he shall have elswhere.

Whereas there is iiii$^{lb}$ and xxx bushells of corne for a rate levyed upon Plymouth and Greens Harbour The Towne [2] appoynt That John Winslow Thom Willett and Thom Clarke shalbe added to the committee to levy men equally for the payment of it.

It is ordered That the Gov$^r$ Mr Thom Prence and Mr John Jenny wth the foure committees and Josuah Pratt shall dispose of lands for the Towne this yeare.

[15.] At a Townes meeting held the 25th March Anno Dom 1640,

It is ordered and agreed upon That all swine above three months old shalbe ringed from the first of Aprill next untill the last of October following upon the penalty of vi$^d$ a swine as often as they shalbe found runing during the said terme pvided that if any shall loose their ringes upon warneing ringe them

---

[1] Rev. Charles Chauncey came to Plymouth in 1638, and was associated with Rev. John Rayner, of the First Church, until 1641 when he removed to Scituate, where he remained until 1654, when he became President of Harvard College.

[2] After the capture of New York from the Dutch, in 1664, Thomas Willett was made its first mayor.

again psently and if any swine be complayned of to be unruly or break into mens grounds that they be yoaked also.

It is ordered that no oxen shalbe kept about the Towne except when they are wrought, upon the penalty of xd a peece.

The like penalty for any young cattell that shalbe kept about the towne except they be kept on the south side the towne with a keeper.

It is ordered and agreed upon that Willm Pontus Thomas Lettice and John Greemes shall repaire the hearing ware and draw yt and deliver out the shares and to have xviiid p thousand and are to hold yt three yeares save that in regard of the charges this yeare in repaireing the ware if they shall not be sufficiently paid for their paines for this first yeare and make it appeare to the Gov$^r$ then at his discretion to allow them iid p thousand on so much as he shall think fitt, but if any of them misbehave himself therein the Towne shall choose another in his steade.

[16.] At a Townes meeting held the xxith Aprill 1641 Concerneing the killing of wolves It is agreed upon that every housholder wthin the Towneship shall pay a half penny for every pson in his famyly to him that shall kill a woolfe for every woolfe that is killed wthin the liberties of this Towneship (except poore psons that have not cattell) and shall bringe the skinn to Mr John Jenney and there receive corne for his pay but Mr Jenney shall have the skinn for his paynes in delivering forth the corne.

Whereas Clarkes Iland is graunted to the Towne of Plymouth and Mr John Jenney is desirous to set up the makeing of salt there The Townesmen of Plymouth to further the said worke doth graunt the said John Jenney and his assignes the wood upon the said Iland for makeing of salt there, and liberty to make use of the said Iland for planting so long as he or his assignes shall make salt upon the said Iland and that none shall cutt wood there wthout consent of the said John Jenney or his assignes and shall sell the Townesmen of Plymouth good salt for two shillings the bushell pvided that the said John Jenney shall not hereafter assigne the said salt works to any man wch not of the Towne of Plymouth wthout the Townesmen's consent.

The Committees for the count are
{ Mr John Jenney
  Mr John Atwood
  Mr John Howland
  Mr W$^m$ Paddy

At a Townes meeting held the xxvith November 1641

It was agreed that Mr Willm Paddy Thom Willett Thomas Clarke John Dunhame & John Winslowe shall make and assesse the Rate for the publike charges of this Towne this yeare.

[Then considerations were pposed about hemp and flax dressing.]

[17.] At a Townes meeting held the second of May 1642,

It is agreed upon that Mr Bradford will fynd a Bull for the Towne Cowes this summer hee shall have vi$^d$ a head for every cowe in the heard that is in the Bill and likely to take proofe.

It is agreed That all that will not remove their yong cattell and oxen and all others that give not milk by the ixth day of May next shall pay xd a head ymmediately to the Townes use as oft as they shalbe found about the Towne during the Summer (except the oxen whilst they work and those to be payed for their keeping according to the Rate for the Townes cowes.

Willm Baker is to keepe the Townes Cowes this sumr. and is to have xxxvi bushells of corne and a paire of hose and shoes and his tyme to begin the fourth of May and to continue to the last October following.

The xxiiith of May 1642

At a towns meeting It is agreed that Mr Winslow shall have power to sell the two oxen at Josias Winslowes (so that he take good securitie for the payment for them and the comodities received for them to be brought to Plym to Mr Paddys house to be disposed by him the rest appoynted for the overseeing and ordering the poores stock.

[19.] 1642

At a Townes meeting held the viith July for disposeing of the Townes stock of cattell called the Poores Cattell before Mr Bradford Mr Thomas Prence Mr John Jenney Mr Willm Paddy Mr Thomas Willett and John Dunhame appoynted with some others to dispose thereof.

| | |
|---|---|
| The Browne Cowe | } had 1 two yere old 1 yere old steere |
| Mr Holmes had | } and a steere and calf. The yeareing steere and the calf with xd was set against the two yeare steere. |

| | |
|---|---|
| | And Mr Holmes had the yereling steere and the calf and the 10d and the two yeare old steere remained to the stock. |
| The Pyde Cowe wth John Shawe was dead | her encrease was onely a yeareling heiffer valued at 4£ John Shawe had the heiffer and is to pay the stock xxd and to bring in her hide to Goodman Hurste to be tanned. |
| The Brown black Cowe Mr Hellot Thom Lettis had is dead | her encrease is a three old steere and i yeareling heiffer The heiffer and 27d were set against the steere and Thomas Lettis had the heiffer and 27d and the stock had the steere |
| Josuah Pratts black heiffer | her encrease is i three yeare old heiffer and i cow calf. Josuah had 40.d and the cowe calf and the stock had the heiffer. |
| The Red Cowe in Mr Smythe's hande is dead | her encrease is one two yeare old heiffer valued at 54.s Mrs Smyth is to have the heiffer and to pay the stock 27.s. |

The Cowes set forth this yeare are these three.

| | |
|---|---|
| Josuah Pratt Thom Savory Anthony Savory | The heiffer they had and Josuah is to have thone half of the benefitt and Thom and Anthony Savory thother half. |
| Mr Holmes Willm Hoskins ffrancis Billington | The browne Cowe and Mr Holmes to keepe her. |
| Edmond Tilson John ffinney | the black cowe Josuah had. |

[20.] The account the division of the stock

| The stock hath oweing to yt | by John Shaw | 01. | 02. | 0 |
|---|---|---|---|---|
| | by Mrs Smyth | 01. | 07. | 0 |
| | | 02. | 08. | 0 |

|  |  | £ | s | d |
|---|---|---|---|---|
| The stock oweth | to Mr Holmes | 00. | 10. | 0 |
|  | To Thom Lettis | 01. | 07. | 0 |
|  | To Josuah Pratt | 02. | 00. | 0 |
|  | To Richard Sparrow for keeping a steer | 00. | 12. | 0 |
|  | To Mr Bradford and Thom Willet for carrying a yoke of steers to greens harbor | 00. | 02. | 3 |
|  | To Mrs Smyth | 00. | 05. | 0 |
|  | more to Richard Sparrow | 01. | 00. | 0 |
|  |  | 05. | 16. | 3 |
|  | more to Josias Winslow for wintering a yoke of steers | 01. | 10. | 0 |
|  | The stock oweth in all | 7. | 06. | 3 |

There is in the stock at this Division July 7th 1642 Three cowes in the hands of Josuah Prate Mr Holmes and Edmond Tilson as before.

It i yoake of oxen in hands of Josias Cooke
It i yoake of steeres came in this yeare
It i cowe in the hands of John Dunham
It i yoke of oxen in the hands of Josias Winslowe
It iii hides to be dressed by James Hurst.

The yoake of oxen in Josias Winslowes hands were sold by Mr Paddy for xvi£ and the cowe in John Dunham's hand for iiii£ 10.s

The totall account

|  | £ | s | d |
|---|---|---|---|
| ffor the yoke of oxen and the cowe | 20. | 10. | 0 |
| It oweing to yt by Mrs Smyth and John Shawe | 2. | 09. | 0 |

|  | £ | s | d |
|---|---|---|---|
|  | 22. | 19. | 0 |
| The stock oweth | 07. | 06. | 3 |

|  | £ | s | d |
|---|---|---|---|
| remayneing to the stock | 15. | 12. | 9 |

|  | £ | s | d |
|---|---|---|---|
| proofe | 22. | 19. | 0 |

In the stock now

There is i yoak of oxen  
three cows  
i yoak of steeres  
3 hides  
In money £15. 12. 9

[**21.**] At a Townes meeting held the xxth September 1642.

It is agreed upon by the genrall consent of the whole Towne that a fortyfycation shalbe made about the ordinance and another peece mounted and that Gov<sup>r</sup> Mr Prence, Mr Atwood Mr Jenney and Mr Paddy shall agree wth workmen to have it donn speedyly and to repaire the watchouse and make a brick chimney to it. And afterwards to make a rate for all throughout the Towneshipp.

Mr Atwood Mr Jenney Mr Paddy John Winslow Manassah Kempton Thomas Clarke and John Cooke Ju<sup>r</sup>: are appoynted to make the rate for the payment of the Clark and messengers wages.

It is agreed upon that the Gov<sup>r</sup> Mr Prence Mr Jenney Mr Paddy Mr Done John Winslow and John Cook or the major pt of them shall dispose of lands for the Town on munday come fortnight wch will be second munday in October.

September 26th.

Whereas Richard Willis by his long sickness is growne very weake and in great want It is agreed that there shalbe a contribucon gathered for him throughout the Towneship and that Manassah Kempton and Thomas Clark do it for that side of the Towne towards the Eele River and Mr Paddy and John Cooke do it in the town and thother side thereof and to take a note what every man will give him.

It is agreed that Mr Jenney Manassah Kempton and John Dunhame shall be added to the comittees to conferr and conclude with the generall Court about the war.

It is agreed that every man shall bring two peeces more of viii foote long to finish the fortyfycacon on the fort hill [1] and that Richard Church shall speedyly make the carriage for another peece of ordinance.

---

[1] Burial Hill was called Fort Hill exclusively until 1698.

[22.] At a Townes meeting holden at Plym the xiiii th of January in the xviith yeare of his ma$^{te}$ now Raigne 1642.

Concerneing the placeing and disposing of ffrancis Billingtons children according to the Act and order of the Court,

It is ordered and agreed upon that John Cooke the yonger shall have Joseph untill hee shalbe of the age of twenty and one years (being now about vi or vii years old) and fynd him meat drink and apparell during the said terme.

It is ordered that Benjamin Eaton his eldest Boy shalbe wth John Winslow upon these conditions untill he shall accomplish the age of xxi years being about xv years in march next and is to fynd him meate drink and apparell during the said terme and pay tenn pounds for his service or xxxiii s iiii d yearely pvided that if he dye before thend of said terme that then the said John Winslow shall pay pportionably to the tyme he lives and no more and the payments to be made in Countrey[2] pvided that if any man els will take him upon these condicons he may wth the approbation of the Governor and Mr. Prence.

It is ordered and agreed also that Gyles Rickett shall take another of his children a gerle aboute five years of age and shall keepe her and find her meat drink and apparell untill she shall accomplish the age of twenty years or be married with consent first so that she marry wth consent of the ma$^{trate}$ and shall have xxx s in hand with her towards the apparelling of her payd him wthin a month after she comes to him.

It is ordered and agreed likewise That Gabriell ffallowell shall have another of his children a gerle about       years of age and shall have her untill she shall accomplish the age of twenty yeares or be marryed (first happening) so that she marry with consent of the ma$^{trate}$ then being and shall fynd her meate and drinke and apparell during the said terme. And shall have wth her xxx s. payd him wthin one month after she is come to him towards the apparelling of her and shall a.so have xxxiii s. iiii d for the first three years next after the takeing of her to be payd out of that wch John Winslow is to pay yearely for Benjamin.

It is also agreed upon that the money remayneing of the poores stock shalbe to buy corne to releeve the psent extreme necessities of such as are ready to pish[2] for want of bread. And

---

[1] Country pay is here intended.

[2] "Pish" is an abbreviation of "perish."

that those that have to do in disposeing the yeares cattell shall pvide the Corne and dispose it where neede is according to their best discretion.

The Towne graunted xxx acrees of the lands of Clarks Iland to the five that make salt for xxi yeares paying a bushell of salt yearely to Josuah Pratt dureing the said terme if it be demanded.

[23.] At a Townes meeting held the xix Aprill 1643,

It is agreed upon that John Smyth shalbe the Cowe Keep for this yeare to keep the Townes Cowes and shall have fourty bushells of Indian Corne for his paynes and a paire of shoes to be equally levyd upon every man according to the number of Cowes that they shall have kept by him and he is to keepe them untill the midle of November next.

It is agreed that no oxen be kept amongst the Cowes longer than they are in worke upon payne x. s. a peece to be levyed to the Townes use.

It is ordered also That the yong cattell shalbe kept wth John Barnes and Georg Watsons cattell on thother side the brooke.

Its ordered That those that keepe two or three Bulls to serve the cattell wthall shall have two cowes kept freely for eich Bull.

The Corne levyed for the Cow Keeps psent use.
The Gov$^r$ i peck and a pottle
Mr Prence i peck and a pottle
Mr Paddy i peck and a pottle [1]
Nath$^l$ Sowther }
Mr Hanbury } i peck
Robert paddock i peck
Mr Jenney i peck and half in bisket. [bread]
Mr Done ½ peck
Thom Southwood ½ peck
Rich : Sparrow ½ peck
John wood ½ peck
Mr Willett ½ peck
Sam Hicks ½ peck
Mr Reynor ½ peck

---
[1] A pottle is a measure of two quarts.

Josias Cooke i pottle
Rich: Knowles i pottle
John ffinney i pottle
Mr Hopkins i pottle

[24.] At a townes meeting holden the xxixth May 1643
[1] It is agreed upon that all housholders wthin the Towneship shall forthwith pvide sufficient Armes according to the act of the Court for themselves and their servants able to beare armes wthin month after the 5th June next on wch day they are to trayne viz Muskett either wth snaphance [2] or matchlocks with match callivers[3] and carbines wch are allowed and also fowling peeces not above foure foote and a half long and of reasonable bore And that Mr Thom Prence Mr W$^m$ Paddy John Barnes and Mathew ffuller to view all such Armes and to certefye such as are defective And those that want either to putt in a sufficient sum or goods to pcure them or els the fyne by the said act to be extended upon them.

Those that contributed to buy Drumheads.

| | | | |
|---|---|---|---|
| Mr Bradford | 6 d | James Cole | 6 d |
| Mr Prence | 6 d | John ffinney | 6 d |
| Mr Jenney | 6 d | Thom Pope | 6 d |
| Mr Attwood | 6 d | Richard Sparrow | 6 d |
| Mr Paddy | 6 d | Robert Paddock | 6 d |
| Mr Hanbury | 6 d | Gabriell ffallowell | 4 d |
| Nath Sowther | 6 d | Richard Wright | 6 d |
| Thom Southwood | 6 d | Thom Cushman | 2 d |
| Mathew ffuller | 6 d | Willm Nelson | 2 d |
| Manasseh Kempton | 6 d | | |

It is agreed upon that ——— Russell shall have 4£ 10s to make the Causey [4] on the marsh to Joanes River bridge and to

---

[1] On the 2d of January, 1632-3, the Colony Court passed the following law: In regard to our dispsion so far asunder and the inconveniency that may befall it is further ordered that every freeman or other inhabitant of this Colony provide for himselfe and each under him able to beare arms a sufficient musket and other serviceable peece for war wth bandeleroes (bandoleers boxes containing charges of powder) and other appurtenances wth what speede may be; and that for each able pson aforesaid he be at all times after the last of May next ensuing furnished wth two pownds of powder and ten pownds of bullets and for each default in himselfe or servant to forfeit ten shillings.

[2] A snaphance was a flint lock. In 1620 the matchlocks were going out of use and the flint locks coming in. In the party of eighteen, landing on Plymouth Rock, December 11th, 1620, old style, there were probably two flint locks, one of which was carried by Miles Standish.

[3] A calliver, or caliver, was a small gun or pistol.
[4] "Causey" means "Causeway."

have ½ cwt of bread for the psent and the said sum to be levyed upon the Towne in Corne at harvest next.

Those that agreed to pvide the said bread,

Mr Prence    14 lb ⎫ and for thother 7 lb
Mr Hanbury   14 lb ⎪ other meanes must be used
John Barnes  14 lb ⎬ to pcure it pvided that it
Mr Paddy      7 lb ⎭ be in pt of payment.

[**25.**] At a Townes meeting held the xxiiiith of September 1643

It is agreed upon by the whole that there shalbe a watch kept in regard of the danger of the Indians. That all the whole Towneship shall joyne in keepeing the watch at Plymouth And that when any cannot come to do his duty in the watch the Captaine of the watch or the Corporall shall put a sufficient man in his stead and he shall pay him and if he refuse to pay he shalbe distrayned for it. That there be six men and a Corporall for one watch wch is to continue xxiiii houres from sunn sett to sunn sett and that he that comes not then to his watch and another be putt in his stead he shall pay him although he come himself.

It is agreed upon that there shalbe a watch house [1] forthwth built of brick and that Mr Grome will sell us the brick for xi s p thousand. That sd ordinance be changed for smaler peeces if they can be had.

That Nathaniell Sowther Thomas Southwood [2] John Dunhame and Thomas Cushman shall divide the number of the Inhabitants into sevrall watches according to the form order.

That Nathaniell Souther and Thomas Southwood shalbe captaines or masters of the watch thone for one weeke and thother for another weeke and so to continue as long as the watch continues. and Thom Southwood to begin.

At a Townes meeting held the ix of October 1643 for elecion of Comittees for the Court and psons to be of the Counsell of warr for the Towne &c

Mr John Done ⎫
Mr Wm Paddy ⎪ Comittee for
John Cooke ⎬ the Court
John Dunhame ⎭

---

[1] The watch-house was built on Burial Hill.
[2] Southworth.

The Govnor  
Mr Prence  
Mr Hopkins  
Mr Jenney  
Mr Paddy  
Nathl Sowther  

To be of the Counsell of war for the Towne.

Mr Hopkins Manassah Kempton John Winslow John Cooke Thom Clarke Richard Sparrow and Thomas Cushman are chosen to be Raters to rate and assesse the charges of this yeare for this Towne for the fortyfycation [1] work doun about the ordinance, for the building of the watchhouse and the officers wages (but not the bridge causey except it be finished.).

[26.] At a Townes meeting holden the xth february 1643

It is agreed That wolfe traps be made according to the order of the Court in manner following,

1 That one trap be made at Joanes River by the Governors famyly Mr Prences and Mr Hanburies and mathew ffuller and Abraham Pearce

2 That one be made at Playne Dealing [2] by Mr Combe Mr Lee ffrancis Billington Georg Clark John Shawe and Edward Dotey.

3 That one be made at Wellingsly by the Inhabits there with the help of Goodman Dunhame

4 That one be made at broken wharfe [3] by Manassah Kempton Edward Banges Richard Higgens Nathaniell Morton Nicholas Snow Anthony Snow John Jenkins Willm ffallowell Robte ffinney John and Ephraim Morton.

5 That one be made at the Towne by Mr Prence Nathaniel Sowther Thomas Southwood Mr Done John ffinney James Cole and Giles Rickett.

All these traps to be made before the next Court.

It is agreed that 50s be levyed by a rate for the Causy at Jones River bridg for the psent and when he shall have donn as much more thereon as by his bargaine he ought to do then to have the rest of his 4£ 10s to be made up by a second rate.

---

[1] On Burial Hill.  
[2] "Playne Dealing" was what is now called "Seaside."  
[3] Broken Wharf was near the head of the Beach.

They that made the rate for the watchouse and also to make these rates

|  |  | £ | s | d |
|---|---|---|---|---|
| Charges the fortyfine the fort last year | ffor the bridge causey | 02. | 10. | 00 |
|  | ffor Richard Church wages | 00 | 16. | 00 |
|  | ffor saw:ng the planks | 00. | 08. | 00 |
|  | ffor iron work to paddock | 00. | 04. | 00 |
|  | To Mr Groomes | 00. | 10. | 00 |
|  | for a paire of wheels | 01. | 10. | 00 |
|  | to Mr :fuller for drawing the planks to the Towne | 00. | 06. | 00 |
|  | for repaire of the stocks to John Groome | 00. | 06. | 00 |
|  |  | 6. | 10. | 00 |

Comittes now chosen
- Mr John Done
- Mr W^m Paddy
- Manasseh Kempton
- John Cooke Ju^r

Stephen Wood and Andrew Ring are to repaire the hearing ware and to have it for three yeares now next ensuing and are to have xiiiid p thousand for drawing the fish and delivering out the shares during the said terme

[27.] At a Townes meeting the xxii June 1644

In case of alarume in tyme of warr or danger these divisions of the Townesh'p are to be observed and these companys to repaire together.

At Joanes River
- Mr Bradfords famyly one
- Mr Prences one
- Mr Hanbury one
- Mr Howland one
- ffrancis Cooke one
- Phineas Pratt
- Gregory Armestrong
- John Winslow
- Mr Lee

| | | | |
|---|---|---|---|
| At the Ele River | { Thomas Little<br>Thom Williams<br>John Smith<br>Robt ffinney<br>Manasseh Kempton<br>Joseph Warren<br>Richard Church<br>Robt Bartlet<br>and the rest | | |
| Plymouth towneship according to order given | | Wellingsly | { ffrancis Goulder<br>Edmon Tilson<br>John Smaley |

And for a watch It is ordered that the watches shalbe observed as they were the last yeare vii men of a night and to beginn half an hower before the sunn sett and to pay iiii d an hower for every one that comes after And if any come not themselves nor send not a sufficient man he shalbe fyned. And Nathaniell Sowthe [1] and Thom Southwood masters of the watch.

Orders agreed upon by the Counsell of warr, That the leade be made up into bulletts and men hyred to do it.

That when an Alarum is made and continued in Plymouth Duxborrow or Marshfeild There shalbe twenty men sent from Plymouth and as many from Duxborrow and tenn from Marshfeild to releeve the place where the Alarum is so continued.

And when any of these places stand in neede of help upon the continuance of the Alarum Then a Beacon to be fyred or els a great fyer to be made from Plymouth upon the Galhouse hill, on the Captain Hill for Duxborrow And on a hill by Mr Thomas his house for Marshfeild. [2]

[28.] At a Townes meeting xxiith July 1644 for the ordering of the poores stock.

By Mr Bradford Mr Prence Mr John Done Mr Thomas Willett and John Dunhame.

Josias Cooke is to have the yoake of steeres wch are in hands untill the first of November come twelve months and is to leade for them fourty loades of wood as he shalbe appoynted.

---

[1] Sowther is here meant.

[2] Galhouse Hill was Gallows Hill, and was the high ground between Murdock's Pond and Samoset Street. The Hill in Marshfield was that lying south of the Webster Place.

There was a browne heiffer wch came in out of the xv£ wch heiffer is putt to Willm Pontus for two yeares and if she have not a calf the first yeare then he is to be payd for the wintering of her this yeare as other have, but if she have a calf then not, and to have her two yeares on the same termes other have thother Cowes.

Josuah Pratt and } Are to have the Cowe (that
Thom Savory } Josuah had) betwixt them
but Josuah to have two parts
and Thom one pte.

The Cowe that Edmond Tilson had hath a cowe calf wch the said Edmond is to winter and to have vi s out his stock for that half wch belongs to the stock.

Edmond Tilson } are to have the Cowe at Edmond
Samuell Eddy } Tilsons betwixt them, but Edmond
to have two pts and Samuel one pt
and Edmond to winter her and
Samuel pay his part thereof.

Mr John Holmes } Are to have the Cowe that is wth
Willm Nelson } Mr Holmes and every of them
John Heywood } equall parts.

In stock two oxen, two steers in Josias Cooke hand three cowes with Mr Josuah Pratt Edmond Tilson and Mr Holmes, and one heiffer wth Mr Pontus, and a cow calf wth Edmond Tilson.

These are put forth but for one yeare.

[29.] At a Townes meeting holden the xxi th November 1644

The Townes men agreed that five men should be chosen to make the Rate for the payment of the publike officers and the lott fell upon Mr W^m Paddy Mr John Howland Manasseh Kempton John Dunhame and Thom Cushman, the Rate they made was for v£ v s

The eight of Aprill 1645

Mr Bradford Mr Prence Mr Paddy Mr Done Nathaniell Souther and Thomas Southwood for and on behalf of the Towne agreed wth James Cole that his sonn Heugh Cole should keepe the Cowes this yeare from the middle of this instant Aprill untill the middle of November following and shall have fifty bushells of corne for his paynes and shall bring them up every morning to bee milked and then carry them forth to feede and bring them hoame at night. The Corne is to be equally levyed according to the number when they are brought together and eich man to pay his pporcon as it shall come to.

[30.] 1646   The disposall of ye poors stock that year.

goodman Tillson (in ye division) hath ye hefer of 2 years olde and ye stock had a yearling bull and a cow calfe. And he was to pay to ye stock 1£ 7s 6d this was paid in corne to ye use of ye pore a year after viz 5 bushells to old goodman pontis and ten bushells lent to John Dunham junior and 2 bushell still remaining in ye hands of John Dunhame which he is redy to pay. This 2 bushels of corne in goodman's donham's hand is alowed to goodman pontis. 1650. Mr Holums [1] had a 2 yearling stear valued at 2£ so he had the stear and ye stock was to have 1£ which is yett unpaid.

Josuah Prate and Thomas Savory had a yearling heafer and a Bull calfe the hefer valued at 2£ 5s and the calfe at 20s The stock is to pay them 1£ 7s 6d   That is to Josuah 18s 4d and to Thomas Saverey 9s 4d

Mr Willett bought at ye same time a yearling heafer and ye bull calfe which came from Josuah's parte and a yearling bull of Tillsons at 4£ 5s paid as folloeth to Josuah 18s 8d and to Tho: Saveray 9s 4d paid more for ye poors use 8 yeards of coten at 2s per yeard 16s 5d more to Tho. Clark for exchange of a beast and 15s for wintering of a beast belonging to ye stock, rest due from Mr Willett.

The cow calfe that came from Tilson was sould to John Dunham and Sam Eedy at 18s John Dunham hath paid his part 9s in a saw which Kenebeck must answer and Eedy is still debtor.

[31.] At a towne meeting the 10 of Desem 1646

It was agreed that whosoever coms not to ye towne meeting being thereunto warned at ye time appoynted shall forfite to ye towns use for every shuch defalte 12d exept he have a sufficent and lawfull excuse.

William Hoggkins [2]<br>Christopher Winter

---

[1] Holmes is here meant.

[2] William Hoskins is here meant.

Ralph Joanes
francis Cooke
Jacob Cooke
William Spooner
Mr Howland
Joseph Ramsden
John Cooke
francis Billington
Mr Lee
Sam. Sturtevant
Edward Gray
John Shaw
Steven Briant
John Winslow
Sam King
Ephrem Tincome
Sam Cutbert
Ed Doty
Mr Holmes
James Hurst
John Howard
Willliam Nellson
John Morton
John Moses
Tho. Letice
lieutenant
Tho Southworth
James Cole
William Browne
Mr Pady
Honoris Attkins
Mr Willett
Mr Bradford
John Smyth Senior
John Thomson
Rich. Sparrow
John Wood
Tho. Sherive
Anderew Ring
Rich Wright
Gabriell ffallowell

Elder Cushman
Jos Pratt
John ffinney
Tho Savorey
Giles Ricket
Tho. Pope
Georg Wattson
John Barnes
Ed Holman
John Donham Sen
Samuell Dunham
James Glace
John Jourden
Sam. Eedy
Steven Woode
Henery Woode
Ed. Tillson
ffrancis Goulder
Tho. Whitney
Nath. Morton
John Dunham Junior
John Churchell
Manasah Kempton
Epherem Morton
Tho. Morton
Robert ffiney
Thomas Clarke
Georg Bonham
John ffance
Rich. Smith
Robert Bartlett
Tho. Little
Nath. Warren
John Smith
William harlow

[32.] At a towne meeting ye 4 Des$^r$ 1647

Mr Howland  
Mr Willet  
Mr Pady  
Manasah Kempton  
and John Donham  

were chosen to make the rate for comon charges being 3£ And allso 25 pounds for ye meeting house.

The 31 July 1652

 The division of the stock of the pore was made between The Gove'r goodman Dunham and Will Paddy. John Heywood is to keepe the cow hee had this psent yeare ensueinge :

 his Increase for ye last 2 years were a stere of year and vantage valued at 34s and a cowe-calfe of this year valued at 22s.

 in ye division he had the cow-calfe at ye prise the stock hath ye steer and is to pay him 6s

 John donham had Increase only one yearling stear valued at 34s he bought ye halfe and is to pay to William Nellson 10s and to John howard 6s.

 William Nellson hath Increase a yearling heafer valued at 50s and 2 cow-calves valued at 40s. he having a young cow before ye half only of her belonging to ye stock, valued at 5£ his part being 50s.

 the stocke is now to have ye said yong cowe wholy ye next year.

 And he is thus paid for his part, 40s in ye yong catle and 10s by John dunham as aforesaid

 John howard is to have ye cow he had this present insuing year.

 John donham is to have ye cow he had in ye same maner and John Smith likewise his.

 The old cow that is at William Nellson's is sould by us to John dunham senior for 4£ 6 bushells of rye being allready gone upon her head to francis Billington ye rest he is to make way for upon demand. William Nellson hath only now in his hand ye yong cowe afforesaid which he is to keep this insuing year.

a smale debt or 2s to
be cleared by Mr Paddys stock

     due now to ye stock 1652
     a yearling stear that came
     from John heawards cowe and
     7s. from Mr Pady and Mr Willett
     for halfe a calfe of John Smiths

[33.] Mr Bradford Governor
  March the 4$^{th}$ 1647

 Such as were apointed by the Towneship of new plymouth to dispose of lands have granted unto Thomas Little of plymouth aforsaid five acres of upland medow beyond Thomas Clarks farme at a brooke comonly called the Indian brooke [1] the medow being mutch of it nought the lower end of the said medow is to be understood the said five acres of upland medow to apertaine unto the said Thomas littell so long as after himselfe or any of his posterity shall Remayn within the limits of the towneshipe of plymouth aforsaid but if both him and them shall all depart the towneship aforsaid then yt the five acres of medow aforsaid is to Return into the lands and disposing of the aforsaid Towne of plymouth.

1646

At a Townesmeeting of the Towne of plymouth which was in october the yeare above written was granted unto John haywood of the towne aforsaid 4 acres of upland ground lying neer unto goodman hursts brooke [2] adjoyning unto the gardin plote of the said John hayward and so to extend it selfe in length into the woods westerly provided yt he alow a suffitient pasage for cattell betwexte the Swampe lying at the nether end of the land and the land it selfe.

[34.]    Christopher Winter
Mr Howland
ffrancis Cooke
Jacob Cooke
William Spooner
John Cooke
Joseph Ramsden
ffrancis Billington
Will. hoskins
Mr Lee
Samuell Sturtevant
Edward Gray
John Shaw
Samuel King
Ephraim Tinkham
Samuell Cutbert
John Dunham Junior
John howard

---

[1] At Manomet Ponds.

[2] This brook was what is now called Cold Spring Brook.

William Nellson
John Morton
John Moses   abs
Tho. Lettice
Lieutenant Southworth
James Cole sen
Willam Browne
Mr Paddy
Samuell Hickes
Captaine Willet
Mr Bradford
John Smith Jun abs
John Wood
Andrew Ring abs
Richard Wright
Gabriell ffallowell
Elder Cushman
Tho. Savory
Gyles Rickard Sen
Tho. Pope
George Watson
John Browne
Edward holman abs
John Dunham Sen
Samuell Dunham
John Jurden abs
Samuell Eedy abs
henery Wood
Edward Tillson
ffrancis Goulder
Tho. Whitney
Nathaniell Morton
John Churchell abs
Mannasses Kempton
Ephraim Morton
Tho. Morton
Robert ffinney
Tho. Clarke
Georg Bonum
Robert Bartlett
Natha Warren abs

John Smith
Willam harlow abs
John Rickard
Gyles Rickard Jun
Richard ffoster
Joseph Warren abs
Arthur hatheway
John Keithe
James Cole Junior
James Shaw
\* \* \* \* \*
Samuel ffuller
\* \* \* \*
Jonathan Dunham
Thomas Lucas

[1] [36.] Plimouth april the 6th 1706 laid out and bounded thirty six acres of land being part of the sixty acre lot of Mr Ephraim Little in the present division of sixty acre lots in said plymouth Township as followeth: lying at a place called the horse neck 31 acres thereof is bounded on the north side thereof by the 58 acres of Caleb Cook; and on the East it is bounded from a stake in the range of said Cooks land in boxberry swamp ranging south and by west sixteen pole to the stake which is the northeast corner bound of the ten acres of Jonathan Bryant and from thence bounded by said ten acres unto the southwest corner bound there being a pine tree marked; and from thence ranging south and by west 28 pole to the stake which is the east corner bound of the 20 acre lot belonging to the heirs of Joshua Pratt; and from thence by the head of said 20 acre lot unto the pine tree marked which is the north corner bound thereof; and from thence by the rang of said 20 acre lot southwest 3 quarters of a point south 14 pole to two small red oaks marked standing together by the edge of the meadow ground at Jones river; and so on the same rang to said river; and from thence bounded by said River up stream unto the 58 acres of Caleb Cook first mentioned. And the other five acres thereof lyeth on the northeast side of Jones River and is bounded by said river from the last mentioned range down stream unto the upper end of the meadow of Jonathan

---

[1] This entry is written on a half sheet of letter paper, and when the first volume of the records was rebound was inserted in this place. The land referred to was in Kingston.

Briant which he bought of Samuel Bryant; from thence bounded by said Jonathan Bryants meadow untill it come down unto the bound between said meadow and the meadow of Samuel Bryant; and from thence on a straight line to the stake which is the southerly corner bound of the land of the heirs of Joshua Pratt and from thence by sd prats land northwest 3 quarters of a point westerly 70 pole to a stake and stones on the side of a hill; and from thence on the same range 45 pole more to a pine tree marked on the * * * * hill near the meadow ground; and so on the same rang home to * * * * * ground; and from thence bounded by the edge of the upland * * * nty two pole to the two small red oaks marked by the meadow side * * * mentioned. There being allowance * * way through gates or bars; cross the last * * ed five acres

John Bradford<br>Samuell Sturtevant

[37.] The 27th 6 mo 1650

Willi Nelson : is to keepe the ould cow that is in his hand this psent yeare.

John Heywood is to keepe the yonge cow that is in his hand for this psent yeare.

Tho Savory is to keepe the cow in that is in his hand for this yeare.

John Smith is to have the Cow that is in goodman Pontus hand for this yeare.

Willi Nelson is to have a heyfer that is a yeare ould and vantidg halfe belonginge to the stock and the other to himselfe; and is to keepe her for three yeare to the halfes.

Willi Paddy is debt to halfe a calfe wh was John Dunhams att 12s to pay to the stock.

[38.] The pors stock being caled in 1648 August 4th

    1 cowe at William pontis. The Increase a yearling steere and a cow calfe.

    1 John Dunham and Sam. Eedy. The Increase a yearling hefer and a bull calfe.

    1 heifer at William Nelson. Increase a cow calfe and 1 cow between Will Nelson and Haward a yearling steere

The stock hath bought goodman pontis halfe of ye yearling stear and a cow-calfe valued at 2£ 10s so he is to be payed

25s, Mr Willet hath bought them and is to pay him 25s. and the stock 25s.

The yearling hefer and a bull calf that was John Dunham and Sam Edy was valued at 3£ 4s the calfe is 18s Mr Pady is to give 9s for ye halfe and either Mr Willet or Tho : Litle is to give 23.s for ye halfe of ye heifer present pay.

The share of Nellsons is valued at 2£ 2.s Mr Wilet is to give 31.s. 6d except William Nellson can make redy pay.

The catle are thus disposed now this year 1648 Aug : 5

To goodman pontis The cowe he had before

John Dunham ye cow that he and Sam : Eedy had before.

William Nellson ye old cow

John Haward ye yonge cow

Thom : Saverey to have a cow yt is to be bought.

[39.] At a Townes meeting holden at plymouth the 4th of November 1648,

The Raters for coman charges were Mr Howland
                                               Manesses Kemton
                                               Thomas Cushman
                                               John Cooke
                                               Thomas Clarke

The towne have apointed Mr Willet and Richard Church to manage the busines at the Court concerning the bridge at Eell river in the behalfe of ye towne

At a meeting of the Townsmen of new Plymouth holden at the meeting house the 17th of May 1649 the Comites chosen weer

|  |  |
|---|---|
|  | Mr howland |
|  | Mr Paddy |
|  | goodman Kemton |
|  | goodman Dunham |
| Constable | John Thomson |
| Surveyors | Mr howland |
|  | Mr Paddy |
|  | Mr Willit |
| Grand Jury | Robert Bartlet |
|  | John ffenney |
|  | Jacob Cook |
|  | Andrew Ringe |

PLYMOUTH RECORDS.    29

At a meeting of the Townsmen of Plymouth holden at the meeting house the * of November 1649 the Raters for the publick charges were chosen

Mr howland
Mannasses Kemton
John Dunham Sen
John Cook
leiuetenant Southworth

Wheras a certaine propryety or privilidg was formerly graunted by the Towne of Plym unto Mr Bradford Govr Mr Willam Paddy Captaine Tho Willet and others in and unto Clarks Iland ; at the Townsmeeting holden by the Townsmen of Plymouth aforsaid the 18th of febreuary 1649 they the said Mr Bradford Mr Paddy and Mr Willet did freely and fully surrender all theire said Right and Enterest which they have formerly had in the said Iland unto the Township of Plymouth.

[40.] The porcs stock was taken notis of by William Bradford and John Dunham senior this 26 day of August 1655.

The cow which John Smith had is dead without any increase.

The cow John Dunham had was also boged and dyed. And her increase kild by the wolf.

The cowe at William Nelsons hath no Increase but one that was lost And we have changed her for a yonger with calfe as is suposed. And he is to paye the stock.

The cowe John Heaward had hath encrease a cow-calfe of this year valued 15s and a two year old stear of which is to have half when sould and he hath the calfe in part thereof.

And let him keepe the cowe still upon the former termes.

And the other is in the hands of William Nelson.

[41.] At a Generall meeting of the Townsmen of New Plymouth holden at the house of Mr Willam Bradford Gouv the 18th of febreuary 1649

Wheras in Regard to the distance of our habitations and sundry other Inconveniencies the whole Town cannot Redyly com together to acte in the Redrese of sundry things in the Towne aforsaid : The said Towne have therfore ordered by these psents yt seaven men [1] bee chosen and deputed by and in the behalfe of

---
[1] In the choice of these seven men the Town anticipated the law passed by the Colony Court in 1665, providing for the choice of a Board of Selectmen.

the said Towne to order the affayers thereof; Videleset the said seaven men to have the disposing of all such lands whether at Clarks Iland Manomet ponds or any other place within the libbertyes of the said Town undisposed of: to the use of such of the said towne as are in want for theire psent nessesityes they to make use therof as long as they please or their heairs after them but not to make sale therof if they depart the towne but to surrender them upp unto the towne agayne at theire departure.

further the said seaven men have power by these presents to make Inquiry into the state and condition of the poor of the Towne and to use theire best descretion and Indeavors that the poor may bee comfortably provided for by contriving and seting them in such wayes and courses as may most probably conduce therunto; and allso to see yt the provisions of the poor bee not unessesaryly Imbezeled misspent and made away in the sommer season before the winter and times of hard things com: And for such poore as are aged or decripped as they cannot work or any other conceaved by the said seaven men to bee in absolute need they have libberty and power by to make a Rate for theire Releefe * shall bee absolute necessity calling them therunto;

And whereas libberty was graunted by the Court holden at New Plymouth * of June last past before the date heerof unto the Townshipe of Plym aforsaid to heard and keepe cattell at Sepecan;[1] the seaven men aforsaid have libberty and * by these prsents to hier and Imploy men as they shall see ocation in hearding wintering of cattell at Sepecan as aforsaid

finally yt the said seaven men bee Annuall and yt every yeare it bee at the Townes libbertye to make a new choise by papers or otherwise as they shall see ocation.

Accordingly at the meeting aforsaid seaven men were chosen which were These following

      John Barnes
      Robert ffinney
      Captain Tho: Willet
      Leiuetenant Tho: Southworth
      John Cooke Juni
      John Dunham Senior
      Tho: Clarke

---

[1] Sepecan became Rochester, June 4, 1686, and included what are now Marion and Mattapoisett.

Allso yt any five of the seaven men men aforsaid in case of the absence of the other two or otherwise shall agree in about or concerning any of the pticulars aforsaid; it shall stand in force as if all were prsent and agreed therin

And that no Rate bee made by the abovesaid 7 men to exceed the sume of 3 pounds for the poore aforsaid. And if there shalbee Reason to make a larger Rate for the end aforsaid that the said 7 men * to the towne that further order may bee taken in that *

[42.] Att a Townsmeeting of the Townsmen of New Plymouth * the house of Mr William Bradford Govenr the 4$^{th}$ of November 1650

It was ordered yt whosoever shall after the day of the date * kill a wolfe or wolves and bring Testimony thereof by the skin or head &c shall have for every wolfe yt shall apeer to be killed within the Townes liberties; fifteen shillings and this to be levied by Rate. And wheras Nathanniell Warren hath lately killed a wolfe before the date heerof yt hee also bee considered in the next Rate as shalbee thought meet.

The Raters for the Publick charges of this Prsent yeare were

Mr John howland     John Cooke Juni
Mannasses Kemton     Tho: Clarke
John Dunham Seni

Gyles Rickard Seni chosen constable for the Towne to serve untell the next June court bee expired.

Att a Townsmeeting of the Townsmen of New Plym: holden at the meetinghouse the first of March 1650 Mr howland Mr Paddy Captaine Willet Mr John Winslow John Cook Juni and Tho: Clarke have engaged to pay two coats a peece to bee in reddynes in the hands and custetie of John Morton to pay any Indian that shall kill a woolfe and make it known to the Govenr upon undoubted Testimony and for such as kill lesser woolves to have an axe or hatchet for every such woolfe; and that the charge of the said coats bee considered and abated unto the abovesaid pties in the publik charges at the yeares end.

It was ffurther agreed by the Townesmen aforsaid that the Court order about woolfe trapps (as it Respects them) bee forthwith put in practise viz: that five trapps or more bee forthwith made by severall companies in severall Naighborhoods in the Townshipp ; and that Nathanniell Morton doe give notice by papers of the names of such as are to Joyne together for the end aforsaid that soe they may bee made and tended

June 1651

ordered that all graves especially for grown persons bee diged five foot deep and that all such as have any ocation * * * graves * * *

[43.] At a Towne Meeting held at the house of Mr William Bradford the 25ᵗ of November 1651

The Raters for publick charges that were chosen were Mr John howland Mannasses Kemton John Dunham Seni John Cook and Tho : Clark.

The seaven men chosen to order the afaires of the Towne febreuary 18ᵗʰ 1649 are to ontinew in theire places by the order of the towne for this following yeare.

An acre of land is graunted unto John Rickard at Welingsley for him to build an house or soe as it hinder no hieway

[1] January 1651 Willam harlow and Benjamin Bartlet have killed two wolves for which the towne is indebted to them.

febreuary 1651 Robert Bartlet also killed a woolfe the same month 1651.

Robert Bartlet hath sence killed another woolf month 1651.

At a Townsmeeting held at the meeting house the 28th of febreuary 1651 it was agreed by the consent of the Towne that the land graunted unto the Towne by the court at Sepecan should bee Purchased of the Indians at the publicke charge of the said Towne ; when the true ppriators thereof shalbee manifested

It was ordered that wheras there is a Neglect of appeerance at Townemeetings when orderly Sumoned therunto : That in case any shall for ye future neglect to com to Townsmeetings when orderly warned shalbee lyable to pay the fine ordered the 10 December 1646 videlect twelve pence a pson for every such default and the said fine to be Required by the Cunstable or som other thought meet by the Towne unless any pson can sufficient reason for his absence.

---

[1] The three clauses relating to Wm. Harlow, Benjamin Bartlett and Robert Bartlett have lines drawn through them in the Records.

## PLYMOUTH RECORDS. 33

At this meeting Nathaniell Morton Requested of the Towne a smale moyetie of land lying betwixt the hieway by his house and the water side or Creeke commonly called and known by the name of hobshole allis Wellingsley the said small moyetie being compased on the one side with the aforsaid hole or creeke and on the other side with the brooke Runing into the said creeke which makes it a necke the said * * * * * * *

[44.][1]

for the Govers Teame
Tho : Lettice
William Nelson
John Morton
for goodman Winters Teame
Willam Hoskins
ffrancis Billington
Nicolas hodgis
Will Spon
for Mr Howlands Teame
Willam Spooner
Benjamin Eaton
Tho : Gray


for ffrancis Cooks Teame
John Cooke
John harmon
Samuell Ringe
for goodman Shawes and
Samuell Sturtivants Teame
They to cut wood for theire owne Teame.
for goodman hursts and
Ephraim Tinkham's Teame
Themselves to cut the wood and John Dunham to bee added to them

for Samuel hickes Teame
Gorg Watson
John Smith Juni
hugh Cole
for Andrew Rings Teame
Richard Wright
henery Atkins
Benjamin Prat

Wheras Nathaniell Warrens Team did nothing in this * the last yeare ; hee and his brethren are to provid wood for themselves and draw proportionable to others
for Tho : Clarkes Teame
Willam Shirtley [2]
Richard Smith
John Smith Seni
for Robert Bartlets Teame
Willam harlow
Richard ffoster
Joseph Green
Gyles Rickard
for Mannasses Kemtons Teame
Samuell Dunham
Ephraim Morton
Tho : Morton

---

[1] A portion of a leaf in the Records containing the preface to this list is torn out. The names of Nicholas Hodgis, Benjamin Eaton, Tho: Gray, Samuell Ringe, Joseph Green henery Wood and John Wood have lines drawn through them in the Records.

[2] William Shirtley means William Shurtleff.

for Mr Winslows Teame
John howard
Samuell Cutbert
John holmes
for goodman Doties Teame
James Cole

Tho : Sherive

Willam Browne

for Robert ffeneys Teame
Tho : Whitney
Edward Tilson
John Churchill
for goodman Rickards Teame
henery Wood
John Wood
John Rickard
Leiftenant Southworth
Samuell *
for goodman Barnes his Teame
James Glase
Jonathan Dunham

1636

[45.] Att a Generall meeting of the Townsmen of Plymouth holden att the house of Mr Edw Winslow The * of ffebruary Anno dom 1636.

1636 Impr wheras great destruction of firewood is by reason of The topps of many trees are only taken away and the * are left behind It is ordered by the towne That whosoever * a tree for firewood upon the Comon grounds shall not only * away the toppes but shall alsoe cutt up the bodys of such and cause them to bee carryed away as well as the toppes * within one month next after they were fallen upon that each that shall doe the contrary shall forfeit five shillings for each tree to be levied to the use of the towne of Plymouth

1641 It is ordered by the Towne that all Swine above * months old shalbee Ringed ;

May 16 1636

this was established to bee in force January 9th 1660

It was ordered by the towne that if any shall absent himselfe from the towne meeting being orderly warned (which is to say * ) before by the constable or his deputie ; unlesse urgent occation Require a shorter warning ; shalbee fined twelve pence for every pson that shall make such defect of non appeerance to the use of the towne unlesse he can make a Just excuse

Richard Wrights grant of

Att a Townsmeeting held att Plymouth the 3rd * The Towne graunted unto Richard Wright twenty five acres to bee layed forth for him at Winnatucksett to him and his assignes for ever in Regard that

25 acres of land at Winatuxet hee was to have had * * in the Township of Plymouth which hee bought of * * as appeers by a Record of Court bearing date * 1638 which hee never was possessed of * * in any place ; In consideration * * of the Towne * * * * * * * * * *

[46.] It was ordered by the towne that all graves especially for elder psons shalbee diged five foot deep and that all such as have any occation to Impioy any in diging of graves shall see that they be diged soe deep ;

It was ordered by the towne that all lands or pcells of lands that shalbee graunted to any within this towneship for the future shalbee graunted openly in towne meetings and that likewise all Rates that shalbee for the poor shalbee made anually by those that are chosen annally to make the Rates for the publicke charges of the countrey.

It was agreed and graunted by the towne of Plymouth unanimously That all such pcells of land both upland and meddow which hath bin formerly graunted by the seaven men apointed to order the affaires of the town ; shalbee the proper Right of such to whom such lands or meddowes have bine Graunted to belong unto them and theire heires and assignes for ever without any exception whatsoever and in speciall a meddow comonly Called Dotyes was graunted to the pties to whom it is disposed to them and their heires for ever without exception ; alwaies provided that notwitstanding this order and graunt ; That whosoever hath any lands graunted unto them upon any either Ilands or beaches belonging to the towne the propryety therof shalbee and Remaine unto the Towne of Plymouth in comon ; and that such said psons as to whom such lands are graunted to have the use therof for a season.

1657
* ember 26
* 7

The Towne agreed that theire land att [1] Punckateesett over against Road Iland shall bee lett unto Captaine Cooke and they have appointed Captaine Willett to lett it in theire behalfe which accordingly was done and the tearmes are elswhere extant in the Records of the Court ;

---

[1] Punckateesett on Seconnett River in Rhode Island.

[47.]

March 1651

The Names of those that have Interest and proprieties in the Townes land att Punckateesett over against Road Iland

    Captaine Willett
    Leiftenant Southworth
    Mr Willam Bradford [1]
    Mistris Allice Bradford
    Mr John howland
    The Elder Thomas Cushman
    John Barnes
    Thomas Clarke
    Gyles Rickard Seni
    Nathaneel Warren
    Joseph Warren
    Mannasses Kemton
    Mistris Elizabeth Warren
    John Rickard
    Samuell Dunham
    Ephraim Tinkham
    Arthur hatheway
    Willam Nelson
    Mr Paddy
    Mr Rayner
    Thomas Pope
    Richard Wright
    Willm Spooner
    John Morton
    Ephraim Morton
    John Smith Juni
    Gyles Rickard Juni
    ffrancis Cooke
    John Cooke
    Willam harlow
    George Bonum
    Mr John Winslow
    James hurst
    Samuell Eedy
    John Dunham Seni

---

[1] The name of Mr. Bradford has a line drawn through it in the Records.

Robert ffinney
Robert Bartlett
Edward Gray
Patience Faunce
John ffaunce
Georg Watson
Edward Doty
John Shaw Seni
James Shaw
Gabriell ffallowell
Nathaneell Morton
Samuell hickes
John Churchill
James Cole Seni
Andrew Ringe
henery Atkins
Thomas Lettice
John Dunham Juni
Willam Browne
Edward Tilson
Mr Lee
Thomas Whitney
John Jourdaine
Jacob Cooke
Thomas Morton
Thomas Savory
ffrancis Billington
John Smith Seni
Jonathan Dunham
John haward
James Cole Juni
Richard ffoster
James Glasse
Mtris Ann Atwood
Samuell Kinge
John Wood
Mistris Margarett hickes
Mistris Jeney
Will: Shirtliffe 74

[48.] Such as were appointed by the Township of Plymouth to dispose of lands did graunt unto Thomas Little five acrees of upland meddow beyond Thomas Clarkes ffarme att a brooke comonly Called the Indian brooke the meddow being much of it nought the lower end of the said meddow is to bee understood That said five acrees of upland meddow to appertaine unto the said Thomas Little soe long as either himselfe or any of his posteritie shall Remaine within the lymetts of the said township of Plymouth but if both himselfe and all his Posteritie shall depart the township that then the said meddow shalbee att the disposing of the towne.

*Thomas Littles 5 acre medow*

foure acrees of upland ground was graunted by the towne unto John haward lying neere unto James hursts brooke adjoyneing unto the garden plott of the said John hayward; and soe to extend itselfe in length into the woods westerly provided hee alow a sufficient passage for cattle betwixt the swamp att the neather end of the said land and the land itself;

*4 acres land to John Haward*

The Towne Graunted unto Nathaneell Morton a small Moyety of land lying betwixt the highway by his house and the waterside or creeke comonly called and knowne by the name of hobshole allis Wellingsley The said smale moyety being compased on the one side with the aforsaid hole or creeke and on the other side with the brooke Runing into the said creeke which makes it a necke the said moyety soe bounded as aforsaid with all the appurtenances belonging therunto to belong and appertaine to him the said Nathaneell Morton hee his heires and assignes for ever;

*Nath{ll} Mortons grant of land t hobshole*

The Towne Graunted unto Richard Wright five and twenty acrees of land to bee aded to that which formerly was alowed to bee his due which was twenty ffve acrees in lieu of a peell of land which hee should have had att Mannomett ponds all which fifty acrees of land are to bee layed forth for him att Winnatuxett[1]

\* 6
\* 1659

---

[1] The Winnatuxett River rises in Plympton, and running through Halifax, empties into Taunton River at Bridgewater. The land referred to is in Plympton, then a part of Plymouth.

by Mr Bradford and the Elder Cushman; and hee the said Richard Wright hath alsoe libertie to looke out some meddow there to accommodate him withall that soe a competency may bee confirmed * * * * *.

[49.] A pcell or Tract of land was graunted unto Mr John howland lying att a brooke within two miles or therabouts of Winnatuxett meddow lying att or about the said brooke; the said pᵣmises with all and singulare the appurtenances belonging therunto was graunted by the towne unto the said John howland hee his heires and assignes for ever.

*The 24th of May 1660.*
*John Howland.*

ffifty Acrees of land is graunted unto the Elder Thomas Cushman neare adjacent unto the place where the land abovesaid graunted unto Mr John howland lyeth : the said fifty acrees of land with all and singular the appurtenances belonging therunto was graunted to the said Thomas Cushman To him and his heires for ever :

*The 24th of May 1660.*

ffour score Acrees of land was graunted unto Stephen Bryant lying on the south branch of Joanses River neare his meddow there provided hee Renounce and Relinquish all his title and Claime to a place formerly graunted unto John Shaw Senr; Called Rehoboth * condition wherof the said four score acrees of land with all and singulare the appurtenances belonging therunto is graunted unto the said Stephen Bryant to him and his heires forever bounded on the Northwest corner at the brooke next his meddow with a white oak att the uper end of his meddow : on the Southeast side bounded with four pyne and one oake tree all marked : on the lower end with two pyne trees marked on the foure sides :

*The 24ᵗʰ of May 1660. The said land called Rehoboth was and is relinquished into the towne by the said Stephen Bryant.*

*The 24ᵗʰ of May 1660,*

ffifty Acrees of land is graunted unto ffrancis Combe lying next to

Stephen Bryants land Neare unto the meddow of the said ffrancis Combe The said fifty acrees of land with all and singulare the appurtenances belonging therunto is graunted unto the said ffrancis Combe to him and his heires for ever; bounded with a great Rid oak tree att the wadeing place and soe Rangeing through a little swamp and * with a white oake by the swamp and soe Ranging to another white oak marked on four sides and soe Rangeing againe to the westeren corner to a Rid oake soe threw the aforsaid swamp to another white oake marked on foure sides; *

* and thence to a Rid oake on the westeren side and soe to his meddow to a Rid oake marked.

The 24th of May 1660.

ffifty Acrees of land was graunted unto ffrancis Billington viz: a Round Knowle of land lying and adjoyning to the hole of meddow belonging to the said ffrancis Billington on the south side of the Cartway goeing to Stephen Bryants meddows; the said ffifty acrees of land with all and singulare the appurtenances belonging thereunto is graunted unto the said ffrancis Billington to him and his heires for ever.

[50.]

1660

ffifty Acrees of land was graunted unto Samuell Sturtivant lying on the North side of Joanes river on the Southeast side of his meddow there the said ffifty acrees of land with all and singulare the appurtenances belonging therunto is graunted unto the said Samuell Sturtivant to him and his heires for ever;

* 24th
May 1660

Three acrees of land was graunted unto Jonathan Dunham and three acrees of land unto Benajah Pratt lying att the heads of theire lands to bee viewed and layed forth for them by George Watson and George Bonum ; the said prmises with all and singulare the appurtenances belonging therunto is graunted unto the said Jonathan Dunham and Benajah Pratt ; to them and each of them theire and each of theire heires and assignes for ever ;

The 24<sup>th</sup> of May 1660

fforty Acrees of land is graunted unto three Indians namly to Acconootus Wanna and Wampocke lying att Shifting Cove [1] to bee layed forth and bounded with all other conditions and cercomstances to bee ordered about it by George Watson Robert Bartlett Nathaneell Warren and Willam Cooke ; and if there shalbee occation to put in another Indian with them that then they shall each ten acrees ;

The 24<sup>th</sup> of May 1660.

It was agreed by the towne that Willam harlowes ffence of Post and Rayles where it now stands next the highway shalbee the bounds of the upper end of his land ;

The 16th of May 1652

The Towne graunted unto Mr John Reyner a smale Moyety of land [2] viz : whatsoever was then Comon lying att the uper end of the acrees formerly layed out to Mr John howland and others on the other side of the brooke against the mill ; a little brook pteing Gabriele ffallowell and it att the uper end ; To belonge to the onely proper use and behoofe of him the said John Reyner hee and his heires for ever ;

---

[1] Shifting Cove was a Cove on the Manomet Shore, South of Manomet Point.
[2] This land included the Poor House lot. Fallowell's land included a part or the whole of the land of the late Stephen Maybury, and the little brook was the outlet of the swamp, which by the raising of the Mill pond has become what is now Slaughter House Pond. This brook was a little later called Dunham's Brook.

[51.]
The 30th
of May 1659

Ellen Cushman

The 30th
of May 1659

Lieut Southworth
Patience Faunce

The 30th
of May 1659

An Inlargment of land is graunted unto the Elder Cushman att the uper end of his land att Joanses river; to goe up in equal proportion for breadth into the woods soe high as the pyny [1] * ;

An adition of land is graunted unto Leiftenant Southworth and Patience ffaunce Widdow att the heads of their lotts of the said Leiftenant Southworth and John ffaunce att the Eel river; this adition to extend a quarter of a mile into the woods from the heads of the said lotts;

In like manor an adition of land is graunted unto Robert flinney and Thomas Morton att the heads of theire lotts they are now possessed of; to extend a quarter of a mile into the woods from the heads of the said lotts

Memorand: That the last graunts above mentioned viz: to Leiftenant Southworth Patience ffaunce Elder Cushman Robert flinney and Thomas Morton; is to bee understood onely of the wood of the said lands to belong to them; but the land to Remaine comon; and that on the graunts to Robert flinney and Thomas Morton any may Notwithstanding take any dry wood within the said bounds;

The 21
of November
1660:
The confeirmation
was on the 20th
of January 1660:
Richard Wright

The 20th
of ffebruary 1660:

A smale peell of land lying neare unto John Cooks att Rockey Nooke was graunted unto Richard Wright to bee a place to sett an house on; and it was layed forth and confeirmed unto him the said Richard Wright as it was bounded by Ephraim Morton one of the measurers of lands appointed by the towne

It was ordered by the towne that all the land lying att the Eelriver swamp betwixt

---

[1] "Pyny" probably means Pine Woods.

Richard Wright

the Eelriver and the shingle brooke [2] shalbee Reserved for comon to the use of the towne; Att the same time it was ordered by the towne likewise that all the land that lyeth betwixt John Cooke and ffrancis Billington not disposed of alreddy to Richard Wright shalbee and Remaine for comon to the use of the towne;

At the same time It was graunted unto Willam Clarke that in case when his land is layed out and bounded there is any that will not be prejuditiall to others that hee shall have enlargement;

[52.]
* *

ffifty Acrees of land is graunted unto Robert Bartlett lying between the sea and the fferne swamp between the Eelriver and Mannomett ponds with all and singulare the appurtenançes to him and his heires for ever;

The 3d of September 1660:

It was ordered by the towne that wheras Complaint is made of great abuse by Reason of the peeling of the Rind of from cedar trees in the swampes belonging to the township whereby much timber is like to bee spoyled and thereby the town much damnifyed; That whosoever shall hentsforth either themselves or any they shall Imploy or sett on worke either English or Indians peele the Rinds of any cedare trees within this towneship or belonging thereunto; and not Imrove the bodyes of such trees soe peeled within halfe a yeare after they are peeled shall forfeite for every such default fifty shillings to the townes use

ffebruary 1660:

It was ordered by the towne henceforth none shalbee pmitted to take into ptenorship any of any other towne to gather knots and make Tarr on the townes lands to the preju-

---

[2] Shingle Brook is the stream on which the zinc factory of N. Wood & Co. stands in Chiltonville.

dice of the town on the penaltie of forfeiting for every load soe gathered in such ptenorship five shillings to the townes use

It was likewise ordered att the same time that none shall gather any knots to make Tarr and lett them lye undrawne together above six months on payne of forfeiting and loosing the said knotes; It being by this order lawfull for any other in such case to take them and Improve them; as they shall see good;

*Aprill 1661*

[1] The guns and swords belonging to the towne were disposed of as followeth:

It to Mr Bradford one gun;

To Nathanneell Morton for the use of Abraham Jackson one short gun and a sword:

To Nathanneell Warren for the use of his man John Rose one matchcock gun with a fier locke since delivered to him for the said gun and hee is to stock it and fitt it up on the townes account.

To Thomas Morton one long gun

To Ephraim Morton one sword

To John Dotey one gun viz. one muskett;

To Stephen Bryant one of the longer sort of guns which was since delivered to Sergeant harlow

To Jonathan Dunham one sword; which hee since hath Returned, these to be kept * * * Mr Southworth Mr Crow and Mr Barnes in the behalfe of the towne Reconed with Gyles Rickard Seni; and George Bonum and there Remaines due to the towne from the said Rickard 2£

*These armes were delivered to the Constable by order from the Towne * 13, 1676*

It from George Bonum    0. 18. 0

three swords belonge to the Towne

Nathaniel Morton    *    sword

Sergeant Tinkham one sword

Leift Morton one sword

---
[1] The clause here inserted relating to the disposition of arms is erased in the Records by marks drawn over the lines.

[53.] Att the Towne meeting held att Plymouth the 10th day of January 1661
It was ordered that a Rate of ten pounds should bee made and levied upon the Towne to bee layed out in bellowes and tooles for a smith and to bee kept for the uses of the towne; The men deputed to make the said Rate were John Cooke, Nathaniell Warren and hugh Cole:

It was likewise ordered att the same meeting by a unanimus voat of all the Townsmen then prsent: That a Rate of sixty pounds should bee made and levied upon all the Inhabitants of the Towne; to bee Improved for the purchasing and procuring of a place for a minnester by those psons formerly deputed by the Towne to enquire out and prepare a place for the end aforsaid: whoe were Captaine Southworth Robert ffinney Ephraim Morton and Nathaniell Warren; The said sum soe to bee levied is to bee payed att two severall payments viz: the former being the one halfe therof is to be payed by the last day of June next following the date heerof; and the other halfe to bee payed by the last of November next following the date heerof in current countrey pay [1] and to bee desposed to the end aforsaid by the psons above named;

Gorg Watson Nathaniell Warren and Joseph Warren are deputed by the Towne to give meeting with Mr Hinckley and Nathaniell Bacon whoe are appointed by the Court to set out the bounds of the Townes lands att Sepecan this to bee done as sone as conveniently may bee

At this meeting fifty acres of land is Confeirmed being formerly graunted unto Edward Gray lying on the west northwest side of Joanes River meddow or therabouts to bee layed out on both sides of the brooke which Runs from the pond through his owne meddow soe as it may bee as little prejudiciall to the Generall as may bee; the said ffifty acrees of land with all and singulare the appurtenances belonging therunto graunted unto the said Edward Gray to him and his heires forever;

[54.]

* 1661

A smale pcell of swamp or meddow is graunted joyntly unto Andrew Ringe and Abraham Jackson lying att the south meddow at the further end of the Cove;
Wheras formerly a smale pcell of land was graunted

---

[1] "Countrey pay" was "pay in produce" at fixed prices.

unto John Dunham Juni: lying on the north side of his feild above plaine dealing in case it should not prove prejudiciall to the Neighbourhood there; and wheras some of the neighbors whom it most conserneth have taken notice of his desire conserning the pmises and have given theire consent unto his said Request; The Towne have therfore graunted unto the said John Dunham three acrees of land lying on the north side of his field aforsaid; to him and his heires for ever this to be layed forth and bounded with all convenient speed and the bounds to bee here entered; provided that the Neighbours shall have libertie to fetch wood from of the said land as they shall have occation notwithstanding this graunt;

 Att a towne meeting held at the meeting house att Plymouth the 24th of March 1661, Conserning the demand of twelve pounds by Richard Church and John Thompson in Reference unto a former bargaine about the meeting house; the Towne agreed by a voate that they would not compound with the said ptes; but will answare the tryall of it by law if the said pties shall see cause to comence suite against the towne or any that have formerly bine theire agents about the said bargaine;

 Libertie is graunted unto John Cooke and Jacob Cooke to looke out some land where it may lye conveniet for them and not prejudicial to others and a Competency therof to bee Confeirmed unto them by the towne.

 Att a Towne meeting held att Plymouth the 24th of 1662,

 Leiftenant Ephraim Morton and George Bonum were appointed by the Towne to be Surveyors for the measuring of land as occation may Require within this Township.

[55.] Att a Towne meeting held att the meeting house att Plymouth the 24th day of May 1662

 The Towne have Refered the busines about our lands att Punckateesett and places adjacent concerning the Incroachment of some of Road Iland upon some pte of the said land; unto the deputies of our Towne together with the messengers of the towne now sent viz: John Cooke and Nathaniell Warren to make our addresses to the Court in the townes behalf and otherwise to to act (conserning the same) as they shall see cause;

 Mr Howland desired a smale hole or pcell of meddow neare his land graunted him formerly by the towne;

 Richard Wright desireth a smale pcell of meddow about

two accers which is over measures of what was alowed to ffrancis Billington ;

Jonathan Shaw desires some Comon land about his house att Lakenham [1] ;

ffrancis Comb Requesteth a smale point of meddow neare the meddow he bought of Edward Gray

Ephraim Tinkham Requesteth a smale peell of meddow lying upon the brooke that Runeth from Doties pond ;

Benjamine Eaton desireth a smale peell of meddow about half an acree lying neare ffrancis Billingtons meddow and some upland to it ;

Ephraim Morton desireth an Inlargment at the head of his lott ;

The Towne have declared themselves Conserning Clarkes Iland that it is now att theire disposing notwithstanding former libertie graunted to pticular psons to Improve it ; It being now deserted and not Improved by any ;

Georg Watson Nathaniell Morton and Willam harlow Renewed theire Request for their former desire of land att Mannomett ponds ; the towne was moved to chos some to dispose of lands and those pticulares are Refered untill the towne shall take further order for the disposal of lands ;

Att this meeting Willam Crow was voated to bee a surveyor for the measuring of lands ;

[56.] Att a Town meeting held by the Townesmen of Plymouth the 30th of June 1662

The Towne made Choise of Robert ffinney and Ephraim Morton to Receive that which is agreed by the Towne to be brought in for the building of a house for a minnester ;

Att this meeting the Towne agreed in Reference unto lands for the disposing therof that there shalbee a meeting on sett purpose for that end ; to bee on the last Munday in October next and that then the towne either together or by a Comittee then to bee chosen for that purpose dispose of lands ; and that in the meantime such as want land have libertie to look out for the supply of their wants in that behalf ;

Willam harlow the Constable of Plymouth for the yeare 1662 gave in his account as followeth :

---

[1] Lakenham was the early name for what is now Carver.

The sixteenth of October 1661 the towne by their Rators made a rate of

|  | £ | s | d |
|---|---|---|---|
|  | 25 | 12 | 03 |

The pticulares wherof were disposed as followeth

| | £ | s | d |
|---|---|---|---|
| Item to the Treasurer | 02. | 06. | 00 |
| Item to ffrancis Goulder | 08. | 00 | 00 |
| Item to Mistris ffuller | 01. | 10. | 01 |
| Item to John Barnes | 02. | 03. | 04 |
| Item to Edward Gray | 01. | 00 | 06 |
| Item to Thomas Savory | 03. | 14 | 02 |
| Item to Ephraim Morton | 00. | 14. | 00 |
| Item to John Cobb | 00. | 14. | 00 |
| Item to John Dunham Seni : | 00. | 12. | 00 |
| Item to Robert ffinney | 00 | 06. | 00 |
| Item to Mr howland | 00 | 12 | 00 |
| Item to Willam Crow | 00 | 06 | 00 |
| Item to Nathaniell Warren | 00 | 12 | 00 |
| Item to charges of Rators att James Coles | 00 | 09 | 00 |
| Item to 4 barrells of Tarr as yett in William harlowes hands | 02 | 00 | 00 |
| Suma totalis | [1] 25 | 13 | 07 |
| Reste due to Willam harlow when the Tarr is delivered | 00 | 01 | 06 |

[57.] At a Towne meeting held by the Townesmen of Plymouth the 27th of October 1662

The Names of those that desire meddow in Sampson's Countrey [2] or therabouts are as followeth

henery Wood
John Jourdaine
Nathaniell Warren
Willam harlow
Gabriell ffallowell
Robert ffinney
Joseph Dunham
Abraham Jackson
Thomas Whitney
Thomas Pope

foure acrees of meddow graunted Jonathan Dunham lying att Sampsons * pond; to him and his heires forever.

---

[1] This footing is a correct copy of the original, but should be 24 19 1
[2] Sampson's Countrey was in the vicinity of Assowampsett Pond in Lakeville

Samuell Dunham
Samuell Kinge
The Names of those whoe desire meddow att the lower south meddow; next unto those that have had former grauntes there

Gorge Watson
Ephraim Morton
Nathaniell Morton    to bee Considered with
John Rickard    some meddow there in lieu
Jonathan Shaw    of that which hee Relinquished
James Cole Juni:    in Joanses River meddow
hugh Cole
Joseph Bartlett
The Names of such as desire Meddow in the * soe called; lying on the south side of Turkey Swamp.

Captaine Bradford
Stephen Bryant    Joseph Warren
Samuell Sturtivant    Willam Crow
John Morton    Edward Gray
Richard Wright    Samuell Kinge
   John harmon
   Ephraim Tinkham
   henery Wood

This is since layed out for him *
* 6 book

Twenty acrees of upland graunted unto Thomas Lettice lying on the Northwest side of a little brook att Doteys meddow being a little above his Comon wast meddow there to him and his heires for ever;

fifty acrees of upland is graunted unto Jonathan Morey next unto Sandwich bounds butting on the sea * * for ever * * and * * ;

[58.] foure acrees of meddow is graunted unto ffrancis Combe lying next unto his meddow which hee bought of Edward Gray on the southerly side therof: to him and his heires for ever;

Twenty acrees of upland is graunted unto John Rickard lying on the northerly side of lakenham with all and singulare the appurtenances therunto belonging to him and his heires for ever;

Twenty acrees of upland is graunted unto James Cole Juni: lying on the northerly side of his land att Lakenham with all and singulare the appurtenances to him and his heires for ever;

The Towne have graunted unto John Dunham Seni: That a graunt of land formerly graunted unto him by the court lying att Swan hold: shalbee layed out to him with the best convenience that may bee;

fifty acrees of upland is graunted unto each of those twelve men that have meddow graunted to them at Winnatuxett to bee layed out to them there

The names of such as desire meddow att the new found meddow in the south side of ¹Turkey Swamp

| | |
|---|---|
| Capt Bradford | Joseph Warren |
| Stephen Bryant | John harmon |
| Samuell Sturtivant | |
| Samuell Kinge | George Bonum and |
| Edward Gray | Andrew Ringe desired |
| John Morton | a peece of meddow lying |
| Willam Crow | southerly from the |
| Richard Wright | cedar bridge. |

Thirty acrees of upland graunted unto John harmon att or neare winnatuxet when those abovesaid twelve men have theire portions layed out for them if then it can bee found with all and singulare the appurtenances to him and his heires for ever

Thirty acrees of upland is graunted unto Samuell Dunham lying att ²Warrens wells on the Easterly side therof with all and singulare the appurtenances to him and his heires for ever:

Thirty acrees of upland is graunted unto Joseph Dunham lying att his brother Samuell Dunhams att Warrens wells aforsaid with all and singulare the appurtenances to him and his heires for ever:

A smale peell of meddow is graunted unto John Barnes lying att the uper end of the south meddow; if it bee not graunted before to any other

[59.] fifty acrees of upland land is graunted unto Nathaniell Warren neare Mannomett ponds neare some meddow formerly graunted to his Mother; the said fifty acrees of upland with all and singulare the appurtenances belonging therunto; to him and his heires for ever;

---

¹ Turkey Swamp was near the line between Plympton and Halifax.

² Warren's Wells—a tract of low land between the South Pond Road and the Russell Mills Pond.

fifty acrees of upland is graunted unto Ephraim Morton lying on the further side of the brooke att Mannomett ponds over against Samuell Ryders land; the said fifty acrees of upland with all and singulare the appurtenances to the said Ephraim Morton to him and his heires for ever;

fifty acres of upland graunted unto Joseph Warren lying att Mannomett ponds neare unto the place above mentioned with all and singulare the appurtenances: to him and his heires for ever;

Graunted unto Gorge Watson Willam harlow and Nathaniell Morton; to each of them fifty acrees of upland lying att Mannomett Ponds at the further end therof; the said fifty acre s of upland to each of them with all and singulare the appurtenances belonging therunto; to belong to them and every of them theire and every of theire heires and assignes for ever; this to bee understood that if there is not enough to make up the same; that is good betwixt the Indians and the pond then to have some to make it up on the other side of the pond;

fifty acrees of upland is graunted unto John Churchill lying att Mannomett ponds on the southerly side of the abovesaid hundred and fifty acrees graunted to Gorge Watson William harlow and Nathaniell Morton when theires is layed out; the said fifty acrees of upland with all and singalar the appurtenances to him and his heires for ever

ffifty acrees of upland graunted unto Joseph Bartlett lying att Mannomett Ponds over against his Unkells land theire with all and singulare the appurtenances to him and his heires for ever

A small peell of land is graunted to Jonathan Shaw * neare his house att Lakenham to bee layed out to him soe as to bee not prejudiciall to the Naighbourhood there; the said peell of land to appertaine with all the appurtenances unto the said Jonathan Shaw hee and heires for ever;

fifty acrees of upland is graunted unto hugh Cole lying betwixt the hither mannomett point and the peece of salt marsh; with all the appurtenances belonging thereunto unto him and his heires for ever;

forty acrees of upland is granted unto John Dunham on the southwest of [1] colchester

---

[1] Colchester was a part of what is now Plympton.

[60.] Att the Towne meeting held att the meeting house and with a Joynt consent agreed that the house for a minnester which hath bin in agitation shall bee built att the Townes charge according to such proportions on each man as they have engaged for the Accomplishment therof; and that such as have not bine spoken to; or have not expressed themselves what they will give towards it bee spoken to in convenient time and that such sumes as they shall contribute towards it; bee aded to the Rest for the accomplishment therof; that soe such as have undertaken to agree with workmen (in the townes behalf) be not damnified; and that the said house may be built according to expectation;

Capt; Southworth John Morton Stephen Bryant and Ephraim Morton were appointed by the Towne to Assist Capt: Willett in defending against Richard Church and John Thompson plaintiffes against him in an action of the case to the damage of twenty foure pounds about our meeting house.

Wheras Complaint is made of some disorder and abuse about takeing of the heerings at the yearly season the towne have proposed to henery Wood that if himself with som others that hee shall agree with all will order by draw or take them and made equall devision of them to the Inhabitants of the town they will allow him or them 9 pence a thousand; onely for full agreement concerning these propositions it is Refered untill the next trayning day after the date heerof;

Herrings

* the said
* to
* p
* for
* ing and
* ibuting

Att a Towne meeting held att the meeting house the 23 of March 1662 It was ordered by the towne that henery Wood and Gorge Bonum with one other whom they shall see meet to be added to them; shall draw or take and devide the herrings to the severall families of the Township of Plymouth whoe shall have theire shares in number according to the number of the persons in theire families and they the said henery Wood and Gorge Bonum etc are to make meanes for the stopage of the said herrings and takeing of them in theire goeing up att theire owe charge; and they are to lett them goe up on fryday nights on saterday nights and on the Lords daies; and the towne doth prohibite all those that have enterest or shalbee Im-

PLYMOUTH RECORDS.   53

* them to the      ployed in the Mill to stopp water when the
* habitants        tide is out of the pond during the time of the
* for said         herrings; and that they the said pties are
* *                hereby authorized to take course for the pre-
* thousand         venting of Boyes swine and doggs from
bee delivered      anoying of them in theire coming up
* mill
* *

Abraham Jackson desireth a smale peell of upland att or neare Warrens wells neare unto some land lately graunted to Samuell Dunham and Joseph Dunham

Robert flinney Nathaniell Warren and Ephraim Morton are appointed by the towne to Run the line and to see the bounds sett betwixt the Township of Sandwich and our Township.

Nathaniell Morton and Nathaniell Warren are appointed by the towne * * * * * :

[61.] The bounds of John Dunham Juni: his graunt of forty acrees of land on the southwest of colchester is bounded as followeth viz : on the northerly end with a white oake tree on the southwest corner and on the other corner of that end two young aspin trees growing * and on the west side with a white oake tree by the way side ; from the said west bound to bee in breadth forty pole broad ;

Att a Towne meeting held att the meeting house att Plymouth the 3th of July 1663

Nathaniell Warren and Ephraim Morton were appointed by the towne to give meeting to those appointed by the Court to Run the line betwixt Sandwich and our Township

     A certaine peell of meddow lying att the lower
     end of the uper south meddow being about 2 acrees
Minister bee it more or lesse is Reserved for the use of a
Lott  minnester

It is likewise ordered by the Towne that Clarkes Iland. Sagaquish and the gurnetts nose the wood of them bee Reserved for the use of a minnester onely John Smith the boates man att Plymouth hath libertie this year to fech from any of the said Ilands what hee needeth ; and if in case any other att any time or the said Smith att the Revolution of this yeare shall fech any wood from of any of those Ilands or places fornamed they shall forfeit all such wood to the townes use ; to bee Improved for the use of the minnester ;

Att the Towne meeting held at the meeting house att Plymouth the 16th day of September 1663 ;

It was ordered and agreed by the towne that the house now in building by the towne shalbee att the dispose of the Towne for the use of the minnester and that for this yeare the sume of sixty pounds bee allowed unto Mr Williams· for his maintainance to be collected out of the Township.

Att this meeting Robert ffinney Nathaniel Warren Ephraim Morton and Nathaniell Morton they or any two of them are appointed by the towne to agree (in theire behalfe) with a workman about the covering of the minnesters house with shingle if it shalbee found to bee the best way of covering

<small>John Jordey & Richard Wright</small>

Att this meeting two sertaine pcells of Meddow were graunted unto John Jourdaine and Richard Wright to each of them a like portion of the said pcells viz : the one pcell lying att the southeast end of Jacob Cookes meddow in the woods ; and the other pcell ; soe much as is comon att the head of Captaine Southworths meddow att Winnatuxett ; and both the said pcells exceed not foure acrees apeece they the said John Jourdaine and Richard Wright to have and to hold to each of them foure acrees of the above said pcells of meddow to them and theire heires and assignes for ever ;

seaven acrees of upland was graunted att this meeting unto Jonathan Bosworth lying att the southeast end of Mr howlands land lying att a place called Colchester soe it prejudice not a highway there ; the said seaven acrees of upland with all and singulare the appurtenances to him and his heires for ever ;

[62.] It was agreed by the towne that such as have meddow att the uper south meddow shall have to each of them a smale portion of upland graunted and layed forth about ten acrees a man to lye as conveniently as may bee unto theire meddowes this to bee done as soon as the land can bee viewed and thinges put into a way for the orderly doeing of the same :

The 20[th] of february 1662.

The bounds of the land graunted to Robert Bartlett is as followeth viz ; fifty acrees of upland lying along by the ferne swamp between the Eelriver and Manomett ponds being bounded on the North norwest end with a Rid oake under the foot of the pyne hills by a little swamp and soe Ranging North northeast fifty pole in breadth towards the sea and soe Runing along by the seaside eight score pole to a little swamppe peece of ground comonly called the grounutt place and soe Runing from the ¹ grounutt place west southwest to a pyne tree standing on the southwest side of a ferney swamp;

² The bounds of the land of Joseph Bartlett the 20th of february 1662. is as followeth viz: fifty acrees of upland lying att Manomett ponds att the brooke side; the easterly end therof being bounded with a little swamp and soe extending it self in the length therof six score pole by the brooke side up into the woods being bounded att the uper end with a walnutt tree by the brooke side; and being in breadth three score and eight pole from the brook; itt is bounded with a marked maple tree standing in a smale swamp on the westerly corner; and on the northerly corner with a little white oake marked; and a stone pitched upright by it: always provided that there is and for ever shalbee a way Reserved through the breadth of the aforsaid land for the conveniency and use of those that have lands lying on the further side of the abovesaid brook att or neare the old way which cattle use to goe over the brooke att which said allowance for the way is foure pole in breadth;

The 2nd of November 1663 the Town mett on some occations not heer enserted; the Towne appointed this day month to bee another Towne meeting

[63.] Att a Towne meeting held att the meeting house att Plymouth the 30th of December 1663.

It was ordered by the Towne that whereas great damage is in the Remote meddowes of the Towne by neat cattle to the Indangering the Improverishing and undoeing of the Towne That in case any neat cattle shallbee found in any meddow that is above four miles from the saltwater viz; the south meddowes Doytes meddowes Joneses River meddow and Winnatuxett meddowes with all other meddowes adjacent or neare the said meddowes within the said

---

¹ "Grounutt" undoubtedly means "ground nut."

² This land is in what is called the Brook Neighborhood, and portions of it are now occupied by descendants of Joseph Bartlett.

limites of the places above mentioned from the first day of Aprill to the last day of August annually; they shalbee comitted to the pound and there to Remaine untill the damage shalbee satisfied or cattle Replevied; and that it shalbee lawfull for any two men of the towne soe finding cattle trespasing as aforsaid to bring them to the pound and to have six pence a head for all such cattle soe brought to the pound as aforsaid and the pound keeper to have four pence a head for all such cattle soe Impounded; and that the owners of the said cattle so Impounded they or some of the naighborhood shall have reasonable notice therof:

It was ordered by the Towne that all swine upon Just Complaint of damage done by them shalbee Ringed or Yoaked; and in case any mans swine being Ringed shall break into any mans corne field or garden being sufficiently fenced the owners of such swine shall pay Just damages:

[1] Att this meeting Jonathan Shaw desired a pcell of upland about twenty acres might bee granted to him lying betwixt land which he bought of Robert Ransom and the pond

Wheras a certain pcell of meddow lying neare the bounds of Plymouth Towards Sandwich hath bine challenged for Correction by Robert Bartlett; which yett notwithstanding hee could not cleare up to bee his by the Record of the court; and that since it doth appeer to bee within the Liberties of our Towne; The Towne have graunted and doth by these presents confeirme unto the said Robert Bartlett eight acrees of the said meddow with all and singulare the appurtenances belonging thereunto To him and his heires forever; The said meddow is a pcell of meddow somtime mowed by Thomas Butler: and on the easterly pte of it is neare a pond and a little swamp and on the notherly pte of it hath another pond neare unto it and on the westerly pte or side of it hath another pond out of which said pond cometh a small Issue or Rundlett of dirty water;

---

[1] This land was on the Wenham Road in Carver.

[64.] ¹The bounds of the lands graunted to Richard Wright att Winatucksett lyeth southwest and Northeast and the western bound by the River side is a walnut tree by a great Rocke and the northermost bound is a white oake and the easterly bound a small white oake ; and the south bound a Rid oak ; and is four score pole in breadth and a hundred in length in all fifty acrees ; fore mentioned in this booke.

¹The bounds of a small pcell of land att Rockey nooke whereon Richard Wright now liveth as followeth viz ; by the Comon Road way with a Rid oake tree from thence to a great cleft Rocke on the northwest side and soe to the sea ; and on the southerly side with the land of ffrancis Billington.

The bounds of the land which John Dunham Juni bought of Benajah Pratt lying above plaindealing viz ; which he now liveth on is as followeth on the southwest corner with a burchen tree marked : on the northwest Corner with a Rid oake tree marked haveing a white oake Joyned to it on the northeast corner with a bush marked and on the southeast corner with a white oak tree marked ; and between the white oake tree last named and the said bush there is a very great Rocke by the brook side standing directly in the Range :

The bounds of the land graunted by the Towne to John Dunham Juni : which was layed out to him by Leiftenant Morton ; lying and being att Winnatuxett which is twenty of the fifty graunted to him there ; is as followeth ; att the southwest corner with an heap of stones lying on a Rocke ; att the northwest corner with a great Pyne tree marked ; att the northeast corner with a Rid oake tree marked at the southeast corner with an heap of stones lying on a great broad stone flatt almost by the ground.

The bounds of Richard Wrights land att Winnatuxett It lyeth southwest and Northeast and the western bound by the River side is a walnut tree by a great Rocke and the northwest bound a white oake ; and the easterne bound a small white oake and the south bound a Rid oake and is four score pole in breadth and an hundred in length.

---

¹ The paragraph concerning the bounds of Richard Wright at "Rockey Nooke" has lines drawn through it in the records,

Richard Wright

The bounds of the land of Richard Wright on which his house standeth at Rockey nooke as it was layed out by Leiftenant Morton is as followeth The bounds on the Northerly side is a great cloven Rocke by the sea side and soe Ranging up towards the woods to a great heap of stones within the feild and soe to the path the breath is to run southerly from the said heap of stones to a great Rid oake marked on four sides; the southerly side to Run from the said Rid oake downward to the sea to a great Remarkable Rocke and soe to the sea the length of it is from the Comon Road way to the sea;

[65.] Att a Towne meeting held att the house of Mistris Bradford att Plymouth the twenty sixt of January Anno 1663.

It was ordered by the Towne that the sume of sixty pounds shalbee levied by Rate for the Inlargement and finishing of the [1] minnesters house provided that in case som few that may scruple the way of gathering or levying the said sume by Rate; that if they shall volentarily pay according to theire proportions to the satisfaction of them that shall undertake for the accomplishing of the worke; it shall be accepted; the said sume of sixty pound is to bee payed the one halfe therof by the first day of May next ensueing the date beerof; either in Tarr or any kind of corn; provided the Tarr bee marchantable and to bee delivered att twelve pence in a barrell cheaper then it shall att that time goe att Boston and the corn att prise then current; the other halfe of the above said sume of sixty pound is to be paid by the * of September next ensueing the date heerof; in wheat barly pease butter or money in any of the aforsaid pticulares; alsoe to be Remembered that in case any one shalbee able and willing to pay his whole Rate att the time of the first payment in Tarr it shalbee att libertie of the undertakers for the worke; whether they will Receive it or noe and accordingly to doe therein as providence shall offer opportunities   the Improvement thereof towards the accomplishment of the said work;

The psons appointed to make the above said Rate were John Dunham seni: Joseph Warren William harlow and William Crow and these or any three of them to make the said Rate and deliver a transcript therof to the Constable with all convenient speed;

---

[1] The minister's house often referred to was situated south of the Unitarian church nearly on the site now occupied by the house of Charles B. Harlow.

The undertakers for the said worke in the behalfe of the Towne are Capt: Southworth Gyles Rickard seni: Robert ffinney Ephriam Morton Nathaniel Warren Edward Gray and Nathaniel Morton: The adition agreed on is to bee 14 or 15 foot in unto the building alreddy erected to bee in equall breath and heigth unto the same and * chimneyes and that the whole house bee covered with shingle upon boards

Wheras there is forty or fifty shillings over plusse of the Countreys of this yeare The Towne aloweth that (bee it more or lesse) it shalbee aded and put into the stocke for the accomplishing of the aforesaid house: and that Nathaniel Warren and Ephraim Morton Require it and cause it to bee aded to the aforsaid stocke:

A quarter of a mile in length was by the Towne alowed and Confeirmed unto each of the naighbours that have land on the * of the Ecleriver viz: Nathaniel Warren Robert Bartlett Joseph Warren and Ephraim Morton and the Rest this to goe from the heads of theire lotts towards the pyne hills a quarter of a mile in length and of equall breadth to the lotts of land they are now possessed of; the said addition with all and singulare the appurtenances to have and to hold to them and theire heirs for ever; Nathaniel Warren hath libertie from the Towne and is deputed in theire behalfe to purchaise a certaine peell of land

Nathaniel Warren and Joseph Warren are appointed by the Towne to goe with the Measurers of land att some convenient time to settle a difference about lands betwixt Robert Bartlett and and hugh Cole This day month is appointed by the Towne on which to have * * about the herrings and * *

[66.] January the 26 1663.

It was ordered by the Towne that for as much as Capt: Southworth having formerly bought about ten acrees of meddow of Mr. Rayner and it being found to bee but five or six Acrees: Rather than to Remove the bounds upon the naighbours the towne have graunted four Acrees of meddow unto the said Captaine Southworth where hee can find it in any undesposed of; and hee hath pitched upon foure acrees of meddow in a hole mowed by

* was      Captaine Bradford neare Munponsettt Pond:
* nted      The Towne have graunted unto Samuell Dunham
* yeares     and Gyles Rickard Juni; a peell of meddow
* but      ground Comonly Called and known by the Name
 forgotten    of Southers Marsh to each of them a like propor-

Recorded by order entered tion therof the whole being estimated att about twelve acrees; to them and theire heires and assignes for ever;

[67.] Att the Towne meeting held att Plymouth the 21 of ffebruary Anno dom 1663.

George Watson Nathaniel Warren and Willam Clarke were appointed by the Towne in their behalfe to manage the business about an exchange of land desired by Acanootus which was then mentioned to the Towne by the said Nathaniel Warren;

It was then ordered by the Towne that if any of the Towne shall make wares unto any of the Remote Rivers of the Towne to take herrings that in case any shall come afterwards to take herrings att the said Rivers and soe come to have benifit of the said wares and likewise of the wares made before they come to take herrings as aforsaid in such Remote Rivers Thatt all such psons shall beare a proportionable charge both of the said wares and wayes made unto them;

It was then ordered by the Towne that whereas att a former Town meeting held att Plymouth the 30 of May 1659 Sundry Inlargments of land onely for the wood therof was graunted unto the Elder Cushman and divers others; Thatt att this meeting the Towne graunted unto all such psons that not onely the wood of such lands shalbee theires but the propriety of the land alsoe moreover that this graunt is generall to all such as have great lotes on both sides of the Towne viz: That to each they shall have an addition of a quarter of a mile from the heads of theire lotes in length; and in breadth to bee in equall proportion with theire said lotes by the great lotts is understood the lotes that were layed out att the first; on the north side of the Towne soe farr as to the south side of the widdow Doties lott and on the south side of the Towne from holmans Rocke to the Eeleriver; this graunt is both of land and wood; provided that this doth not prejudice any former graunts;

Att this meeting ten acrees of land was graunted unto Thomas Savory att the [1] foure mile brook lying next unto his other land there

John Jordan Att this meeting a smale peece of wood land viz: that peece of wood land lying betwixt the feild of

---

[1] Four Mile Brook crosses the Carver Road.

Gyles Richard Seni; and the [1] little town is granted unto John Jourdaine;

Att this meeting a little peece of upland ground about an acree was graunted unto Benajah Pratt lying eastward from his barn To bee layed forth by John Dunham seni; and Gorge Watson the bounds wherof is to the eastward or northeast corner of a wall att John Dunham seni; his feild and soe eastward of a Round hole to a smale Rocke:

Att this meeting the Towne granted unto Samuell Dunham Joseph Dunham Abraham Jackson and Jonathan Pratt to each of them six acrees of meddow; lying in a meddow neare the lower south meddow.

[2] Wheras a certaine peell of meddow hath bin for sometime challenged by Robert Bartlett lying neare unto the bounds of Plymouth towards Sandwich it being graunted him by the court which yett notwithstanding hee could not prove by the Record and that since it doth apeer to bee within the liberties of our towne The Towne have graunted unto the said Robert Bartlett eight acrees of the said meddow to him and heires for ever;

[68.] ffebruary 1663.

Att this meeting twenty acrees of meddow was graunted unto Robert flinney lying att Sampsons Countrey if it be there to bee had

The Remainder of the meddow formerly graunted to Gyles Rickard seni; lying between Doties meddow and a place called Colchester is graunted unto his sonnes John Rickard and Gyles Rickard juni;

Thirty acrees of land was graunted unto Robert Ransome lying on the south side of Lakenham pond next adjoyning unto the land hee hath there;

fforty acrees of land is graunted unto Jonathan Shaw lying att Lakenham next adjoyning unto that land hee hath there alreddy

Ten acrees of land was graunted unto every of those that have meddow in the uper south meddow and ten acrees of land is graunted unto every of those that have meddow in the lower south meddow;

---

[1] The little town was on the road leading from the Sandwich road at Hobs Hole Brook.

[2] These seven lines have marks drawn through them in the records.

Ten acrees of land is graunted unto Robert Bartlett lying adjoyning to his meddow that Thomas Butler mowed

A little peece of swamp was graunted unto Andrew Ringe lying between the [1] pond on the backside the fort hill and Gabriell ffallowells ffence

Ten acrees of land graunted unto Stephen Bryant adjoyning to his meddow formerly graunted by the towne :

Thirty acrees of land was graunted unto Gorg Bonum lying southerly to that land which hee bought of Edward Gray :

Thirty acrees of land was graunted to Gyles Richard Juni : lying next adjoyning to his fathers meddow before mentioned

Thirty acrees of land is graunted unto Willam Nelson lying on the North side of Jonses River meddow on both sides of the brooke that goes from Mr. Joseph Bradfords : soe as it bee not prejudiciall to the naighbours ;

In case it soe fall out that there is more meddow in the place where Robert Bartlett hath meddow above expressed that then the towne have graunted that which Remaines unto Joseph Bartlett soe it exceed not six acrees :

[69.] March the 22 cond 1663

| The owners names Impri Mr howland Mr Cushman | 1 | [2] The severall lotes on Puncateesett Necke are as followeth Lott is ffoggland bounded with a well or springe and a Cedar bush on the north beach therof; and one share lying on the east side of the South point of the necke; bounded att the South end with the highway; and goeth downe to the creekes mouth; the west side bounded with the highway; the north end bounded with a pyne stake at the west side and on the east with a stake standing by a stone in the marshy ground ; |
| --- | --- | --- |
| Thomas Clarke William | 2 | Lott lyeth on the southend of the south point and west side therof; the north end is bounded with a walnutt |

[1] The pond here referred to is Murdock's Pond and Fort Hill was the Burial Hill and extended across Russell Street.

[2] Puncateesett Necke was on Seconnet River and is now in Rhode Island.

| | | |
|---|---|---|
| Shirtliffe | | stake standing by the highway the said highway is three pole in breadth and goeth betwixt this lott and the share of the first lott to the creekes mouth south fourteen degrees westerly; and goeth from this lott and share to a springe att the head of the Cove the south end and west side of this lott is bounded with the sea.

Memorandum that on the 12th day of June 1672 that Elizabeth sometimes the wife of Willam Shurtleffe deceased came before the Govr and freely surrendered up all her right and Interest shee had in the land att Punckateesett which was the land of her former husband Willam Shurtliffe forenamed; unto Thomas Clarke above named and acknowlidged her selfe to be satisfyed for the same: and the Gov$^r$ gave orders it should be soe recorded. |
| Samuell Eedy Thomas Savory | 3 | Lott is on the west side of the south point bounded on the south end with a walnutt stake standing att the highway side betwixt the 2cond lott and this att the north end buteth to the highway att the cove as farr as a white thorne bush: att the East side bounded with the highway at the west side with the sea and ffogland beach: |
| Joshua Pratt Gyles Rickard Juni: | 4 | Lott lyeth on the south end and west side of the body of the necke and is on the east side of the highway that goeth to the Cove bounded with a Pyne stake and a Rid oake stake att the south end therof and att the north end it butts to the east and west highwayes and is bounded with a walnutt stake and a dry pyne stake. |

| | | |
|---|---|---|
| Ephraim Tinkham John Smith Juni; | 5 | Lott lyeth on the easterly side of the fourth lott and att the south end bounded with a Rid oake stake and a walnutt stake and att the North end with a dry pyne stake and a stone sett up att the highway. |
| Nathaniell Warren John Smith Seni: | 6 | Lott lyeth on the East side of the first lott bounded on the south end with two walnutt stakes and on the north end next the highway with a stone sett up and a Rid oake stake |
| Gyles Rickard Seni: John Rickard | 7 | Lott lyeth on the east side of the first lott bounded on the south end with two walnutt stakes; and the north end with two Rid oake stakes next the highway. |
| [70.] Gabriell fallowell Andrew Ringe | 8 | lyeth on the east side of the seaventh lott and att the south end is bounded with a walnutt stake and the waare and att the north end is bounded with a Rid oake stake |
| Mistris hickes Sam: hickes | 9 | lott lyeth on the east side of the body of the necke and on the north side of the east and west highway att the east end butteth on and bounded att the said end with a stake and a little walnutt tree in swampy ground; and att the head being the west end and next the highway that goeth through the body of the necke and soe to the maine it is bounded with a smale Rid oake and a pyne tree; |
| Thomas Lettice Rich: Wright | 10 | Lott lyeth on the north side of the 9th lott and buteth home to the waar bounded att the east end with a little walnutt tree in swampy ground and a Rid oake stake and att the west end with a pyne tree and a walnutt stake, |

| | | |
|---|---|---|
| Mistris Jenney<br>Joseph Ramsden | 11 | Lott lyeth on the north side of the 10th lott and is bounded att the east end with a Rid oake stake and a burch tree and goeth to the waare and att the west end on the south side it is bounded with a walnutt stake and the north side bounds at the head to bee Regulated att the head in the swamp according to this walnutt stake |
| Mistris Warren<br>Joseph Warren | 12 | Lott is on the North side of the eleventh lott: att the east end it buteth to the waare and is bounded with a burch tree and and an alder stake: and att the west end it is butted to the highway; and the bounds to bee Regulated according to the south head bounds of the 11[th] lott which is now a walnutt stake and the north head bounds of the thirteenth lott which is a burch tree in the swamp |
| Willam Browne<br>Edmund Tilson | 13 | Lott is on the north side of the 12th lott goeth to the waare att the east end and is bounded with an alder stake and a white oake stake standing by the end of an alder tree and att the west end and north side it is bounded with a burch tree standing in the swamp the south head bounds of this lott to bee Regulated according to this burch tree; and the north head bounds of the 10[th] lott which is a walnutt stake; |
| John Wood<br>Thomas Pope | 14 | Lot lyeth on the north side of the 13[th] lott on the east side is bounded with a white oake stake and a beach tree buteth to the water and att the west end is bounded with a burch tree in the swamp and a white oake stake; |

5

[71.]
Robert Lee
Edward Doutey

15  Lot lyeth on the north side of the 14th lott and on the east end is bounded with a Beach tree and a great dry white oake and goeth to the water; and att the head next the highway with two white oake stakes ;

Francis Billington
James Shaw

16  Lott lyeth on the north side of the 15th lott att the east end bounded with a great dry white oake tree and a great white wood tree; and goeth to the water; and the west end bounded with a white oake stake and a Rid oake stake ;

John Dunham seni :
Jonathan Dunham

17  Lott lyeth on the north side of the 16th lott and att the east end is bounded with a white wood tree and a flatt blake stumpe that stands by the water side; and att the head and west end therof; with a Rid oake stake; and a walnutt stake ;

Francis Cooke
John Cooke

18  lott is on the north side of the 17th lott and att the east end is bounded with a blacke flatt stump by the water side and a great white-wood tree and att the west end with a walnutt stake and a Rid oake stake

Samuell Sturtivant
Edward Gray

19  Lott is on the north side of the 18th lott and att the east end is bounded with a great whitewood tree and a Rid oake tree and att the head and west end therof it is bounded with a Rid oake stake and a walnutt stake. The 17: 18 and 19: lotts are 96 pole in length which is to be measured from the west end and then what land falleth att the foot betwixt the water and them is to be equally devided to them in Respect of theire Inferior quallitie to other lots ;

| | | |
|---|---|---|
| * Winslow Gorge Bonum | 20 | lott lyeth on the west side of the body of the necke and is bounded with a Rid oake bush att the west end therof att the east and west highway side and on the north side and west end it is bounded with a willow stake by a smale Rocke stone it extends from the Cove highway to the way in the body of the necke and lyeth on the north side of the east and west highway ; |
| Robert ffinney Samuell Kinge | 21 | Lott is on the north side of the 20[th] lott; and extends from the Cove to the highway in the body of the necke and on the south side at the west end is bounded with a willow stake ; and on the north side of the south end with a Rid oake stake ; |
| Gorrge Watson John Shaw senier | 22 | Lott is on the north side of the 21 lott bounded at the west end with a Rid oake stake and a pyne tree and extends from the water to the highway in the middle of the necke ; |
| Willam harlow henery Attkins | 23 | Lott lyeth on the north side of the 22 lott bounded att the west end with a pyne tree and a walnutt stake and extends from the water to the highway in the middle of the necke ; |
| James Cole seni: Robert Bartlett | 24 | Lott lyeth on the north side of the 23 lott; and att the west end is bounded with a walnutt stake and a walnutt bush and extends from the water side up to the highway in the middle of the necke ; |
| [72.] Samuell Dunham James Cole Juni: | 25 | Lott on the north side of the 24th lott and att the west end is bounded with a walnutt stake and a walnutt Bush and extends from the water side to the highway in the middle of the necke ; |

| | | |
|---|---|---|
| Arther Hatheway<br>John Howard | 26 | lott is on the north side of the 25 lott and att the west end is bounded with a walnutt stake and a smale Rid oake bush and extends from the water side to the highway in the middle of the necke ; |
| John ffaunce<br>Thomas Whitney | 27 | lott lyeth on the north side of the 26 lott and at the west end is bounded with a smale Rid oake bush and a Rid oake tree by the bank and extends from the water side to the highway in the middle of the neck. |
| John Barnes<br>John Morton | 28 | lott lyeth on the north side of the 27th lott and att the west end is bounded with a Rid oake tree on the banke and a white oake tree on the banke and extends from the waterside up to the highway in the middle of the necke : |
| John Dunham Jun<br>Willam Spooner<br>* * | 29 | lott is on the north side of the 28th lott and att the west end is bounded with a white oake tree on tne banke and a white oake tree a smale distance of : and extends from the water side to the highway in the middle of the necke : |
| Mistris Bradford<br>Mistris Attwood | 30 | lott is on the north side of the 29th lott and att the west end is bounded with a white oake tree a smale distance of from the bank and a Ride oake bush on the line on the north side of this lott it extends from the waterside east southerly 14 degrees eighty six pole to a walnutt stake that stands by the highway ; |
| Jacob Cooke<br>John Jordaine | 31 | lott is on the north side of the 30th lett and on the south and west end is bounded with a Rid oake bush and on the east end and south side with a wal- |

| | | |
|---|---|---|
| | | nutt stake and from this walnutt stake the line to Run betwixt this lott and the highway north 14 degrees westerly for a highway to the 32 lott and to the meddow the north bounds to bee ordered by the owner therof and the owner of the 32 cond lott |
| Captaine Willett Mr Paddy | 32 | lott lyeth on the north side of the one and thirtyeth lott and is bounded with the said 31 lott to bee equall in quantitie with the 31 lott: and the bounds betwixt to bee sett as the owner shall agree: and this lott is to have a highway to the marsh on the east side it being the north point |
| Ephraim Morton John Churchill | 33 | lott lyeth on the east side of the North point and highway that is in the body of the necke att the south end is bounded att the highway with a white stone and a walnutt stake and from the said stake extends notherly to the meddow to a white oake tree |
| Mannasses Kemton Nathaniell Morton | 34 | lott lyeth on the east side of the 33 lott and is bounded att the south end att the highway with a walnutt stake and a walnutt bush and from the said bush the line extends north 14 degrees easterly: |
| Thomas Morton Richard ffoster * | 35 | lott lyeth on the east side of the 34 lott and is bounded att the sout hend of the highway with a walnutt bush and a smale walnutt tree and from the said walnutt tree extends north 14 degrees east to a younge Rid oak sapline: taking all upland: |

| James hurst  Willam Nelson | 36 | lott lyeth att the goeing unto the necke on the mane upon the east side of the thirty fift lott and is bounded att the south end with a smale walnutt tree and a smale white oake tree; and att the north end with a young Rid oake sapline and a smale walnut bush; his breadth 45 pole : and in length seaventy eight ; |
|---|---|---|

[73.] Memorandum That against the east side of the eight lott and against the east end of the 9th lott there is a peece of meddow estimated att about three acrees that doth not appertaine unto those lotts but Remaines undevided as the measurers doe testify and declare ; furthermore the said measurers have declared that conserning a certain hill on the southwest point of the 2 cond lott that wheras it is badd they allowed for itt in the measure ; and therfore wheras there are stones on it that may bee usefull for the generall ; that it is left comon ; and wheras there is certaine vaines of stones lying about the first lott ; called ffogland ; that they are left comon for the good of the whole in consideration that they may prove usefull for the generall ;

Wheras the measurers of the said land att Punckateesett etc layed out but thirty and six lotts ; and that it doth appear by the list of the Names of the Purchasers that have enterest in the said lands ; that there should have bine thirty seaven lotts layed out ; and one single share more ; Captaine Southworth expressed himselfe to bee willing to bee left out for the present in taking his pte with the other ptenors ; and to take a share for himselfe and one for Mr. Rayner (which two shares make one lott) in the lands adjoyning as yett not layed out ; provided the rest of the ptenors would cleare it from the Indians in point of purchas or such troble as might arise from them or others in that behalfe which they joyntly engaged to doe ; and likewise for the odd single share not layed out henery Wood expressed himselfe willing to accept of it and to take it when layed out for his share on the tearmes and conditions that was engaged to Captaine Southworth for his ;

Att a Towne meeting held at the meeting house att Plymouth the 17$^{th}$ of May 1664

Wheras much prejudice acreweth unto the towne by the non appeerance of the townsmen att Town meetings when lawfully warned therunto and that this abuse ariseth by the neglect of the execution of former orders made by the towne for the Redresse heerof :

It was att this meeting further ordered that whosoever shall absent himself from any towne meeting being orderly warned therunto shall pay twelve pence for every default according to the aforsaid orders : unlesse hee can make a Just defence approved of by the towne and that the cunstable of the Towne shall carfully levy the same for the townes use ;

Wheras the Towne hath formerly ordered in Reference unto horses or horse kind belonging to other places and townships Runing within our Townes bounds that the owners of such horses or horse kind should pay for every one they have Runing in our townes liberties : the some of two shillings and six pence p anum ; and that in case any of our Towne or others shall att any time take up and carry away any such out of the towne to bee Responsable to pay the said sume for every horse kind they shall soe carry out : and that by the neglect of the Improvement of the said order the towne is much damnified ; it was nowe ordered by the towne that whosoever of other Townships or places that have any horse kind goeing withm the liberties of our Towne shall pay the sume of 2 shillings and six pence for every of them for every yeare which according to their age or otherwise they shall apeer to have bine in the Township or towns liberties : and this for the time past : and for the Time to come that the above said order to bee strictly observed in the ptes of it : and that whosoever shall carry out of the Township any such horse kind as have bine for some time therein shall pay * * :

[74.] Att a Towne meeting held att the meeting house att Plymouth the 8th of July 1664

It was ordered by the towne concerning the Eelriver bridge that our deputies be fully Impowered to treat with the court and carry on the busines about the building of it

The Raters chosen were Robert ffinney Willam Clarke and Willam Crow

Att a Towne meeting held att the meeting house the * of October 1664 The Raters chosen were John Morton Robert ffinney Willam Crow

Wheras great Inconveniency hath accrewed to the Towne by pmiting of sundry psons to take the benifitt of the Townes Comons in a promiscuous and disorderly way; It is ordered by the Towne that noe one Shall Improve any benefit on our Comons except householders approved by the Towne up on paine of forfeiting whatsoever shallbee Raised to the townes use; and in case any under pretence of hiering of servants shall Improve and Imploy any man or boy that hath noe Right to the Comons of the Towne; that shallbee found to bee in ptenorship in Improveing the said Comons by Raising any benifit thereon; that whatsoever benifit or proffitt shallbee soe Raised as aforsaid shallbee wholly forfeit to the townes use

four acrees of meddow is granted unto John Jourdaine att the south meddow out of that meddow there undisposed of

Mr Prence
Capt Southworth
Nathaniell Warren
Ephraim Morton

were appointed by the Towne in due and convenient time to meet together to consider of such propositions and pticulars as may probably tend to the Comon good and welfare of the towne;

It was ordered by the towne that in case the Constable Samuell Sturtivant shall faithfully and carefully collect what is yett unpayed of the last yeares Rate to the minnesters house hee shall have halfe of his owne Rate viz: of the last Remited unto him that is to say to the last Rate to the house aforsaid

The last Munday in December next is appointed for a Towne meeting day for the disposing of lands etc

Att a Towne held att the meeting house att Plymouth by the Townsmen of Plymouth the 27th of May 1665

Certaine of the naighborhood betwixt the towne and the Eelriver were appointed by the towne to view the highwaies in the naighborhoods aforsaid and to Consult and Compound with the naighbors for the settling of them for the best conveniency that may bee both to the generall and each pticulare; and what conclusions they Come to of any wages that they make Record thereof to the Court that soe they may bee entered upon publicke Record with the markes of them; and soe to bee pmanent

Robert flinney     Nath : Warren
Willam Harlow     Nath : Morton
hugh Cole     Ephraim Morton
                 Willam Clarke

Conserning the land att Punckateeset it was ordered that Capt : Southworth Nathaniell Warren and Edward Gray doe treat with Phillip the Sachem Conserning our Interest therein (soe much oposed) and to Procure of him an evidence for it besides what wee have or a full Confeirmation thereof : and to Indent with by giving him some gratuitie for his satisfaction Reward and Incurragment and that John Cooke Nath : Warren and Edward Gray doe lett out our meddows therein in the behalfe of the ptenors for this yeare to the best advantage they can

[75.] heer followeth the bounds of severall pcells of land belonging to Gyles Rickard seni : graunted unto him in severall places.

     Imprimes a Lott of Land lying a little from Lakenham Necke on the easterly side of Winnatucksett River begining att a great Rocke and soe Runing eighty pole Northwest downe the River and the other Rangeth northeast one hundred pole to a great heap of stones upon the southeast corner : and on the Northeast end a brooke and soe to another brooke by the end of a swamp : and southwest untill it comes to Winnatucksett River unto a white oake tree there marked

     The bounds of the meddow belonging to Gyles Rickard seni : in Winnatucksett meddow is as followeth viz ; twelve acrees wherof eight lyeth next Mr John howland between the said John howland and Edward Gray ; bounded on the easterly corner with a maple tree : next to the said John howland with another maple tree : on the westermost Corner next to Edward Gray with an oake : and on the northermost Corner next to Edward Gray with a pyne tree ; three acrees and an halfe more therof lyeth at the uper end of the meddow next above Captaine Southworth ; and halfe an acree that lyeth adjoyning to these three acrees the said Gyles Rickard bought of John Cobb and Edward Gray soe the whole of the aforsaid amounts to twelve acrees ; furthermore there lyeth by this meddow that lyeth above Captaine Southworths meddow an acree and an halfe that doth belonge to John Morton : soe this five acrees and an halfe is bounded on the nothermost Corner next to Captaine Southworth with a white oake marked : and on the westermost corner is bounded with a great blacke oake standing in the meddow the uper end is bounded with the upland there being noe more above it belonging to that meddow;

Those peells of land above mentioned were layed out according to order pmee Gorge Bonum

John Morton and John Cobb have acknowledged the sale of these smale peells of meddow above mine att Winnatucksett to goodman Rickard; and I thinke Edward Gray alsoe but hee hath sold it before witnes                  Thomas Southworth
Plymouth the 30th of December

1664

The bounds of the land of Gyles Rickard seni; lying att his meddow in the woods which was graunted him by the court; the length of it is half a mile the easterly end buteth upon pte of the meddow and a peece of low swamp ground the brooke that Runs out of the meddow bounds the land all along the south side; the north side upon the comon; the Range of the land lyeth west in length att the west end by the brooke it is bounded with a marked white oake: and from thence north to a marked Rid oake about fifty pole in breadth; the east end is bounded on the north side with divers marked oakes and soe to run on a line to meet with a marked Rid oake that stands on the north side att the west end of the land mensioned;

pme Thomas Southworth

May the 1: 1663

The bounds of twenty acrees of land graunted unto Thomas Lettice by the towne the 27 of October 1662 was layed out by Willam Crow the first of ffebruary 1664 as followeth

This graunt is formerly Recorded in this booke

Att the Request of Thomas Lettice I have measured and bounded the said land att the north end on the east side with a young Rid oake tree; and from the said tree the line goeth nearest due south unto a great pyne tree marked and standeth on the west or norwest side of the said little brooke and from the said Pyne tree the line goeth directly to the meddow and at and from it the line extends to a younge white oake sapling growing upon the Root of a

Pyne tree and soe home to the meddow; allowance being given for a highway threw the said land

William Crow

[76.] A true Record of the Amesurement of severall lotts or portions of meddow aloted to severall psons in the lower south meddow in the township of Plymouth which was done the 14$^{th}$ of Aprill 1664 as followeth

The six acrees belonging to Gorg Watson which hee bought of Gorge Bonum lyeth betwixt the meddow of John Wood on the north side and the meddow of Thomas Pope on the south side; and all the meddow that lyeth on both sides of the little brooke which cometh from towards Lakenham and Runeth into the maine brooke is graunted and layed forth to the said Gorge Watson for three acrees of that six which was formerly graunted him by the seaven select men; and wheras there is a smale peece of meddow which is thought to be Comon if it shall appeer not to belonge to any lott alreddy layed out which small peece of meddow lyeth upon a smale brooke higher up in the same meddow calle l the beaver dam brooke; if as aforsaid it doe not appertaine to any other alreddy layed forth then the said Gorge Watson is to have it for two acrees more of the said six acrees graunted by the seaven men aforsaid; and the other two therof below Willam harlowes meddow; on the west side of the said River

Geo Watson of these two acrees see 13 pages forwards these two acrees of meddow is otherwise ordered for Gorg Watson is to have it in another place

Nathaniel Mortons Lott is bounded on the northerly end on the East side with a smale white oake tree formerly marked and now Renewed and on the northerly end on the west side with a great Pyne tree marked the River trending in att that place neare

to the upland ; there is a Certaine Cove lying on the easterly side
of the said lot Runing into the land there being meddow graunted
to Nathaniel Morton hee Renounced it lying att Jones river ; and
tooke it att this meddow soe that this pcell of meddow became
six Acrees hee having six acrees there graunted him by the
Court before this was layed out to him

    Gorg Bonums Lott lyeth next unto Nath : Mortons Lott
on the southerly end and is bounded on the northerly end on the
east side with a greate pyne tree marked standing on the southerly
side of the Cove fornamed in Nath : Mortons lott neare unto the
entery thereof ; and on the northerly end on the west side with a
smale Pyne tree marked

    henery Woods lott lyeth next to Gorge Bonums Lott on
the southerly end and is bounded on the northerly end on the east
side with a pyne tree standing on a point marked and on the
northerly end on the west side with a white oake tree marked :

    John Churchills Lott lyeth on the southerly end of henery
Woods lott and is bounded on the northerly end on the east side
with a pyne tree marked and on the northerly end on the west side
with a pyne tree marked ;

    Willam harlowes Lott lyeth on the southerly end of John
Churchills Lott and is bounded on the northerly end on the east
side with a pyne tree marked and on the northerly end on the west
side with a pyne tree marked and on the southerly end on the west
side with a pyne tree marked standing in a grove of pynes and on the
southerly end on the east side with a smale pyne tree on a point
      pme Nath : Morton
          Towne Cleark

  1664 In Reference unto the desire of Jonathan Morey to
have the meddow land graunted to him that was sometimes
Thomas Littles being upon the Indian brooke beyond Mannomett
ponds : The towne did give libertie unto the said Jonathan Morey
to use and Improve the said meddow untill they shall see Reason
otherwise to dispose of it : Reserving still the propriety thereof
unto themselves ;

 [**77.**] Ten acrees of land is layed out to Stephen Bryant by
his meddow on the westerly side begining att the Path goeing to
Bridgwater ; bounded with a great Rid oake att the pathside ; and
Runs Northerly alonge by the meddow side to a white oake which
is betwixt ffrancis Combe and him ; soe Rangeth to a Crooked

walnutt by the meddow side; att the Northermost Corner; soe Ranging westward to a white oake and soe Ranging south backe to ffrancis Combe; is marked with a smale Rid oake itt Runs forty pole square

Att a Towne meeting held at the meeting house the eleventh day of September anno dom 1666 the towne of Plymouth did with one unanimous consent agree to alow unto [1] Mr Brinsme seaventy pounds a yeare besides his fierwood;

And wheras in consideration that the said Mr Brinsme is like to leave good acomodations to come hether and therin shall much deny himselfe and that in case he should change his condition and by death bee taken away from amongst us and leave a family behind him; hee haveing nothing assured to him in point of proprietie beside the said sum yearly abovementioned; in Reference to acomodation of house and land or farme etc; The Towne have Refered the matter with like unanimouse consent unto the Gov$^r$: Capt: Southworth Capt: Bradford the Elder Cushman Nathaniell Morton John Barnes Robert ffinney Nathaniell Warren John Morton and Ephraim Morton to treat with Mr Brinsmee about it and to come to Composition with him either to accomodate him with land etc; according to what wee have or to engage to alow him a sume to procure acomodation himselfe soe that the said sume exceed not an hundred pound;

Wheras att the said meeting Complaint was made by divers of want of acomodation of lands; especially meddow It was agreed that the next towne meeting which is to bee on the next training day after this date that then there shalbee a Consideration of such in som proportionable way to such as are alreddy accomodated

Att which day the towne agreed and gave libertie to Nathaniell Warren and Joseph Warren to Purchase thirty acrees of meddow with * * graunted by the Court unto the towne at Sepecan which is for * * Likewise it was agreed and ordered then by the Towne that Nathaniell Warren and Willam harlow shall alsoe Purchase such other lands as are yett unpurchased besides those fornamed in the behalfe of the Towne with the Courts

*

The bounds of Gyles Rickard seni: his land lying next the land of Gorg Watson lying above the head of Wellingsley brooke

---

[1] Rev. Wm. Brimsmead is here meant who supplied the pulpit of the First Church a short time after the departure of Rev. John Rayner.

is as followeth: on the south corner with an heap of stones and
soe Runing forty pole up upon a west southwest line to a smale
heap of Rockes with some stones on the topp of them; which is
the bound of the west corner: on the south corner it is bounded
with a smale Red oake tree: and on the east corner with an heap
of stones

This
layed out
August
1667

The bounds of a certaine addition of land graunted
unto the said [1] Gyles Rickard seni: aded to his garden plott hee now liveth on is as followeth viz; forty
foot in breadth on the southerly syde below from his
ffence southerly or therabouts and Twelve foot
from his fence southerly att the uper end or therabouts as it is now staked and layed out: and soe
for the length Run upon a straight line from the
lower end to the uper end is the bounds;

[78.] Att a Townmeeting held att the meeting house att Plymouth 27th of Dember 1665 Capt: Southworth engaged to assist
the Constable of Plymouth in procuring in the Remainder of the
Rate levied for the finishing of the minnesters house.

Robert ffinney
Ephraim Morton
Nathaniell Warren
and Willam harlow
} were appointed by the Towne to
take speedy course for the
finishing of the said house.

Att this meeting It was generally voated by the Inhabitants that the sume of seaventy pound formerly engaged unto Mr
Brinsme to bee alowed to him yearly bee Raised by way of Rate
and that the said sume bee payed att two severall payments Annually viz; the one halfe by the fiifteenth of May and the other
halfe thereof by the fifteenth of December and that one third pte
or one pte of three of every such paiment of seaventy pounds bee
payed in money or wheate att prise Current the said money or
wheat to bee delivered by the fifteenth of June anually and the
other two thirds to bee payed in Corne or Tarr att prise Current:
to bee payed att or before the times forementioned yearly;

Att this meeting a [2] garden plott was graunted unto Jacob
Michill adjoyning unto the homestead of Gyles Rickard seni: in

---

[1] Gyles Rickard lived on the south side of Sandwich Street on land including the house lots of the late John Chase and the late George Harlow.

[2] This garden plott included the lot on which the Carver house stands on the South. westerly side of Sandwich Street recently owned by the late Barnabas H. Holmes and Jacob Michill built a part of the present house.

case hee build theron; the said garden plott to be layed forth by Nathaniell Warren and Willam harlow; with as little prejudice to any of the naighbours as may bee:

Att this meeting it was agreed by the towne that the southeast side of Captaine Southworths land att the Eelriver bee bounded with the said River from the lower end to the uper end of the said land;

The eight day of January 1665 Wheras John Morton Leiftenant Ephraim Morton Robertt ffinney Stephen Bryant and Sergeant Tinkham and Willam harlow were formerly appointed by the Towne to dispose of such peells of meddow as are yett undisposed of to such especially as are in want in the Towneship; did accordingly meet on the day and yeare next above named and disposed of meddow to severall psons as followeth

Impr That wheras Gorge Watson expended forty five shillings in money towards the paying for the south meddowes; six acrees of meddow was appointed unto the said Gorge Watson in lieu therof; lying in the lower south meddow in case the said forty five shillings bee not satisfyed betwixt the date heerof and the last of Aprill next; and in case it bee then paied that the said meddow is to returne to the Towne

The bounds of Robert ffinneys meddow when it is determined by the Towne next wee dispose unto Gabriell ffallowell three acrees of meddow in the meddow last found out lying neare the south meddow

And unto John Jourdaine foure Acrees to lye next to Gabriell ffallowell

And unto henery Wood three acrees next to John Jourdaine

unto Edward Dotey three acrees att the turkey swamp
unto Samuell Sturtivant two acrees att the turkey swamp
unto Thomas Pope two acrees next unto henery Wood as above said
unto Jonathan Shaw two acres on the brooke where his father Watson hath meddow att the south meddow
unto Gabriell ffallowell three acrees
unto Samuell King three acrees att the Turkey swamp
unto Jonathan Morey three acrees next unto Thomas Pope
unto John Dotey three acrees
unto Richard Willis two acrees next to Jonathan Morey

unto James Cole Jun: three acrees next to Richard Willis
unto Samuell Kinge Jun: three acrees next to James Cole
unto John harman two acrees att the Turkey swamp

[79.] unto Willam Nelson four acrees att the lowest of the lower south meddow

unto Samuell Dunham halfe an acree next unto his other meddow

unto Benajah Pratt two acrees of swamp

unto Joseph howland two acrees alreddy measured att the Turkey swamp

unto Stephen Bryant att the Turkey swamp three acrees or where Robert Latham mowed on the Townes meddow

unto Gorge Bonum that pte of swamp between his owne meddow to the Ceader Bridge and another pcell of swampy meddow att Andrews Bridge lying a little above the said bridge ;

unto Ephraim Tinkham four acrees next to Willam Nelson as above named ;

unto Leiftenant Morton foure acrees next to Ephraim Tinkham

unto William harlow foure acrees next to Leift Morton

unto Joseph Bartlett one acree of meddow att the second Pond beyond the Indian brooke towards Sandwich and two acrees more att the south Countrey if it bee there to bee had

unto Nathaniell Morton one acree of meddow in holes on the North side of the Cove which land is layed out to him and Joseph Dunham and others att the lower southmeddow It being a smale slip of meddow which Runs out of the said Cove on the north side of the ffathermost slip if it bee an acree but if not to bee made up by the next slip up the Cove easterly on the said north side

We graunt unto Ephraim Tinkham and Willam Nelson two acrees of meddow att Taspequans Pond :

Those who have proportions of meddow att the south Countrey are to pay one shilling and six pence an acree by the last of march next or otherwise to forfeit theire graunt ;

The bounds of Stephen Bryants meddow above expressed is as followeth viz : it is bounded with a pyne tree marked betwixt Edward Doytes meddow and a stake on the other syde Right opposite ; and att the other end betwixt the meddow of Samuell King and it is bounded with a pyne tree marked : and oppo-

site against with an oake tree marked standing att a little cove or slip of meddow att the upper end of the said Cove ; opposite to the aforsaid pyne tree between the said Samuell King and him ;*
The bounds of Captaine Bradfords meddow att Naponsett pond is as followeth viz : foure acrees lying att the uper end of Turkey swamp on the westerly side of the Iland and is bounded with a maple tree marked standing on a hill side betwixt his meddow and the said swamp and soe Rangeth Crosse the meddow on a southwest line to a white oake tree marked ; cerculated with a swamp att the northwest end

Alsoe to Joseph howland two acrees of meddow there layed out to him lying on the westerly side of Capt : Bradfords meddow abovesaid and is bounded with the aforsaid white oake on the southerly end of the said Iland and soe to another white oake standing in a swamp on the westerly side of the said meddow :

I Gorge Bonum being appointed by the Towne of Plymouth to lay out such lands as was given out : as to the Elder Cushman fifty acrees lying upon the brooke by Jonathan Bosworthes about halfe a mile downe the said brooke or therabouts : did with the Elder and his son and Jonathan Bosworth lay out the same begining att a smale spruce upon the aforsaid brooke it being the corner bounds and soe Runes Northwest six score pole unto a smale oake bush from thence Northeast unto a smale Rocke neare a spruce swamp side : it being the next Corner bound and from thence eastward to a great spruce tree

A lott of land layed out for Jonathan Shaw containing forty acrees from the old bounds to the pond 44 pole to Range up by the pond side above the head of the pond to a smale Red oake neare the cartway that comes from the south meddow on the westward side It Rangeth over from that unto two smale Red oakes about the northeast end of a deep bottome : and soe it Rangeth north to his bounds of his lands

[80.] a lot of land layed out to Robert Ransom thirty acrees from the easterly of the pond side begining att the brooke that Runs out sixty pole and Runs away east northeast unto two Pynes that stands in a swamp att the very Corner and soe Rangeth to the brooke that Runs by the side of his owne land :

The bounds of the upland graunted by the Court unto John Dunham seni : lying att a place called swan hold ;

as it was layed out by Leiftenant Morton is as followeth; viz: bounded on the westerly end with a Pyne tree marked standing on the northwest side of a little swamp; and on the Northerly to a marked tree on the south side of Dotyes Pond and on the southerly Corner it is bounded with a black oake marked and soe Runing downe betwixt the said swan hold and Dotyes pond aforsaid to a marked tree on the Easterly Corner; In Reference unto the bounds of his meddow att Swan hold; Leiftenant Morton judged that all the meddow there either Respecting quantity or qualitie was but competent and scarsly soe: to answare the Courts graunt to the aforsaid John Dunham seni; and soe the whole that is there is alowed unto him in Respect unto the said graunt;

*John: Dunham Seni*

Att a Towne meeting held att the meeting house at Plymouth the fifth day of ffebruary 1665;

Capt: Southworth  
Leift Morton  
Mr John howland  
Gorg Watson  
and Robert ffinney  

were chosen by the Towne to bee the select men for the Towne of Plymouth; and Impowered by the towne to call Towne meetings as the occations of the towne may Require and to take Course about Idle and extravigant psons and to graunt lands either upland or meddow as occations of the yeare may Require within our Township;

The Rators Chosen by the Towne to make a Rate of forty pounds for and towards; as pte of the charge alowed to Mr Brinsmed; for this yeare were

Willam harlow  
Willam Clarke  
and Samuell Dunham

Leift Morton  
Nath: Warren  
Gorg Bonum  
Willam Clarke  
and Hugh Cole  

were appointed by the towne to settle two severall graunts of lands lying att Manomett Ponds viz: the one unto Samuell Ryder and the other unto the said Will: Clarke which graunts was to each of them twenty acrees:

Benajah Prat was Chosen by the Towne to bee a Receiver of the excise according to Court order

The Towne have graunted unto Mr Thomas Prence six acrees of upland meddow lying on the west side of Joneses River meddow next unto that meddow which was formerly graunted unto Mr John Winslow ;

Jonathan Barnes and Jabese howland } are graunted libertie to looke out ffor accomodation of land within the Township both upland and meddow ; in order unto theire accomodation :

Edward Gray
Will : Clarke
and Willam Crow
} were appointed to Repare to the Inhabitants of the towne with the first conveniency they can to see what may be collected for the Releife of ffrancis Billington hee haveing lately suffered great lose by the [1] burning of his house ;

June the 20th 1666 the Surveyors for the highwaies Chosen by the Towne were Jacob Cooke Thomas Lettice and Robert ffinney whoe were chosen the last yeare to the said office but forasmuch as they did nothinge in the mending of the wayes they were Required to serve this yeare againe

[81.] Att a Towne meeting held att the meeting house att Plymouth the fourth of July 1666.

The cellect men chosen were

John Morton
Leifte : Morton
Robert ffinney
Nathaniel Warren
Willam harlow
} these approved by the Court and sworne July the 5 : 1666

The Rators chosen were Willam harlow
Willam Clarke
Willam Crow

The pticulares the Celect men are to take into theire Cognizance and charge besides what the Court orders to them : is as followeth

Item to looke into the Towne bounds that none encroach on them

Item to the settleing of the bounds betwixt Plymouth and Sandwich

---

[1] This was probably the first fire in Plymouth after the destruction of the Common House, January 14, 1620-1, old style. Billington's house was at Seaside.

Item to take some Course with Idle psons and to see them follow some lawfull Implyment

Item to finish the settlement of the bounds of Agawam

Item to mind the Townes Consernes in Reference to the Comons and unnessesary spoyle of wood theron :

It is ordered That wheras there is due from the Towne unto Gorge Watson the sume of 47 shillinges in money That in case the said sume bee payed unto him by the 16th day of October next; that the six acrees of meddow bound over unto him for the payment of the said sume shalbee then Released to the Townes use or then to bee his proper Right; and in case it bee then Released as aforsaid that then the said six acrees of meddow shalbee at the Townes dispose for a publicke use and not to bee appropriated to any pticulare and that the Towne shalbee att the Charge of the laying of it out;

October 17 1666

[1] The waies layed out by Leift Ephraim Morton Nathaniel Warren Robert ffinney hugh Cole Willam harlow and Nathaniel Morton Apointed by the Towne of Plymouth for to lay them out; are as followeth : viz : from the Towne bridge up the hill as the way now is onely a little on the turning on the Right hand on the banke to be taken downe and soe up to three stones piched into the ground together on the tope of the hill; and soe upon a line to another greate stone pitched up on the westerside of the way and soe bounded by another neare the southeast Corner of Giles Rickards garden and soe up the hill to a great Rocke which is the bigest on the tope of the hill neare the Corner of John Barnes his garden place ; and from thence on a line to a heape of stones ; and from thence on a line to a heap of stones in a valley ; and from thence to a Rocke by the swamp side with a great stone on it lying neare Willam harlowes ; and from thence to a heap of stones on the southerly side of the gutter that Runs downe to the watering place ; and from thence onward to another heap of stones in Alkarmus feild ; and from thence to a heape of stones on the Northerly side of Wellingsley brooke and soe over the said

---

[1] This is the laying out of Sandwich Street. The town bridge was just above the level of the brook and consequently there was a hill on its southerly side. Giles Rickard's land was on the right, the land of John Barnes was on the left opposite to the Green, and Alkarmus' field extended from Sandwich Street to Gallows Lane at Mount Pleasant Street. From John Churchill's land at Jabez Corner the laying out includes two roads, one along shore to the Cliff and the Warren farm, and thence to the old Manomet Road, and the other by George Bramhall's, and to the left across Eel River and intersects the other on the south side.

brooke to an heape of stones on the topp of the hill by Wellingsly; and from thence to a heape of stones on the southermost end of the said hill; and from thence to an heape of stones along southerly to a Corner of a field which was formerly Ralph Wallens and from thence to another heape of stones onwards to the topp of a hill southerly and from the stones a long Rocke with a dent in the topp of the southwest end of it; lying on the southerly side of John Churchills feild which was somtimes the land of Anthony Snow and from the said Rocke towards the waterside northeast or thereabouts to an heape of stones and soe alonge the hyeway as it is now in use and soe along the waterside as it is now in use to an heape of stones att the lower end of Gorge Mortons land and soe bounded with heapes of stones on the westernside of the said way that is now in use unto Robert Hinneys Clift and soe to the flishing point; lett it be understood that all the heapes of stones named are to be named as markes of this way doe lye on the western side of the said Way; but to proceeed, The way from the flishing point is to goe to the end of Nathaniel Warrens Land to an heap of stones and soe by heapes of stones up threw his feild to his barne and soe on the southwest side of his house downe to the way that Comes over the Eelriver bridge and soe to a peece of Comon land which lyeth between the lands which formerly were Mr Winslows and Mr Warrens; But to returne to the aforsaid Rocke by the side of John Churchills feild and from that said Rocke the way is to goe up the valley and soe towards the Eelriver as it is now in use to an heap of stones on the westerly side of the said way att the head of Willam Clarkes feild; and soe bounded by severall heapes of stones on the westerly side of the said way to a Certaine great Rocke lying neare the foot of Eelriver bridge leaveing James Clarkes house on the westerly side of the * and soe from the said Rocke over the said bridge and soe directly to meet with the way on the southerly side of the said Bridge fornamed;

[82.] Att a meeting of the Celectmen of the Towne of Plymouth the scond of October 1666

It was ordered by them that hensforth noe wood or timber be spoyled by barkeing within a mile and an halfe of any naighborhood but they that fell trees shall carry away both top and body on the penalty of eighteen pence a tree;

It is further ordered by them that whosoever shall carry or sell any barke out of the towne shall forfeite thee prise therof to the townes use :

It is further ordered by them if any of our Township shall find any Incroachment upon our Towne by any of any other towne ; It shalbee lawfull for any of our Towne forthwith to take out an attachment upon any timber or knots or Tarr etc soe felled or taken and shalbee payed for his paines and the benifitt to Redound to the Towne

### October 22 1666

It was ordered by the Towne that the Celect men of the Towne of Plymouth or any two or three of them agreeing together shall have power to give order to the Constable to warne Townemeetings as often as occation shall Require Respecting the townes occations and that the Constable shall give seasonable warning therof by order from them ; according to the time appointed by the towne formerly in that Respect

Nathaniel Warren  
Joseph Warren  
Willam Clarke  
and hugh Cole  
} are deputed by the Towne to Purchase all such lands as are to be Purchased of the Indians att or about Agawaam

Nathaniel Morton  
John Morton  
and Leift: Morton  
Willam Clarke  
Willam harlow  
and ffrancis Comb  
} were appointed by the Towne to lett and to farme, sett and lease out the Townes lands att Agawaam for the Townes use for any tearme of time under seven yeares

Att a meeting held by the townsmen of Plymouth the 2cond of January 1666 ten acrees of land was graunted unto Benjamine Eaton lying above ffrancis Billingtons house neare Rockey nooke ;

hugh Cole to be accomodated with meddow att the lower south meddow downe that River below those that have meddow there alreddy graunted

October 1666 — the land above expressed graunted to Benjamine Eaton was above the land that was somtimes Gorge Clarkes and is to be layed out as to the best conveniency to him soe to as little prejudice to the naighbors as may bee ; the land lyeth between ffrancis Billingtons and that which was John Cookes graunt above Gorge Clarkes ;

New Plymouth

This ordered to be Recorded pr Thomas Southworth

haveing order att a Townemeeting held the second day of January 1666 for the bounding of ten acrees of land graunted to Benjamine Eaton lying above the lands that was formerly Gorge Clarkes and betwixt ffrancis Billingtons lott and the lotts that were John Cookes: have layed it out on the westward side of the swamp called Bradfords Marsh and on the south side and east end of the said land have bounded it with a swamp wood tree standing att or in the swamp: from thence the line extends nearest southwest and by west to a Red oake tree marked and standing on the westward side of the Topp of a hill; and on the north side and east end next to the swamp with a young walnutt sapling and from the said walnut the line extends nearest southwest and by west unto a forked Red oake sapling; bounded Aprill 11<sup>th</sup> 1667 pr Will: Crow:

[83.] Att a Townemeeting held att the meeting house att Plymouth the * day of July 1667; It was agreed and concluded as followeth

viz:

That the sume of fifty pounds shalbee alowed to Mr. Cotton for this psent yeare and his wood To be raised by way of Rate to be payed in such as god gives ever onely to be minded that a considerable pte of it shalbee payed in the best pay; and Willam Clarke and William Crow are appointed by the Towne to take notice of what is payed and brought in unto him and to keep an account therof: Joseph howland and ffrancis Combe are agreed with by the Towne to find the wood for this yeare for the sume of eight pounds

Robert ffinney  
Willam Clarke  
and Joseph Warren  
{ are appointed by the towne to take some speedy course for the finishing of the <sup>1</sup> minnesters house:

Willam Clarke  
and William Crow  
{ are apointed by the Towne to take the account of Edward Gray in the

---

<sup>1</sup> It is probable that the minister's house here referred to stood on the lot given to the church in 1664 by Bridget Fuller for a parsonage and on its southeasterly corner about where the house of Isaac Brewster now stands. The old house and lot seem by the records to have been sold in 1667 by Rev. John Reyner's son John, to George Bonum.

behalfe of the Towne; and also all other accounts that doe belong unto the Towne in pticular to demand that which is due to the Towne for the Rent of Agawam;

The Rators chosen to make the Countrey Rates and other for the Towne were John Morton serjeant Willam harlow and Willam Clarke;

<table>
<tr><td>this land is neare the bounds of Sandwich</td><td>ffifty acrees of land formerly graunted unto Jonathan Morey layed out unto him by Gorge Bonum was att this meeting Confeirmed to him and his heires and assignes for ever; the bounds wherof are as followeth viz; begining at a * swamp lying att the northeast end of the said land the northermost bounds of the said land is a whit oake standing on a little brow of a hill and Rangeth from the said oake for the length therof on a west southwest line nearest unto a pyne tree by the herring pond soe called; and soe Ranging for the southermost bounds to a pyne tree leaning over the said pond; and soe backe for the eastermost bounds to a little Rid oake standing by the swamp</td></tr>
</table>

The bounds of hugh Coles Land lying neare the hither mannomett pointe soe called is as followeth viz: bounded att the easterly end with a great Rocke by a place comonly called the salt marsh and soe Ranging up into the woods upon a southwest line halfe a point westerly; which is from the great Rocke spoken of 72 pole to a heap of stones; and Runing along by the sea one hundred and two pole; and there att the northerly end bounded with a heap of stones; and there Runing into the woods south- west half a point westerly 72 pole and there bounded with a heap of stones;

Layed out to Gyles Rickard Juni: a pcell of land lying betwixt the meddow of his father which is neare Dotyes meddow in the woods and a spott of meddow lying on the northwest side which pcell of Land is ninteen acrees and is bounded att the north end with three white oakes marked: and another pcell of eleven acrees on the south side of his fathers said meddow and on the west syde with a Rid oake marked and a white oake and a Rid oake on the south corner and is bounded in with a swamp;

Six acrees of meddow was graunted unto ffrancis Combe ying att the south meddow brooke

An addition of land was graunted unto each of the naighbors on the north syde of the towne att and about plaine dealling viz ; to Run a quarter of a mile into the woods from the ends of theire lotts this is to be understood of all the great lotts towards Jones River

[84.] Ten acrees of meddow was graunted unto hugh Cole lying att the south meddow brooke

Eight acrees of meddow was graunted unto Joseph Bartlett lying at the south meddow brooke

Six acrees of meddow was graunted unto John Cole lying att the south meddow brooke ;

four acrees of meddow was graunted unto Daniell Dunham lying att the south meddow brooke

five acrees of meddow is graunted unto John ffallowell lying att the south meddow brooke ;

six acrees of meddow is graunted unto Samuell Eedey lying att the south meddow brooke ;

a peece of swamp is graunted unto Robert Bartlett to make meddow of lying adjoyning to his meddow att the Eelriver

ffour acrees of meddow is graunted unto Benajah Pratt lying att the brooke Comonly Called Crane brooke ;

Samuell Sturtivant is graunted to exchange his fifty acrees of land graunted unto him by the Towne for fifty acrees lying att Monponsett pond to the south end of the pond ;

The swamp lying att the path by John hawards house (that was) is graunted to William Nelson

A peece of meddow lying on the southeast side of Captaine Bradfords meddow being a peece between some meddow alreddy layed out is graunted unto Thomas Cushman Juni ;

Att this meeting it was ordered by the Towne that noe Cattle either horses hoggs or other Cattle shall not be put turned or Carryed to the [1] salth »use beach from the first of May untill the first of November Annually ;

> The bounds of a garden place or homsteed layed out to Jacob Michell according to a former graunt expressed in this booke is as followeth

It adjoyneth to Gyles Rickards garden plott on the southeast syde of the garden plott of the said Gyles Rickard ; and is

---

[1] Salthouse Beach is Duxbury Beach.

bounded on the other syde att the lower end and att the uper end therof with two stones sett into the ground ;

The Towne have ordered and engaged to Refrayne from sending any hoggs to the gurnett beach att any time ; and horses or neat cattle to the said beach from the begining of Aprill unto the last of October Annually : and that this order be Comunicated to the Towne of Duxburrow desireing and expecting that they should doe the like ;

[85.] Att the towne meeting held att Plymouth the 13th day of October 1667

Leiftenant Morton
Gorge Bonum
Joseph Warren
Willam Clarke
and hugh Cole

That wheras the sume of twenty-two pounds is alowed by the Court with that which is alreddy expended towards the building of a bridge over the Eelriver ; which is accepted by the towne These are appointed by the Towne to Receive the said sume ; and to serch the old bridge and to take Course and agree with the workmen for the Rebuilding or Repaireing therof in the place it now is in the most prudensiall and frugalest way that may be ;

Wheras by a former Towne order William Clarke and William Crow were appointed by the Towne to take the account of Edward Gray in theire behalfe as alsoe all other accounts appertaining to the Towne ; but were not Impowered to prosecute by Law for the Recovery of any debt due therunto : These are to certify that the Towne of Plymouth hath Impowered and doe by these prsents Impower the said William Clarke and William Crow to demand Receive and in any case of none payment of any debt or debts due to the Towne by due course of law to Recovering any such debt or debts in the behalfe of the Towne aforsaid and will alow and approve of theire Regulare acting Respecting the prmises as nesessitie may Require

In Reference unto the proportion made by the Celectmen that some prudentiall Course might be taken for and about the Receiveing of Townsmen and stating of theire prividges : the Towne have appointed and doe Request

| | |
|---|---|
| The Gov[r] | as a Committee in due and |
| Edward Gray | convenient time to meet to- |
| Nathaniell Morton | gether and to treat of and con- |
| Gorg Watson | trive such pticulars as may be |
| Leift: Morton | thought meet to be proposed |
| Serjeant Tinkham | unto and voted by the Towne |
| Serjeant harlow | for theire more orderly pro- |
| Joseph Warren | ceeding in that behalf : |
| Will Clarke | |
| and Willam Crow | |
| Joseph howland | |

In Reference to the proposition Concerning a more Just and equall way to be thought on for the makeing of Rates ; It is refered to the next meeting of the Celect men and that then such as shall see good to propose any thing Respecting the premises shall Repaire to them and Comunicate the same and Consult with them in Reference therunto

Att this meeting the Towne graunted unto Robert Barrow and Edward Dotey to each of them six acrees of swampy meddow lying att or not far from the uper south meddow betwixt Andrews bridge and the new meddow soe as it doe not Infring any former graunt nor hinder any highway flifty acrees of land was graunted unto John Jourdaine lying towards the north end of Sandwich herring pond Joyning to Jonathan Moreyes swamp ; soe as in case hee sell it to some of the Towne of Plymouth

A privilidge of grasse or sedge is graunted unto John holmes att the [1] Reed pond in case hee can make meddow of the whole pond or any pte therof it is to be his owne :

[86.] The 30th of November 1667 The Towne agreed to send for Mr John Cotton and to leave the charge of the Transportation of him and of his family and goods from [2] Martin's Vinyard to Plimouth ; Morover they haveing formerly agreed to alow him for this yeare the sume of fifty pounds : to be Raised by Rate

---

[1] Reed pond was flowed ground on Cold Spring Brook between the country road and the railroad.

[2] Up to the latter part of the 17th century the Island now called Nomans Land was called Martha's Vineyard and what is now called Martha's Vineyard was called Martin's Vinyard. The name undoubtedly came from Martin Pring who visited it in 1603. Nomans Land probably derived its name from a christian Indian chief named Tickanoman who flourished about 1650 on Martin's Vineyard. A point of land on Martha's Vineyard nearly opposite Nomans land is laid down on a pen and ink plan of the Island dated 1693 as Tickanoman's Point. In an old deed it is called Noman.

It was agreed by the Towne that the sume of fifty pounds shalbe speedily Raised by Rate wherof twenty-five pounds to be delivered to Mr. Cotton as pte of the abovesaid fifty; and the other twenty-five pounds to be Improved by the psons deputed: for the defraying of the charge of his Transportation and the other nessesary charges about the house etc: The Rators Chosen to make this Rate were Leift: Morton Willam Clarke and Willam Crow

The lands which I layed out for Samuell Sturtivant att Monponsett pond of fifty acrees abutting upon fifty acrees of Mr Willam Bradford's lying on the east end of the said Willam Bradfords; and is bounded with a Pine tree by the pond syde and Runes easterly from the corner of the pond to a blacke oake on the north syde of the path; and Rangeth southerly to a smale blacke oake and soe to a little white oake marked; and so Rangeth by the swamp syde to a blacke oake that standeth on a plaine; which oake is the corner bound answarable to the forenamed pyne tree by the pond syde; between the said Willam Bradford and Samuell Sturtivant:        pme Gorg Bonum:

The bounds of Capt: Willam Bradford's land att Monponsett pond is as followeth

| | |
|---|---|
| * should | (viz) fifty acrees of land bounded on the |
| * been laid | northwest with a pyne tree marked by the pond |
| * Captaine | syde; and the westermost bound a smale Rid |
| * * | oake tree marked: the southermost bounds a |
| * * | tree marked standing between him and Samuell |
| lying on | Sturtivant: and another pyne tree marked |
| * * | standing by the ponds syde betwixt Samuell |
| att Monpon- | Sturtivant and him for the eastermost bounds |
| sett * * | |
| * * | |
| * * of | |
| January 31st | |
| 1667 | |

The bounds of James Clarke's farme is as followeth viz: bound on the easterly end with the pond and soe Runs one hundred ninety two pole northerly to a Rocke upon a Rockey-hill with stones upon it; and soe Runs in westerly an hundred pole to a great Rocke and a white oake tree by it marked and on the southerly corner marked with a smale Red oake tree; but sd tree being Roted down a heap of stones is set in ye place By Thomas faunce surveyor to the Towne of Plimouth Aprill 5 1675

The twenty acrees of Land the Towne graunted unto James Clarke lyeth against pte of his farme land abovesaid ; and is bounded on the easterly corner with a Rid oake and on the southerly corner with a Rid oake tree, and on the westerly corner with a Rid oake and on the northerly corner with ⅞a Rocke and stones upon it ;

(Aprill 5th 1695 A Raing run and settled between Samuell Riders land below mentioned and James Clarkes farm land sd James Riders northerly corner bound is a heap of stones by the swamp sid and soe to Run a strait corse to James Clarkes southerly corner bounds of his farm land and from thence upon a straite course to the sd Riders head bound in his record mentioned, Raniged and settled on the day and yeare above written by Thomas faunce surveyor to the Towne of Plimouth) The bounds of Samuell Ryders Land att Mannomett ponds is as followeth viz ; on the easterly corner bounded with the pond and brooke and soe Runing Northerly to a heap of stones ; and so Runing westerly one hundred pole and there bounded with a Rid oake tree and thence for his southerly corner to a smale Run of water that Runs into the brooke and there marked with a swampy oake ; ffor the twenty acrees graunted unto him by the Towne it is bounded as followeth ; ffor his easterly bounds therof it is a stone sett into the ground by a Cartway syde and bounded on the south corner with a Red oake ; and the westerly corner with a Rid oake ; and on the northerly corner with a Red oake by a Rocksyde

the bounds of Thomas Popes land is as followeth the north end bounded with a great white oake by a little brooke and soe Runing southerly six score Rod and bounded on the east syde of a pond with a Rid oake tree ; and from thence Runing easterly three score and six pole marked with a bush ;

Awanno the Indian and Awampocke theire land is bounded on the easterly corner with a Rid oake tree and soe Runing Southerly one hundred Rod to a great pond ; and from thence westerly to a little pond which is fifty rod distance and soe bounded on the north corner with a bush ;

[87.] Att the Townemeeting held att the meeting house att Plymouth the one and thirtieth day of January ann" dom 1667

Joseph howland  } agreed with the Towne to be the standing
Joseph Bartlett  } troopers for the Towne for the tearme of
and ffrancis Combe } five yeares from the date heerof full to be

expired and to be alowed the sume of four
pounds and ten shillinges which is in the
hands of the former troopers viz ; Capt :
Bradford Willam Clarke and James Clarke
belonging to the towne ; and to be assisted
by the Towne for the procuring therof ;
Joseph Warren } are appointed by the Towne to forwarne
and Jonathan Morey } the Indians not to make use of our lands
lying neare sandwich bounds ; and to
oppose them in makeing use therof : and
to signify unto them that they shall not
soe doe unles they can make Just
title therunto ;

  Att this meeting libertie was graunted unto all such as have land graunted to them att Winnatucksett to Remove theire said graunts a mile and an halfe from theire meddows towards Monponsett pond ;

Saml Kinge    fiifty acrees of land is graunted unto Samuell Kinge lying neare to his meddow at Monponsett pond ;

Edwd Dotey    fiifty acrees of Land is graunted unto Edward Dotey lying neare his meddow att Monponsett ; next unto the fifty acrees graunted unto Samuell Kinge ;

John Andrew & Saml    Graunted unto John Andrew and Samuell Mylam to each of them thirty acrees of upland somwhere about Mannomett ponds if they can find it in any such lands as not graunted unto any others

Abraham Jackson    Thirty acrees of land is graunted unto Abraham Jackson where John Andrew and Samuell Mylam shall have theires if it may be there had if not any wherelse wher hee can find it ; not prejudiciall to others ; within this townshipp

Joseph howland    Thirty acrees of land is graunted unto Joseph howland lying betwixt the Indian pond and Billington's tree ; on the northsyde of the said pond

John Dotey    Thirty acrees of land is graunted unto John Dotey lying next unto Joseph howlands att the same place ;

| | |
|---|---|
| Thos: Cushman | Thirty acrees of land is graunted unto Thomas Cushman Juni: lying next to John Doteys att the same place; |
| Jona: Shaw | Ten acrees of land is graunted unto Jonathan Shaw lying next unto his land at Lakenham; |
| This is otherwise * * * * * from * * * * | [1] Graunted unto James Clarke a certaine pcell of sedge or a pte of the pond att Mannomett ponds viz: all that pte of the pond or sedge ground which lyeth between a place there called the Gurnett and the bounds of Samuell Ryders land and soe upon a straight line unto the beach |

The Towne have ordered

| | |
|---|---|
| Richard Wright | That flifty acrees of land graunted unto Richard Wright lying att Winnatucksett shalbe layed out and ordered by Captaine Bradford and the Elder Cushman; |

The Towne of Plymouth haveing ordered us whose names are heerunto Published soe to measure and bound unto Richard Wright fifty acrees of upland att or neare Winnatucksett as by theire Record doth appeer dated October 16 1659 wee have accordingly done the same; upon the east syde of Winnatucksett River where the said Richard hath begun to settle or Improve; and have since bounded the said land on the northerly syde next the River with a great Rocke: and from the said Rocke (which may be Knowne) by nother great Rocke that stands in the line by him; The line extending nearest northeast and by north unto a stone sett or pitched into the ground for the length of the said land and from the said Rocke the land goes soe farr up the said River unto and is bounded by a stone sett into the ground by the said Riversyde neare a live oake that stands on the banke of the River and from this stone it extends nearest northeast and by north to a Rid oake marked on four sydes these four markes are the bounds of the aforsaid fifty acrees of land; which land butts home to the River; pformed the 12th day of february 166 *

Pme Willam Bradford,
Thomas Cushman.

---

[1] This clause has lines drawn through it in the records.

[88.] The bounds of Gorge Watsons meddow att the Lower south meddowe is as followeth viz: on the south syde of a little brooke: bounded with a pyne tree betwixt the meddow of Thomas Pope and the said Gorge Watson and soe Runing westerly to a great spruce tree; and on the easterly end with a pyne tree which stands betwixt the meddow of John Wood and Gorg Watson; The aforsaid brooke Runing through the said meddow of the said Gorge Watson from the maine River westerly up unto the aforsaid spruce tree the said meddow soe bounded as aforsaid was layed forth by Leiftenant Ephraim Morton unto the said Gorge Watson for ten acrees be it more or lesse;

ffurthermore there is two acrees graunted and ordered to Gorg Watson lying att the lower southmeddow: att a place called the beaver dam brooke: bounded att the easterly end with a pyne tree: on the north syde: and a spruce tree on the south syde; att the easterly end next the meddow of Robert Ransom: and att the westerly end with a pyne tree: a smale brooke Runing through it into the maine River: this peell soe bounded the said Gorge Watson is to have for two acrees of meddow be it more or lesse;

Three score acrees of land is layed forth by Gorge Bonum unto Thomas Savory att the four mile brooke on the northwest syde therof: bounded on the easterly corner with a white oake tree marked standing on the syde of a hill neare the brooke; and on the southerly corner with a great pyne tree marked upon the topp of a hill neare the brooke: and soe Rangeth northwest neare to a great blacke oake marked standing on the northwest syde of the cartway that goeth to Swan hold: and soe Rangeth to a white oake marked standing on a point of land att the northwest corner of a pond called beaver pond: and on the southeast syde of the said pond to a pyne tree marked standing neare the pond syde which is the bound of the said land on the easterly corner:

New Plymouth
ffebruary 19[th] 1667

The bounds of thirty acrees of land graunted unto Joseph howland the 31 of January 1667 by the Towne of Plymouth on the northsyde of the Indian pond the said land att the south end and east syde: is bounded with a white oake tree which stands on the north syde of the cart way; and att the end and east syde it is bounded with a smale Red oake sapling standing neare a swamp soe to a white oake tree standing on the south syde of a hill; and is on the north and westward syde of the said land and on the southward end and westward syde it is bounded with a smale Rid oake tree standing on the south syde of the aforsaid cart way; the line is north forty degrees to the eastward and south forty degrees to the westward; length one hundred pole breadth forty eight pole more or lesse; bounded as aforsaid

pme William Crow

A pcell of sedge ground is graunted unto Joseph Bartlett lying att a pond by Thomas Clarke's ffarme on the easterly syde therof; bounded on the western end with a Ceder bush; and soe Ranging into the pond; and on the easterly syde with a place or gutt comonly called the Gutt; which pteth the ponds and soe Ranging from the said Gutt over to the clifts of the beach;

[89.] Att a Towne meeting held at the meeting house att Plymouth the 16th day of March 1667;

The Towne have graunted unto Mr Thomas Prence a smale psell of land lying att his meddow att Jonses River being about twelve acrees be it more or lesse which is a psell of land Invironed about with swampes; to be layed forth for him by Edward Gray and William Crow;

Jona; Barnes    An acree and an halfe of land is graunted unto Jonathan Barnes in Alcarmus feild to be layed out to him by William harlow and Nathaniel Morton

grant to Indian    A libertie is graunted by the Towne unto the Indian called Caussetan and his Relations to Improve a smale psell of land about ten acrees about [1] breakeharthill and for the acknowlidgment of the Towne to be the true propriators therof the said Caussetan or some one of his Relations is to pay yearly halfe a pecke of Indian Corne;

Thirty acrees of land is graunted unto Ephraim Tilson lying att the head of Nahucked near Lakenham

Thirty acrees of Land is graunted unto William holmes for the accomodation of his son: the said thirty acrees to be att the said Nahuckett;

---

[1] Breakehart hill is the hill on the Sandwich road south of Ellisville.

Willis        ffifteen acrees of Land is graunted unto
Richard Willis lying neare Warren's wells

The Towne have agreed that a leantoo and a Cellar shalbe made and erected to the minnesters house ; to bee about halfe the length of the house ; It being left unto Leiftenant Morton and Serjeant harlow to agree with workmen to doe it ; as they shall Judge most Convenient ;

It is ordered by the Towne that notice be given to those that are the owners of the mill That the Towne Requires them either by a flood gate or otherwise to take Course that the herrings or Alwives may have free libertie to goe up to spawn att the season therof according to a former agreement and Ingagement ; and in case they shall Refuse or neglect soe to doe that then the Towne will take Course that it shalbe done ;

The Towne have agreed with Abraham Jackson to make and sett up some fence or a psell of ffence about the minnesters gardens next unto the street which is to post and Railes viz ; five Railes in a post the postes to be oake and if the Railes be Ceder that they shalbe sufficient halfe Rounds and this to be done soe farr as the gardens doe Reach or extend next the street and alsoe that it be done seasonably for sowing of garden seeds ; and hee is to have two shillings a Rod ; alsoe provided that the Rails shalbe but ten foot longe or eleven foot with the ends entered into the postes ; and in case that hee shalbe found not to make wages therof that hee be Considered more as Reason shall Require ;

The Towne have further agreed with the said Abraham Jackson to find Mr Cotton with wood this following summer for six shillings a Cord ; The Comittee appointed by the Towne to Consider of such propositions

Graunted unto James Clarke a Certaine psell of sedge ground att Mannomett pond bounded upon the southerly Corner with a Rocke ; with an heap of stones on it by the said pond syde ; and soe Runing on a line unto a place Comonly Called the [1] Gurnett ; unto the easterly point of it ; and soe Runing on the same line over to the beach ; and soe extending in breadth home to his meddow formerly graunted to him and unto his owne upland on the Northwest syde ;

---

[1] It is difficult to say whether this line ran in the direction of the Gurnet across the bay or whether there was a place at Manomet called by that name. If there was such a place the editor has never seen it referred to elsewhere.

[90.] Plymouth

Measured and bounded thirty acrees of upland unto John Dunham Juni: and is pte of fifty acrees of upland graunted by the Towne aforsaid unto twelve acrees of meddow lying att Winnatuxett which was graunted there to John Dunham seni : The said thirty acrees lying on the Northwest syde ; and the Southwest syde of the path that goeth to Bridgwater ; the said land is bounded at the Northeast end and the Southeast syde with three spruce trees growing up together or out of one Root which trees stand on the Northwest syde of the said brooke ; att the Northeast end and the Northwest syde of the said land it is bounded with a stone sett into the ground on the Southwest syde of the aforsaid path ; att the Southwest end and on the Southeast syde the said land is bounded with a smale ash tree marked in the swamp ; and att the said end and Northwest syde it is bounded with a great white oake there growing another from the Root therof ; These four markes are the bounds of the said land : being one hundred pole in length and forty eight pole in breadth    Aprill the 27 : 1668
pme Willam Crow Surveyor.

Att a Townmeeting held att the meeting house att Plymouth the 18th day of May 1668

Liberty was graunted by the Towne unto Edward Dotey Thomas Dotey and Thomas hewes to sett up a stage for ffishing att Clarkes Iland and to Improve such wood as they shall need theron for the makeing or building of the said Stage and other nessesaries for the makeing of flish but not to Transport any wood of from the said Iland except to keep fier in theire boates ; and That they be prohibited to keep any doggs there soe to anoy or Course such sheep as shall att any time be put upon the Iland by any of our Towne ; and the Towne doth heerby prohibitt that noe hoggs or other Cattle except sheep shalbe put on the Iland ; and this privilidge or libertie to be and appertaine to the psons above named for the tearme of seaven yeares from the date heerof and noe more unlesse the Towne shall see Cause to give further liberty ;

Att a Townmeeting held att the meeting house att Plymouth the sixteenth day of June 1668 In Reference to a Complaint that many horses are Rid and driven threw the Towne by Strangers some of which horses are * to be taken up and sold or made away in a disorderly way and probably therby many wronged ; The Towne have appointed hugh Cole Serjeant harlow and Stephen Bryant to take notice of such horses as are soe carryed threw the Towne and are heerby Impowered to examine them whether they have a passe for them and all of them and in case they find them to be carrying of them away disorderly to take speedy Course to have them seized on that soe the law may be followed on them; That is to say they are heerby Impowered to seize on them and forthwith to bring them before some one of the majestrates of this Jurisdiction for tryal;

William Crow and Joseph Warren are appointed to Run the line of our grant of land att Sepecan in the behalfe of the Towne:

Thirty Acrees of Land is graunted unto Daniell Ramsden lying on the southeast syde of Lakenham by John Rickards Tarr pitts by a swamp syde neare Doties plaine;

a smale psell of sedge Ground was Graunted unto Joseph Bartlett lying and being att Mannomett ponds lying neare unto the sedge Ground graunted to James Clarke; on the easterly side therof; being about halfe an acree be it more or lesse;

[91.] The names of such as have voated in Towne meeting in the Towne of Plymouth

[1] Mr Thomas Prence
Capt: Thomas Southworth
Capt: Willam Bradford
Mr John Cotton
The Elder Thomas Cushman
Mr John howland
Jacob Cooke
Samuell ffuller
ffrancis Billington
William hoskins
Samuell Sturtivant
Edward Gray
Stephen Bryant
Joseph Ramsden
John Dunham juni:
Samuell Kinge

---

[1] In this list the names of Thomas Prence, Thomas Southworth, John Howland, Francis Billington, Joseph Ramsden, Henry Wood, John Morton, John Wood, Gabriell Fallowell, Thomas Savory, John Dunham, seni: Jonathan Dunham, Thomas Pope, John Barnes, Thomas Whitney, Thomas Clarke, Nathaniell Warren Hugh Cole and Jonathan Bosworth have lines drawn across them in the records.

PLYMOUTH RECORDS. 101

Ephraim Tinkham
henery Wood
John Cobb
Willam Nelson
John Morton
John Moses
Thomas Lettice
James Cole seni:
James Cole juni:
John Smith
Gorge Bonum
John Wood
Thomas Lukas
Andrew Ringe
Richard Wright
Gabriell ffallowell deceased
Thomas Savory
John Dunham seni: deceased
Jonathan Dunham
Benjah Pratt
Gyles Rickard seni:
Willam Crow
Thomas Pope Gone from Towne
Gorg Watson
John Barnes
Edward holman
Willam harlow
John Jourdaine
Benjamin Eaton
Jonathan Barnes
John Rykard
Gyles Rickard juni:
Samuell Dunham
Samuell Eedey
Thomas Whitney
Nathaniell Morton
Leift: Ephraim Morton
Thomas Morton
Robert ffinney
Thomas Clarke
Willam Clarke

Robert Bartlett
Nathaniell Warren
Joseph Warren
hugh Cole
Jonathan Shaw
Samuell Ryder
James Clarke
Abraham Jackson
Joseph Dunham
John holmes
Joseph Bartlett
Mr Joseph Bradford
Jonathan Pratt
Edward Dotey
Gorge Morton
Thomas Cushman
ffrancis Combe
Joseph howland
Jonathan Bosworth
John Barrow
Robert Ransom
Jonathan Morey
John Bryant
Jabez howland
Daniell Dunham
Richard Willis
Ephraim Tilson
John ffalloway
John Bradford
Robert Barrow
John Dotey
Joseph Churchell
Nathaniell Southworth
Mr * *
Thomas Faunce
John Drew
John *
Samuell Gardner
Josias Morton
Nathaniell Morton
Thomas Clarke jun:

[92.] The bounds of the land of John Andrew and Samuell Mylam is as followeth viz; it is bounded with Mannomett Ponds brooke on the Northerly end; and on the Northerly Corner with great white oake tree standing by the brooke syde and soe Runeth by the said brooke four score and twelve pole; and then Runeth away south southeast or therabouts four score and twelve pole; and there bounded with a Red oake tree marked and soe Runeth east northeast or therabouts four score and twelve pole and there bounded with a smale Red oake bush which standeth on the southwest syde of an old Indian path;

The bounds of the Land of Wecanucked allies Tantarega is as followeth viz; bounded on the southerly Corner with a Red oake by the Cliff; and soe Runeth Northwest or therabouts fifty pole and there bounded with a smale Red oake att the northerly Corner; and soe Runeth Northeast down two and thirty pole to a Red oake tree marked; and soe away southeast fifty pole or therabouts to a whit oake tree marked neare the Clift;

The bounds of Richard ffosters Land viz: it is bounded with the beaver dam brooke on the southerly syde and soe Runeth down four score pole easterly; and then Runeth fifty pole Northerly and there bounded with a Red oake tree; and soe Runeth up westerly four score pole to a Red oake tree; and at the southwest end bounded with a swamp that Runeth into the beaver dam brooke;

A neck of land compased with swampes Containing twenty six acrees layed out between William hoskens and Ephraim Tilson to each of them thirteen acrees viz; Thirteen acrees to Ephraim Tilson bounded upon the northerly corner with a white oake tree Runing eight pole easterly; bounded with a white oake soe Runing away southerly four score pole to a pyne tree marked by a swamp syde and from thence westerly and the westermost bounds a white oake; Ephraim Tilsons easterly bounds is Willam hoskins northerly bounds being a white oake and from thence eight pole to a heape of stones placed by a corner of a swamp and from thence four score pole Runing southerly to a spruce tree marked by a swamp syde and from thence westerly to the aforsaid pyne tree that is Ephraim Tilsons southerly bounds;

To Ephraim Tilson seaventeen acrees lying on the westerly syde of the head of Nahuckett Brooke; the easterne bound marke is a white oake and soe Runing alonge by a swamp four score pole in length to a great Rocke from thence thirty six pole to a Red oake; from thence four score pole to a maple tree which is the Northermost bounds

To Willam hoskins seaventeen acrees lying on the easterly syde of the said Nahuckett Brooke and a smale Red oake for the Northermost bounds from thence easterly four score pole to a shrub on a plaine; and from thence thirty six pole to a white oake tree; and from thence alonge the brooke to a Red oake by the meddow syde which is the westermost bounds

Layed out by order by Leiftenant
Ephraim Morton

[93.] New Plymouth

Measured unto Mr John howland and Joseph howland ten acrees of land graunted by the Towne unto Jonathan Bosworth att the southeast end of sixty acrees hee then lived on att a place comonly Called Colchester the said ten acrees is bounded on the Northwest syde with a white oake tree which is one of the bounds of the aforsaid sixty acrees and with the brooke when it goes into the said sixty acrees on the southeast syde of the said land att the northeast end is bounded with a young white oake and att the southwest end with a great Cleft Rocke haveing a little Rocke standing close to him June 13th 1668

p<sup>r</sup> William Crow Surveyor

New Plymouth

Measured unto Mr John howland fifty acrees of upland att a place Comonly Called Colchester and it adjoynes unto the land that the said howland and his son Joseph bought of Jonathan Bosworth being measured and graunted for his Lott belonging to his Winnatuxett Meddow the length therof extending Northeast nearest one halfe easterly from the aforsaid bought land bounded at the Northeast end and southeast syde with a maple tree standing by or neare a spring and on the said syde att the southwest end with a white oake tree neare the meddow; att the northeast end and northwest syde bounded with a maple tree being on the westward syde of a swamp on the said syde; and southwest end is marked a white oake neare the line of the aforsaid bought land

June 13th 1668
prme Willam Crow Surveyor

Att a Townmeeting held att the meeting house the sixt day of July 1668 It was ordered by the Towne That if any pson or psons within this Towne shall find any barke lying upon the Comons of this towne or knoweth of any Barke that is gott upon the comons That it shalbe lawfull for him or them to seize upon it acording to law for the Townes use and to be payed his paines for his prosecution therof;

<ins>Stephen Bryant desenteth</ins>    And that no pson or psons from the date of these presents shall load Transport or carry away or cause to be loaded Transported or carryed away any barke out of this Towne by land or water without lycence under the hands of two of the Celect men of the Towne upon the penaltie of the forfeiture of the said barke or the prise therof to the Townes use and that the said Celect men shall forthwith graunt such lycence to such as shall make it appeer that they have cut such barke on their owne land;

Twenty Acrees of land was graunted unto Thomas Dunham lying on the North syde of the Towne about Jonses River to be layed forth for him by the Elder Cushman Jacob Cooke and Stephen Bryant as conveniently as they can to his benifitt and as little prejudiciall to others as may bee;

Leift: Morton Serjeant harlow and William Clarke } are appointed by the Towne to take an account of William Crow in the Townes behalfe and to give him or alow him Reasonable satifsaction out of the Townes stocke for his paines in the Townes business Respecting the said accounts

Townsmen    The second Tuesday in September 1668 is appointed for a full Towne meeting to treat and settle the busines about Townsmen;

The Towne have (with the Consent of John Everson) disposed of Richard Everson his son unto Willam Nelson seni: of Plymouth to be and Remaine with him untill hee hath attained the age of one and twenty yeares hee being att the date heerof about two yeares old

[94.] Att a Townmeeting held att the meeting house att Plymouth the 29th of October 1668 the Towne agreed to alow unto Mr John Cotton the sume of eighty pounds for this following yeare out of which said sume hee is to find and provide for himselfe firewood without any Charge to the towne untill the yeare is expired the manner of the pay of the said four score pound is to be one third pte therof in wheat or butter and one third in Rye or barly or pease and the other third in Indian Corne to be payed att two severall payments one halfe therof by the first of January next and the other halfe by the last of September next; the prises of the pticulars above expressed to be as followeth viz:

| | | | |
|---|---|---|---|
| wheat att | 4s | 6d | a bushell |
| Rye att | 3 | 6 | a bushell |
| pease att | 3 | 0 | a bushell |
| Indian Corne att | 3 | 0 | a bushell |
| Barly att | 4 | 0 | a bushell |
| Mault att | 4 | 6 | a bushell |
| Butter att | 0 | 6 | a pound |

It was alsoe agreed by the Towne that the said sume should be levied by Rate on the severall Inhabitants of the Towne

The Rators Chosen by the Towne on the third day of December 1668 were

Nathaniel Morton
Joseph Warren
Samuell Dunham

Att the Townmeeting last above written

It was ordered by the Towne; that the Celect men shall hensforth have full power to Require any that shall Receive any stranger soe as to entertaine them into theire house to give Ceeuritie unto them to save the Towne harmles from any damage that may acrew unto them by theire entertainment of such as aforsaid;

It was likewise agreed that John Everson be forthwith warned to depart the towne with all Convenient speed;

Att the Towne meeting held att Plymouth the 15th of ffebruary 1668 The Towne appointed Robert ffinney and Willam Crow to take notice and Require all those that are Rated to pay the aforsaid sume to Mr Cotton to bringe it in seasonably and in the specye agreed on and to take and keep an exacte account therof; as alsoe to take some Course that the ground appertaing to the house in which hee liveth be ffenced seasonably that soe it may bee Improved to the use and benifitt of Mr Cotton;

Liberty is graunted by the Towne unto Leiftenant Morton and Edward Dotey to sett up a stage att ¹Sagaquas and to have the use of soe much land on the upland upon the Rockey point

---

¹ Sagaquas was Saquash.

there on the Northwest syde of the said Leiftenant Mortons Meddow as may be Convenient and Requisite for two boates to make flish on the shore;

[95.] The bounds of the lands graunted by the towne of Plymouth on the 21 of october 1662 unto Gorge Watson Willam harlow and Nathaniel Morton being an hundred and fifty acrees viz; to each of them fifty acrees lying together att Mannomett ponds as is elswhere expressed in this book; which was layed out to them according to order by Leiftenant Morton; is as followeth; viz; a necke of land lying to the Northeast (or therabouts) of the Indians Land which said necke is bounded to the Northwest (or therabouts) with the lands of Leiftenant Morton and Joseph Warren leaveing an highway betwixt the said lands of Leift: Morton and the said Necke downe to the sea; The said Necke is alsoe bounded on the west southwest end with the Indians lands and Runeth over to the Northwest westerly to a marked oake tree; the said Necke being estimated att fifty acrees or therabouts be it more or lesse; the Remainder of the aforsaid land being an hundred acrees; Runeth from the Indians land on the west southwest syde or therabouts; lying by the sea on the Clift; and extendeth itselfe in length two hundred pole west southwest or therabouts to a white oake tree in the plaine neare the pond; and is bounded on the Northwest syde with a marked walnut tree standing on the west syde of a little swamp and Runeth four score pole over east Northeast or therabouts to the aforsaid Marked trees

Att a Towne meeting held att the meeting house att Plymouth the fifteenth day of ffebruary 1668

The ffollowing proposition was Read unto the Towne

The Comittee appointed by the Towne being assembled or the Major pte of them after much agitation of pticulars thought meet to offer these following propositions to further consideration;

In Reference unto the terminateing and stateing of Townsmen of Plymouth that only such be deputed Townsmen that were Inhabitants and ffreeholders therof att that time when as the court alowed it to be a Townshipp and theire successors and that it be att theire libertie to admitt such others into such there society as are houskeepers of honest life and are like to approve themselves soe as they may be benificiall to the commonwealth according to theire capasitie and abilities;

The Towne approved of the said propositions and voated it to be the Rule and was for the admition of Townsmen for the present and accordingly tooke an exact view of the list of the names of those that were formerly called and had voated in Townmeeting and established such as were found to be Townsmen according to the said order and admitted some few more unto them; and Refered others to further consideration;

The names of those who were found to be Townsmen of Plymouth according to the abovesaid order which Relates unto the time of the establishment of the Towne of Plymouth and the bounds therof sett by the court which was in the yeare 1640:

Thomas Prence
Capt: Thomas Southworth
Capt: Willam Bradford
The Elder Thomas Cushman
Mr John howland
Jacob Cooke
Samuell ffuller
Samuell Sturtivant
Edward Gray
Steven Bryant
Samuell Kinge
Serj Ephraim Tinkham
John Cobb
Tho: Lettice
James Cole seni:
Gorge Bonum
John Wood
Gabriell ffallowell
Rich: Wright
Willam Crow
Tho: Pope
John Barnes
Gorge Watson
Benajah Pratt
John Jourdaine
Gyles Rickard Juni;
Giles Rickard Seni:
Samuell Dunham
Samuell Eedey
Tho; Whitney

Nath: Morton
Leift: Ephraim Morton
Tho: Morton
Robert flinney
Willam Clarke
Robert Bartlett
Nathaniell Warren
Joseph Dunham
John holmes
Mr Joseph Bradford
Edward Dotey seni:
Edward Dotey Juni:
Gorge Morton
John Barrow
Richard ffoster
John ffaunce
James Cole Juni:
Joseph Churchill
These following were admitted att the same time
Willam hoskins
Willam Nelson seni:
John Dunham
Joseph Warren
Serg Willam harlow
Andrew Ringe
hugh Cole
James Clarke
Joseph Howland
Jonathan Pratt
Jonathan Barnes
Joseph Bartlett
Daniel Dunham
Abraham Jackson
John Cole
Samuell Kinge Juni:
Richard Willis
Jabez howland
John Doty

Att the same meeting a Comittee was chosen further to Consider of such pticulars as may be proposed and thought meet to be observed in Reference to Towne privilidges whoe are to meet for that purpose on Munday the 21 of this Instant ffebruary;

Mr Thomas Prence ⎫  these with any others of the
Capt: Thomas Southworth ⎪  Townsmen that shall please to
Nathaniell Morton ⎪  give them meeting to propose
Leift: Ephraim Morton ⎪  and agitate matters Relating to
The Elder Thomas Cushman ⎪  Towne privilidges and to
Edward Gray ⎬  acquaint the Rest of the
Samuell Sturtivant ⎪  Townsmen with what they
Willam Clarke ⎪  thinke meet in Reference to
Joseph Warren ⎪  the primises att the next
serg William harlow ⎪  Towne meeting and then to be
Robert ffinney ⎪  Rejected or established as the
Willam Crow ⎭  whole or Major pte shall thinke meet

Nathaniell Morton

Att this meeting the Towne graunted unto Nathaniell Morton seni: what lands are or may be suppos'd to be comon between his lands lying by the lands of John Churchill; and the Creeke comonly Called hobshole in the Township of Plymouth; alwaies provided That hee leave a competency of Land without the ffence to sett up on the said land next unto the Creeke syde for the landing of hay or other goods and alsoe provided that hee and his heires and assignes give libertie unto the naighbors to cart up hay or other goods from the said Creeke through his land there unto the Comon Road way att any time soe as not to goe through or spoyle any Corne theron

Att this meeting likewise the Towne graunted unto Richard Willis a smale pcell of comon land lying att the end above the smale psell of land which hee bought of Nathaniel Morton bounded with two heapes of stones att the uper end provided; alsoe that hee give libertie unto the Naighbors to Cart hay or other goods up through the land hee hath there; both that which hee hath now graunted him and that which hee bought as aforsaid; from the Comon highway to the litle Towne and not to be Interupted by him nor his heires or assignes att any time when they may Cart; and not spoyle or damage any Corne thereon;

The bounds of the land of Mr Joseph Bradford att Winnatucksett is as followeth It abuteth on the Northsyde of the River haveing Richard Wrights land lying on the southsyde of it and it Runs fourscore pole from the River haveing a swamp on the northwest syde the whole length of it and soe Rangeth to a smale pyne tree standing in low swampy ground; and soe Rangeth to a white oake marked standing on a hillsyde;

The bounds of the Land of Samuell Kinge Seni: being fifty acrees it begins att the bound marked tree that standeth between the meddow of Steven Bryant and the meddow of the said Samuell Kinge; the said tree being a white oake tree marked; and soe it Rangeth along by the meddowsyde of the said Samuell Kinge eight score pole to a white oake standing by a swamp syde which is his southermost bounds and soe Runeth fifty pole into the woods from the said swamp to a blacke oake which is his westermost bounds and soe to a smale white oake which is his Northermost bound

Att the Towne meeting held att the meeting house att Plymouth Monday 21 of february 1668 fifty acrees of land was graunted unto John Lukas lying neare the land of Samuell Kinge above mensioned to be viewed and layed out by Gorg Bonum for him the said John Lukas and if it can not there be had; then it is to be had elswhereif it can be found;

[97.] Att a Towne meeting held att the meeting house att Plymouth the 12th of May 1669 Leift Morton and Robert ffinney were Chosen to be deputies to serve in the Towns behalfe att June Court next and the severall adjournments therof;

Mr Willam Clarke was Chosen Constable for the Towne;

Samuell Dunham and Andrew Ringe Chosen Grandjurymen

Leiftenant Morton Serj harlow and Willam Crow were Chosen to be Celect men.

Thomas Cushman Juni: Benajah Pratt and Gorge Morton Chosen Surveyors of the highwayes

In Answare unto a proposition made unto the Towne in the behalfe of Mr Cotton That wheras God by his good Providence hath soe ordered that hee is likely to Continue amongst us and to preach the word of God unto us That in case hee should end his life in that worke amongst us and leave a family behind him that for as much as the house hee liveth in is the Townes for the use of the minnestry successively and that The Towne Cannot accomodate him with any farme or liveing to leave behind him for his family The prmises Considered; The Towne have unanimously voted to alow unto his wife or family the sume of fifty pounds and that shee or they be prmited to live in the said house untill the Towne shalbe provided of another minnester incase God doe soe dispose that hee end his life in this Towne before them;

Att this meeting it was ordered by the Towne that the Constable shall have fifteen shillings alowed him by the Towne for the yeare hee is Constable; and that hee be Rated according to his estate in all Respects as others to any Comon Charges and that hee give a true account to the Towne yearly of his proceedings in his office and that the said account be Recorded;

Att a Towne meeting held att Plymouth the 29[th] day of July 1669

The Raters Chosen to make the Country Rates and Rates for the Townes Concerns were Leiftenant Morton Serjeant harlow and Samuell Dunham;

Att this meeting a quarter of an acree of land was Graunted to Willam harlow being a little [1] Knowle or smale psell of land lying neare his now dwelling house on the westerly syde of the Road way To sett a new house upon

Steven Bryant and John Waterman are appointed by the Town To view and make Report to the Towne of severall psells of land desired by Serjeant Tinkham Willam Crow and John Jourdaine and to make Report thereof to the towne

Leiftenant Morton and Samuell Dunham were appointed by the Towne and Invested with full power in theire behalfe to sue and Implead the case against those that have hiered the Townes land att Agawaam; and the Towne to beare the Charge of the said action; and to stand to the award that shalbe given by law upon the said suite;

The 29[th] of July 1669 John Everson Came before Captaine Southworth and acknowlidged that hee hath disposed of his daughter Martha Everson unto Robert Barrow of Plymouth to be to and with him as his owne Child from this time forward to be provided for looked unto and desposed of by him the said Robert Barrow as his owne Child;

---

[1] This is the lot on which a house belonging to Professor Lemuel Stephens stands, on the west side of Sandwich Street beyond Fremont Street. This house is the one which William Harlow built.

[99.] Att the Towne meeting held att the meeting house att Plymouth the 15th day of December 1669 The Rators Chosen to make the Rates for Mr Cottons Maintainance were

Nathaniell Morton
Serjeant harlow
Willam Crow

The prsons appointed to see his Rate layed on were

Willam Crow
Samuell Dunham

In Reference unto a Controversy between Captaine Bradford and the Towne about his usuall Rate to Mr Cottons maintainance It is mutually agreed by and between the said pties that for three yeares from this date this yeare being encluded that hee shall and will annually pay unto Mr Cottons Maintaintance the sume of fifteen shillings; and when the said time is expired that then the towne and him to come to a further agreement about the same; and in Reference unto his pay to Mr Cotton for the last yeare not yet payed hee hath engaged to pay the sume of twelve shillings and for what is behind of former years that what is due hee will pay it;

Att the Towne meeting held att the meeting house att Plymouth the 15th of ffebruary 1669 It was ordered by the Towne That if the Constable doe Receive an order from either the Majestrates Residing in the Towne or from the court or from the Celect men of the Towne att any time to warne a Townmeeting and neglect to give due warning viz: by himselfe or others to every one written in the list of the Townsmen The said Constable soe neglecting shall pay twelve pence for every one that hee neglecteth soe to warne to be levied to the Townes use by the Constable succeeding the yeare following after such defects are made

Samuell Dunham and Willam Crow are deputed by the Towne to Receive that which is behind due to the Towne from the Constables of Plymouth for the two yeares last past before the date heerof and are heerby Impowered to prosecute in law what shalbe nessesary in the Townes behalfe for the Recovery theerof; and likewise by vertue of this order to Require what is behind due to the towne on sepecan account untill august the fift 1672 this addition being then added;

It was ordered by the Towne that all meddowes in our Township or belonging to the Towne shalbe Ratable to all our comon charges of both Towne and Country

Memorand: That the Rators be minded

To Remember Myles Blacke or any other that Keepes Cattle on the Townes Comons to be Rated for;

Joseph Bartlett hath agreed with the Towne to pay for the Rent of Sepecan forty shillings which is in the Custody of Willam Clarke and engageth to the Towne to pay forty shillings in currant Country pay by the fifteenth of November 1671 and doth freely surrender the said lease of the land att sepecan and the Towne accepts of it on the payment of the said sumes

Att the Towne meeting held att Plymouth
the fffteenth of May 1670

The Towne have voted that such as have made a wast Gate for the letting of the ffish goe up shalbe ffully supplyed with ffish for theire owne pticular use in the first place for this yeare; and that the hedge they make to stopp the ffish shall stand untill such time as none appeers to take ffish when ther is ffish before the said hedge or weire and that it shall not be pulled downe att that time untill the Miller is Reddy to stopp water;

[100.] Att a Towne meeting held att the meeting house att Plymouth the seaventh of July 1670.

This was Rattifyed att the meeting of the Towne on the 8th of August 1677 att the said meeting Mr Gray and John Bradford were appointed by the Towne to look to the execution of the said law

Wheras Complaint is made of Great stray and wast of Timber in the swamps or the Comons belonging to the Towne; It is ordered by the Towne that henceforth noe bolts boards or shingle shalbe transported out of the Townshipp either by our owne or others; on paine of forfeiting the said bolts boards and shingle or the worth of them to the Towne use;

Edward Gray and } are appointed by the
Joseph howland } Towne to see that this order be duly and strictly pformed and observed;

Serjeant harlow ⎫ were Chosen by the
Willam Clarke ⎬ Towne to make the
and Willam Crow ⎭ Country Rates and
the Rate for the
Comon Charges of
the Towne for this
yeare ;

Att this meeting the Towne graunted unto John Cole one acree and an halfe of salt sedge ground ; lying att Jonses River to be for his use as longe as hee continueth there ; and ordered Joseph howland to lay it out to him which was don as followeth :
The bounds of John Coles sedge ground ; the acree is twenty pole in Length and eight pole in breadth and is bounded on the eastsyde with the River ; and on the westsyde with three stakes ; the syde line extends North and south the halfe acree extends twenty pole in Length and four pole in breadth it is bounded on the Northsyde with the River and on the westsyde with two stakes ; this sedge ground lyeth att a place Comonly Called Mr howlands point ;

Att a town meeting held at Plymouth the 13[th] day of december 1670

The Rators Chosen to make the Rate for Mr Cottons Maintainance was Leift Morton Serjeant harlow and Samuell Dunham ;

Att this meeting ;

The Towne graunted unto Thomas Dunham twenty acrees of Land lying on the Northsyde of the smelt brooke

The Towne likewise graunted unto Edward May twenty acrees of Land lying att Naponsett ponds there two psells to be layed out to the pties above named by Willam Crow and Joseph howland soe as it may not be prejudiciall to any former graunt ;

Att this meeting a psell of Land was graunted by the Town unto John Morton lying in Alcarmus feild to sett an house on to the vallue of four acrees if it may there be found if not ; hee is to have it in any other place within the township as is not disposed of alreddy to others

Schoolmaster
Att the said meeting the said John Morton proffered to teach the children and youth of the towne to Read and write and Cast accounts on Reasonable considerations

Att this meeting Nathaniel Morton Leift Morton and Joseph Warren were appointed by the Towne to agree with Tatoson about a psell of Land desired by him att Sepecan.

An acree and an halfe of Land is graunted by the Towne unto Thomas Doten lying in Alcarmus feild to sett a house on in the most Convenienetest place soe as it may not be prejudiciall to others

A smale peece of land lying and being att the Towne of Plymouth by the watersyde att the foot of the hill below Mr Cottons was graunted by the Towne unto Mr Willam Clarke of Plymouth to sett his ware house on; with free egresse and Regresse therunto without Interuption;

[101.] Ordered made and Concluded by the Towne of Plymouth att theire Towne meeting held att the meetinghouse att Plymouth on the 26$^{th}$ of December Ann$^o$ dom 1670 as followeth;

That every one shall bringe in an exact bill of his estate to the Rators that shalbe att any time orderly Chosen; and incase any doe neglect heerin; It is left to the descretion of the Rators to Rate them as they shall see cause; and if any one shall bring in any false bill of his estate; the Rators suspecting it to be soe upon special grounds; shall Keep it untill the next Towne meeting and there prsent it to the Towne and it being there proved to be false the prson that sent it in shalbe fined twelve pence on the pound for whatsoever Ratable goods etc he hath omitted to enter into his said bill: to the use of the Towne;

Ordered that all uplands be vallued in Rateing att 20 s an acree viz: plowed lands and hoed lands and all meddowes att 20 s an acree if within foure miles of the place where the hay is used; but if more Remote att ten shillings an acree; and that such Rates as are made upon meddowes be levied on the owners of the meddowes onely this to be understood of such as lett hay by the load; or from yeare to yeare

*horse Kind to be Rated*

Ordered that all neat Cattle be Rated for as followeth: viz: a Cow to be vallued att fifty shillings and all heiffers of three yeares old equall to a cow; a paire of oxen att seaven pound twoo yeare olds both heiffers and steers att thirty shillings apeece; and all yearlings att twenty shillings apeece; and that * horses and mares be vallued att three pounds apeece all two year

as neate
Cattle

olds of horse Kind att forty shillings a peece; and yearlings att 20 s * and that all such Cattle both neate and horsekind soe to be Rated for and vallued to be payed for that are in each man's Costody though not his owne;

Ordered that all sheep be vallued att six shillings apeece in Rateing and that Rames be exempted

Ordered that all swine from halfe a yeare old and upward be vallued att five shillings a peece and bores to be exempted;

It is ordered that all single men that have not prsented above eighteen pound stocke to be Rated; that they shall Notwithstanding be Rated to the same vallue

Ordered in Reference to the weavers of the Towne that they be Rated for every loome that is Improved as for thirty £ stocke viz: Gyles Rickard one loome John Wood one loome John ffalloweys loome not soe Constantly Imployed vallued att 5 £ stocke and Daniell Dunhams loome les Imployed vallued att 5 £ stocke

Ordered that every Tayler in Reference to his facultie be vallued att 20 £ stocke

Ordered that all such as are Improved in any publicke place That what sallery they have it be accoumpted as Ratable stocke

Ordered That whosoever hath and Improveth any facultie besides his Rateable estate be Responsible to be Rated for the same proportionable to what they shall Rationally give in an account of to the towne which if they shall Refuse or neglect to doe; That it be left to the descretion of the Rators to doe therin as they shall thinke meet;

That all such as have bin or shalbe Improved about fish or flishing theire Improvement therin to be vallued att 20 £ : estate a peece

Edward Gray to be Rated for six score pound stocke this yeare Improved in trading

William Clarke fourscore pound;
Gorge Watson ten pound
Willam Crow ten pound
Joseph Warren ten pound

[102.] This following order beares date the fift of August 1672
It is ordered by the Towne that whosoever shall Neglect to bring in his bill of his estate to the Rators att the time appointed shalbe fined two shillinges for every such default to the use of the Towne to be levied by the Constable with the Rate that the said delinquent is Rated att that time ;

| | |
|---|---|
| Serjeant harlow his facultie being a Copper vallued at | £40 |
| Joseph Bartlett his facultie being a Cooper vallued att | 30 |
| Samuel Ryder being a Cooper his facultie vallued att | 30 |
| Joseph Dunham for his facultie being a carpenter vallued att | 30 |
| James Cole for his facultie Keeping an ordinary att | 80 |
| Thomas Lettice for his facultie Keeping an ordinary att | 20 |
| Thomas Lucas his facultie being a Smith att | 50 |
| Jabez howland his facultie being a smith att | 40 |
| Edward Gray and serjeant harlowes and Edward Doties boate att | 25 |
| Another boate of Edward Grayes att | 25 |
| Jonathan Barnes his boate att | 18 |
| Gorge Watsons boate att | 12 |
| Leift Mortons boate att | 18 |

Att this meeting it was voated by the Towne that the Elder Cushman be ffreed from paying any Rate to the Minnestry for the future in Regard of his many emergent occations and expence of time; therin Improved for the publicke good ;

A comittee was Chosen by the Towne to Consider and draw up some propositions to Restraine the eregulare Improvement of the Townes Comons viz: Willam Clarke and William Crow to give meeting with the Milletary officers att theire next meeting ; to acte with them in Reference to the prmises

[103.] Att the Towne meeting held att Plymouth the 2cond of ffebruary these following orders were made and Concluded by the Towne

Impr : That there shalbe noe Tarr made ; by any prson but such as are Townsmen or their order ; whose names are entered in the townes list bearing date the fifteenth day of february 1668 or shalbe heerafter entered into the said list; and incase there shalbe any Tarr found to be made by any that are not Townsmen as aforsaid; and have not order from some one of them for the makeing of the said Tarr; all such Tarr to be forfeite; the one halfe to the enformer and the other halfe to the use of the Towne

2 That there shalbe noe pyne knot picked or Tarr Run or made within this Township by any person: but by such as are the proprietors as aforsaid or theire order; and incase there shalbe any such knotes picked or Tarr made by any except such proprietors or theire order; that all such knotes or Tarr to be forfeite the one halfe to the enformer and the other halfe to the Towne

3 That every such proprietor or his order may make ten barrells of Tarr by the yeare and noe more

4 That any prson whatsoever of our owne Township that shall find any knots gathered or Tarr made within this Township by any prson whatsoever; That is not a proprietor as aforsaid; or theire order shall seize the said knotes and Run them out alowing one third to the Towne and incase they seize and gett any such Tarr Reddy made; then to alow the Towne two third ptes; but in case such knotes be onely drawne and sett then they to have the one halfe and the Towne the other halfe; the Towne allowing theire proportion of the charge of the draught and barrells;

Willam hoskins Joseph Warren James Clarke Joseph howland Joseph Bartlett Thomas Cushman Juni: John Barrow and John Tilson; are appointed by the Towne to see the above written orders duely and truely executed in the Townes behalfe;

John Rosse prmited by the Towne to make as much Tarr as hee can; himself notwithstanding the former orders;

whales

[104.] Ordered by the Towne That whatsoever whale or pte of a whale or other great ffish that will make oyle shall by the Providence of God be Cast up or Come on shore within the bounds of this Township That every such whale or pte of a whale or other such ffish as will make oyle; two ptes of three therof to belonge and appertaine to the Towne viz: the propriators aforsaid; and the other third pte to such of the Towne as shall find and Cutt them up and try the oyle; provided they be of the said propriators that doe soe find and cut up and try them; but incase any other that are not propriators as aforsaid whether Inhabitants of this Towne or forranguers shall find any such whale or flish and bring word or give notice therof to the Towne; they are to be sufficiently satisfyed for the same;

The Towne have graunted unto Peter Risse a psell of swamp ground or meddow lying att the easterly syde of Nahuckett brooke neare Lakenham being somthing above three acrees; Measured and bounded unto Edward Maye twenty acrees of Land adjoyning to and lying on the Northward syde of the Land of Samuell Kinge Seni; att Moonponsett meddow; at the Easterly end; the said twenty acrees is bounded with a spruce tree: which is in the said Kinges Range neare a spring; and att the said end on the Northward syde is bounded with a Red oake on the said syde; att the westward end with a swamp white wood tree; standing in a swamp; and att the said westward end on the southward syde; It is bounded with a Red oake tree; the length therof is eighty pole; the breadth forty pole;

ffebruary the 8[th] 1670

By Willam Crow Surveyer

The bounds of Edward Dotens Land neare Moonponsett is as followeth

viz: bounded with a white oake tree marked standing by a swampsyde on the easterly Corner in the Range between the land of Samuell Kinge and his land; this Range Runs away Northwest an hundred pole; to a white oake marked which is the Northermost bounds att the Northermost Corner and soe extends upon a Range southwest to a maple tree fourscore pole which is the westermost bounds; and soe Runs upon a southeast line an hundred pole; to a white oake; which is the southermost bound marked tree;

The bounds of the Land of John Lucas lying neare Moonponsett viz: bounded with a white oake tree marked standing on the Northsyde of a smale brooke which is the westermost bounds and soe Runs an hundred pole upon a Northward by east line to a maple tree which is his Northermost bounds; and soe Runs upon an east and by south line four score pole to a white oake tree marked which is the eastermost bounds; and soe Runs south and by west an hundred pole to a maple tree ; which stands in the bounds between him and Edward Dotens land ; this to be understood that there is a smale slipe of meddow in the said land encluded which is a part of his land graunted and bounded as aforsaid ; to the said John Lucas ;

[105.] The bounds of a smale psell of meddow layed out to John Doten near Moonponsett is as followeth : it lyeth between tew swampes ; Runing upon a southerly line unto the end of Captaine Bradfords meddow ; and is bounded on the westward syde with a spruce tree ; and on the easterly syde with a spruce tree ; and a stake standing in the midest between them ;

The bounds of Thomas Dunhams land graunted by the Towne and layed out by Gorge Bonum is as followeth ;

his east bound is a spruce tree standing by the smelt brooke syde ; and Rangeth away Northwest to a small Red oake ; and soe Rangeth away southwest to a smale pyne tree standing upon a hill ; and southeast to a Red oake by the brooke and this Land lyeth forty pole one way and seaventy six pole the other way ;

Gorge Bonum Surveyor

Richard Wright & Thomas Michell

The bounds of Richard Wrights and Thomas Michells Land ; lying by a path comonly Called Colchester path in the Township of Plymouth ; on the Northwest syde of the path ; and his east bound is a white oake neare the path ; his south bound is a blacke oake standing upon the topp of a hill by a Great Rocke ; his west bound is a smale white oake standing by a swampe ; his North bound is a white oake standing by a Rocke ; it Runs eight score pole in length and three score pole in breadth ;

Gorge Bonum Surveyor

The bounds of Samuell Kinge sen: land ; the east bounds of his meddow is a pyne tree ; the west bound is a white oake : the bounds of his land and meddow both ; The North bound is a white oake by a swampsyde ; the west bound of his land is a blacke oake ; the south bound of his land is a white oake ; a smale pyne on the east syde of his meddow is his east bound of his meddow : the sume of all is three acrees of meddow and fifty acrees of upland

Gorge Bonum Surveyor

Att a Towne meeting held att the meeting house att Plymouth the 24th of May 1671 The Towne Ratifyed and Confeirmed unto Gyles Rickard seni: a smale psell of upland ground lying by and adjoyning unto his land above the little Towne allies Wellingsley which said addition of land was formerly graunted by the Court; to the said Gyles Rickard;

Att the meeting above said the Towne graunted unto Edward May a smale psell of Swampy ground about two or three acrees (more or lesse) to make meddow off; lying att or neare Moonponsett pond or att the lower end of a meddow called Moonponsett Meddow; and is next a peece of meddow Called Edward Doteys addition; with a spruce tree and a pyne that is the bounds of the said addition; from which trees the said two or three acrees extends downe stream on both sydes the brooke unto a swamp white wood tree marked on the eastsyde of the said brooke; and to the aforsaid pyne tree which stands on the westward syde of the said brook;

layed out by Willam Crow Surveyor.

[106.] Att a Towne meeting held att the meeting house att Plymouth the 24th August, 1671

Leift Morton serjeant harlow and Willam Crow } were Chosen to be Rators for the publicke Charges of the Country

Att this meeting the former orders made by the Towne about Rateing were ordered to be observed in Reference to this Rate

Att this meeting Samuell Dunham was invested with full power in the behalfe of the Towne to Require in and Recover such debts as belonge to the towne as yett unpayed by severall prsons and to prosecute law for the Recovery of them if hee shall see cause

Att this Meeting John Morton appeered and tendered himselfe to bee in a Reddines to erect and keep a scoole for the teaching of the Children and youth of the Towne to write and Read and Cast accounts according to a former proposition to the towne expressed and Inserted in this booke

Att this Meeting Gorge Bonum had libertie to sett up a [1] ffulling mill soe as it anoy not the Corn Mill; nor hinder not the Alewives in goeing up in theire season;

---

[1] This fulling mill was set up near where the factory of the Bradford Joint Company stands.

Corn Mill vote thereabout

Att this Meeting the towne Requesteth and appointed the Gov<sup>r</sup>: Nathaniell Morton and Leiftenant Morton to treat with and give Notice unto the owners of the [1] Corn Mill att Plymouth that they provide a good and sufficient house att the said Mill to Cecure the Corne that shalbe brought thither to be ground and that they keep the Mill in Repaire soe as to grind Corne well and sufficiently and for that end alsoe to provide an honest and skilful man to tend the mill Constantly that prsons bee not wronged on that behalfe as they have bine; or otherwise that the towne will procure another Mill to be sett up;

Att a meeting held att Plymouth for the Towne of Plymouth the 30<sup>th</sup> of August 1671

The lawes of the Collonie were publickly Read; Att this meeting the Gov<sup>r</sup>: Mr howland Willam Crow and Joseph howland was appointed to view a smale moyety of land desired by Edward Gray to sett a warehous on; att or neare the end of his ground att Rocky nooke and make Report therof to the Towne It was agreed and voated by the towne att this meeting that those that made the last Rate for the Country shall make the Rate for Mr Cotton for that which is behind of the last yeare;

The bounds of the land layed out to Richard Willis lying att Warren's wells as followeth; the southeast end of it is bounded with the Eelriver brooke; and the Northeast syde with Warrens Wells brooke and soe Runing fourscore pole along the said brooke and there bounded with a pyne tree marked; and it Runs up southerly six acrees breadth along the Eelriver brooke; and there bounded with a Red oake tree marked; The west bound is a Red oak tree marked;

The bounds of the land layed out to Joseph Churchill and Eliezer Churchill att the Great south pond is as followeth

The Northwest end abuteth on the said pond and is bounded att the Northerly Corner with a Red oake tree Marked and soe Runeth southwest ten acrees breadth; and there bounded with a Pyne tree marked; and soe Runeth eight score pole southeast and there bounded with a Pyne tree marked close by a smale Rocke; and the easterly corner bounded with a Pyne tree marked

---

[1] The corn mill was on the site of the factory of Loring & Parks.

[**107.**] The bounds of an addition of land formerly Graunted unto Gyles Rickard Seni : lying adjoyning unto his old feild att Wellingsley allies the little Towne lately layed out by Leiftenant Morton is as followeth ;

viz : the westermost bounds is an heap of stones being forty pole or therabouths up into the woods from his said old feild The bounds of the southerly Corner is a smale Red oak tree marked ; and the southeast syde of it Runs downe alonge the little Towne valley leaving a sufficient cartway in the said valley the easterly end is bounded with an heap of stones lying by the said Cartway and the Northeast end of it is bounded with the Cartway which leadeth from the said valley towards the Towne ; and Runeth along the said Cartway to the Land of Gorge Watson and these is bounded with a smale Red oake marked ;

Att a Towne meeting held att the meeting house att Plymouth the 15$^{th}$ day of January 1671 the Rators Chosen to make the Rate of forty pound for Mr Cotton was Leift Morton serjeant harlow Willam Crow ;

And Edward Gray and Willam Clarke were Chosen to see the same duely payed

It was ordered by the Towne that the ancient order about the fine for non appeerance att Towne meetings be duely levied according to the tearmes of that order for the future ;

Thomas Whitney is graunted by the towne to take in and Improve a small necke of land att the easterly end of his feild soe as it appeer not to be any ones propriety it being about halfe an acree more or lesse

Att a towne Meeting held att the meeting house att Plymouth the 20$^{th}$ day of May 1672 ; The Towne did agree and unanimously voate and Conclude that theire lands Att Sepecan Agawaam and places adjacent ; the proffitts and benifitts therof shalbee Improved and Imployed for and towards the Maintainance of the free Scoole now begun and erected att Plymouth ; and that the proffitts and benefitts therof shall noe way estranged from the said use ; soe longe as ther shalbe occation to use it for that end ; and in that behalfe ; and the Towne have made Choise of and do Request Mr Thomas Prence and Captain Willam Bradford together with the Celect men of the Towne to Improve it the best they Can for the end aforsaid ;

Att this meeting

The Gov<sup>r</sup>
Capt: Bradford
Elder Cushman
Nathaniel Morton
Robert ffinney
Edward Gray
Mr Willam Clarke
and Joseph Warren
And Stephen Bryant

} Together with the Celect men of the Towne are appointed by the Towne to meet together in due and Convenient time to agitate and Contrive the best and equallest way that may be for the payment of such Rates as are to be payed in one Respect or other; and to make Report of theire doeings thereon to the Towne;

Att this meeting the Towne Graunted unto Edward Gray a Certaine smale psell of Land on which his warehouse now standeth att Rockey nooke by the watersyde; being about three quarters of an acree be it more or lesse; as it is now bounded and staked out by Mr Prence and Joseph howland whoe were appointed by the towne to view it and settle the bounds therof;

Att this meeting the Towne Graunted unto Gorge Watson a smale addition of Land att the head of his Land lying above the little towne be it three quarters of an acree be it more or lesse;

[108.] Att the Towne Meeting held att the meeting house att Plymouth the 20<sup>th</sup> day of May 1672 The Towne Graunted unto Alexander Kennedy twenty five acrees of Land Lying on the Northerly syde of Edward Mayes Land att Moonponsett;

Att this Meeting the Towne Graunted unto John Waterman an acree and an halfe of land lying in Alcarmus feild To be layed out to him by Nathaniel Morton Leift Morton and Mr Willam harlow;

Att this Meeting a smale slip of Land be it more or lesse The Town Graunted unto Nathaniel holmes lying betwixt his land in Alcarmus feild his house now standeth on and a psell of land belonging to Benjamin Bartlett in the said feild;

Att this meeting the Town Graunted unto Gorge Bonum a necke of land lying att [1] ffresh lake on the Easterly syde therof; extending from the brooke that Runeth out of ffresh lake to Lout pond; and the swamp lying betwixt the pond and ffresh Lake is the bounds of the said Graunt att the southerly end;

July the 22 1672

---

[1] Fresh lake was Billington Sea.

Alex
Kennedys
25 acrees

Measured and bounded unto Alexander Kennedy twenty five acrees of Land lying on the Northsyde of Edward Mayes Land: att a place comonly Called Moonponsett; att the westerly end therof; Its bounded with a swamp white wood tree from which tree the line extends easterly to a Red oake tree which is Edward Mayes bound mark att his North Corner; and from the said Mayes bound mark the line extends to a Red oake tree which is the said Alexander's east Corner Mark; from which the line extends Northwest and by North nearest to a white oake tree Marked; which standeth att the syde or end of a swamp: from which white oake the line extends westerly to a spruce tree standing by the syde or in a swamp; from the said spruce tree the line extends to the aforsaid swamp white wood tree which makes an angle att the head of the aforsaid Land

p$^r$ Willam Crow Surveyor

[109.] Att a Towne meeting held att the Meeting house att Plymouth the fift day of August 1672 the Rators Chosen to make the Rates for the Country charges and Mr Cottons maintainance were
Serjeant Willam harlow
Willam Clarke
Willam Crow

Att this meeting thirty acrees of Land was Graunted to Leiftenant Ephraim Morton lying about the head of the Eelriver

fifteen acrees of Land was Graunted to serjeant Willam harlow to be att the same place

fifteen acrees of Land was Graunted unto Gorge Morton att the same place

Att this meeting the Towne Graunted unto Willam Crow a psell of Land lying on the eastsyde of Moonponsett pond between the swampes which is to be layed forth and bounded to him by Capt: Bradford and stephen Bryant

Att this meeting the Towne Graunted unto Steven Bryant a peece of Land lying and adjoyning to his meddow att Moonponsett meddow bounded on the westsyde with the land of Samuell King seni: and a swamp; and on the eastsyde with a swamp as the swamp Runs; and att the North end likewise with a swamp

A smale psell of Meddowish Ground lying neare Daniell Dunhams meddow att Swanhold being about two acrees be it more or lesse Runing by a smale brook which Runeth into the south-meddow brook; is Graunted unto Daniell Dunham

Twenty acrees of Land is Graunted unto James Barnabey lying att the Eelriver att the southwesterly syde of the double brooke

Three quarters of an acree of upland is Graunted unto John Waterman lying in Alcarmus feild att the upersyde of the land graunted to him by the Towne in that feild the $20^{th}$ of May Last past before the date heerof; the said three quarters of an acree of land to goe alonge even with his said former Graunt and to Joyne therto on the aforsaid side therof;

A small psell of Land is Graunted unto Thomas hewes lying and adjoining unto the uper end of his Land hee now liveth on which is bounded on the Northerly or Northwest syde with the highway that Goeth to the Eelriver or more properly with the highway which Goeth from the said Thomas hewes his house to the Eelriver path and to goe for the breadth of it square with his other land and in length to goe as high as to a stone pitched into the Ground; onely there is to be a lane left between this and his other land

The swamp att Wellingsley lying up the brooke is Graunted wholly unto the Naighbors there viz: John Jourdaine Gyles Rickard Juni: Nathaniel Morton seni: Abraham Jackson and Samuell Eedey;

A psell of upland is Graunted unto Jabez howland lying by the mill brooke att Plymouth viz: all that upland which lyeth att the head of the land given him by his father Mr John howland and soe to Run square with the said land up into and to Close with the ffence of Gyles Rickard seni: as also a little peece of Meddowish Ground; att the foot of the land given by Mr howland as aforsaid to Run on a square with the said land to the brooke

[110.] Graunted unto Andrew Ringe

Graunted unto John Dunham Seni: a smale psell of Meddow or meddowish ground lying att Winnatucksett; being three acrees be it more or lesse; lying on the Northeasterly syde of the Iland and is bounded with the meddow of Gyles Rickard seni : on the one end and the meddow of Richard Wright on the other end ; and with a brook and a swamp on the easterly syde therof ; and with the said Iland ; on the westerly syde therof

New Plymouth ffebruary 7$^{th}$ 1670

Measured and bounded unto Serjeant Ephraim Tinkham fifty acrees of upland lying and being on the Northsyde of Winnatucksett River ; neare Robert Lathams stacking place ; and on the eastward syde and south end of the said land it is bounded with a white oak tree standing neare the said stakeing place ; and on the said end and westsyde the land is bounded with another white oake ; and att the North end and westsyde it is bounded with a pyne tree ; the breadth fifty six pole and the length extends north one halfe point easterly from the said River

p$^r$ m Willam Crow
Surveyor

New Plymouth february the seaventh 1670

John Jordaine

Measured and bounded unto John Jourdaine fifty acrees of upland lying on the Northsyde of Winnatucksett River ; and on the westsyde of Ephraim Tinkhams Land ; bounded on the south end and east syde with a white oake tree and on the said syde and North end with a pyne tree which two trees are alsoe the bounds of the said Ephraim Tinkhams Land ; on the westsyde therof and on the westsyde and north of the said Jourdaines Land It is bounded with a pyne tree standing on the westsyde of a swamp ; and on the said west syde and south end its bounded with a Red oake tree standing neare the River and in the head line of the aforsaid Towne ; which tree hath eighty markes theron : the said fifty acrees extends from the River north one halfe point easterly nearest ; and is fifty six pole in breadth

pme Willam Crow Surveyor

1667 layed out to Edward Gray by Gorge Bonum 4 acrees more or lesse of meddow att Winnatucksett River ; bounded as followeth viz : on the Northwest syde of the said River with a forked white oak tree marked which tree is alsoe the bounds of John Mortons Meddow in that place and the bounds of the said meddow of Edward Gray on the southsyde is a Red oake Marked standing neare the River; and it is bounded downe the River with a Red oake marked on eight syde or sydes which tree standeth as low as there is any meddow Considerable and att the south corner with a pyne tree that leaneth over the said meddow and ten acrees of upland which lyeth by the said Meddowsyde; bounded with the said white oake tree which bounded the said meddow; and on the Northerly corner with a Red oake Marked and on the westeren corner with a white oake marked and on the southerly corner with a white oake leaning over the said meddow

[111.] Plymouth

Bounded for and unto Jabez howland a psell of land be it more or lesse Graunted and Given unto the said Jabez by the aforsaid Towne and his father Mr John howland which land lyeth on the southsyde of the Mill brook in the towne aforsaid next to the Garden spott of Gyles Rickard seni:

Att the Northerly end and the easterly syde of the said land it is bounded with a great longe Rocke that lyeth Close home to the aforsaid brooke; and on the said end and west syde the said land is bounded with a smale Rocke which lyeth neare the brook on which is layed an heap of stones; and att the south end and west syde the said land is bounded with a stone sett into the Ground and on the said end and easterly syde; it is bounded with a stone sett into the Ground; and Notwithstanding these bounds: According to the Towne Graunt the land att the North end is to butt home to the said brooke as the brooke Runeth; and att the south end the land is to Joyne home to the Land or line of Gyles Rickard seni: and on the east syde therof the land is to Come home to the Garden spotts that lyeth on the said syde; alwaies provided That the highway att the Northeast Corner shall not be Infringed or any wayes straightened; and that (if the Towne Claime it) the owners of the said Land shall maintaine a Coupple of Styles

October the first 1672        pr William Crow

Surveyor

Wheras the Towne of Plymouth have graunted unto Willam Crow a psell of land lying on the Eastward or east syde of Moonponsett pond and ordered the laying out and bounding therof to be don by us whose names are heerunto subscribed therfore wee underwritten have bounded the said psell of land;

att the south end and west syde therof with a little brooke where it goeth into the said Moonponsett pond The west syde of the said Land buteth home to the said pond alsoe on the west syde and North end it is bounded with the herring brooke where the said herring brooke goeth into the said Moonponsett pond and att the said North end and east syde the said Land is bounded with a three cornered Rocke that stands on the upland and from the said Rocke the line extends southward to a great white oake tree marked on four sydes; and soe home on the said line unto a brooke in a swamp; and where the said line Cutts the brooke there the brooke is the bounds of the said Land, for the southeast Corner therof

   dated the 27[th] of January
    Ann° 1672

      pr me Willam Bradford
      Stephen Bryant his W marke

 The bounds of the Land of Willam Clarke of Plymouth lying on the southerly syde of the Eelriver by a place Comonly Called the double brooke is as followeth;

 The easterly Corner is bounded with a stump marked and a heap of stones about it; and soe Running Northwest to the River forty pole; and soe Running southwest by the River syde eight score pole; and there bounded upon the westerly corner with a maple tree neare the River and soe Runing southeast forty pole and there bounded with a pyne tree;

 The bounds of Leift: Ephraim Mortons Land lying on the southerly syde of the shingle brooke; The Easterly Corner bounded with a smale Rid oake and soe Runing forty and eight pole Northerly and there bounded with a maple tree neare the shingle brooke syde and soe Runing seaven score and twelve pole southsouthwest or therabouts and ther bounded with a Red oake tree, and soe Runing forty and eight pole east southeast, or therabouts; and ther bounded with a Red oake tree;

[113.] ffebruary the 27[th] 1672

 It being found by Captaine Southworth formerly and others with him That Samuell ffuller Came short of his first Grant of Land five acrees below and the Cartway Runing through the length of his land from his house to the head of his lott; Therfore there is ten acrees aded for a supply which is extended forty pole higher into the woods Containing the same breadth with the former lott according to what was Graunted to him by the Court as appeers upon Record; The southsyde from the old bounds being a white oake standing att the southermost Corner soe Ranging to another white oake; and from thence over the brooke to a maple tree and from thence to a Red oake standing in the swamp; and from thence to a white oake standing on the south syde of the brooke neare the foot of a great hill and from thence to a pyne tree on the side of a great hill being marked on four sydes; The Northsyde bounds from the bounds between Elder Cushman's Land, being a heape of stones on the Northsyde the path; and soe along to a smale Red oake; from thence by severall Marked trees to a pyne tree; and soe on to a white oake marked on four sydes being the westermost bounds and soe Crosse the head by severall trees marked throw the smelt River swamp to a pyne tree on the syde of the hill marked on four sydes

           pr me Gorge Bonum
             Surveyor

of this Graunt which is the Ground of the above mentioned ameasurment see Great booke of evidences of lands enroled folio 100 & folio 159

  Att the Towne meeting held at the meeting house att Plymouth the 22cond of Aprill 1673 The towne appointed and Requested Capt: Willam Bradford to be moderater att all towne meetings att Plymouth and that the principall matteriall thinges to be proposed att Towne meetings be for the future drawn up in writing and openly Read;

  Att this meeting the Towne ordered that every man in the Towne shall procure twelve black birds heads six of them by the first of June next and six of them by the first of October next on paine of paying a fine of two shillings for every defect to the use of the Towne or 2 pence apeece for soe many as shalbe wanting of the dozen and if any bills more than a dozen then to have pence apeece for them out of the Townes stocke and that the said heads bee brought in by the times prefixed unto Willam Crow Jabez howland Willam harlow and Willam Clarke;

  It was ordered by the Towne that the ffish Called the alewives be not hindered by the mills or otherwise in theire goeing up; and that they be afforded water sufficient to Repaire to the salt water when the fflood Gates are shutt downe and that none shall take any such ffish in theire Goeing up except for eating; and that the wastgate be drawn up every Night in the season the flish are goeing up and that butt one ware be made for them in theire Coming downe

And serjeant harlow and Jabez howland are appointed by the Towne to see these orders Respecting the flish be duely executed and pformed;

[114.] Att a Towne meeting held att the meeting att Plymouth the 16 of May 1673

The Celect men Chosen were Leift: Morton Serjeant harlow Willam Crow

The deputies were Leift: Morton Willam Crow

The Constable John ffallowell

The Grandjurymen serjeant harlow and Gorg Morton

Andrew Ringe  
Jonathan Shaw  
Joseph Warren  
Nathaniel Southworth  
} Surveyors of the highwaies

The Towne have graunted unto Willam Crow four acrees of meddow or meddowesh Ground lying att the uper end on the East Corner of the widdow Sturtivants meddow att Monponsett to be layed out to him by Capt: Bradford; which said meddow or meddowish ground lyeth likewise on the east side of Tho: Cushmans Meddow and soe up stream on both sydes of the maine brooke;

Twenty acrees of upland is Graunted to the widdow Sturtivant lying on the Northerly syde of her Meddow att Monponsett to be layed out to her by Willam Crow

four acrees of Meddow is Graunted unto John Lucas lying att the south Meddow; Andrew Ringes and Abraham Jacksons being first layed out in the Cove

John Jordan

Two acrees of Meddow is Graunted to John Jourdaine lying in the abovesaid Cove when the abovesaid Andrew Ringe's Abraham Jackson's and John Lucas his is layed out

Two acrees of Meddow is Graunted to John Waterman Andrew Ringes Abraham Jacksons John Lucas his and John Jourdaines being layed fourth

eight acrees of land is graunted unto ffrancis Curtice lying att the second place of Goeing over Jones River by the Indian bridge by the herring weire;

Memorand That thirty acrees of land apeece be graunted to Samuell King Juni : and Isaac Cakebread where they desire it if it be not found prejudiciall To Steven Bryants and Edward Doties meddowes

Memorand That a competency of land be Graunted to Robert ffinney att the head of the Eelriver neare his meddow ;

John Dotey desireth ten acrees of Land att Monponsett Graunted unto Benajah Pratt six acrees of upland lying att a place Called Pontuses Meddow there being a swamp Included in it ;

[115.] Thirty acrees of land is Graunted unto John Waterman lying between Alexander Kenadaies land and John Cobbs land by Lathams Cartway to Winnatucksett ; and the way goeing to Bridgewater

Twenty acrees of land is graunted to Peter Risse att Winatuxet Brooke on the Northwest syde of the said brooke ;

Richard Wright
fifteen acrees of land is graunted unto Richard Wright lying next his land att Monponsett ; in leiu of a psell of land by him surrendered lying att the Towne of Plymouth neare John Woods land

Jacob Cook Sen
Six acrees of land is graunted to Jacob Cooke seni : lying neare his meddow att Winnatucksett on the Westerly syde therof ;

Wheras Great Complaint is made of much abuse by the ffeeding of neate Cattle and horses in the ffresh meddowes belonging to severall of the Towne of Plymouth ; It is ordered by the Towne that if any neate Cattle or horses shalbe found in any of the fresh meddowes viz : Winnatucksett meddowes Jonses River meddowes Dotyes meddowes or either of the South meddowes either upper or lower or Monponsett meddowes or in swan holt meddowes whether the said Neat Cattle or horses be belonging to either the Inhabitants of the Towne or fforraignors from the 15[th] of March untill the fifteenth day of July Annually It shalbe lawfull for any that shall find such Cattle or horses soe treaspassing to bringe them to the Towne's pound, and that the owners of such cattle or horses shall pay for every neat beast two shillings, and for every horse kind five shillings for every default to be payed to them that bringe the said Cattle to the pound, provided they pay the Charge of Impounding them

Capt: Bradford serjeant harlow Willam Crow Joseph Warren and Joseph howland of the Towne } are appointed by the Towne to view lay out and bound certaine psells of Wood land for the use of the Towne lying on the Northsyde of the Towne, and when that is done, That John Bryant seni : be accommodated with some land if it be there to be had ; if not elsewhere if it may be fond ;

Capt: Bradford Willam Crow and Willam Nelson } are appointed by the Towne to Run the Townes bounds on the North end and west syde of the Township ;

Att this meeting the Towne Graunted unto John Attwood seni : a smale slipp of Meddowish Ground and upland together lying between the highway and the brook att the end of his orchyard ; which was somtimes the orchyard of Mr Cushman which said smale slipp is to Run up the brook as high between the highway and the brooke as [1]

[116.] New Plymouth January the 31 1672

Wheras the Towne aforsaid Graunted unto several men fifty acrees of land apeece that had meddow att Winnatucksett off whom Captaine Thomas Southworth was one of those men and Now Joseph howland being in posession of the said Captaines Meddow ; have therfore measured and bounded unto the said Joseph howland ten acrees of land lying on the eastward syde of and butteth home to the said Captaines Meddow ; att Winnatuxett Att the North end and Westerly syde of the said ten Acrees it is bounded with a white oake Marked ; att the North end and Eastward syde it is bounded with a smale white oake Sapling ; That hath now two graines from the Roote ; and on the westward syde and south end it is bounded with a Great spruce tree And on the eastsyde and south end It is bounded with a Red oake sapling that standeth on or by the syde of a hill ; Alsoe in or by the said Right ; measured and bounded unto the said Joseph howland forty acrees of land

*Capt Southworth*

---

[1] The brook here referred to has in modern times been called Shaw's brook. It is a little south of Samoset Street, and is what was called in the earliest days "First Brook."

on the westward syde of Winnatuxett River; where the River bounds Richard Wrights land; At the Eastward end and Northeren syde it is bounded with a smale white oake tree next or neare the River and on the said Eastward end and Southward syde it is bounded with a longe Rocke which lyeth on the westward syde of a swamp and att the westward end Northward syde, it is bounded with an oake; and att the sd Westward end and southward syde it is bounded with an oake; The Northward syde of this land is layed home and abuteth to the River; The lines att the end of this land are not alike, there being an Angle att the eastward end therof

pme Willam Crow<br>
Surveyor

Joseph Howland

[117.] The bounds of thirty acrees of upland or therabouts which was Graunted by the Towne unto Jacob Cooke seni: in Leiw of the land taken away from him att the head of his land att the smelt brooke in the Townshipp of Plymouth by the Runing of the line of Edward Grayes and Samuell ffullers Lands which thirty acrees of land is bounded as followeth; viz: att the southeast end with an ash tree marked and with three stones att the foot of it; and att the southwest end nearest, it is bounded with a blacke oake tree marked haveing alsoe three stones att the foot of it; and the soatherly syde is bounded with the smelt brooke; and on the westerly syde betwixt Samuell ffuller and him; It is bounded with a white oake tree and three stones att the foot of it

The bounds of the Lands of Jacob Cooke Graunted by the Towne and layed out By Gorge Bonum, lying against Joneses River meddow upon the southsyde of the way Goeing to winnatucksett; it is bounded by a white oake tree Marked standing on the south syde of the way against Brewsters hill and soe Rangeth up into the woods to a blacke oake tree with three stones att the Root therof, and soe Ranging for the breadth of it to a white oake tree with three stones pitched att the Root of it upon a little Iland in a pond;

The bounds of the meddow of Edward Gray lying att Moonpousett brooke being two acrees, be it more or lesse is as followeth

viz: next unto Captaine Bradford it is bounded with a white oake marked; att the eastern end of an Iland which is the said Edward Grayes Northeren bounds; and his easteren bounds is a smale Cedar standing att the edge of a swamp marked, his westeren bounds or his westeren corner is bounded with a white oake standing on the edge of a swamp and soe Runs downe the brooke to the meddow of Samuell Sturtivant and is bounded ther on the westward syde and on the Eastward syde with a spruce tree between Samuell Sturtivant and him; and also ten acrees of upland abuting on the said meddow; the easteren bounds therof, is the westeren bounds of the meddow aforsaid, his westermost bounds of it is a Red oake; and soe it Rangeth downe by the side of Goodwife Sturtivants Land; to the aforsaid white oake which stands betwixt them in theire meddow,

Att the meeting house held att Plymouth the 23 of July 1673

Leift Morton } were appointed by the Towne to goe
Willam Crow } with those that shall Goe by the order
Joseph Warren } of the Court to Measure theire land
att Sepecan

Att this meeting the Towne voated that theire house in which Mr Cotton lives shalbe Repaired att theire charge; and that it be declared to him that they expect that hee should keep it in Repaire all such time as hee lives in it;

Joseph Bartlett engageth to pay forty shillings due to him from the Towne unto the psons appointed to Receive it, as soon as Corne is payable;

Edward Gray Willam Crow and Samuell Dunham; are appointed by the Towne to Receive what debts are due to the Towne from any pson or psons and alsoe in the Townes behalf to take accoumpt of the Constable;

The Rators Chosen att this meeting were { Leift Morton
Serjeant harlow
Will: Crow

[118.] The bounds of the land layed out by Gorge Bonum unto Edward Gray on the 14[th] day of ffebruary 1673 belonging to the said Edward Gray by vertue of a Graunt unto the propriators of Meddow att Winnatucksett which land lyeth att the Northwest corner of Monponsett pond, is as followeth viz; by the said pond syde with a pyne tree marked and att the uper end with a spruce tree marked by a swamp syde; and soe bounded Round with the said swamp which said swamp Runeth downe to the said pond on the Northwest; the said proportion of land is fifty five acrees bounded as aforsaid;

Twenty acrees of land which was Graunted to James Barnaby lying on the southwest syde of the double brookes att the Eelriver; is bounded as followeth viz: the Easteren bounds therof is a burch tree marked by the brooke syde, att the Corner of a swamp; on the southerly syde it is bounded with a beach tree marked; on the westerly corner itt is bounded with a white oake Marked on the Northerly syde or Corner therof it is bounded with an ash tree marked standing by the brook syde; on the Northeast end; it is bounded by the brooke and on the southerly syde by a swamp;

Willam Nelson haveing Relinquished his Graunt of thirty acrees of land graunted unto him, neare Joneses River meddow; To have soe much land on the North end and east syde of John Cobbs land which lyeth somwhat distant from Moonponsett brook have measured and bounded as followeth; beginning att a Great white oake tree which Standeth on the south syde of the way that Goe to Bridgwater which is one of John Cobbs bound markes the line extends to a Great fflatt Rocke that stands about twenty Rodd distant from John Cobbs North corner marke and from the said Rocke the line extends Eastward to a white oake tree marked standing in or close to a swamp, and from the said white oake tree the line extends to a white oake tree, that is the said John Cobbs east corner marke of his land ffebruary the 24$^{th}$ 1673,

By William Crow Surveyor

Measured and bounded unto John Waterman thirty acrees of upland lying on the westward of monponsett pond; and is between the lands of John Cobb and Alexander Kenedey as followeth att the west corner therof It is bounded with a white oake tree marked standing in a swamp att the North corner with a white oake Marked standing by the New way that Goes to bridgwater; att the east Corner is marked a pyne tree, standing on the westward syde of a hill; and att the south corner is marked a white oake tree standing close to or by a swamp near Allexander Kennedys land; the length lyeth Northeast a quarter of a point easterly eighty pole, the breadth lyeth southeast one quarter of a point southerly; that is from the west end and North syde, allowance of land being made or Given, that if occation be there shalbe a way through this land and that by Consent of the said John Waterman,

p Willam Crow Surveyor
Plymouth the 12 of ffebruary 1673,

[119.] Att a Towne meeting held att the meeting house att Plymouth the 16th day of ffebruary Ann° Dom 1673

Wheras Notwithstanding for what upon serch is or Can be found in the Records of the court for the Jurisdiction of New Plymouth The land which Samuell Ryder bought of Samuell Eedey lying att Mannomett ponds in the Towneshipp of Plymouth; is found to be Comon and att the Towns dispose; The Towne have Graunted unto the said Samuell Ryder all theire Right and Interest in the said land, which is twenty five acrees of land lying att Mannomett ponds aforsaid; as it is now bounded and in the possession of him the said Samuell Ryder, To him and his heires and assignes for ever;

Att this meeting the Towne Graunted unto Jabez howland, That wheras Gorge Bonum is Interrupted by him in his way to the ffulling mill; that in case he doe Relinquish an acree of his land below by the brooke wherby the said Gorge Bonum may have a way threw it, to his said mill; that then the said Jabez howland shall have an acree in leiw therof out of the townes land on the top of the hill,

It is ordered by the Towne

That every Inhabitant that is a Townsman and expect town privilidges shall pticularly engage for him or themselves to pay theire proportions to all towne charges that the towne in Generall shall conclude of to disburse and Rate for; and that all such psons as shall Refuse to pay such Rates shalbe denyed of all and every the Towne privilidges they make use of according to order of the Towne upon herbage, wood Timber Tarr ffish or what else may be in the Towne; And that none be pmited to be Inhabitants in the Town before they Ingage to beare theire proportions of all Town Charges

And that all lands meddows and other Ratables within our Township shalbe Rated to all Towne Charge

ordered by the Towne that the Celect men of the Towne be Impowered to call such younge men or others as live Idelely and disorderly to an accompt for theire mispending theire time in ordinaryes, or otherwise and to take Course for their Reformation as shalbe by them thought meet;

The Towne expressed themselves Content that the Naighbours about the Middle of the Towne shall have the benifitt of the ffish called Alewives which goe up att the season att the mill brooke, soe as they take a course that they may Goe up without Interuption;

The bounds of Gorge Watsons Meddow lying in the meddow Comonly Called Doties meddows, and is bounded on the easteren end with a stake, standing the west syde of a spring brooke and soe Runeth westerly to another stake standing about the middle of the meddow; and from thence still westerly upon a straight line to a Grove of bushes standing by the brooksyde; and it is bounded on the south syde with the brooke, and on the North syde; It lyeth adjoyning to James Coles meddow;

[120.] Att a Towne meeting held att the meeting house att Plymouth the 18$^{th}$ of May 1674;

The Towne have voated and do Graunt unto Leiftenant Ephraim Morton heerby a Confeirmation of four lotts breadth viz: four score pole of land in breadth lying on the southerly syde of the Eelriver in the Township of Plymouth, bounded on the Easterly syde with a highway Runing up by the land which was somtimes Richard Churches land; and extending in length to the ffoot of the pyne hills; The like liberty of Confeirmation is Graunted to any of the Inhabitants of the Towne Respecting theire antient proprietyes, if they shall see cause to desire it;

Capt Bradford
Leift Morton
Elder Cushman
Nathaniell Morton
Serjeant harlow
Willam Crow
Willam Clarke
Joseph howland
and Joseph Warren
Edward Gray

were appointed by the Towne to meete together on the next training day which wilbe on the third monday in June next; To Consider of pticulars in Reference unto equall makeing of Rates;

The fifty acrees of land Graunted unto Mr Thomas Cushman belonging to Winnatucksett meddow; or neare a place called Colchester in the Township of Plymouth; is bounded as followeth viz : with a smale Red oake standing neare Colchester brooke ;

The Southermost bound is a Red oake marked standing neare a Rocke on the southwest syde

The westermost bounds is two smale Red oakes neare a spott of meddow Ground

The Northermost bounds is a white oake standing by the same brooke that is comonly Called Colchester brooke; and Joyning to that; which was formerly Graunted and layed out to the said Thomas Cushman

The bounds of a psell of land Graunted unto Gorge Bonum being a necke of land Joyning att ffresh Lake in the Township of Plymouth, on the Northesterly syde of The said lake is as followeth

It adjoyneth to the Lott of the said Gorge Bonum which hee bought of John Rickard, which was somtimes the lott of Steven Deane ; the said necke of land, Runing alonge on the same Range as the said lott doth betwixt the pond and the swamp, and soe Runeth to lout pond ; and a Certaine swamp that Runeth betwixt the said lout pond and ffresh Lake is the southermost end therof ;

four acrees of land was Graunted unto Thomas Lucas lying between [1] Mr Prences Bottome (soe Called) and deep water if it be there to be had if not to have foure acrees in some other place where it may be found not disposed of to others

[**121.**] Att a Towne meeting held att Plymouth on the 15th day of June 1674 It was ordered as followeth ;

schools     Wheras att a Towne meeting may the 20th 1672 the proflitts and benifitts of the lands att Sepecan Agawaam and places adjacent were given toward the maintainance and Incouragement of the free Scool att Plymouth the Towne declares that theire graunt was onely of the lands there and therabouts which were purchased by the Towne of the Indians before the said May the 20th 1672 and they doe desire and Authorize Capt: Bradford the Secretary the Celect men William Clarke and Joseph Warren to doe theire uttmost to Improve the said Lands for the attaining

---

[1] Mr Prences Bottome was a piece of low or valley land granted to Thomas Prence. It is now owned and occupied by B. M. Watson.

of the ends propounded Namly that their Children be pfected in Reading when they are entered the bible; and alsoe that they be taught to wright and Sifor; besides that which the Country expects from the said Scool

Att a Towne meeting held att the meeting house att Plymouth the 14th day of october 1674

Andrew Ringe and Jonathan Barnes } appointed by the Towne to see unto and procure in Mr Cottons maintainance

The names of the men that engaged to draw the wood;

| | |
|---|---|
| Samuell Dunham | 9 load |
| Andrew Ringe | 8 load |
| John Wood | 6 load |
| Daniell Dunham | 4 load |
| Joseph Churchill | 3 load |

in all 30 load

Daniell Dunham, Joseph Warren and Jonathan Barnes were appointed and authorized by the Towne; and Invested by them with full power for and in theire behalfe legally to demand and Recover whatsoever is or shalbe due to the Towne from any pson or psons and are Responsible to give an accoumpt to the Towne from time to time of theire actings in the prmises as occation shall Require

And the Towne have ordered and deputed Nathaniel Morton the Now Town clarke for them and in theire behalfe to give full power to them and to any that shalbe by them and under them deputed, by a legall letter of Attorney signed by his hand to acte in the prmises from time to time as occation may Require untill the Court shall see Reason otherwise to order

Att this meeting Gyles Richard Jun: Requested a smale psell of land up above the Naighborhood, and Andrew Ringe and Benajah Pratt were appointed to view the said land desired and to make Report therof to the Towne in order to a graunt therof;

This Towne haveing formerly and now seen the great damage that hath and will arise unto the Townes Inhabitants in the Generall by Graunting of Great psells of land to pticular men; and suffering of pticular men to make use of the Townes comons as they please therby turning the Generall advantage of the Townes comons to theire private benifitt which was and is more to the hurt and damage of the Towne then the benifitt of the said pticulars ; The Towne haveing therfore ordered some prsons to view theire comons and they haveing made Report to the Towne in open Towne meeting It is therfore ordered acceded and concluded, and they doe heerby sett apart all the uplands and swampes that are surrounded by the wayes lines and places heerafter mensioned ; and that they shall Remaine for ever for Generall Comons for the Townes Generall use, for wood and Timber for the Inhabitants to make use of in the Towne for building ffencing and fierwood ; and that not any waies the said lands or swampes to be graunted to any pticular men ; hereby alsoe prohibiting all trees not to be felled for barke or to be cutt downe or carried away out of the Township either in whole trees or wrought up ; the said lands bounded as followeth To Remaine for ever to the Generall use of the Towne ; provided this acte and order not to hinder or disturbe any pson or psons in theire pticular proprieties

[122.]
proved that a graunt of land to John Barrow in this tract is excepted and some speech likewise of a psell of land

Graunted by either the court or Towne within the bounds as followeth, viz : begining att the smelt brooke where Samuell ffullers house standeth or where the Kinges Road therby croseth ; and from the said River the line to extend to a brooke that is called colchester brooke ; where Mr howland hath lands ; as the cartway goeth to and from the said brooke and River ; and from the said colchester brooke to extend as the said Colchester brooke Runeth untill it comes unto Winnatucksett River ; and soe downe Winnatucksett River untill it comes to a brooke that comes out of a meddow Called Monponsett meddow and soe from the said Meddow to the Eastside of Monponsett pond and from thence to Joneses River pond where the Towne line cutts the pond ; and soe to the brooke that Goeth out of the said Joneses River pond and the line to extend as the said brooke Runeth untill it comes to Joneses River

John Bryant
desireth

bridge; and soe to the first Station att the smelt brooke or smelt River fore named;

And whatsoever pson or psons Inhabitants or others that shall Treaspas in any of the afore mentioned pticulars shall pay to the Generall use of the Towne And if the Treaspas be one more then twenty trees a yeare then to pay

At the Towne meeting held at the Meeting house at Plymouth the 13 th of ffebruary 1674 It was unanimously agreed and voated by the Towne that our meeting house shalbe speedily Repaired att the Townes Charge

And Mr Gray and } were appointed and deputed by
Mr Clarke } the Towne to take speedy Course
that the said meeting house be Repaired; and the Towne heerby engageth to see the Charge therof faithfully defrayed in such [1] specue as they shall agree with men for the doeing of it; and that such pay as is due from ffrancis Combe Jonathan Morrey John ffallowell and Samuel Ryder, and all pay as is alreddy payed by them, to the Townes agents, be improved Towards the effecting of the said worke; alwaies provided that the twenty seven shillings due in money to Leiftenant Morton be first defrayed out of it;

Extravagant
Persons
warned
out of Town

It is ordered by the Towne that henceforth the Celect men of the Towne are fully Impowered successively to take effectual Course That all extravigant psons that have or shall Come into the Townshipp or any such as the selectmen or any two of them shall or doe not approve off That they shall warne them out of the Towne; and take a speedy and effectual course that they depart the Townshipp: or take sufficient Cecuritie to save the Towne harmles from such damage as may acrew to them by theire staying therin; Leiftenant Morton and Joseph Warren were appointed by the Towne to settle the Matter between the Towne and Acanootus the Indian about the exchange of lands

---

[1] The editor does not feel sure of the exact word in the original records. If "specue," as here printed, it means "specie," not as we use that word, but in the sense of "kind" of payment.

The 16 of ffebruary 1673

Att this meeting the Towne Graunted unto Jabez howland That wheras Gorge Bonum

Aprill 29<sup>th</sup> 1674

The Towne of Plymouth haveing graunted unto Jabez howland by way of exchange an acree of land on the topp of the hill next the said Jabez his land, that is on the south syde of the mill brook: for soe much lands to be Relinquished by him of his land there; next the said brook; and on the west syde of his land; I therfore have measured of the Relinquished land: from the said Jabez his lands: and bounded his other lands; from it by one stone sett into the Ground neare the fulling mill: and brooke from which stone the line extends up the hill southward to another stone sett into the Ground, next to a Rocke; on the topp of the hill; from the stone sett into the Ground neare the topp of the hill: the line that Compaseth; the aforsaid one acree Graunted by the Towne extends westward to a stone sett into the Ground; and from this stone; the line extends southward to a stone sett into the Ground by Gyles Rickard Seni: his ffence; and lands and from the stone sett into the Ground by the said Rickards land, the line extends eastward till it meet the head line of the said Jabez his land att the southwest Corner therof Aprill 29 1674

         pme Willam Crow Surveyor

[123.] Att a Towne meeting held att the meeting house att Plymouth the 24<sup>th</sup> day of May 1675 it was ordered by the Towne That notwithstanding all former orders made by the Towne prohibiting the Cuting or Transporting any barke out of the Township; Great Spoyle and stripp of Timber is made on the Townes Comons by that meanes The towne therfore ordereth that whosoever shall or doth Cut any barke on the townes Comons within this township: that all such Barke shalbe forfeite to the use of the Towne: and Andrew Ring Benajah Pratt and Jabez howland are appointed by the towne or any two of them is appointed to take some Reall and serious Course that the said order be duly executed:

Att this meeting it was ordered and unanimously agreed that the Towne doe freely Give unto Mr John Cotton theire p<sup>r</sup>sent minnester and to his heires and assignes for ever The house and land upon which hee now lives; incase the said

Mr Cotton liveth and dieth in this place; in the worke of the minnestry: In Consideration of which the said Mr Cotton and his wife doe fully and freely quitt and discharge the said Towne of that fifty pounds which they had promised to mistris Cotton formerly incase of her husbands decease in this place;

Morover It is agreed that the said house shall now be viewed by four men; mutually and Indifferently Chosen; by the said Towne and Mr. Cotton: and they shall Judge in what condition the said house is: and sett a Just vallue therupon: according to theire best Judgments: and if God by his Providence shall Call Mr Cotton from his worke in this place during his life time; That then four men be by the said Towne and Mr Cotton mutually and Indifferently Chosen to view the said house and what the said house is better and the additions of building upon the land shalbe vallued by them and accordingly shalbe payed by the Towne to the said Mr John Cotton or his order;

The prsons Chosen to acte according to this order in vallueing and Judging of the worth of the house etc; are

Leift: Morton and Joseph Dunham Chosen by the Towne and serjeant harlow and Joseph howland Chosen by Mr Cotton:

Att a Towne meeting held att Plymouth the 7[th] of January 1675

The Towne haveing Received by theire Constable two warrants the one Injoyning them to presse eleven able sufficient men to goe forth as souldiers against the Indians our enimies the other Requireing a Rate of eleven pounds to be made for and towards the Charge of the souldiers to Goe forth

In obedience and in order wherunto the Towne primarily made Choise of a Councell for the Towne to advice and order the affaires of the Towne Respecting the prmises whose names are as followeth viz:   Capt Willam Bradford    Joseph Warren
                 Mr Thomas Cushman   Willam Crow
                 Leiftenant Morton     Willam Clarke
                 Serjeant harlow

Accordingly alsoe they Chose Rators to Levy the said Rate
viz:                        Joseph Warren
                          Willam Crow
                          Willam Clarke

The men appointed by the Towne to make and provide Clothing in the behalfe of the Towne for the souldiers now to Goe forth were
   Mr Gray
   Joseph Warren
   Jabez howland
   Willam Clarke
   Joseph Bartlett
and the Towne stands hereby Ingaged to satisfiy for which they shall order disburse in that Case

[124.] Measured and bounded unto John Cobb fifty acrees of land lying on both sydes of bridgwater path betwixt two swampes where Robert Lathams way Comes into the said Path, and is bounded with a white oake that stands on the South syde of the North swamp att the eastward end of the said land, and on the said syde; and on the westward end it is bounded with a smale Red oake tree, on the Northsyde of the south swamp the said land is bounded att the eastward end with a forked young Red oake; and att the westward end of the said Land, on the said syde it is bounded with a great white oake tree standing, on the southsyde of the Path
  ffebruary 18$^{th}$ 1667
         p$^r$ Willam Crow Surveyor

att the Towne meeting held att the Meeting house att Plymouth the 19 day of ffebruary 1675
  Leift Morton } appointed by the Towne to see
  Robert ffinney } to the Gathering in Mr Cottons
  and Joseph howland } sallery

It was ordered by the Towne that there shalbe forthwith a fortification build upon the fort hill att Plymouth: to be an hundred foot square the pallasadoes to be 10 foot and one halfe longe: to be sett 2 foot and an halfe in the Ground; and to be sett against a post and a Raile; every man is to doe three foot of the said ffence of the fortification the Pallasadoes are to be battered on the backsyde one against every two and sharpened on the topp to be accomplished by every male in each family from sixteen yeares old and upwards and that there shalbe a watchhouse erected within the said ffence or fortification and that the three peece of ordnance shalbe planted within the said ffence or fortification;

Agreed with Nathaniell Southworth to build the said watchhouse which is to be sixteen foot in length and 12 foot in breadth and eight foot studd to be walled with board; and to have 2 fllores the uper flore to be six foot above the lower fllore; and he is to batten the walls and to make a smale paire of staires in it and to fram two smale windowes below to make 2 gables to the Roofe or eachsyde one, to Cover the Roof with shingle; and to build a Chimney in the said house; and to do all the worke therunto; onely the frame is to be brought to the place att the townes Charge; and for the said work hee is to have eight pounds to be payed either in money; or other pay equivolent;

Att this meeting the Treasurer promised to procure Carriages for to mount the ordnance, or to pay for the makeing of them;

Att the meeting held att the Meeting house att Plymouth the 4[th] of May 1676 The Celect men Chosen were

    Leift: Morton
    Willam Crow
    Willam Clarke
    Joseph howland
   The Deputies
    Leift Morton
    Mr Gray
   The Constable
    Gorge Morton
   Grandjurymen
    Serjeant harlow
    Serjeant Tinkham
   The Surveyors
    Steven Bryant
    Isacke Cushman
    Ephraim Tilson
    Mordica Ellis

Att this meeting the Town voated that 30 £ more shallbe Rated for to be aded to the former Rate to pay the souldiers etc;

[125.]

Major Willam Bradford
Mr John Cotton
Mr Thomas Cushman
Samuell ffuller
Edward Gray
Steven Bryant
John Dunham sen:
Samuell Kinge sen:
Serjeant Ephraim Tinkham
John Cobb
John Mores
Thomas Lettice
James Cole
Gorge Bonum sen:
Andrew Ringe
Richard Wright
Gyles Rickard sen:
Willam Crow
Gorge Watson
Serjeant Willam harlow
John Jourdaine
Benjamin Eaton
Jonathan Barnes
Gyles Rickard Jun:
Samuell Dunham
Nathaniel Morton
Leift Ephraim Morton
Thomas Morton
Robert ffinney sen:
Willam Clarke
Joseph Warren
Jonathan Shaw
Samuell Ryder
James Clarke
Abraham Jackson
Joseph Dunham
John holmes
Leift Joseph howland
Joseph Bartlett
Mr Joseph Bradford
Nathaniel Southworth

Thomas ffaunce
John Bradford
John Drew
Jonathan Moray
John Doten
Joseph Churchill
Gorge Morton
Robert Barrow
Eliezer Churchill
Samuell Sturtivant
Samuell harlow
Isacke Cushman
Elkanah Cushman
John Bryant sen:
Nathaniell holmes
Baruck Jourdaine
Joseph ffaunce
John Rickard
John Bryant
Jacob Cooke
Ephraim Morton Jun
Robert Ransum
Ephraime Tilson
Caleb Cooke
John Morton
Samuell Dunham Jun
Willam Bradford Jun
John Gray
Thomas Clarke Jun
John Sturtivant
Samuell Gardian
Nathanell Wood allias Attwood
Isacke Lobdell
Joshua Pratt
Thomas Cushman
Edward Doten
Jonathan Pratt
Gorge Morton
John Barrow

[126.] Att the meeting held att the meeting house att Plymouth the 13$^{th}$ of June one thousand six hundred seventy and six

   The Raters Chosen were   { Leift Morton
                 serjeant harlow
                 Willam Crow ;

 Att this meeting the Towne ordered that all the Guns and swords belonging to the Towne shalbe delivered in unto the Counstable

 The Towne voated alsoe att this meeting that all Inhabiting in this towne or within the bounds of the Townshipp shal be Rated to publick Charges except such as live on the almes of the Towne ;

  Willam Crow    ) were appointed to present to the
  Jabez howland    } Court in the townes behalfe what
  and ; Joseph Warren ) charges is due to them from the
              Country ; in order therunto to pre-
              pare the said accoumpt against the
              next Court and then to present it

 Att the Towne meeting held att Plymouth the 19$^{th}$ day of August 1676  Leift : Ephraim Morton
    and Leift : Joseph howland
were chosen Deputies to attend the next Generall Court and to acte in the Townes behalfe in the Concernes therof

  serjeant harlow    ) were chosen by the Towne to take
  Willam Crow    } the accoumpt of each manes estate
  and Joseph Warren ) in the Towne in order unto the
settleing of matters Relating to the Raiseing of means by Rates in this Colonie for defraying of the publicke Charges of the Collonie ;

  Leift Morton    ) were Chosen Rators to levy the
  Serjeant harlow  } Rates for the publicke Charges
  and Willam Crow  ) fortwith to be Raised by Rates ;

 It was ordered by the Towne that Joseph Warren and William Crow shall take the accoumpt of the last years Constable, and to Give it in att the next Towne meeting ;

 Att a Towne meeting held att the meeting house att Plymouth the 15$^{th}$ day of September Ann° Dom 1676 the Towne did agree and voate That Mr Cotton our Minnester shall have alowed unto him for this year, the sume of sixty pounds to be payed in Current silver money of New England the one halfe therof to be payed by the last of october next ensueing the date heerof and the other halfe att or before the first day of Aprill Next ensueing the date heerof

The men appointed by the Towne to see the said engagement pformed that is to say to Collect and cause to be payed ; by the Inhabitants are ; serjeant harlow and Nathaniell Southworth

It is agreed by the towne that the said sume shalbe levied by Rate on the said Inhabitants ; and the Rators Chosen were Serjeant Willam harlow Mr Willam Crow, and Joseph Warren ;

Att a Towne meeting held att the Meeting house att Plymouth the 15th June 1677 the Rators Chosen to make the Rate for the payment of the souldiers were

    Mr Willam Crow
    Joseph howland
    Willam Clarke

The Comittie Chosen to take an accoumpt of what is due from severall psons Relateing to the warr since the last expedition under Major Bradford are

    the said Major
    the two Deputies
    Leiftenant Morton
    Mr Crow ; serjeant harlow
    Nathaniel Morton

[127.] Att the Towne meeting held att the Towne of Plymouth the 15th of May 1677 Mr Edward Gray and Joseph howland were Chosen Deputies to serve att the next Court and the severall adjournments therof

Leift: Morton | were Chosen to serve in the office
Serjeant harlow | of Celect men
and Mr Crow |

Jonathan Barnes was Chosen Constable

Andrew Ringe and | Chosen Grandjurymen
Benajah Pratt |

Leiftenant Morton | were Chosen Surveyors
Serjeant Tinkham | of the highwayes
and Serjeant harlow |

Mr Crow and | were appointed by the Towne
Joseph howland | to take an accoumpt of the

estates of each man of this towne soe as it may be in a Reddines to be presented to the Next Court

Memorandum that all the Male Inhabitants Capeable of Workeing have pformed theire dutyes of worke to the highwaies viz all such of them as live in this Towneship from and between Major Bradfords and John Cobb

The Towne have ordered the Deputies of this Towne Now Chosen to make enquiry Concerning the Graunt of Saconett Lands unto the [1] servants and to declare that the towne find themselves agreived; in that Larger Portions of Land by farr are distributed than was att first Given to them by the Court and this towne doth order the Secretary Leiftenant Morton Mr Crow and Serjeant harlow to Joyne with the Deputies of our Towne Now Chosen to serch the Records of the Graunts of the lands aforsaid and to prepare the Case by drawing up a draught of the pticulars of theire agrievantes Respecting the pmises soe as it may be in a Reddines to be psented to the Next approaching Generall Court In Regard that the Graunt of Land Att Agawaam is found deficient and that Notwithstanding wee are Rated according therunto as fully as if wee had a full Graunt of the propriety therof;

It is ordered by the towne that our Deputies Now Chosen: shall endeavor to procuie the said Graunt fully pfected;

Gorge Bonum and Andrew Ring are appointed to view a smale Moyety of land lying in Alcarmus feild between Thomas Dotens Land and the Land of Joseph ffaunce: desired by Gyles Rickard: and to make Report therof to the Towne att the Next Towne Meeting; that if it appeer not to be Matterially prejudiciall to the Naighborhood: that it shall then be Graunted to him by the Towne;

In like manor they are desired to view a smale Moyety of Land desired by Nathaniel Wood and to make Report therof to the Towne;

In Reference unto a smale psell of Land & a smale Cottage theron formerly posessed by Thomas Dunham deceased: Now desired by Benjamine Eaton the Towne have ordered

---

[1] In early times the word "servant" did not necessarily mean what it does today. This should be remembered in connection with the statement that William Brewster was the servant of Sir William Davison.

that the said Benjamine Eaton enter upon the same and posesse and Improve it, being willing to Graunt and surrender up theire Right therin unto him, the said Benjamine Eaton to him and his heires and assignes for ever :

[128.] Att a Towne meeting of the Towne of Plymouth held att the meeting house att Plymouth the first of August 1677 The Rators Chosen to make all the Rates viz : for the minnester and the Country charges and the Towne Charges were

Leift : Morton
Serje : harlow
Willam Clarke

The Towne have Graunted unto Gyles Rickard Jun : a smale psell of upland Ground being aboute two acrees be it More or lesse Lying and being in Alcarmus feild between the land in the possession off Joseph ffaunce on the southerly syde ; and the land of Thomas Doten on the Northerly or Northwest syde or end ; and abutting on the Kinges highway, which leads from the towne of Plymouth to Wellinsley Brook ; and extending from the said highway westerly or southwest nearest up towards the woods, untill it meets with a psell of land appertaining to Gorge Watson : provided withall that hee his heires and successors is to leave an [1] highway to Goe from the aforsaid Comon Road between The aforsaid Thomas Dotens land and his said land ; up towards the woods, viz : an highway of forty foot wide for egress and Regresse, of horse and foot and Carts, to and from as occation may Require

The Towne have Graunted unto Thomas hewes a Certaine swamp Called hurtleberry swamp lying above serjeant harlowes between the uper old footpath as did formerly lead from the Towne of Plymouth towards Wellingsley Brooke and the path that Goeth from the Towne to the Naighborhood Comonly Called the little Towne : which swamp is Graunted to him to make tryall to make Meddow therof but not speedily to make sale therof provided alsoe that incase hee ditch or ffence about it hee shall not hinder Crosse nor stopp any high way that Goeth by it or lyeth Neare it pticularly hee shall not hinder nor Interupt the highway by which Serjeant harlow and others of the Naighbors doe usually Cart wood out of the woods ;

---

[2] This highway was probably what is now Mt. Pleasant Street.

The Towne have Graunted unto Jonathan Morey three score acrees of upland Ground lying and being att the salt water pond by the way between Plymouth and Sandwich and six acrees of Meddowish Ground by the said pond adjoyning or neare unto the upland for a place for him to build and settle on: provided hee keep two sufficient Gates on the said land that soe Notwithstanding this Graunt passengers may passe through it; on the highway that Goes through the same as formerly;

Att this meeting it was ordered agreed and voated that the sume which shalbe payed to Mr John Cotton our p$^r$sent minnester shalbe four score pounds for this yeare which sume shalbe payed in Country pay one third to be payed in wheat or butter or tarr or shingles, another third in rye pease or mault; and the other third in Indian Corne the wheat att four shillings six pence per bushell, butter at six pence a pound Mault att four shillings a bushell, pease att three shillings and six pence a bushell Rye att three shillings and six pence a bushell Indian Corne att three shillings a bushell Tarr and shingle att prise Current with the Marchants The payments to be made: the one halfe by the first of November, the latter halfe by the first of March to those appointed to Collect it; and this to Continue till God in his Providence soe Impoverish, the Towne that they shalbe nessesitated to abate of the said sume;

It is further agreed that if any will pay theire Rates or pte thereof in money they shall have liberty soe to doe;

The Towne have Chosen Mr Edward Gray and Joseph Bartlett to Collect the Rate for the minnester for this p$^r$sent year; and the said Edward Gray and Joseph Bartlett doe engage and promise to the Towne that the said sume as above mensioned shalbe payed Reasonably to the minnester att the times above appointed, provided like Course be taken for the future;

[129.] Att the Towne meeting held att the meeting house att Plymouth the 8$^{th}$ of August 1677 It was ordered by the Towne that such woulves as have bine killed by any before this date unpaied for shalbe payed for twenty shillings a peece that is to say old woulves; and that for such woulves as shalbe killed by any of the Towne after this date within the Township they shall have butt ten shillings a woulfe viz: an old woulfe but nott soe for cubbs;

Att this meeting thirty acrees of Land was Graunted, and fully Confeirmed unto John Bryant son in law to Steven Bryant; lying att or neare a place Called Billingtons holes neare unto or upon Jonses River in the Township of Plymouth to be layed forth to him by Leiftenant howland and William Crow;

Att the Towne meeting held att the meeting house att Plymouth on the 17th day of September 1677, The Towne Impowered and authorized Mr Edward Gray in theire behalfe to demand of the Towne of Scittuate, or such as are more emediately Concerned to make payment to him, the said Mr Gray the sume of nineteen pounds, sixteen shillings and eight pence for the said Towne of Plymouths use which is a debt due to the said Towne of Plymouth from the Towne of Scittuate soe ordered by the Country and upon Receipt of the said sume to give Receipts or acquittances for the same; and the Towne doth heerby Impower the Towne Clarke, incase there shalbe occation to give a letter of attorney in theire name to sue for our due in that behalfe; morover The Town doe heerby Impower the said Mr Gray to make payment of such pte of the said sume as is due to any souldier or souldiers unto whom it is assigned Retaining that which is his owne due therof and be heerby Responsible to produce the Remainder for to be Improved for the publicke use of the Towne; and what charge the said Mr Gray shalbe att in procuring and Transporting of the said sume to be payed by the Towne

morover The Towne doe Impower Mr Edward Gray in theire behalfe to demand the sume of 2£ 4s of Steven Bryant and 2£ from Willam Nelson Sen : and 3£ from Jonathan Morey ; and 2£ from Mr Clarke & 4£ from Samuell Ryder and to Improve the same ; or soe much of it as hee shall see Cause for the Repaireing of the meeting house ;

The Towne have Graunted unto Andrew Ringe a smale psell of upland near his house about halfe an acree more or lesse to plant an orchyard or otherwise to use as hee shall see Cause

Att a Towne meeting held at the Meeting house att Plymouth the 7th of January 1677

Wheras att a meeting held att the meeting house att Plymouth the 15th day of ffebruary 1669 : It was ordered by the Towne that if the Constable doe Receive an order from either the Majestrates or any Majestrate Resideing in the Towne or from the Court or from the Celect men of the Towne att any time to warne a Towne meeting and Neglect to Give due warning viz: by himselfe or others to every one written in the list of those who doe acte in Town meeting the said Constable soe Neglecting shall pay twelve pence for every one that hee Neglecteth soe to warne, to be levied to the Townes use by the Constable succeeding the yeer following, after such defects are made; as alsoe that many whoe have bine orderly warned to towne meetings have frequently Neglected to appeer theratt: wherby the Towne 's much damnifyed;

It is further ordered by the Towne that if any shall absent himselfe from the Towne meeting being orderly warned; which is to say a week before by the Constable or his Deputie unless occation Require a shorter warneing, shalbe fined two shillings for every such defect of non appeerance to the use of the Towne unless hee Can make a Just defence for his said absence; and that such fines for such defaults be forthwith made known to the Constable by the Towne Clarke; and forthwith levied by the Constable for the use of the Towne;

A smal Moyety of land was Graunted by the Town to Mr Edward Gray lying att the foot of the hill below Mr Cottons att the watersyde viz: about 40 foot square to sett a ware house on; with libertie of Convenient egrese and Regresse therunto It was ordered by the Towne that Jonathan Morey be Invested with full power from the Towne to defend our Just Rights Incroached upon by others on our Comons towards Sandwich;

[130.] Att a Towne meeting held att the meeting house att Plymouth the 20th of May 1678

The Towne have sett and to ffarme lett Clarkes Island for the tearme of seaven yeers unto Richard Willis of Plymouth; to begine from the fifteenth of october 1678 and from that time the said tearme of seaven yeers to be fully and compleatly ended, for and in Consideration of the full sume of three pounds pr yeer to be yeerly payed in Currant silver mony of New England To the Towne of Plymouth or to theire order: notwithstanding this lease any of the towne may fech what wood of the said Iland they pleas either for building fierwood or otherwise; but are heerby prohibited from puting any Cattle of any kind theron:.to the said Willis his Anoyance or to the Anoyance of any that hee may take in under him to Improve the said Iland for the said Tearme of seaven yeers; In Reference unto the Request of James

Cole that hee may Reataine and Improve two acrees of land by him lately Inclosed with other land of his lying below the land of Daniell Dunham on the south syde of the Towne of Plymouth which said two acrees of land: is for the prsent att the Townes despose: In Regard that the Court Record doth not pfectly and clearly demonstrate the proprietors to whome Att the first it was alloted;

The Towne doe heerby give libertie to the said James Cole his heires and assignes to Improve the said two acrees of land to his or theire pticular use and benifitt, untell any other true propriators doe appeer to lay Claime therunto; viz: The Towne doth heerby surrender up unto the said James Cole his heires and assignes all the Right and Interest they have unto or in the said two acrees of land untill any other doe appeer to have better Right therunto, provided that hee the said James Cole doe leave out to the Townes use other two acrees of his owne land att the same place, to be att the Townes dispose soe longe as hee Retaines the aforsaid two acrees of land;

Att a meeting of the Towne of Plymouth held att the Meeting house att Plymouth the 26th of June 1678

The Rators Chosen to make the Rates for the Minnester and other charges for the Country Rates were

{ Leift: Morton
  Mr Crow
  Will: Clarke }

Att this meeting the Towne Graunted unto John Morton a smale peece of upland for an homsted to build an house on lying and being by the little brook where the old prison stood between that Cartway that Goeth allonge by the place, where the old prison stood; and the land of Andrew Ringe above and the barne of John Wood;

The Collectors to Gather the minnesters maintainance for this yeer are Willam Clarke and Abraham Jackson whoe are to doe it on the same Conditions as it was pformed the last yeer; five shillings was allowed to Goodman Edey viz: Samuell Edey for work don by him in time of the warr in makeing Clothes for souldiers

Serjeant harlow }
Mr Crow         } were ordered by the Towne to sett and to farme lett our Right of lands
Joseph Warren   } att Agawam etc for the tearme of seaven yeers from the date heerof;

It was ordered by the Towne that all such Cattle as are or shalbe wintered in the Towne or Townshipp tho otherwise disposed of afterwards shalbe Rated for that yeer in which they were wintered;

[131.] Att a Towne meeting held att the meeting house att Plymouth the 15th day of December 1678

The Towne have sett and to ffarme lett unto Edward Gray of Plymouth Clarkes Iland; for the tearme of seaven yeers; to begine att the date heerof and from thence to be Compleatly ended; for and in Consideration of the sume of three pounds and nine shillings yeerly to be duely payed in current silver mony of New England to the said Towne or theire order for the said tearme of seaven yeers and that hee alsoe pay unto Patience Willis widdow the Relict of Richard Willis of Plymouth late deceased: the sume of twenty shillings silver money for that the said Willis had an Interest from the said Towne for the tearme of seaven yeers as aforsaid, the Towne haveing and Retaineing liberty Notwithstanding this Lease, they or theire order to ffech what wood they need from off the said Iland, as they shall see cause, either for building ffencing or fierwood; but are herby prohibited from Leting any Cattle of any kind therupon, To the said Leasser his Annoyance or the Annoyance of any that hee may be in ptnershipp with: or take in under him for the Improvement of the said Iland, for the tearme aforsaid; the Conditions above expressed being duely observed: he the said Edward Gray is to have and Injoy the said Iland for the said tearme of seven yeers, and although the said Edward Gray should decease before the said tearme of seaven yeers is expired; yett Notwithstanding his heires successors, or assignes shall or may Injoy it on the like Conditions as above expressed, for the aforsaid tearme of seaven yeers It is likewise agreed by and between the towne and the said Edward Gray that hee may keep sixteen neate Cattle on Clarkes Iland Rate ffree and no more Edward ( ) Gray his
marke.

The Towne have Graunted unto Mr Cotton that incase any Comon land Can be found fitt for pastureing about the first brook, as is Conceived there may, that hee shall have a Competency therof, Graunted and layed forth to him and his heires for ever;

The Towne haveing Graunted the 16th of May 1673 unto ffrancis Curtice eight acrees of land att the second place of Goeing over Jones River by the Indian Bridge by the herring ware; I have measured and bounded the said eight acrees; which lyeth on the eastward syde of the said River ware and bridge: and att the southwest Corner of the said Land it is bounded with a Red oake tree standing by the River att or neare a Row of Rockes or stones that lye a Crosse the River; and from the said tree the line extends to a stone sett into the Ground att the southeast Corner of the said Land by a Red oak sapling marked on four sydes; and from the said stone and line extends North and by west nearest unto another stone sett into the Ground; att the Northeast Corner of the said Land by a pyne tree Marked; and from the stone att the Northeast Corner, the line extends west and by south unto a stone sett downe Neare the bankes of the said River by a Red oake Sapling Marked; soe to the River And on the west syde of the said Land the said River to be the bounds: from the Northwest Corner stone to the aforesaid Red oake tree; att the Southwest Corner the Length fifty four pole; the breadth twenty-five pole; allowance being made for the highway;

December the 18th day pr me Willam Crow
Surveyor 1678

[132.] The bounds of a Graunt of Land Graunted by the Towne unto Benajah Pratt lying att a place in the Townshipp of Plymouth called Pontuses meddow; It is as followeth viz; 8 acrees of upland bounded att the North end with two acrees of Land which belonges to Joseph Churchill; and on the east end or eastermost Corner it is bounded with a young Red oake standing by the cart way; The south bound with a stone sett into the Ground on the syde of a Ridge; The west bound is a smale Red oake marked standing on the syde of a hill; this Last bound pteth the said 2 acrees fornamed from the said Benajah Pratts Land;

Att the Towne meeting held att the meeting house att Plymouth the seaventh of Aprill 1679,

The Town Graunted unto Samuell Jenney the watchhouse upon the ffort hill in Respect of his destitute Condition to be for a house for him to dwell in; and not to be sold or estranged to any other use; and hee hath liberty to Remove it to any other place for the end aforsaid, when he pleaseth;

Att this Meeting the Towne Graunted unto Joseph Warren sen: twenty acrees of Land lying att The Eelriver on the Southerly syde of Ephraim Mortons Land, there, bounded on the westerly syde with the Cart way that Goeth to the herring pond, comonly Called the halfway pond, And on the easterly syde by a smale brook or Run of water Comonly Called the shingle brook;

Likewise the Towne Graunted unto Ephraim Morton Jun: Att this Meeting a smale psell of Land lying att the Eelriver on the southerly syde of his other Lands on which hee Now dwelleth viz: Joyning to his said Land and soe Runing to the brook which Runeth through the swamp and soe to the Road way that Goeth to the herring pond Comonly Called the halfe way pond; and soe to the Land of Robert Bartlett his Land or the Lands there which belonge unto the heirs of Robert Bartlett aforsaid deceased

A smale psell of Land was Likewise Graunted by the Towne To Nathaniel Wood lying and being att the first brook on the Northerly syde of the brook Neare unto house lately erected between the said house and the Comon Road;

August 4 1679

The Towne then voated to pay to Mr Cotton out of the Townes Corne in the hands of Gorge Morton the sume of six pound and three shillings as due to him for all arreares of Rates made for his Maintainance untill May the 30th 1677: upon the payment of which Mr Cotton doth wholly acquitt and discharge the Towne of all former arreares and acknowlidge himselfe fully satisfyed with Reference therunto; I underwritten having received the said summe above mentioned of George Morton doe fully acquit & discharge the towne of Plymouth as a Towne of all the summes due to me for my maintenance till the said 30th of May 1677

Witness my hand John Cotton

Att a Towne meeting held att the meeting house att Plymouth August the 4th 1679 Nathaniel Morton was sworne Clarke of the Towne of Plymouth for this prsent yeer

Att this Meeting it was ordered by the Towne and voated that all actes and orders and Graunts of lands and all other pticulars formerly entered in our Town book shalbe as Authenticke and Good in law as if they had bine entered by a Clark under oath

Att this meeting Major Bradford was Chosen Moderator to acte as such as there May be occation att our Town Meetings
Leift: Morton Willam Crow } Raters to make the and Willam Clarke were Chosen } Rates of all kinds to be now Rated

The Collectors to Gather the Minnesters Maintainance for this yeer are   Steven Bryant sen:
and Samuell Dunham sen:
and the Towne hath engaged to stand by them in the procuring of it;

Att this meeting the Towne voated that the one halfe of Mr Cottons Rate shalbe payed into the Collectors by the first of october next; memorandum that the Collectors are to acte in the procuring in the Maintainance for Mr Cotton on the same Conditions as it was don the last yeer;

The Constable is ordered by the Towne to take Course for the settleing of the bell and the Turrett and the sweeping of the meeting house and the Ringing of the bell and to pay for the doeing of these pticulars; and likewise to pay Kokawehewan an Indian for the killing A woulfe

The bounds of a tract or psell of land which was Graunted by the Towne of Plymouth unto Mr Nathaniel Warren deceased, which said Graunt of land beareth date the 27$^{th}$ day of october Ann$^o$ Dom 1662 lying neare Mannomett ponds, in the Township of Plymouth aforsaid neare unto some Meddow Graunted unto Mistris Elizabeth Warren the mother of the said Nathaniel Warren; sould by Mistris Sarrah Warren of Plymouth aforsaid ;► to Joseph Bartlett the 4$^{th}$ of August 1679 The bounds therof is as followeth; on the southwest Corner with a Rocke and stones layed upon it on the southeast Corner with a pine tree standing upon a hill by the side of a little pond: on the Northwest Corner bounded with a Great white oake in A maple Swamp by the brooksyde; on the southeast Corner with a smale Red oake standing on the side of a hill; the brook being the foote bounds of the said land; and It Joyneth on the Northerly syde to the land of Benjamine hammon which hee bought of ffrancis Curtice;

New Plymouth;

Wheras the Towne Graunted unto John Bryant son in law unto Steven Bryant thirty acrees of land, lying att or Neare

a place Called Billingtons holes, as appeers by theire Graunt the
eight of August 1677; wee have by order in the said Graunt
measured and bounded the said thirty acrees of Land; Att the
southeast Corner therof, with a Red oake tree standing on the
Northerly syde, of a little brook, att the Roote of which Red
oake tree there is a stone pitched into the Ground; Att the
Northeast Corner with a little Red oake sapling att the Norwest
Corner with a smale Red oake Sapling; and att the southwest
Corner with a smale Red oake tree; Layed out for thirty three
pole in breadth; and one hundred forty six pole in length; and
due allowance Given for the highway that Goes through the said
Land the 23 day of July 1679

pr Willam Crow Surveyor<br>Joseph Howland

[134.] New Plymouth

Measured and bounded unto John Morton fifty Acrees of
upland graunted to him by the Towne to his Meddow att Wnna-
tucksett: The said land lyeth between Allexander Standish his
meddow Abraham Jacksons Land and the Path that Goeth to
Bridgwater: The bounds of the said land is as followeth; Att
the Northeast corner therof is Marked a younge white oake tree
which standeth in or Near a swampp which is the said Abrahams
bounds marke from the said white oake tree the line extends to a
maple tree standing in a swampp and soe the line extends hom
to Allexander Standish his Meddow; and then the line extends
as the meddow lyeth, to a fforked spruce tree marked; and from
the said spruce the line extends westward as the swamp lyeth
untill it Comes to or Crosseth a south line; that Comes from a
white oake tree marked standing on the south syde of Bridgwater
Path; then as Bridgwater Path lyeth soe the line Runeth untill
it Cometh to Abraham Jacksons Land att the said Path; then to
a Red oake tree which is Abraham Jacksons southwest Corner
marke and from thence the line extends to the aforsaid white
oake tree which standeth in or Neare a swamp;

June the 7[th] one thousand six hundred<br>seaventy and nine Willam Crow<br>Surveeyor;

Att a towne meeting held att Plymouth for the Towne of
New Plymouth att the meeting house the sixt day of January
1679
Willam Crow Joseph Warren<br>Leiftenant Morton Edward Dotey

Major Bradford, Leiftenant Morton, Willam Crow And Joseph Warren } or any three of them are appointed by the Towne to Run the southeren line of the townes bounds according to the Court order; are appointed by the Towne to demaund in all the townes debts due to them from any and Incase of Non payment the towne heerby Impowers them to make suite of Law for the Recovery therof and that they keep a due aocoumpt of what they Receive and are Impowered heerby to Give legall Receipts and acquittances for what they Receive of Any and that they give in a true and faithfull accoumpt to the Towne Respecting the prmises when by them Required and the Towne doe heerby Impower Nathaniel Morton Clarke in the behalfe of the Towne to Give forth a letter of Attorney to Anny two of the psons above named to make suite and plea for any debt dew to the town for any psons as occation May Require;

It is Agreed between the Towne and Edward Gray (as an Apendix to his Lease for Clarkes Iland) that hee may keep sixteen Neat Cattle; on the said Iland Rate free; And noe more:

The bounds of Serjeant Ephraim Tinkhams land viz: that which was somtimes the land of John Dunham is as followeth; Att the North Corner a blacke oake tree marked and soe Runing forty pole south and by East to a smale Pyne Marked att the East Corner and soe Runing four score pole southwest and by west to a white oake tree marked; and soe Runing forty pole North and by west to a Red oake tree on the west Corner. Measured and bounded by Gorge Bonum and Ephraim Morton;

[135.] Att a Towne meeting held att the meeting house in Plymouth the 20<sup>th</sup> of January 1679

Leift: Morton, Mr Edward Gray, Joseph Warren and Mr Crow } are appointed by the Towne to Run any line of the bounds of the Townes lands as they shall see cause

And alsoe to treat with the purchasers of Sepican soe called of and concerning our title to the said Lands and places adjacent; and to Come to Composition with them Respecting the controversy betwixt the said Towne and them about it as they shall see Reason, and in case they Can not Close in a mutuall composition they are heerby Impowered by the said towne and

in theire behalfe to Answare or prosecute a suite with them
Concerning the said lands as they shall see cause; and that the
Clarke of the said Towne shall in the behalfe of the Towne make
and seale a letter or letters of Attorney in the townes behalfe to
Answare or prosecute a suite or suites Respecting the pmises:
and the said Comitte are heerby Impowered to Appoint and
Constitute one attorney or more to be healpfull to them Respecting the prmises as they May have occation And that the
mony belonging to the towne that is or may be in the hands of
William Crow be Improved for defraying the Charge of the said
expedition as occation may Require;

  Att a Towne Meeting held att the meeting house att
Plymouth the 26th day of Aprill Ann" Dom 1680: The Towne
agreed to allow Mr Cotton four score pound pr yeer: the one
halfe therof to be payed in Currant silver Mony of New England
and the other halfe in Corne and provisions att prisses yeerly
sett by the Country: The one halfe of both specaes to be payed
by the first of october; and the other by the first of Aprill
yeerly; The said sumes to be put into and Raised with the
Country Rates: and Gathered in by the Constable: And this to
continew soe Longe as the Towne shalbe Inabled to pforme it;
And the Towne doe allow unto the Constable fifteen shillings for
the procuring in the said sumes in season; for the following yeer:
on Condition hee see the said sumes duely and fully payed; in
time and specue The Towne have voated to hier a pasture for the
depasturing of Mr Cottons Cattle for this prsent yeer; And to
Indeavor to buy a Pasture for the use of Mr Cotton for the
future:

  furthermore severall Men have underwritten to healp him
unto wood according to such psells as is expressed in a List of
theire Names;

  It is ordered by the Towne that every housekeeper of
this Towne shall bring in six blacke birds heads or two Crowes
heads unto the Grandjurymen of our Towne betwixt this and
July Court Next on paine of forfeiting twelve pence for every
Neglect therof to the Townes use;

  The Deputies Chosen Att this meeting to serve att the
Court were       Leift Morton
            Will: Clarke
  The Constable      John Doten

The Celect Court          Mr Gray
                          Mr Crow
                          Leift: Morton
The Grandjurymen          serjeant harlow
                          Thomas ffaunce
The Surveyors of the highwayes James Clarke
                          Abraham Jackson
                          Ephraim Tilson
                          Elkanah Watson

It was voated by the Towne In Reference unto pay for the killing of woulves between Mr Crow and the Towne that Mr Crow shall have twenty shillings for killing every of those woulves in controversy as aforsaid;

[136.] 16 may 1667

The bounds of lands graunted to William Hoskins at ye head of [1] mohutchett at a towne meeting as is to be seen in ye grant 1667 it being thirtie acrees is as followeth a spruce tree marked standing by ye syde of a browne swamp being the northerly corner & soe extending westerly four score pole & there marked with a pine tree standing by another browne swamp & thence extending southerly to a cedar swamp & so following ye cedar swamp that comes into ye said pond

The bounds of Ephraim Tillsons lott of land graunted att ye same time & is alsoe thirty acrees lying at ye head of mohutchett meddow & lyeth on ye northerly syde of William Hoskins is as followeth The north corner is bounded with a white oake Tree Soe runneth westerly eight pole to another white oake from thence ye range runneth southerly sixty pole to a pine tree & from thence easterly eighty pole to a spruce tree standing by a browne swamp;

[137.] Att a Town meeting held att Plymouth att the meeting house the 16[th] day of August 1680 The Rators Chosen were Leiftenant Morton serjeant harlow and Willam Crow, these are to Rate for the Country and for Mr Cotton and such other Rates as may fall within this yeer;

---

[1] Mohutchett brook," a stream a short distance southwest of Carver Green. The district about it is now called "Hutchett."

In Answare to Mr Cottons paper put into the Townmeeting Respecting the house and Ground hee lives on; and Reparation therof etc; The Towne have Referred the Issueing of an Answare to the Next Towne meeting;

The Towne have ordered that the order about Non appeerance att Towne meetings be vigorous put in execution and for that end an exact list was taken of the names of such as made defect att this meeting by Non appeerance

The Town have Graunted unto Samuell King Jun: a smale psell of land about ffresh Lake or [1] Sparrows plaine; to build and plant on That is to say ten acrees Absolute; and if the Naighboors about the Towne and hee Can agree about it, then hee is to have ten acrees More as hee shall have need therof to Improve it;

Wheras att a Towne meeting held att the meeting house att Plymouth the 12$^{th}$ day of May 1669 the Towne then unanimosly voated to allow unto mistris Joanna Cotton wife unto Mr John Cotton our minnester; or his family the sume of fifty pounds Incase God should soe dispose that hee end his Life in this Towne before them;

Att the Towne meeting held att the Meeting house att Plymouth aforsaid the eight day of November Ann° Dom 1680, The Towne then voated and doe heerby give unto Mr John Cotton theire present Minnester the house hee then lived in and the homsted it Now standeth on att Plymouth aforsaid but not that which was Mistris Bridgett ffullers and Samuell ffullers which is not Intended in this Gift; and bequest; The said house and homsted on which the said house standeth; (excepting the homsted of Bridgett ffuller and Samuell ffuller aforsaid) To have and to hold unto the said Mr John Cotton To him and his heires and Assignes for ever: on Consideration wherof the said John Cotton and the said Joanna Cotton his wife doeth both for themselves and theire heirs and successors ffreely discharge and Relinquish and quitt claime unto the above mensioned fifty pounds; as Not payable nor to be demaunded nor Required of the said Towne of Plymouth nor theire heirs executors nor administrators for ever;

Moreover it was further voated by the said Towne att

---

[1] Sparrow's Plain" was a tract of land near the westerly end of Billington Sea, or Fresh Lake, where forty acres were granted to Richard Sparrow in 1637. The hill near it still bears the name of "Sparrow's Hill."

the abovesaid meeting That (after the Conclusion of this prsent
yeer for which this Rate for the minnesters Maintainance is
alreddy made) that then they will add ten pounds pr annum to
his eighty pounds yeerly sallery formerly allowed him, which
amounts to Ninety pounds: as it was eighty pounds the Last
Rate; and the said Mr Cotton is to flind Pasture and fierwood for
himselfe and family for the future; and Nathaniel Morton
Secretary and Willam Clarke are appointed: in the behalfe of
the Towne to give sufficient Legall evidence of the said house
and land; unto the said Mr John Cotton

[138.] The bounds of Jacob Cookes land layed out by
Gorge Bonum Three score acrees Att Moonponsett is as followeth
The Easterly bounds is a black oake tree Marked
The bounds Northerly is a blacke oake tree Marked,
which is the Corner bounds of Major Bradfords Land
the southerly bounds is a white oake tree standing by
a peece of meddow the west is a white oake Marked
standing by a swamp These are the bounds of fifty
acres of the said land. The Remainder which is ten
acrees is bounded by a pyne tree marked standing by a
pond syde shore, that is alsoe the west bounds of Major
Bradfords Land the southwest bounds of the ten acrees

Jacob
Cook

Runes to the Northeren bounds of the aforsaid fifty
acrees, and the west bounds of the said ten acrees is a
pyne tree standing by the pond syde, and the southwest
bounds of the said ten acrees is a spruce tree standing
by a swamp syde; and soe from the said spruce tree
the Range Runs through a swamp; which is the
westernmost bounds of the aforsaid fifty acrees

Gorge Bonum;

Att a Towne meeting held att Plymouth the twenty
third day of May 1681 It was ordered by the Towne
in Reference to the Corn mill That Mr Edward Gray
Leiftenant Morton and Willam Clarke are authorized
by the Towne To treat with Samuell Jenings and the
Rest of the ptnors about buying the Mill of him and
to come to a prise with him about it if hee be willing

Mills

to sell it and incase hee Refuse to sell it; that then
they signify to him that they Intend to Build another
mill; and the Towne doe alsoe authorize them the

said Edward Gray Leiftenant Morton and Willam Clarke to put things in such a posture as that theire may be another Mill Built Incase Samuell Jenings Refuse to sell his:

Atwood   Measured and bounded seaventy Acrees of Land formerly Graunted unto Mr John Attwood in the yeer 1637 on the fift day of March as by Record may and doth appeer, att the Northeast Corner therof it is bounded with a Red oake ·sapling standing on the North syde of a ditch Called Attwoods ditch and from the said sapling the line extends west and by North Nearest unto a young Maple tree, standing in the swamp between three Maples; And from the said Maple, which is Marked the line extends to a young Red oake sapling tree Marked, standing on the North syde of James Coles Land; and the west syde of an old ditch formerly· Made by the said Attwood; and from the said Red oake sapling; the line extends East & by North Crosse a point of upland to the swamp, and soe eastward as the swamp lyeth till the above said first sapling beareth North and by west; I say Measured and bounded the 15$^{th}$ day of ffebruary 1681 by

Mee Gorge Bonum<br>Surveyor

[139.] Att a Towne meeting held att the meeting house Att Plymouth the 22cond of August 1681

The Rators Chosen were
serjeant harlow } these are to make the Rates
and Willam hoskins } both for Mr Cotton and the
Country Rate for this yeer

This
* other
likewise
ordered

Att this meeting the Towne voated that our pte of the mony due for mount hope shalbe Improved for either the Repairing of the Meeting house or for the building of A New one as occation May Require

In Reference unto John harmon the Towne ordered that Incase any should come and sett him downe in the street of Plymouth; that a warrant shalbe in a Reddines to arrest the man that shall bring him and sett him downe in the street aforsaid; or any pte or place within our Townshipp to answare for brach of law in that behalfe.

It was ordered by the Towne that Noe foraigne Indians be prmitted to hunt within the precints of our Towneship and that if any shall soe doe that they be first warned to desist; and incase they goe on therin; that Complaint be made of them to the Court;

Att a Towne meeting held att the Towne of Plymouth by the Inhabitants of New Plymouth the 30$^{th}$ day of January Ann" Dom 1681

The Towne have voted Leift Morton Mr Willam Clarke Joseph Warren and Joseph Bartlett To be a Comittee to take a view of the meeting house; and to take some speedy Course either that it may be Repaired; or to build a New one as they shall see cause and the Towne of Plymouth doth heerby engage to defray the charge seasonably and in such specue as shalbe Requisite;

It is enacted by the Towne that noe houskeeper or other in this Towne Resideing in the Towne shall entertaine any stranger into theire houses above a fortnight without giveing Information to the Celect men or some one of them therof upon the forfeiture of ten shillings a weeke for all such time as any such stranger shalbe soe entertained and stay without the said Information: To be levied on the estate of such house keepers or others that shall neglect to Informe as aforsaid:

strangers regulated

And incase the Celect men upon Information as aforsaid shall see cause to either take bonds for every such stranger either: to keep and save the Towne harmles from any damage that may acrew unto the Towne by the stay of such stranger or strangers in the Towne or expell them out of the Towne; The Celect men are heerby Impowered to doe either as they shall see Reason and cause:

The Towne have Graunted unto Samuell Savory twenty acrees of upland between Johns pond and the Cedar swamp neare Swan hold in the Towneshipp of Plymouth; and incase hee sell it, that hee pte with it to none but an Inhabitant of the Towne

Major Bradford
The elder Cushman
Nathaniel Morton
Leift Morton
Mr Willam Crow
Mr Willam Clarke
and Joseph Warren
Joseph Bartlett
} were Chosen to be a Comittee to agitate and prepare some pticular proposition to be proposed to the Towne they are to meet on the 2cond of ffebruary concerning the prmises ;

[140.] Att a Towne meeting held att the meeting house att Plymouth the 13th day of ffebruary 1681 The Towne doe agree that the money due to the Towne the prsent payment therof shalbe devided according to every ones proportion of Charge expended in the warr and to be devided by Major Bradford and Mr Willam Crow ;

It is enacted and ordered by the Towne that noe ffreeholder or Townsman shall sell or allianate theire privilidge in the Townes Comons unto any of any other Towne except hee sell his land therwith

It is enacted by the Towne that noe ffreeholder or Townsman of the Towne of Plymouth shall have but one Right in the Comonage of the said Towne ;

Att a Towne meeting held att the meeting house att Plymouthe 24th of May 1682

The Celect men Chosen were     Leift Morton
                                Willam Crow
                                Willam Clarke

Leift Morton and Joseph Warren Were Chosen to be deputies

To be Remembred by the deputies that some Course be taken for the Restraint of soe many Indians Assembling sometimes att the North side of the Towne att the later ends of the yeer and theire abusive Carriages there ;

Serjeant harlow and Willam Hoskins Chosen Grand Jurymen

Elkanar Watson Chosen Constable

Nathaniel holmes
Nathaniel Southworth
And Nathaniel Atwood
} were Chosen Surveyors of the highwayes

It is ordered by the Towne that thirty pounds silver mony be forthwith levied by Rate for the Repaireing of the

## PLYMOUTH RECORDS.    171

Meeting house and to be delivered to the overseers of the worke
The Raters Chosen were    Serjeant Willam harlow
                          Willam Crow
                          and Joseph howland
Concerning the Mill the Towne have ordered that
Leiftenant Morton    } shall treat with Charles Stock-
Joseph Warren and    } bridge about and Concerning the
Joseph Bartlett      } building of a New Mill and to
                       make Report therof to the towne

[141.] Att a Towne meeting held att the meeting house att Plymouth the 4th day of September 1682
The Towne voated that theire land att Agawaam shalbe sold and that the prise therof shalbe Improved for the building of a New meeting house and for the defraying of other Necessary uses behoofull to the Towne ;
Major Bradford    } are Chosen and appointed by the
Leift : Morton    } Towne to make sale therof for
and serjeant harlow } the Townes use as aforsaid ;

It was likewise agreed and ordered by the Towne that the Jurisdiction of the said Land shall belonge to the Towne of Plymouth onely ;

Moreover att the said Meeting the Towne engaged each to other seriously That the alewives or herrings soe Called shall not be stoped in theire Goeing up either in the half way pond River or in any other River or Runett belonging to the Towne in theire Goeing up to spaune ;

John Bradford and Thomas ffaunce are appointed by the Towne to be Collectors of Mr Cottons Rate

Serjeant harlow is appointed by the Towne to Graunt Ticketts according to Law in such Case provided unto such as are Nessesitated to travell on the Lords day incase of danger of death or such like Nessesitons occations etc

Morover it was voated att the Towne Meeting held att Plymouth the 4th of September 1682 That they will take Course that they that legally bought any Shares of Land of any Townes men att Agawaam before the said Towne Meeting shall have theire money Returned againe ;

Att a Towne Meeting held att the Meeting house att Plymouth the 30 day of October 1682 It was Joyntly agreed by the Towne that the former Comittee viz : Leift : Morton Joseph

Warren and Joseph Bartlett to Agree with Charles Stockbridge about the dam ; and the passage to be Left for the flish to Goe up or any other pticulare Respecting the Mill brooke or any other Thinge that may be Respecting the prmises ;

Aprill the 7<sup>th</sup> 1684 att a Towne meeting; The towne have voted the sume of fifty shillings which they will ffreely Give and allow unto William Green towards his Cure in Meer Pitty and Compassion to him in his prsent misery ; and not as theire Charge ;

the towne have agreed with Gorge Bonum to take the alewives and to foraigners have them for 9 pence a hundred and our Townsmen for 6 pence a hundred and take some Course with unrully persons that hinder them from goeing up and Coming downe the brooke

The Towne have Graunted unto Acannootus fifteen acrees of Land att a place Comonly Called washanest Joyning to a Pond to be layed out for him ;

The Towne have Graunted unto Thomas Cushman Jun : three acrees of Meddow att the head of Jones River meddow to be first Layed out for him and that what is left shall be to supply others that have desired it soe farr as it will Reach ;

Joseph Warren } are a Comittee Chosen by the
Nathaniel Southworth } Towne to Lett out Clarkes Iland
and serjeant harlow } to the best advantage they Can
for the Town

Richard Wright

a Certaine smale psell of land is Graunted to Richard Wright to sett a house on being att the lower Corner of the New Street and to have it as longe as hee lives and when hee Endeth his life to leave it to the Towne ;

[142.] Att the Towne meeting held att Plymouth the second of January 1682 The Towne agreed and voted that noe Indians shall henceforth be sett to worke in any of the Townes for the wast in Cuting donne of any of the Timber of the Towne, as makeing of Shingles or bolts ; or any way to the wast of the Comons ; and that noe Indians shalbe Imployed upon any such accompt on the penalty of whomsoever soe Imploys them to forfeitt five pounds silver mony, to be levied upon theire estates for the Townes use ; nor that any Indian shall for the future be Imployed about or worke any timber brought out of the Comon upon the same penalty and that this order to be in fforce and to take place from the first of March next; and it is further ordered and agreed upon that the Celect men for the time being, be heerby Impowered by the Towne To see to the strickt execution of this order and to demand the forfeiture of the fines: for breach of the same: and to prosecute the same to effect:

Leift Morton } were deputed by the Towne to Agree
Joseph Warren } with workmen for the building of a
and Willam Crow } New meeting house: att Plymouth
the length wherof is to be fforty five foot; and the breadth 40 foot; and 16 foot in the wall

And These men to agree with workemen fully to finish the same with seats Galleryes &c in every other Respect:

[143.] At the Towne meeting held att the meeting house att Plymouth the 27th of May Ann° 1681

The Towne have Impowered the Deputies to make defence in plea Concerning John harman and doe heerby engage to stand to what they shall Conclude in that Respect and the Towne likewise engaged to pay the Charge that may arise in that behalf

Leift: howland; is appointed by the Towne with the Celect men to take the Constables accoumpts that have not yet brought in theire accoumpt to the Towne:

The Towne have Graunted unto Leift: Morton twenty five acrees of land on a place Called Warrens Wells plaine:

Thomas ffaunce was Graunted att this meeting ten acrees of land lying on the southwest or southerly syde of the said Land Graunted to Leiftenant Morton

Leift: Morton }
Will: Crow } were Chosen Celect men att this
Willam harlow } meeting;
Leift Morton and } were Chosen Deputies
Joseph Warren }
Andrew Ringe and }
Isacke Cushman } Grandjury men;
John Bryant sen: Was Chosen Constable

Serjeant Tinkham }
Thomas ffaunce }
Jonathan Pratt } Surveyers of the high wayes
Elkanar Watson }

William Bradford Jun: \
Elkanah Watson \
Nathaniel Wood \
Isacke Cushman \
Willam Shirtley \
Steven Bryant Jun: \
Samuell Gardiner \
and John Gray

tooke the oath of fidellity and desire to be proposed to the Court to take up theire ffreedome Willam Shirtley stands propounded to take up ffreedome

Att the Town meeting held att the meeting house att Plymouth the 17<sup>th</sup> day of June 1683 the towne voted to allow 25£ silver mony towards the building of a Cart Bridg att the Eelriver provided that the foure southeren Townes by order of Court feirmly oblidged, not onely to Give twenty pound att the prsent: Therunto; but alsoe that ever for the future the said Townes be Ingaged: to pay theire Just proportions as the Townes are Rated in the Country Rates towards the maintainance of the said Eelriver bridge, and Joneses River bridg alsoe:

*Eelriver & Jones river bridge vote about them*

Att this Meeting Joseph Bartlett and Ephraim Morton Jun: agreed with the towne for the sume of twenty five pounds to build a bridge over the Eelriver which together with the twenty pounds allowed by the four southeren townes; wilbe full satisfaction for the building of the said bridge;

The towne have likewise engaged to allow three pounds silver mony for and towards the building of a bridge over Jones River for the use and Conveniency of the Naighborhood which bridge shalbe for hoof and foot provided the Conditions and proportions doe suckseed Concerning the Eelriver bridg above written:

[144.] Deputies Chosen \
Leiftenant Morton \
Joseph Warren

Leiftenant Warren \
serjeant harlow \
Joseph Warren \
Joseph howland \
William Clarke

} Celectemen

Constable \
John Bryant Jun:

Grandjurymen \
Thomas ffaunce \
Jonathan Shaw

## PLYMOUTH RECORDS.   175

Surveyers of the highwayes   Joseph Bartlett
                                        John Rickard Jun
                                        Robert Ranson
                                        Samuell Sturtivant

    Att the Towne meeting held att the meeting house att Plymouth the 14 of July 1684

    Joseph Bartlett and Ephraim Morton Jun : accnolidged that they had Received the full and Just sume of twenty five pounds in silver of the Constable for theire makeing theire bridge att the Eelriver

    thirty acrees of Land was Graunted to Joseph Warren buting upon the 20 acrees of land formerly Graunted unto him by the Towne and Runing up by the brooke comonly Called the double brookes; hee allowing a Convenient highway through or by it;

    Wheras in the yeer 1673 the sixteenth of May; the towne did Graunt unto Mr Willam Crow 4 acrees of meddow or Meddowish Ground lying on the uper end att the east Corner of the widdow Sturtivants meddow at Moonponsett to be layed out to him by Captaine Bradford, which said Meddow or Meddowish Ground lyeth on the east syde of Thomas Cushmans meddow ; and ; soe up stream on both sides of the maine brooke

    It is Now ordered and Graunted by the Towne that Mistris Crow shall have her meddow Land where it is Granted upon that brooke or elsewher ; if it be not there to be found ;

    John Bryant was allowed by the Towne fifteen shillings for Gathering in the minesters Rate the last yeer ; and for gathering in all the Rates of this prsent yeer as towne Country and Minnesters Rate : hee is likewise allowed : thirty shillings ;

Robert Barrow Meadow

    The bound Marks of Robert Barrows meadow lying upon southers Marsh Brook at the Easterly End of a seder swamp on the westerly or southwest End A spruce tree marked standing in a swamp and soe to the shore to a maple tree Marked on foure sides & from thence up the brook to a pine tree Marked on 4 sides standing in the meadow on the northerly side of the brook and from thence to a maple tree neare the shore standing on the southerly side of the brook marked on 4 sids

    William Rings Meadow Lying upon southers marsh brook is bounded by Robert Barrows ; on the North-

Will:
Kings
Meadow

erly side of y̆ brook is a pine tree marked on four
sids standing in the Meadow and from thence to a
maple tree Marked standing neare the shore on the
southerly side of the Brook & soe from thence up
the brook neare an old beavour dam on the northerly
side of the brook A spruce and a pine tree Marked
on foure sids on the southerly side of the brook
A pine tree Marked on 4 sids standing by the upland
This Meadow was laid out and bounded

By Mc George Bonam Junior

Surveyor

[145.] Att a meeting of the Towne of Plymouth on the
24[th] of November 1684

The Towne desired and Appointed Major William Bradford John Bradford Nathaniell Southworth Leiftenant howland and
Isacke Cushman to be agents in theire behalfe : That if any shall
or doe Intrud within the Northerly line of the Towne Graunted by
the Court as doth apeer upon Record that they shall oppose
them and the Towne by these prsents doe engage to defend them
in that Case :

The Towne did order Joseph Warren and Joseph Bartlett
to finish our southerly Line betwixt Sandwich and the Towne of
Plymouth :

Att this townemeeting the towne Graunted unto John
Barrow thirty acrees of Land lying between the path that Goeth
from Plymouth to Bridgewater and the path that Goeth up to
Joseph Kinges farme, and the Towne have appointed and desired
Major Bradford to Lay it out for him ;

Att the meeting held att the meeting house att Plymouth
the 18[th] day of May 1685 the officers chosen to serve were

Cunstable John Rickard senior Cunstable
Leift Morton
Leift Joseph howland } Celectmen
Isacke Cushman
Joseph Warren sen : } Surveyors for high wayes
James Cole
Grandjurymen    serjeant harlow
                Barach Jourdane

Major Bradford  
Leiftenant Morton  
Left: howland  
John Bradford  
Joseph Warren  
} Commissionated to Run a west line on the North side of the Towne

The Land of John Barrow layed out nere Monponsett according to the order of the Towne of plymouth the 3d of August 1689 The bounds Westerly is a Red oake tree Marked of foure sides by Bridgwater path on the south syde so Rainging southerly to a white wood tree standing neere a swamp from there Rainging by the swamp side Easterly to a white oake Marked on foure sides and soe Rainging northerly for want of lands Crose Bridgwater paith home to the land of frances Curtice Laid out

    by William Bradford  
    and Georg Bonum Sr

[146.] Wee whose Names are under written being Chosen by the Towne of Plymouth and sworn in the yeer of our Lord 1684 to Lay out the Kinges highway Throughout our Towneship have Layed them out as followeth ;

ffrom our Towne Bridge to a heape of stones att our [1] New street end on the westward side of the old way ; from thence to a heape of stones at the first brooke on the southwest side and a Rocke on the North East syde from thence to the second brooke the ffence on the Northwest syde and an heape of stones on the southwest syde soe to [2] strawberry hill to a heape of stones on the Westward side of the aforsaid old way ; soe to the Mile Rocke on the eastward side of the aforsaid old way from thence to a Sapling marked Against John Doties allies Dotenes feild forty pole bounded with a stake and an heap of stones soe to the Land of Goodman Tinkham alonge the old Road ; Leaveing his ffence on the east side and from that ffence 40 foot westward soe to a heap of stones bounded on the Eastside against Samuell Kinges orchyard soe to a heap of stones on the east side of Nathaniell Southworth ffence soe to the house of Goodman Bryants bounded with a heape of stones on the west side ; and soe alonge the old Road to [3] Mr Crowes land to a heape of stones on the west syde and soe alonge the old Roade to a smal pecked Rocke on the

---

[1] " New street " is what is now North Street.  
[2] " First Brook " is the small brook which crosses Court Street south of Samoset Street. " Second Brook " crosses Court Street in front of the estate of Roswell S. Douglass, and " Strawberry Hill " is the hill on the easterly side of Court Street, on which stands the Summer cottage of Charles S. Davis.  
[3] Mr. Crowes land was at Seaside.

east syde and soe along the old Road to the land of [1]John Gray bounded on the eastward side with a heap of stones and soe along the old Road leaveing William Shurtleyes house on the eastside and soe to smelt Brooke to a heap of stones on the west syde soe by an heape of stones on the westward side on Samuell ffullers to a heap of stones on the eastward side in Isacke Cushmans ffence; soe to a stump with a heap of stones about it in Elder Cushmans land so to a heap of stones on the westward side soe to the end of the Causway of Joneses River Bridge bounded with a Rocke on the west syde and soe along the Causway to the bridge; and the way to bridgwater to Run up from the old Road betwixt Elder Thomas Cushmans and Elkanah Cushmans land Marked att the old Road that Goes to Jones River with a heap of stones about a stump on the southerly side to a Red oake tree on the southerly side And soe along the old Road that Goes to [2]Pimkin Bridge with severall bound upon the southerly side and Northerly syde:

ffor the westward Bounds Next Midlebery

A white oake tree on the southward side of the way marked with P and soe alonge the old Road to a Red oake tree att Mahuckett broke soe along to the old Road to the house of Daniell Ramsden: bound with an heap of stones soe to a white oak on the south side of the way to an oak sapling against Ephraim Tilsons Land and soe to a great tree marked on the south side of the way and soe to the Corner of Robert Ransoms ffence bounded on the south with an heape of stones neare lakenham brooke; soe allong the old Road to hunting house brooke with a white oake tree marked on the south side of the way and allong the Road to Arthers swamp a white oake tree marked on the south side of the way and soe along the Road to spring hill: a white tree Marked on the south side of the way and soe along the old Roade to the pting wayes a Red oake marked with a heape of stones

[147.] about it and soe along the Road to sparrowes hill a pyne tree marked on the south side of the way & soe along the old way to woods feeld a white oake marked on the south side the way. and soe to Goodman ffinneyes land a heap of stones

---

[1] The land of John Gray was at Rocky Nook.
[2] The location of Pimkin or Pipkin Bridge it is difficult to determine. It is quite probable that it crossed Fountain Head Brook, which crosses the Bridgewater road in the westerly part of Kingston.

laied about a walnut sapling and soe along the old Road to [1] Squirrills Rocke & soe along the old Road to Plymouth towne brook leaveing the bridge on the East side soe allong the old Road way to a tree marked on the south side of the way neare Gyles Rickards land soe to the Northerly end of the training Green a heap of stones on the westward side of the way and soe along the old Road to Wellingsly booke bounded on the west side with a pecked Rocke with som stones about it and soe to the southerly end of wellingsly hill bounded with an heap of stones the west syde the way; soe to the southeast side of Eliaezer Churchills land a heap of stones on the west side of the way and soe up the valley to a Grat Rocke on the west side of the way and soe along the old Road to Left: Mortons Land a Red oake marked on the west side the way and soe along the old Road to goodman flinneses land, a Red oake marked on the west side of the way and soe along as the way Now Runes to Mr William Clarkes brooke and soe over the brook to a heap of stones on the south syde of the brooke on the west syde of the way soe to a white oake tree neare the house of Thomas f'rnces on the south side the way soe to a heape of stones on the south side of the way and soe over the Eelriver bridge to a heap of stones on the south syde of the way neare the bridge and soe along the old Road to a heap of stones near the Corner of Joseph Warrens Barne on the southwest side of the way and soe along the old Road to two Rockes in James Barnabes land on the west side of the way soe to a white oake marked and soe to a Red oake Marked and soe to the old Road and there a Red oake tree marked all on the old westerly side of the way soe to a Red oake tree Neare the woolf trape soe to a walnute tree marked both on the south side the way soe to Run throw the land of Joseph Warren att the Eelriver Swamp ther a spruce tree Marked on the west side the way and soe over the brook to a Red oake tree on the west side the way; and soe along the Eelriver swampside leaveing the swamp on the east side of the way soe to a pyne tree marked on the west syde of the way soe to a Red oake marked soe to the old path soe along to [2] Clam Pudding pond leaveing the pond on

---

[1] Squirrel Rock stood on Summer Street near the Long House, so called, above Robinson's Iron Mill.

[2] "Clam Pudding Pond" is on the easterly side of the Sandwich road, as it now stands between the old Cornish tavern and the Thrasher neighborhood. It is sometimes called in the records Clampudder, and its name is not thought by the editor to have any reference to either clams or pudding.

the west side of the way soe alonge the old way to [1] saltwater pond severall trees marked on the west side of the way are there 2 white oake trees marked on the way west side of the way soe along the pondsyde leaveing the pond on the Eastward side of the way soe along to the white oak tree marked and an heap of stones on the westward side of the way soe to a smal Run of water Neare Jonathan Moreyes and soe to a white oake tree Marked on the east side of the way soe to a Rocke and a pine tree tree Marked on the west side of the way soe over a smale neck of land with a Red oake tree marked on the westside of the way and then to a pyne tree marked on the westerly side of the way and soe bounded by the Clifts & Saltwater to the southerly end of Plymouth bounds:

     Leift Ephraim Morton
     Jonathan Shaw sen:
     Abraham Jackson sen:
     Barach Jourdaine
     Gorge Morton
     Isake Cushman
     Leift Joseph howland
     Joseph Warren sen
     Jonathan Barnes
     Willam harlow sen:
     Nathaniell Southworth
     Joseph Bartlett

[148.]    Major Will: Bradford
     Mr John Cotton
     Mr Thomas Cushman
     John Bradford
     Samuel Bradford
     Jacob Cooke
     Mr Joseph Bradford
     Thomas Cushman
     Isack Cushman
     Elkanah Cushman
     Leftenant Joseph howland
     William Shertly
     Caleb Cooke

---

[1] Saltwater Pond is at Ellisville.

Francis Cook
Benjamine Eaton
Benjamen Eaton Ju
John Gray
John Barow
Richard Wright
John Sturtevant
Steven Briant Senor
John Briant Junor
Samuel fuller
nathaniel Southworth
Samuell Kinge senor
John Doten
John holmes
John Cobb
nathaniel wood alies atwood
Edward Doten
Sergeant James Cole
Abraham Jackson
Samuell Dunham senor
George Bonom senior
Goorg bonam Junior
Andrew Ringe
George Watson
Jonathan Barnes
John Briant Sen :
Robert Barow
serjeant will : harlow
Joseph Dounham
Joshua pratt
John Jordain
Barock Jordain
Gyles Rickard senor
John Rickard senior
Joseph faunce
nathaniell holmes
Samuell harlow
John Drew
Eliezur Churchill
Joseph Churchill
George Morton

Leftenant Ephraim morton
Thomas morton
Robard finny
Samuell Gardian
Josiah morton
nathaniel morton
Will: Clarke
Thomas ffaunce
Ephraim morton Junior
Samuell Rider
Thomas Lasell
Thomas Clarke
James Clarke
William harlow
Joseph Bartlet
Jonathan morey
John morton
Samuell Dunham Junor
John Dunham senor
Jonathan Shaw
Robert Ransom
Ephraim tilson
Jonathan prat
John Rickard Junor
Elkanah Watson
Will Ring
Eliazur Ring
Giles Rickard Junor
Stephen Briant Junor
John pratt
Elkiah tincom
Eleazer Downham
Eliazier Cushman
John nelson
George Bonam
John Waterman
James Warren
Joseph Warren
Robert Bartlet
Samuel Lucas
Benony Lucas

Ephraim Cole
John Mordo
nath : harlow
John Cole
John Churchill
William Churchill
Jonathan shaw Junior
Joseph Bartlet Junior
John foster
John Carver
Benjamin Warren
Thomas Clarke
James Winslow
John Barnes
Ebenazar holmes
Will : barnes
James Clarke Junior
on the 19th of December 1698
Nathaniell Warren
was voatted a Townsman

[149.] At a towne meeting held at the meeting house at Plymouth by Townsmen Thierof July 6 1685

The Towne Chose Thomas faunce To be their towne Clarke

Then allso the towne Chose major bradford and Joseph warren to be thier agents at the Court to answer the townes presentment Relating to Joneses River bridge, and to acte on the townes behalf with the agents of the foure other townes who are ingaged with this towne to repaire said bridge for its reparation

At a towne meeting held at plymouth the 27 day of July 1685

serjeant harlow  }
Isack Cushman   } was Chose by the towne to be their
Jonathan Shaw   } Rators for the hole year

At this meeting the towne granted to Mr John Cotton Thirty acers of land Liing on the norwest side of the Land that Edward Doten Bought of mr will : crow; and soe to extend northerly to thee walck path and soe to Run up in to the woods for thee Length

At this towne meeting the towne granted to nathaniell wood 2 aceres of Land Ling at the first Brook nere to John Rickards Land only A Cart way to be left betwen them for the neighborhood to goo up into the woods

At this meeting Leftenant morton and serjeant harlow were Chosen to tack an acouent of those Constabels that have not yet geven in their acounts of Rates Commited to them to gather

At this towne meeting the towne voated to alow to widow warren 3 shillines per week for diating will grene deuring the time hee is with her to diate

At this towne meeting It was Agreed uppon by thee towne That thee Rates Both for Cuntrey & towne Charge should be made in one & the same speasey; and that the Deputies and Grand jurymen shall have but 2 shillings per day Apeece for theire servis At the Courts

At a towne meeting held at plymouth the 12[th] day of october 1685 Thee Towne Chose and Comisianated major Bradford Leftenant morton Lefton: howland Joseph warren & John Bradford Either to agree with the Ageants of Medelburrow with Respect to the head line or to Run It Acording to Court grant soe far as to take in the south meadowes

[150.] The bounds of Nathanell Woods 2 Acres of land granted to him by the towne of plymouth one the south side off the first Brouck soe Called is as folloeth the north Corner A Rock stone set into the ground and Ranging twenty poule one the southwest side of the Common Road to a stone set into the ground and soe Runing sixteene poule southwest to a stone set into the ground and soe Ranging Northwest twenty poule to a stone set into the ground

Mesured By mee Ephraim morton senior ordered By the towne

The Bounds of the 12 acres of Land Laid out by George Bonam and andrew Ring unto Samuell King Junor is as folloeth buting uppon deepwater swamp bounded with a stake uppon a hill at the southwest Corner and Runeth northwest 38 pole to a small Red oake by the Cartway at the westermost bound from thence to a small Red oake at the north East Cornour upon a side hill above princes botom and Runeth along to a small pine tree upon the side hill & soe Crosing the Cartway that Cometh from depe-water & that Cartway is to be alowed and it Roneth along one the west side of a letle Round Swamp and to a small white oke by deep water swomp March ye 11 1683[4]

The bounds between John Gray and Caleb Cooke are as folloeth Att the East end a small Rocke and a heap of stons about it and ffrom that bound to the Common Rode & ther bounded by a Walnut tree marked one fouer sides and a heape of stons att the foot and from that bound to a Run astraite Corse to A heap of stons by the Cart way that goeth up to Joneses River medow and to John Grais land from that bound Last Expresed Raingeth With Samuell ffullers land to A heepe of stons one the southward side of the above sd way to the Red swamp and ther bounded by a heape of stons and from the wester Cornor bound which is a pine tree marked one four sids standing uppon [1] Reyboth hill these bounds last Exprd is the Raing between Caleb Cooke and John Grais land at the head of sd Grais land Rainged and bounded the 9[th] day of March 1685[86] pr mee Ephraim Morton senor surveior to the towne of plymouth

[151.] Att a town meting heild att plymouth the 17[th] day of may 1686

The Celect men Chosen were Leftenaut Morton serjant harlow & Joseph warren senor

The Deputies were Leftenant morton and Joseph warren senor

The Grand Jurymen were Isack Cushman and Eliazur Churchill Isak Lobdell

The Constable is John Doten

The survairs Chosen were Samuell Rider John Doten samuell sturtevant and Jonathan Shaw ;

John Doten sen[r]   Att this meting the towne granted unto John Doten senor of plymouth ffouer acrees of medow lying uppon mahuchet broke and the sd Doten shall take it one both sides of the broke and the sd Doten shall hold it by vertew of the towns Wright

in Respect to William hoskins and Ephraim tilsons Request for the towne to stand by them to defend theire wrights of lands that John tomson and John soule Challenges to be the

---

[1] " Reyboth hill," sometimes in the records called Rehoboth and Raabath hill is on the southwest side of the old road round Spirit's pasture at Rocky Nook.

propriators of a sertain tract of land purchised by Captain Thomas southworth of Josiah Wompatuck the towns answer is that they are Resolved to stand for ther Whrits which they have both from grant of the Court and alsoe by posession above this 40 years

Att A towne meting held at plymouth the 9th day of June 1686 major Bradford and Leftenant Morton Were Requested and Impowered by the towne to goe along With those Gentellmen appointed by the Court to setle the northerly bounds of the towne At this meting the towne Requested Major bradford to answer the towns presentment for the Want of a pound as alsoe the towne agreed with John Rickard senor to build a pound of forty foot square 6 foot hy the posts to be white oake the Rails to be substainshall sedor Rails Every top Raile to be pined and to set this pound above the Rode at the head of [1] new streete End

John Prat

Robt Ransom

John Rickard Junior

Thos Hewes

Att a towne meting held at plymouth the 19th day of July 1686 the town graunted unto John pratt twenty acres of land lying upon the westerly side of Dotens pond and to be laid out by the descresion of the survaior so as to take in his now dweling house att this meeting the towne granted to Robert Ransom twenty foot of land square ne re to the ware houses below John Rickards

At this meting the town graunted unto John Rickard Junior thirty foott of land square below the hill by the shore side nere to the Ware houses

Att this meting the towne granted unto Thomas Hewes the Improvement of five acrees of upland att saaquash for five years provided that he Carry nothing to prigudice the medows there nor Cut downe the wood Within forty foot of the bank on the southerly side therof

Major Bradford Elder Cushman Leftenant morton Isack Cushman and John Bradford these or aney 4 of them are authorized to act for the town as agents in there behalf With Reference to the northerly bounds of the town

[152.] Att a towne meting held at plymouth the 30th of august 1686 Gorge Morton is graunted ten acres of

---

[1] New Street was North Street.

Geo: Morton

land at a place Comonly Caled & Known by the name of the [1] hy Ridg together with a small percell of swamp land Joyning to it be it 3 acres more or Less At this meting Jonathan Barnes and Robert Ransom had the towns aprobation to keepe ordenarys for this present yeare Att this town meting Elkanah Cushman Was graunted 4 acres of meddow be it more or less Joyning unto the brook that comes out of Jons river meddow on the northerly side of the brook

Elk[a] Cushman

Measured and bounded unto Elkanah Cushman foure acrees of meddow Which was graunted unto him by the towne Which sd meddow lyeth on the northerly syd of the brook that Cometh out of Jons river meddow the bounds of the sd meddow are as followeth begining at a stake & a heape of stones it being the south bounds by the brook and soe Runing norwest to a Red oake sapling which being Crows bounds and soe Runing along the side of the Hand to a mapell bush marked on 4 sids which sd bush standeth in the meddow being the West Cornor and soe from thence northeast to a white oake tree marked on 4 sides standing on the upland and soe Runing down East to a white oake tree marked on foure sids standing upon the upland and soe from thence southeast to a stake and heap of stons by the brook and soe Runing down the brook to the stake and heap of stons first Expresed the brook being the bounds on the southeast end September the 2 1686

pr mee Gorge Bonam senor

An agreement Made between Isac Cushman and John Gray and Jacob Cooke each of them Inhabetants of the towne of plymouth as Respecting the setteling the bounds of their lots of meddow lying on the Westerly end of Jons River meddow is as followeth the Corner bounds on the south side of the meddow between sd Jacob Cooke and sd John Gray is a Red oake marked on fouer sydes standing on the upland and soe Rainging from thence to the north side of sd meddow to a small Red oake marked on 4 sids With severall staks standing in sd Raing also on the other side of the sd Grays loot the Corner bound between

---

[1] The "High Ridge" here referred to was near the nook at the head of Hobs Hole Brook.

the sd gray and the said Cushman on the south side of sd meddow is a Red oake marked on fouer sids standing on the West side of a small Iland or hummach of upland & soe Rainging northward to a stake standing on the meddow in the Westerly side of sd Cushmans [1] loot; of meddow which he bought of Mr Joseph bradford of plymouth with severall stakes standing in sd Raing and soe Rainging from that sd stake Westerly to a white oake marked on fouer sids standing on a point of upland unto Which Agreement Wee the above Written have set to our hands the Eighteenth day of august 1686

      Isac Cushman
      Joh Gray
      Jacob Cooke

[153.] Leftenant Houland John Sturtevant and Nathaniell Southworth were Chosen by the town to serve at the County Court upon the Jury

 John Downham William Shurtly Elkanah Cushman and John Briant Junor Were Chosen to serve at the Court of assistants

 At a town meting held at plymouth the 27th of September 1686 the town voatted and ordered the Removeall of Sarah Downhams houce and to be set up at the houce of Giles Rickards senior

 At this town meting [2] James Cool Jonathan Mory senior Abraham Jackson senior John Rickard and the Widdow Rickard had each of them the towns aprobation to keep ordenaryes for this present yeare

 At this meting the town agreed With Samuell Downham Junior for the Ringing the bell and sweeping the meting house for this present yeare and the towne is to alow the sd Downham twenty five shillins for his worke

 The Bounds of the land settled between Steven briant senior and Nathaniel Southworth by Georg Bonham survayor as ffolloeth first a stone set up by a stump which was the antient bounds upon the Eastward side of the high Way upon the south side of the Brooke 2 and so it Runneth upon a west southwest poynt a little southerly to a hummuck that stands upon A hill at the head of the afore: sd Steven briants loot and soe to Run

---

[1] "Loot" evidently means lot.
[2] James Cool means James Cole, who kept a tavern in Leyden Street, on the site now occupied by the house of W. H. H. Weston.

upon the same poynt from that humack Eighty pole further to a Red oake tree upon the north syde of the brooke which is the uppermost head bounds Betwixt them

At A town Meting held at plymouth the 9<sup>th</sup> day of febuawary 1686 87 Joseph Bartlet John Bradford & Ephraim Morton Were Chosen to serve upon the Jury at the County Court

The Bounds of a Certain tract or neck of land Graunted by the town unto Gorg Bonam senor lying near unto fresh lake is as followeth the northermost bounds on the south side of the brook is a mapell tree marked on four sids and from thence to a smal Red oake southward standing upon a point of land lying on the North side of the Cart Way that goeth into the above sd neck of land and soe Rainging southward to a spruce tree standing by [1] lout pond side and so from sd spruce tree Runeth along the pond side to a swamp that lieth betwen lout pond and fresh lake the pond being the bounds on the West side and the brook that Cometh out of fresh lake is the bounds on the North side

[154.] At a town meting held att plimouth the 6<sup>th</sup> day of June 1687

The Celect men Chosen by ye town Were
Leftenant Joseph Howland
Joseph Warren senor
and Isaac Cushman
Mr William Clarke Chosen Constable
The survairs Were
Abraham Jackson senor
John Gray
Jams Warren
Jonathan praat
The 9<sup>th</sup> day of June 1687 8

It is Agreed Betwen Gorge Bonan senor as overseer unto Ruhamah Willis estate and Jonathan Barns both of plimouth before Major bradford serjeant harlow & Joseph Warren senor That the bounds betwen Jonathan baruses Ware houce and the land of Ruhamah Willis That the sd Barnes shal Com no farther upward towards her houce then three foott from his Ware houce at the Easterly Cornor Wher A stone is sett into the ground and

---

[1] " Lout " is an obsolete word derived from the Latin word " lutum," and means probably " muddy."

soe to Run towards the southwest to Another stone set into the ground Against the sd barneses fence and then the sd barnes is to Run upward to the Cornor of his fence where is another stone set into the ground and soe from thence we are bounded by goodman Watsons garden spot where is a stoone set into the ground 4 foott or therabouts at the Southwest Cornor of the sd barnes ground unto Which Agreement the above sd Gorge Bonam and Jonathan Barnes have meutually set to there hands

Gorge Bonam
Jonathan Barnes

The bounds betweext ye land of John Doty and John holmes Is as folloeth  A stone set into the ground by the Water side and Another stone sett into ye ground forty pole up West southwest And on the same point to the Comon Rode and there bounded With A Walnut tree marked

Ephraim Morton
Joseph Warren
Joseph houland

[155.] At a town meting held at plimouth the 15$^{th}$ day of august 1687

Leftenant Morton Was Chosen Comisioner by the town to act With the Celect men of said town with Referance to orders from the Counsell Respecting the Celect men of the town of plimouth

Att this meting the town Imployed Joseph Bartlet senor to provid the Measures Scales and Weights for ye towns use accordding to order of the Councell Relating to the town of plimouth Which the sd bartlet doth promise to do Within A month after the date above Written and to Return an account of the Cost thereof unto the town and the town doth promise to Repay the sd Bartlet With all Convenient speed

At this meting Samuell Downham senor deClared himself sattesfied for his servise in Ringing the bell the last yeare

At this meting Leftenant Morton and serjant harlow were desiered by the towne to take the acount of the Constable of the Rats Committee to him to gather

At A town Meting held att plimouth the 24$^{th}$ day of August 1687  At this meeting it was propounded to the town whether they Judged them selves able to pay to Mr Cotton the summe of 90 pd as they had done of late years the affirmative being put to voate but som hands were held up the Negative vote being Called for many more hands were held up upon which it Was farther voted that the maintenance of the minester for this present yeare 1687 should be by the free subscription of Every one & those promises to be ackowlidged A dew debt and that the sd summes promised are and shall be duly paid in october and Aprill as was in former years promised

It was further voted that the prises of grain shall be Wheat at 4 shillings a bushell; Ry and barly at 3 shillings Indian Corne at 2 shiling 6 pence

The men appointed by the towne to see what persons would give) (for Lakenham Wenatuxet and munponset Jonathan Shaw & Robert Ransom senor; for the north end of the towne John Bradford and Elkanah Cushman and from the town brook southward Ephraim Morton Junior and Thomas ffaunce

The Towne have made Choice of the Celect men to make the Rate Relating to the town Charges

[156.] New plimouth ffebruary the 10th 1679

Measured and bounded unto Joseph Warren senior twenty Acrees of land granted him by the towne of plimouth Lying and being on the southward side of Ephraim Mortons land att the elleriver and on the Eastward side of a Cart way that Leads to the Hering pond att the Westward End and Northward side thereof It is bounded with a stone set into the ground betwene and nere the Kings Road and the aforesd waie that goes to the hering pond Also by Which is a Red oake tree marked from Which stone the Line Extends east southerly Nineteene degrees one halfe unto A stone set Into the ground on the Westward sid of the shingle brooke from which stone the line is soe to Extend home to the sd brooke as the brooke Runeth to be the Eastward End bound of the said land and on the Westward end and southside of the sd land It is bounded With a stone set into the ground in the duble Brooke swamp on the Eastward side of the aforesd Cart Way that goes over the afore said duble brook and from the said stone in the swampe the line Extends Eastward to a stone set into the ground Aboute the midle of the south side line from which stone the line extends to A stone set into the ground on the Westward side of the shingle brooke and so home to the Brooke and this land is at the westward end therof to butt home to the Cart way or path that goeth to the afor sd heren pond; Within the Compasse of these bounds is alowance made for the Kings Road that lyeth through the land The East end is Broader then the west end by Reason of the swomp

for this grant se page 91

per William Crow surveior

The dimentions of the bounds of the Elder Thomas Cushmans six lotts of land lying betwen Samuel fuller on the south side and Joseph Bradford on the North side by an old ditch att the foot and by a stake and a heap of stones att the head being twelve score pole from foot to head and from sd ditch att the foot or scirt of the squar Raing six score pole to the Northward to A white oake Marked on 4 sides & thence terning About and Runing twelve score pole to A pine tree Marked on 4 sides thence Runing directly six score pole to the heape of stones and stake Above mentioned

The ditch and heap of stones first mentioned is the mutually Ackowledged bounds betwen Thomas Cushmans land & Samuel ffullers land & the bounds last mentioned are the bounds Mutually Acknowledged betwen sd Cushman and Insine Bradford the land Abuting on the saltmarsh at the Easter end, March 22ᵈ 1686 Bounds setled by me Ephraim Morton senior ther survior for the Towne of plimouth for the Elder Thomas Cushman of plimouth

[**157.**] Att A towne meting held att plimouth the 23ᵈ day of January 1687, 88

[1] Att this meting an order from his Excelency was published Whereon hee did Require the sd towne of plimouth to appere before his excelencey To make out there title to Clarks Island Whereupon a voat being Caled for to know the towns answer The towne haveing Considered thereof do Answer that they are Resolved to defend there Rite in the above sd Iland to there utmost according to law and therefore Chose a Committey

---

[1] Sir Edmund Andros declared the titles of all public lands vested in the crown. The town expended so much money in resisting the claim of Andros to Clark's Island that it was finally obliged after the accession of William and Mary and the deposition of Andros, to sell the Island.

to Consider of and fully to act in the towns behalfe to defend there Rite in the above sd Iland Ither by sum one of them or by sum other person Whom they shall think meete to Improve therein and the towne doth promise to take Care to defray the Charge therof And thereupon did Agree that a Rate of ten pounds in silver should be forthwith made

The Committy Chosen to act in the towns behalf to defend the towns Rite In Clarks Iland Were

Leftenant morton
Joseph houland
Joseph Warren Senor
Isaac Cushman
Nathaniell Southworth
Joseph Bartlet
John Bradford

Att the above sd meting on the 23$^d$ of January Serjant Harlow was Chosen by the Celect men and Cunstable to be the Sealer of Weights and measures for the towne of plimouth

Att This meting the towne ordered that the Records of sundrey psels of uplands and medow lands should be Trancescribed Into the towne book That was formerly granted by a Committe Chosen to graunt lands & lay in loose papers

The bonds of fifty Acrees of land Graunted by the Towne to Mr. Thomas Cushman is as followeth lying in the Towneship of plimouth and on the northerly side of a lettle brooke Comonly Caled and known by the name of Colchester brook the southermost bound att the East end is A maple tree Marked on 4 sides and soe along the brook 6 score pole to A Red oake tree Marked on 4 sides and from sd tree Rainging Northwards 78 pole to A white oake tree Marked thence Rainging Eastward 6 score pole to A birch tree Marked on 4 sides standing in a swamp

    Survied and measured By
     Georg Bonam Surveyor
    to the Towne of plimouth

The bounds betwen the meadows of deacon Nathaniel Wood and John Barrows which sd meadow Lyeth at the south meadow & is bounded as ffolloweth from A pine tree Marked on 4 sides on the south side of the meadow & soe staked across the meadow to a stump on the North side

[158.] These are to Witnes That John harman have sold to Edward Gray my Grant of upland & the medow lyes where Robert Lathum mowed upon monponset meadow medow given mee by the towne Thirty acrees of upland and Two Acrees of medow lying about monponset pond upon Consideration of A Reckning betwen him and I; and so do by these presence Resigne up unto goodman Gray all my Rites and Intrest of my grant above mentioned unto all Which I John hermon do sett to my hand this 11th of June 1667

John Hermon
Witnes Will: Hoskins

This was Acknowledged the 22th of September before Thomas Prence Gov r

Two acrees of meadow Laid out for John harmon att turkey swamp Below Mr William Bradford below that which was laid out for Joseph Houland and is bounded on the north with a white oake standing in upon the Iland and on the west with a white oake standing in a swompe and lyes by the swomp syde to the bounds of Samuell Stirtevant and on the north with a seder and a stake on the side

Ten acrees of land lying on the Northwest syde of Wenetuxet and is bounded with a Red oake on the foot and on the East with A white oake by the River side and with a white oake on the north Corners with a white oake Twenty acrees on the northwest end of Turke swomp Round about with the swomp and a white oake marked on the west end

Gorg Bonam survair

New plimouth laid out to Ephram morton on the 12th day of March 1691 forty Acrees of upland lying on the southerly side of the shingle Brook and is bounded as followeth bounded at the northerly Corner with a Red oake tree Marked on four sids and from sd tree the line extends south souwest eigh score pole to A white oake tree Marked on 4 sids and a heap of stones by it which is the northermost Corner bound at the southerly end and from sd tree the line to extend east southeast forty pole to a small pine tree marked on four syds which is the eastermost Corner bound at the southerly end and from sd tree the line extends North and by east eigh scor pole to A standing pine tree

on a hill side marked on four sids which is the easterly Corner bound at the Northerly end and from sd tree the line to extend west and by north 40 pole to the Red oak tree first mentioned
Surveyed and Measured pr me
Thomas ffaunce Surveyor

[159.] Att a Town meting of the Inhabitants of the Town of plimouth on the 21<sup>th</sup> of May 1688 The officers Chosen for the town of plimouth were

    The Select men Were
    Joseph Waren senor
    Isaac Cushman
  Serjant William harlow
    and John Bradford
    Elkanah Watson Comitioner
    John Stirtevant Cunstable
  The surviors were Jacob Cooke
    Benony lucas
    Robert Bartlet
    and John Pratt

The men appoynted to go to see What persons would Contrebute towards Mr Cottons Support for his Labour in the ministree for this present year Were
  Jonathan Shaw senior
  Robert Ransom senior
  Thomas Cushman
  Jacob Cooke
  Josiah morton
  and Tho : ffaunce

and that what is promised by each person shall be payed both as to time and Specey as Was Agreed on the last yeare

At A towne meeting held att plymouth May the 28<sup>th</sup> 1689 for the Choyce of Court and towne officers The Deputies Chosen Were Isaac Cushman and John bradford

The Grand Jury Were Jonathan Shaw senior Thomas Cushman & Elkanah Cushman

  The Select men  Serjeant Harlow
         Joseph Bartlet &
         Nathaniel Southworth
 The Cunstables Chosen Were Josiah Morton &
         Wiliam Shirtleif

The town agreed that the surveyes of the high wayes the last yeare Chosen should serve this yeare again

Att this meeting the towne doe agree that there shall be a declaration presented to the Generall Court that the Cuntrey mite help to beare theire proportion of charge to Relive those persons that have ben Grevios sufferrors for defending the [1] Comon Write

Att this meeting the Towne voated for two Cunstabls to be Chose to serve this yeare At this meeting the Towne do Impower the Celect men to take care for the Reparation of the Meeting house

[160.] An Agreement made betwen Robert & Josiah finney both of The Town of plymouth in New England Respecting a division of those lands that was given to us by our uncle Robert finney of plimouth deceased as doth appeare by his Will to be devided eaqually betwen us both Wee doe therfore Thus Agree mutualy that The Lane that now is that leadeth downe to the sea side along by The dweling house shall be the bounds betwen us and Robert is to have all the lands from the above sd laine home to Thomas Mortons land on the north sid of the above sd lane excepting A Certain peece of land That which by oure agrement Josiah is to have out of the foot of Roberts part which is att the foott of Roberts land att the southeast end of sd land hom to the water side and is bounded next the Water sid upon the banke With A heap of stones and soe Runeth up to another heap of stones standing att the head of the Above sd pece or tract of land and thence Croseth over to Another heap of stones by the above Expresed laine and we doe further Agree that Josiah Shall maintain the head fence and half the side fence of this land soe bounded and this pese of land soe bounded Together with all That land that was our uncles on the southward sid of the above sd laine hom to the land of Mr Wiliam Clark is to belong to Josiah and this division of land betwene us is to extend in heigte to the head of the above sd laine where wee have mad a heap of stones and from thence to square of both Wayes and wee doe further agree that If we find the laine two narrow for oure use there to leave out on both sids our proportion to make it wider that so we may have Cumfortable egress and Regres to

---

[1] The "Common Right" here referred to was the title to land which it was necessary to defend against the claim of Andros.

our housing and wedoe further agree that Robert shall have all those persels of medow that was our uncls both at small gains and att the Ealriver head excepting a certain peece Comonly Caled and known by the name of knolesses medow which is to belong to Josiah

This devision of Lands above expressed we the above sd Robert and Josiah doe Agree shall be binding both to us and our heires for ever as Witness our hands and seales on the lift day of June 1689

    In presence of     Robert ffinney ()
    Thos : ffaunce     Josiah ffinney ()
    Joshua ffinney     and there seales

[161.] Att a meeting of the Inhabitants of the towne of plimouth on the 22$^d$ of June 1689 They did then voat and agree that all Nesessary Charges that hath ben expended about defending the Towns Wright in Clarks Island shall be Repayed

2 they doe voat and agree that some of the lands in Commonage belonging to the Towne shall be sold for to defray the Charges above expresed

3 they do voat and agree that If Aney of the Inhabitants of the Towne are minded to bye aney lands that shall be sold out of the Comons belonging to the towne; that any such persons soe minded shall have the Refusall of such land as shall be sould for the use Above sd

Att this meeting A Committe were Chosen to make saile of Clarks Island Saquosh and the Gurnet together with aney small prsels of uplands or meadows lying in Commonage belonging to the Inhabetants of the towne of plymouth as alsoe a Certain seder swomp Caled by the name of Colchester Swomp to help to defray sd Charge.

The Comittee Chosen to make saile of the lands above exprest Were
    Serjant harlow
    John Stirtevant
    John Doten senior
    Jonathan Shaw senior
    Ephraim Morton Junior
    John Gray these or aney foure of them agreeing are to act fully in the particulars Abov expresed as also they are to

take account of the Charges that hath ben Relating to Clarks Island

Att a towne meting held att plimouth on the 9<sup>th</sup> of August 1689 John bradford and IsaaC Cushman Were Chosen Deputyes for the Whole year

att a towne meeting held at plymouth the 26<sup>th</sup> of August 1689 the Inhabetants then Chose A town Councell to act with the Comition offecers According to Court order

The Councell Chosen Were
Serjent harlow
John Bradford
and Tho : ffaunce

Att a Meeting of the Enhabitants of the Town of plymouth on the 4<sup>th</sup> of November 1689 they then Chose Raters to make A Rate of sixty pounds acording to the Warrent of the Govenor

The Raters Chosen Were  Serjant harlow
IsaaC Cushman
Elkanah Watson

[162.] An Agreement Made Betwen James Warren and Joseph Warren both of the Towne of plimouth on the first day of ffebruary 1689 or 90 with Refferance to a devision both of uplands and meadow lands that before was in partnership betwen us which said lands was formerly the land of Capt Tho : Southworth and Constant Southworth Lying on the Northwest side of the Eele River betwen the lands of Tho : ffaunce and the sd Rever Wee doe therefore Agree upon a devision as followeth of the above sd lands and medows begining att the lower meadow the first devision belonging to James Warren and is bounded with a stake and a stone att the Rever side and A mapel Tree and A heap of stones by it att the upland side and all the other part of the meadow below the grat Rock by the Rever side by Clam's Island meadow hom to the bound above expresed doth belong unto Joseph Warren ;

The first devision of swamp and upland belongeth unto Joseph Warren and is bounded att the upland side with an [1]odizar bush and a heap of stones by it and soe Runeth upon A west Norwest poynt to a Red oak tree and a heap of stones by it and soe on the same poynt hom to the land of Tho: faunce and from these bounds to extend southerly to a stake and heap of stones by it standing by Clams Island medow and soe to Run on the same poynt of Compas as is above exspresed to a heap of stones in the swamp and soe to a red oake tree and a heap of stones by it on the upland and so a Cross the lot The Nex devision belongeth unto James Warren and from these bounds last mentioned to extend southerly to a stake and a ston by it by the Rever side and so to a Red oake tree and a heap of stones by it and from that Red oake to Run acros our land on the same poynt of Compas to a Red oake tree and a heap of stones by it and so to another tree and a heap of stones by it The Next devision belongeth unto Joseph Warren and is to extend southerly from the bounds last mentioned to a white oake tree and a heap of stones by it by the Rever sence we side nere over against where the dubble brooke find the tree Cometh into the Rever and soe to Run acros mentioned is our land on the same poynt to another White lower down oake tree and a heap of stones by itt and soe the river to severall other trees with heapes of stons by itt and soe to severall other trees with heapes of stons by them acros the lots. And from these bounds last mentioned James Warren is to have all the lands to the head of the lotts; and we do further Covenant and agree with Thomas faunce That hee shall have that slipp of upland that lyeth betwen his owne upland

---

[1] This is a new word in the records, and Mr. B. M. Watson of Plymouth, a competent authority, thinks it a word unknown to botanical nomenclature. The same gentleman suggests that it may mean "osier," the willow.

and his half acree of meadow soe Called to begin at a great Rocke at the half acree bars and soe to Run acros to an other grat Rock on the hill side and soe to his own bounds and from thence downward to the Cart way alwayes provided that we may have free pasage for Carting through his land betwen that and the bridg either by Gats or barrs And All these uplands and meadows soe devided and bounded as is herein above exspresed shall stand good and Remaine firme and Inviolable for us and our heirs for ever and In Witnes to our free and full Concorrance herein Wee the above said James Warren and Joseph Warren have set to our hands on the $3^d$ of ffebruary 1689 or 90 in presence of us Witnesses

Tho: ffaunce     Joseph Warren
Joan ffaunce     James Warren

    Att A meeting of the Inhabitants of the Town of plimouth July $12^{th}$ 1690 Isaac Cushman and Thomas ffaunce Were Chosen Surveyors for the Town of plimouth for the measuring of land.

[163.] Att A town meeting held att plimouth on the $10^{th}$ of March 1690 Leftenant Morton and John Bradford were Chosen by the Inhabitants of the Towne to assist Nathaniel Southworth at the Court Conserning the Whale attached by the Celect men in the Towns behalfe to defend the Towns write therin so far as they Can

    Att the meeting above sd the Town did voat to stand by the Celect men of the Town in prosecuting their Intrest In the Whale attach: by the Celect men for the Towns use as above sd but seing serjant harlow & Joseph Bartlet did somwhat decline the Thing there upon the persons above named were Chosen to act with nath: southworth therein in the towns behalfe

    At the meeting above mentioned the town Chose 7 Jurors 4 to serve at the County Cort at march and 3 to serve at the Cort of assistants in Aprill

John Stirtevant
Barack Jordan
[1] John Mordow
and Jonathan Barns
} were to serve at the County Court in March $\overline{90}$

Ephraim Morton
John Doten
& John Murdo
} were to serve at the Cort of assistants in Aprill 90

att the meeting Above sd the Town doe Impower and Request the Celect men to take an account of the late Cunstables that have not yet given in theire accounts to the towne of Rates Committed to them to gather

At a town Meeting held att plimouth on the 19$^{th}$ of May 1690 The Deputies then Chosen were John Bradford and Isaac Cushman to serve att the next Court and att severall adjurnments and for the whole yeare

The Celect men Chosen were
Lef: Morton
Serjant Harlow
& Thomas ffaunce
John Murdow
& Samuel Harlow } were Chosen Cunstables

Barach Jordan
James Warren
and John pratt
} Grad Jurors

The surveyors Chosen were
Thomas Clark  Georg Bonam
Jonathan Shaw Junior  John Gray
& Isaac King

John Murdock

Att this meeting the Town granted unto John Murdow 30 foot of land square under the hill below John Rickards leaving a Considerable ditch betwen that and John Rickards Ware house

---

[1] John Murdock, whose name is found spelled in the records Murdow or Mordow or Murdo, was a Scotchman, who appeared in Plymouth not far from 1687. He built the house which formerly stood on the north side of Town Square, and which should have been called the Murdock House instead of the Bradford House,—a name by which it has been known to the present and the last generation. Situated as it was on the old Governor Bradford lot the name Bradford House improperly associated the house itself with the Governor. The origin of the name Bradford House is a recent one. In 1767 Thomas Davis came into the possession of the house and occupied it until his death in 1785, when it became the property of his daughter Sarah, the wife of LeBaron Bradford of Bristol, who, after the death of her husband, occupied it until her death in 1821. From her the name Bradford House was derived.

Att A meeting of the Inhabitants of the Town of plymouth December 3ᵈ 1690 They then Chose Raters to make A Rate of for the defraying Chargs Relating to the Warr The Raters then Chos Were Serjent harlow John Bradford & Tho: ffaunce

The bounds of the land that Joseph Howland sold unto Thomas Lazell lying in the township of plimouth at A place Comonly Called and known by the name Colchester the south Corner bound is A white oake marked standing neer a Rock Marked on 4 sides the West bound is A mapel tree marked on four sides the North bound is A white oake marked on 4 sids standing in or neere swampe Ground the east bound is A mapel tree standing in A swamp Marked on 4 sids

<table>
<tr><td>Joseph Howland<br>Thos: Lazell (Bounds)</td><td>Survied and measured by Georg Bonam surveior to the Town of plimouth</td></tr>
</table>

[164.] At a Towne meeting of the Inhabitants of plimouth february the 23ᵈ 1690/91 The Towne Joantly voted it was their desire that utmost endeavores should be used to obtaine A [1]Charter of his majesty that wee might be and Continue A distinct Goverment as formerly

Agents — The Towne also then voted that they would bear their proportion of five hundred pounds & more if need Require for the obtaining A charter and at present to Raise their proportion of two hundred pound for that end and purpose to be sent to those gentlemen that shall be Improved as our agents and the Remainder to be Ready upon tidings from them to be delivered for the accomplishment of our desires

New Plimouth

Measured and bounded unto Joseph Warren fifty Acrees of land formerly Granted unto Joseph Warren

---

[1] Plymouth Colony never had a charter, but managed its affairs under the Patent from the Council of Plymouth, and the compact signed in the cabin of the Mayflower. After the revolution of 1688 and the accession of William and Mary, efforts were made to obtain a charter. Sir Henry Ashurst was made the agent of the colony, and he was assisted by Rev. Ichabod Wiswall, of Duxbury. Increase Mather and Messrs. Cook and Oakes were at the same time in England, acting for the Massachusetts Colony. Through the influence of Gov. Sloughter, of New York, it was at one time decided to include Plymouth in the New York commission; but it was finally embraced in the Massachusetts charter which bears date October 7th, 1691.

Joseph
Warren

senior lying att Monnoment ponds on the easterly side of left Ephraim Mortons lot bounded on the Northerly Corner with a Rock neere the bank side and A heap of stones on it thence Rainging south and by west eigh score pole to A heap of stones thence Rainging on a east and by south line fifty pole to A small white oak Marked on 4 sids and from sd oake the line extends north and by east eigh score pole to A rock and A heap of stones upon it by the pond sid and from sd Rock to extend west and by north fifty pole to the Rock first mentioned

Measured and bounded on the 13<sup>th</sup> of March 1691 pr me
Thomas ffaunce surveyor

New Plimouth April 13[th] 1691

*
Harlow

Where as A knowle of land was formerly graunted to William Harlow senior containing 2 or 3 acrees lying on the southerly sid of his land he bought of samuel hicks Therefore laid out to the above sd William Harlow 2 Acrees begining att the Corner of the sd William harlows fence Rainging eastward 12 pole along the Road to a stone set into the ground neer the bank on the westerly sid of the spring and soe to extend from said bound to A heape of stones by the stone wall fence belonging to Samuel Harlow that is About his meadow and from sd heap of stones to extend along by the detch and fence Aboute the meadow belonging to nathaneel holmes and so home to the fence of William harlow above sd

Measured and bounded on the day and yeare above mentioned per me<br>Thomas ffaunce,<br>Surveyor to the Towne

[165.] At a meeting of the Inhabitants of the Towne of plimouth May the 25[th] 1691 for the Choyce of Cort and Towne officers

The Deputies Chosen by the Towne to serve at the next Cort and the severall Adjournments were
John Bradford and Isaac Cushman

the Select men were Serjant Harlow Nathaniel Southworth & Thomas ffaunce

the Grand Jurors were Jonathan Shaw senior William Shurtleff and Elkanah Cushman

the Cunstables were John Gray and Ephraim Coole

the surveyors for the high wayes were Ephraim Morton Junior Joseph faunce John Waterman and John Pratt

At A towne meeting held at plimouth on the 31 day of Agust 1691 The Jurors Chosen to serve at the County Court were John Doty John Murdo Samuel harlow James Warren

Serjant harlow being deceased that was Chosen Select man for the yeare at this meeting the Inhabitants of the Town Chose Leftenant Morton to serve in his place this following year

At this meeting the Towne being Informed of some persons that Intended to lay out lands within our Township which were not Inhabetants of our Town The Inhabitants of the Towne then made Choyce of John Bradford Isaac Cushman and John Doty to serv warne oppose and hender any persons that should Attempt to lay out any of the Towns Comons or settle boundarys thereon

Joseph Bartlett Sen<sup>r</sup>
At this meeting The Town Graunted unto Joseph Bartlett Senior 70 foott of land along the shore where his warehouse now standeth below John Rickards dwelling house and downe towards the sea so far as he shall se Cause to Whorfe

Att A town Meeting held at plimouth March 9<sup>th</sup> 169$\frac{1}{2}$ the Jurrors Chosen to serve at the County Court were Ephraim Morton John Stirtevant John Nelson and John Doty; and for the Court of assistants Abraham Jackson James Warren Nath: holmes and Nathaniel Harlow

At A towne meeting held at plimouth May 30<sup>th</sup> 1692

Leften Morton and John Bradford were Chosen Deputies to Represent the towne in the grate assembly to be holden at Boston on the eight day of June 1692

John Foster
at this meeting John ffoster had 30 foot square of land granted to him by the towne below the path next the bank sid betwen the sd bank and the highway if it be there to be had and not interfere upon the hig way

Att the Towne meeting on the 9<sup>th</sup> of March 92 above mentioned John pratt desired that his land

John Pratt — formerly Granted to him att wenham and laid out on the easterly side of the brook mite be Removed and laid out upon A square on the other side of the brook for his better Convenience of fencing of it which Request was granted him by the Inhabitants then present

John Foster — The bounds of the land granted by the Town of plimouth unto John ffoster are as followeth by a Rock by the high way to the southward end of his shopp and soe alonge the hig way to A stone sett in to the ground and from thence Rainging to a tree standing on the bank marked on 4 sydes and from thence Rainging to an other tree on sd bank marked on 4 sides

Measured and bounded
pr me Thomas ffaunce

[166.] Att A Town meeting held at plimouth on the 25<sup>th</sup> of July 1692 for the Choyce of Towne officers The Select men then Chosen Were William Shurtlef Isaac Cushman and Thomas ffaunce & left Mory was Choysen Commissioner, The Grand Jurors were Ephraim Morton Junior Thomas Cushman and Jonathan Shaw Junior The Constables are samuel Lucas and Eliazar Ring The Surveyors for the high wayes are James Warren Caleb Cooke Samuel Stirtevant Giles Rickard Junior & Robert Ransom Junior

At A Town meeting held at plimouth on the 3<sup>d</sup> day of october 1692 It was ordered and Agreed By the Inhabitants of sd Towne to make A Rate of 80 pounds for Mr Cotton of which one half is to be paid in money the other halfe in Corrant Cuntery pay sd payments to be made in october and the other half in Aprill ffollowing which sum is ingaged to him for his labour in the Ministry ffor the present yeare 1692

Its alsoe voated that the Select men shall make the Rate for the minester

voated that 5 pounds be Rated for the Repairing the meeting house in sd Rate

voated to pay former Charges to Deputies and Grandjurors

voated that the propryetors of Winituxet meadows shall have liberty to sett A fence one Monponset side of the brook to secure their meaddows

J. Dunh^m   At this meting flifty Ackers of land was Granted to Joseph Dunham

At a town meeting held at plimouth September 14^th 1693 Johon Nelson was Chosen to be the towns Representative at the Grate and General assembley at Boston the Jurors Chosen were Abram Jackson John Dotey John Mordo & John Sturtevant

voated att this meeting it was voated that the Select men should make the Rate for the Minister for ye yeare Insuing

*The bounds of Elder Thomas Cushmans—12 Acres Meadow*

The Bounds of the twelve acrees of meaddow belonging to the Elder Thomas Cushman at Wenatuxet is as followeth bounded with a white oake tree at the Northerly Corner sd tree is marked on 4 sides and thence Rainging across the Meaddow westward to a Red oake tree marked on 4 sides which is the bounds betwen the sd Elder Cushmans Meadow and Mr John Howlands meaddow and from sd Red oake Rainging up the Meaddow southward to a pine tree marked on 4 sides and from thence Rainging aCross the meaddow to a bunch of maples standing by the meadow which is the bounds betwen John Dunhams lot and the above sd Elder Cushmans

[167.] New Plimouth

Att A meting held att plimouth the 22^th of february 1650 by Mr Howland Mr Willett John Dunham John Cook William Paddy & Thomas Clarke

Wee grant to mr howland Elder Cushman John Cook John Dunham senior Twelve Acrees Apece of meddow ground att Wennituxett To take it on both sides of the River so as others that shall have more grants theare be not prejudiced

Wee further grant that Mr Bradford may have twelve Acrees of meaddow att the above sd River to ly opon both sides of The River

Wee Graunt unto James hust Twelve Acrees of meddow ground Att Winnituxett

The 29^th of the 10 month 1651 Wee grant unto Leftenant Thomas Southworth Twelve Acrees of meaddow ground att Winnituxett

The 24th of the 10th mon 1651 Wee grant unto Edward Dotey four Acrees of meddow ground att Winnetuxett and If there be any more left undisposed we grant him four Acrees more

We grant unto John Winslow Twelve Acrees of meddow ground att Winnatuxett upon both sids of the brook as the above sd men are granted

Wee Grant unto Jacob Cooke Twelve Acrees of meddow att winnituxett upon both sides the brooke as the other graunts

The 29th of the 10th month 1651

Wee grant unto Geyles Rickard Senior Twelve Acrees of meddow ground att Winnituxett

Wee further Grant to the above sd Geyles Rickard senior An enlargment of his ground lying Southward of his house provided the neighborhood be willing to it & this upon the view of Mr Thomas Willett and Mr Paddy

The 29th of the 10th 1651

Wee Grant unto Georg Bonam twenty Acrees of upland lying att the head of his lott att the Eyle River above the upper foord

The 29th of the 10th 1651

wee grant to John morton ten Acrees of meaddow att winnetuxett to be layd out by the measurors

The 17th of march 1654

we grant to good Watson A little slip of medow above the bridge that is upon the Cedar swamp brook att the south-meadow

Wee Grant to Andrew Ring A percell of meadow upon * Brooke by Josh Pratt soe it extend not six Acrees

Wee Grant to Samuel Dunham and Giles Rickard * * * the meadow att Souther Marsh

[168.] The 25th of December 1655

Wee Grant unto George Bonam and Andrew Ring three Acrees of meadow Apece lying att the Southeast end of the Cedar Swamp neer the south meadow

Wee Graunt to Thomas Clarke The Scerts of meddow lying uppon The pond att Monument from the Creicke Round abound

Wee Graunt to Thomas Clarke five Akres of meddow lying in the same meddow with Thomas little Tho: littles being first layed out According to his graunt in the town book

We Graunt to Samuel Stirtevant four Akers of meddow lying upon the North side upon A branch of Jonesriver and that Mr Lee have the Remainder provided that it exceed not foure Akers

Wee Graunt to frances Cooke 3 holes of meddow lying at the Hither end of the Greate meddow Caled Jons River

Wee graunt to Ephraim Tincom three spots of meddow that lyeth next James Hursts at the easter end of James hurst soe that there be not above four akers october 14 1653

The 17th of March 1654

Wee Grant to Goodman Watson A lettle slip of meadow above the bridg that is upon the Ceder swamp brook att the South meadows

Wee grant to Andrew Ring a percell of medow upon Craine brook by Josiah pratts soe it exceed not six Acrees

This is above Recorded

We Grant to George Bonam and Andrew Ring three acrees apece of meadow lying att the south-east end of the Cedar swamp nere the south meadows

[169.] The first of february 1648

It is granted That Thomas Cushman Gabrill fallowel and Richard Write shall have an acree of meddow apeece att the West meddow at Edward Dotyes farme

It is further Granted that John Wood Henry Wood and Stephen Wood should have an Acree of meddow apece att the same meddow next to them

Its fur granted That Goodman golden Samuel Downham and John Downham shall have an Acree Apece next to them and these 9 acrees be layed out to the above sd persons betwen Mr fuller and Mr Atwood

Its further granted that the persons following have an Acree of meddow apece lying above Mer Atwood to be devided by *

| Andrew Ring | | Thomas Whitten | |
| John Morton | } 3 | Nath: Morton | } 3 |
| Ephraim hicks | | George Watson | |
| Robert Padducke | | Edhraim Tinkum | |
| Tho: Letice | } 3 | John holmes | } 3 |
| John Dunham | | Will: Nelson | |

| | | |
|---|---|---|
| Mer Lee | ⎫ | John finney |
| good Stirtevant | ⎬ 3 | Rob: finney |
| good Kinge | ⎭ | John Thomson |

These sd meddows granted to the sd persons to them and theire * soe long as they live in the Town and noe longer and then to Returne to the Town Acording to the directions att the Town meeting

William Paddy
John Donnham
Richard Sparrow
Thomas Southworth

[**170.**] The Bounds of John pratts Land at Wenham on which his house now Standeth are as followeth bounded by the brook which Cometh out of Dotyes pond on ye southerly side and soe along as the brook Runeth till it Cometh where the brook turneth an other way and there marked with a maple tree & so from sd tree along the swampe to two white oak saplings marked on 4 sides & from thence across sd land and there marked with a White oak tree marked on 4 sides and from thench Rainging down to sd Dotens pond and marked with severall pine trees in sd Rainge and at sd pond sid there bounded with a pine tree & a heape of stones by it Measured and bounded on the 8[th] of June 1692 pr mee Thomas ffaunce Surveyor

New plimouth measured and bounded unto Ben pratt on the 8[th] July 1692 twenty acrees of land Abuting on the path that goeth from John prats to lakenham on the southerly side of said path and is bounded as followeth Neere the path bounded with a white oake bush and A hea of stones by sd bush & from thence Rainging up the plain 4 score pole to a lettle bush & A heape of stones & from thence to extend 40 pole to a pine tree and a heap of stones by it and from thence to extend towards sd path foure score pole to A pine tree Marked standing Neere sd path & a heape of stones by sd tree

pr mee Thomas ffaunce Surveyor

The bounds of three Ackers of meadow more or less Measured and bounded by George Bonam for Thomas Cushman lying att the head of Jons river meadow bounded by A Red oake att the ffoott marked on four sides thence Rainging to a stake by the brooke and from sd stake to a maple tree standing on the southeast side of an Island and from sd tree and stake at the foot Rainging up the brooke on both sides to an ash tree on the east sid of the brooke and A white oake on the west side of the brooke both marked

The bounds of the land of Thomas Cushman lying at the Indian pond the bounds on the Northern side is A red oake tree standing or neere a small Island on the edge of the pond marked on 4 sides thence Runing Eastward to a Red oake marked on four sides and thence Runing southerly to a white oake standing on the ffot of a hill Caled halfway hill marked on 4 sides thence Runing Westwardly to the pond again to a black oake marked on 4 sides standing by a sloaping Rock by the pond side and thence Runing Noitherly to the bounds first mentioned Thirty Acrees more or less This lyeth Joyning to the pond att the Western end

    Surveyed and bounded by mee
                George Bonam Surveyor to the
                Town of plimouth

[171.] A list of those nams of those that toke the oath of fidelety at the town meting held at plimouth the 17[th] day of May 1686

    Samuell Downham Junor
    John Coob Junor
    Abraham Jackson Junor
    Robert Bartlet
    Nathaniell harlow
    Elkiah tincom
    Isack King
    Joseph King
    Frances Curtes
    Francis Cuke
    George Samson
    Samuel lucas

The bounds of that tract of land which was granted unto Stephen Bryant Junior for Conveniencc of fenceing his meadow in the woods where he now liveth sd land is bounded as followeth at the uper end it is bounded by a tract of land granted by the towne unto his fath Stephen Bryant senior and on the southeast syde by the meddow belonging to sd Bryant and down along and bounded by sd meddow till it Cometh to a pine tree Marked on foure sides staning neere the brook th t runeth through sd meadow and from sd tree Rainging westward to A white oake tree marked on 4 sides standing neare A swampe and soe up along and bounded by sd swampe till it Comes to his fathers land above Mentioned alwaies provided that John Bryant and his heires shal have free liberty and in no wise hindered at any time from haveing free passage through said land unto his meadow or farm fencing of his meadow allong the scirts of upland as ocasion may Call for this tract of land above Mentioned Contaignes 16 acrees be it more or less September 16$^{th}$ 1693 bounded out unto the abov named Stephen Bryant pr me Thomas ffaunce Surveyor To the towne of plimou

The Mark of Samuel Bradfords neate Cattle & horses & swine is as followeth A Cropp of the neare eare

The marke of nathaniel Mortons Cattle horses & swine is as followeth A hapeney out of the foreside of the Rite eare

Joseph Bartlet Junior his mark for his neate Cattle horses & swine is as followeth A half cropp cut out of the furr eare behind and a half cropp cut out of the neare eare before

Elnathan Bartlets Mark for his Neate Catle horses and swine is an half Crop on farr Ear before and an Whole Crop on ye Nere Eare

Benj$^{in}$ Bartlets Mark for his Neate Catle Horses and Swine is an Arow head on ye Top of Each Eare

[173.] The 13$^{th}$ of June 1659 John Barnes sold a blaek horse unto Mr John Saffin about three yeares old or

The 14$^{th}$ of June 1659 William Clarke sold a Red horse unto Mr Thomas Dexter for about foure years old ;

The 28$^{th}$ of ffebruary 1659 John Barnes sold a blacke horse of about five yeares old had a little starr in his forehead ; to Mr Gibbs of Boston Marchant and likewise a mare of a Chesnutt Couller about nine yeares of age with one wall eye and a white strip between her nostrills was sold by the said John Barnes to the said Mr. Gibbs the same day :

January the first 1661 The markes of Mistres Elizabeth Warrens horses are as followeth one Red mare about thirteen yeares old with a white blase in her face marked with two slits in the neare eare and soe the bitt cut out which marke is on the out side of the said eare and alsoe the

these horses were entered

said mare is branded with a P on topp of the buttocke

2condly a Coult of about a yeare old of the same Couller and the same marke

3dly a Bay mare with a black tayle and maine with a little starr in the forehead about five yeares old of the same marke

4 ly a blackeish horse Coult with one white foot behind and a fayer starr in his forehead of the same marke

5 ly one young mare neare two yeare old blackish with gray heires of the same marke

one blacke mare neare 4 yeare old with a few gray heres in her forehead which belonges to Nathaniell and Joseph Warren of the same marke as Mistris Warrens above said

and one Rid horse Coult with a white blasse downe his face of the same marke belonging to the said Nathaniell and Joseph Warren;

The marks of Thomas Morton horses a mare of about six yeare old of a whitish Gray Couller Cropt on the Right eare with a P on the left buttock

1661 a mare of a yeare old Coult of a blakish Couller with a speck or starr in her forehead and a little blase that Comes downe her nose marked with a slitt upon the topp of the Right eare and a P on her left buttocke

[174.] ffrancis Combes marke of his Cattle is an halfe moon Cut out of the farr eare on the farr side of that eare and an hole in the same eare

November
1662     Nathaniel Mortonss markes of his horses are as followeth: a black horse of foure yeares old or therabouts with all foure white feet and a blase downe his face most on the left side and his artificiall markes are a pece cut of the left eare on the tope somwhat hollow in the midds or somewhat deeper in the midds; with a smale bitt cut out of the same eare on the outside therof somwhat halfe Round like a halfe moone; and a mare coult of a yeare and vantage old of a blackish browne culler for the prsent with a starr in her forhead with a little white on her

left hinder foot below her fetlocke on the edge of her hough or therabouts and for her artificiall marke she is as the horse is crop on the left eare on the topp and a little bite cut out halfe round of the same eare on the out side therof: onely the Crop is not soe deep in the midds as the horse and is not cut Right of but a little on one side:

1669    The marke of a horse of Nathaniel Mortons which had from Barnstable of a whitish Couller of about three years old; marked with a slit on the topp of his left eare and a little peece Cut out of the back syde of his said ear: towards his body much like a half moone.

Joseph Bartletts marks of his Cattle is an halfe Cropp on the far eare before.

John Andrews Marke of his Cattle is a little Cutt or noch on the hinder part of the neare eare:

Joseph Warrens marke for his Cattle both neat Cattle horses &c is a peece Cutt out behind the topp of the Near eare like unto an Arrow head: or like unto a V

Aprill the 13th 1683    The markes of Mr John Bradfords Cattle is the topp of the Right Eare Cutt off; and a Slitt on the under side of the Left Eare;

May the tenth 1683    The Marke of John Grayes Cattle is a half peny Cut out of the Right Eare on the under side of the Eare and an half penny Cutt out of the left Eare on the under side of the Eare;

[175.] Georg Bonams Senor marke and Georg Bonam Juniors marke of theire Cattle and horsies is a half pence Cut out of the hind part of left Eare

Robbert Bartlets Marke ffor his Cattell is a half Cropp cutt out of the ffarr eare before and a halfe Cropp Cut out of the nere eare behind

James Warren's marke for his Cattell is a halfe Cropp Cutt out of back part ye Left eare and A hapenny cutt out of the backside of the Right eare

William harlows Marke for his Cattle and swine is as followeth A Cropp on the Rite eare and a half Cropp on the hind part therof

Benjamin Warrens Marke for his Neete Cattell swine and horses is as followeth A half Crop Cut out of the fore part of the left eare

Ebenazer holmes Marke for his Neate Cattle horses and swine are as followeth is A halfe Crop Cut out of the Right care before

Joseph Bartlets Jun Marke for his horses and Neate Cattle is two half Crops one on the fur eare behind and the other on the nere ear before

John Doty his eare Marke for his neat Cattle horses sheepe and swine is as followeth is a hapeney Cutt out of the back part of the ffarr ear

Joseph holmes his eare marke for his Cattle horses sheepe and swine is as followeth (viz) a half Crop on ye under side of Right eare & a half Cropp on the uper sid of the left eare

John Morton his marke for his neate Cattle horses shepe and swine is a half peney cut out of the under side of the Rite eare

The mark of Thomas Mortons Neate Cattle horses shepe and swine are as followeth (viz) a half Cropp of the under side of the farr eare and a slitt in ye neere eare

The eare mark of Isaac Dotys Neet Cattle horse kind sheep and swine is A haponey Cut out of the under side of ye left eare

The ear mark of Mr John Sturtevants neat cattle & sheep * * upon the Left Ear and a Round hole in the Right ear

[176.] Plimouth December The first 1699

Then It Was ordered and Agreed too by The Major of The Rigements of the County of plimouth and The Comishion officers of Each of The Millitary Companies of the Town of plimouth Thatt The high way Leading downe from Midleboreough Through sd Town of plimouth To The Chois Landing place & whorfs att The Bay or Waterside shall be the dividing bounds Between The souldiers of each Company

        Major Nath Thomas
        Cap$^t$ John Bradford
        Cap James Warren
        Lef Nath Southworth

Insg John Watterman
Insg Nath Mortton

Plimouth March 15<sup>th</sup> 17 15/16

Wheras The Honorable the Left Governor hath Granted Commissions to milletary officers for Two Companies in the Town of plimouth These are to certyfy all whome it may Concern That ye Deviding line betwen ye Two Companies in sd Town shall be as followeth (viz) Begining at ye [1] Town bredge and from sd bredge as ye Road or highway leads Toward Wenham in plimton and from sd bredg Downward by The brook To ye sea and all the solders on ye Northerly side of sd line to belong to ye Northerly Company and all on ye southerly side of the line to belong to ye southerly Company

pr us Isaac Winslow Colnor
John Cushing Left: Colnor

[178.] Complaint being made to the Cort of quarter sesscons of the want of a Road or highway throw the towne of plimouth to Rochester the sd Justices did think it Conveniant for the Select Men of the town of plimouth aforesaid to lay out the way towards Rochester soe far as sd towns bounds extended that way upon which we the select men of plimouth aforsaid with the desire of the towne that we should undertake the worke did on the last day of 1698 went up and vewed the land & we aprehended that the most Conveniant way is from plimouth towne along the old south meadow path to the sedar bridge & soe leaveing Benoney Lucas house on the Right hand and soe goeth on the eastward sid of sd Lucas his land & leaving Samsons pond on the eastward and along the way that now goeth to the River where the bridg useth to be Above John Bensons house This we determine to be the Roade from plimouth to Rochester

William Shurtlif
John Mordo Selectmen

voted an act vallied by the Inhabitants of the Town

[179.] James Clarke Junior of plimouth did on the 25<sup>th</sup> of Agust 1718 Take up in my Corne feild A sorrel Collored * of about 12 hands high & neere 14 years of age and much wind galed Marckt I G upon his shoulder

---
[1] The bridge here referred to crossed town brook at the foot of what is now Spring Hill, and the highway referred to was Mill Lane with its continuation Summer Street. A way down Spring Hill was not laid out until 1716.

Taken up by William Swiff of plimouth A stray horse * hands & a half high he is a Red horse With a White face and is * with a O upon ye neere thigh if aney person shall lay a Right to him they may have him paying ye Charges Dated at plimouth * of March 1719 William Swift

Taken up astray horse of a black Culler brand marked * nere side on ye sholder with a T and on ye hind thy on ye * side with ye letter M if aney person lay a Right Clame for him paying the Charge said horse was Takein up by Elehazar Cobb of plimouth on the $2^d$ Day of June 1719.

Taken up a stray Mare of a lite bay Culler or a dark brown Judged to be about four years old no artificall Mark Desernable if any person lay aney Right Clame to her paying the Charges he or they may have her said mare was taken up a stray by Ebenazar holmes Junior of plimouth about the begining of Desember 1720

plimouth october 16 1721 Then taken up by Jonathan Bryant of plimouth a stray Heifer of a year and vantage Red and white spotted no artificall Mark to be Deserned

plimouth November $8^{th}$ 1721 Then Taken up by James Clark Junor A smal Black * a stray Noe Natural nor artificall marke Judged to be five or six yeare old

The markes of Nathaniell Mortons

Samuell Savory's markes of his Cattle, is a half Crop cut out of the topp of the Right eare on the fore pte of the same eare and a half Moone Cutt out of the backsyde the same eare * * of a blacke Couller * horse coult belonging * Eedey is marked with a hole burned in each eare

Marke of ffrancis Combe

his Cattle is a halfe moone Cut out the farr eare on the under part of *

Markes of a horse sold by Jonathan Barnes the fift of June 1667 : a mouse coullered horse with a peece cut out of the Right eare about * yeares old

The Markes of John Dunham the younger his Cattle is a Cutt under the eare and an O sett upon the fore hoofe with an Iron

The markes of Jonathan Mawry his Cattle is a slit on the topp of the Right eare; and a halfe moon Cutt out on the same eare on the out side

John Bryants senor Marke for his Cattle is a Cutt Cross the neare Eare

Samuell Kings Senor his marke is a slit on the topp of the Right eare

The Towne brand mark of Briston is B on the off shoulder this was Ientered the 20 of ffebruary 1681-82

The mark of Thomas faunces Cattle and horseses is a halfe Crop on the outside of the Right eare Like to an arrow head

The Eare Mark of Josiah Mortons nete Cattle horses sheepe and swine is a half peney cut of y fore side of the Right eare

The mark of John Washbons Cattle horses sheep and swine is a half Crop on the under side of the Right eare & a little Crop on the Top of the left eare

The eare mark of the neat Cattle shepe and swine of Thomas Morton ye * * A Crop of the Top of ye Rite eare

The eare Mark that Jacob Mitchel hath for his catel horses and sheep is a hole punched out of the Rite eare

The eare mark of Samuel Hoskins neat Cattle sheep and swine A Crop on ye Topp of the Rite eare and a hapeny cut out of the under side of the left

The care mark of Elkanah Churchills neet Cattle sheepe & swine is a hole made in both eares

Plimouth Towne
Book
Thomas Faunce
Town Clerk
of plimouth
1697

[Vol. 2.
     2.] This Writting Made the Ninth day of January
1673 betwen William Clark son of Thomas Clark
of the Town of New plimouth in The Collony of
New plimouth on the one party and Thomas ffaunce The son of
John ffaunce of the afforsd Towne deceased on the other party
Wittneseth, That Whereas The said William Clarke and Thomas
ffaunce are personally posesed of sundry Lots of land lying on
the Northward side of Ele River in the Towne of plimouth
aforesd Which were formerly posesed and Improved by The
aforesd Thomas Clarke and John ffaunce and Whereas the
bounds of and line or Rang betwixt the said persons and lots are
very dubious & well knowne whereby trouble and dammage thereby
may arise to the aforsd partyes there heirs or assignes for the
prevention thereof It Is Therefore by these presence freely and
also fully Covenanted agred and Concluded by and betwen The
said William Clark and Thomas ffaunce Mutually for themselves
and there heires and assignes for Ever that the bounds that thay
the said William & Thomas have Made This day betwen there
said lots and land and herein Inscribed and discribed shall
Remaine for Ever to be bounds and land Marks betwixt the said
lots or lands to be keept observed and Remaine Involiable for
Ever by the said William & Thomas theire heires and assignes
for Ever The bound Rang or Line Is as ffolloweth The first land
Mark Is a stone sett into the ground at the Northeast End of
the said lots by the Marsh side about which Is laid a heap of
stones and from ye said stone by the sd Marsh the line Is to
Extend to a prety big Rock standing Neare the swamp side and
from the said Rock the line Is to Run or extend unto a stone sett
into the ground on the       of a small hill about Which Is laid
a heap of stones from Which stone ye line Is to Extend to another
stone sett into the ground by a Red oak sapling standing neare
The North Corner of the Now dwelling house of the said Thomas
ffaunce about which is laid a heap of stones & from the said
stone at the North Corner the line Is to Extend to a small Rock
standing in a bottom which Rock hath on the south side therof a
small flat Rock and from the said small Rock the line Extends
Nearest southwest unto a stone set downe in the ground upon a
long Ridg of land about which Is laid a heap of stones and from
the said stone on the Ridg the line Extends unto a stone set downe

into the ground on the Northward side of a hill which Is neare
the half mile End about Which Is laid a heap of stones and from
the said stone set on the side of a hill the line Extends unto a
stone sett into ye ground on a small hill that Is on the North side
of the southward most half of those that are Called gileses holes
and from the said stone the line Extends to a pine tre Marked on
fouer sides from the head bounds standing on the Westermost
side of the southermost hole of giles holes Comonly Called giles
holes and the said William Clark doth by these prests frely give
[3.] and Enfeoffe to the said Thomas ffaunce his heirs and assignes
in fre privelege Benifitt and use of a spring of Water that Is at
the Northward end or Corner of Thomas ffaunces house in
William Clarkes land with Egres & Regres to and from the said
spring for Ever provided alwayes that in Case the said William
his heirs or assignes shall fence in the said spring the said Thomas
his heirs or assignes shall mainetaine Either gate or stile for theire
use to and from the said spring and so to have It Without
Mollestation; for the true performance of all and every of the
abovesd agrements The said William Clark and Thomas ffaunce
have hereunto Joyntly and severally set to theire hands the day
and yeare first above Ritten and doe Joyntly agree that these
presents be Recorded in the Court Records of the Colony aforesd.

The land bounded and these     William Clarke
signed in prescence of these     Thomas ffaunce
Witnesses
William Crow
Joseph Warren

[5.] plimouth february 16$^{th}$ 169$\frac{2}{3}$

    Measured unto M$^{er}$ John Cotton 30 acrees of land Granted
unto him by the Towne of plimouth lying on the Northerly syde
of the land of edward doty late of plimouth deceased sd land is
bounded as followeth the Northerly Corner att the westerly end
is bounded with a white oake marked and a heap of stones by sd
tree; sd bound is on the Easterly syde of a grate hill in a little
doak or valley and from said tree The line to Extend East and by
North to a small white oake marked and a heap of stones by sd
tree which is a bound between the land of John Cobb Sen and
John Nelson and from the white oake first mentioned the line to
Extend south and by East 44 pole to a white oake marked and a
heape of stones by sd oake standing on the Northerly syde of a

grate hill and soe Rainging East and by North till it Cometh to
the westerly end of Edward dotyes land and soe to the Norwest
Corner of sd Land and soe along sd dotyes Rainge
Mr John   untill a grate Rock or Rocks that lyeth on a hill on
Cotton    the Northerly syde of sd dotys land will beare from
sd dotyes Rainge East and by North and from sd
Rock the line Extendeth east and by North to the
lands formerly laid out and soe along sd lands till
it Comes to the bound above named belonging to
the abovesd John Cobb & John Nelson Measured
and bounded on the day and yere above mentioned
pr me Thomas ffaunce Surveyer
to the Towne of plimouth
New plimouth January 6$^{th}$ 169$\frac{2}{3}$

Measured unto James Barnebe twenty acrees of upland
formerly granted by the Towne of plimouth unto his father James
Barneby late of plimouth deceased sd land is bounded as followeth
with a spruce tree standing nere the duble brook in the Corner of
the swamp and soe Rainging along the swamp west and by north
unto a beech tree Marked on 4 syds standing on a hill syde neere
sd duble brook and from sd beach tree South and by West to a
white oake marked on 4 syds standing in a swampe and from sd
tree the line Extends East and by South to a maple
James     tree marked standing neere the duble brooke sd
Barnaby   land is bounded by the duble brooks on the Northern
syde & easterly end of sd land with allowance of
four pole in breadth for a highway to goe through
sd land where the way now goeth through it

Measured and bounded on the day and yeare above
mentioned pr me Thomas ffaunce Surveyor

The settlement of the bounds of a Certain Tract of land
belonging to John Cobb and John nelson ye said Nelson haveing
asined his right in sd land to sd Cobb yet have other lands
bordering upon sd land and adjoyning to it doe therfore agree
upon the settlement of the bounds as foloweth sd land lyeth on ye
westerly end of hawards swamp and is bounded on the Northerly
Corner with a Rock and heap of stones by sd Rock & soe to
Rainge southerly to a white oak tree standing on

John Cobb
John Nelson

the syde of a hill nere the sd hawards swamp syde & from sd tree upon a straite line to the walke path and there bounded with a white oake bush and heap of stones The settlement of the bounds above mentioned was done by John Cobb and John Nelson the parties therein Conscerned January $30^{th}$ $1692\tfrac{2}{3}$

[6.] January $6^{th}$ $1692\tfrac{2}{3}$

6 acrees
and 3 quortors
of

Joseph
Warren

Measured and bounded to Joseph Warren 30 acrees of land formerly granted by the Towne of plimouth unto Joseph Warren senior late of plimouth deceased sd land lyeth adjoyning to his other lands on the westerly syde of the Roade that goeth to sandwedg on the southerly syde of said land & is bounded as followeth with a white oake tree marked and a heape of stones by sd tree neere sd Rode and soe Rainging west and by north to a spruce tree standing neere the duble brook soe Caled and from sd tree Rainging North and by east to a maple tree marked adjoyning to his other lands and twenty acrees of sd land lyeth on the Westerly syde of the Roade that goeth to Sandwich and is bounded with A spruce tree marked on 4 sydes standing neere where the shingle brooke Cometh in to the duble brooks and from sd spruce tree Rainging south and by East four score and six pole to a white oake Tree Marked on four sydes and a heap of stones by sd Tree and from sd bound Rainging west and by south to A grate Rock neere to the brok and soe home to the brok and soe downe the brok as it goeth untill it Cometh unto the spruce tree first mentioned and the other 3 acrees of sd 30 akers lyeth adjoyning unto his other lands on the easterly side of sd Sandwedg Road on the southerly of sd land bounded by sd land on the Northerly syde and on the southerly syde with a red oake tree Marked on 4 sydes standing neere sd Roade and thence Rainging Easterly to another Red oake tree marked and soe home to his other lands

Surveyed and measured by me Thomas ffaunce Surveyor to the Town of plimouth on the day & yeare above Written

An Agreement Made the 25th day of february 169$\frac{2}{3}$ betwen Robert Bartlet & James Warren Respecting the setling of the bounds of their lands betwen them; which are as followeth from a stone sett in the ground on the southermost point of upland Abuting upon the sd Robert Bartletts Meadow & from sd stone Rainging Northerly along by a ditch till it Cometh to the bounds of the meadows belonging unto the sd Robert Bartlet and James Warren & from the bounds first mention Ranging south-easterly to A white oake tree Marked & soe Rainging thence to the meadow And we further Agree that the sd James Warren shall make and maintaine A good sufficient fence from the southermost Corner of his orchard & soe along the meadow syde to A heape of stones on the syde of A hill Against the midle of bogles Cropp soe Caled & from sd heape of stones the said Robert Bartlett is to make and Maintaine likewise a good sufficient fence along his said meadow side to the bounds first mentioned and soe along sd bounds as above Expresed and soe westward to the River and as to the settlement of the bound betwen their lotts begining upon the hill on the Eastermost end of James Warrens house & is bounded up along as follows Begining att two Rocks on the side of a hill neere the sd Robert Bartlets fence and soe Ranging North Easterly to an other Rock nere the fence & soe from sd Rock on the same point to an other Rock neere sd fence and from sd Rock to Raing Easterly to a heape of stones neere sd fence & from sd heape of stones to 3 stones sett into the Ground on a hill nere sd bartlets fence & soe from thence to the Raing as the lotts were formerly settled by; We doe further agree that ye bounds as they are here mentioned shall be binding to us and our heires for ever as Witness our hands and seales on the day and yeare above Mentioned

*Robert Bartlett & James Warren Bounds settled*

            Robert Bartlett
            James Warren

[7.] At a towne Meeting held at plimouth on the 13th of March 1693 for the Choyce of Towne officers for the yeare The Select men Chosen were Isaac Cushman William Shurtly Nathaniel Southworth John Stirtevant and Thomas ffaunce

The Cunstables were Robert Bartlet and Richard Cooper

The Gran Jurors John Nelson Elkana Cushman and Thomas Clarke

The surveyors for the high wayes are Samuel Bradford Samuel ffuller William Ring Benjamen Warren and Edmond Tilson

At this Meeting Thomas ffaunce was Chosen Towne Clerk for the folong yere

The Jurors for the quorter sesions are Nathaniel Wood John Mordo Jonathan Barnes and Joseph Stirtevant

At this meeting the Town voated that the Select Men shall herby have full power to Constitute & make such orders in the Towns behalf as they shall think most likly to prevent the grate stray and Wast that is made of the Timber upon the Comons belonging to the Towne of plimouth

The bounds of the lots betwen Robert Bartlet and Benjamin Warren are as followeth begining at a heape of stones on the southwest syd of the watch house hill soe Caled & soe Rainging to a heape of stones in the land betwen sd lots on the brow of the hill and from thence Rainging as the lotts Run up to an other heap of stones in the lane and from sd bound Rainging to an other heap of stones att the half mile end and soe Rainging as the lotts Run to a heape of stones att the head of the lots and a Red oake tree marked on 4 sides sd tree standeth neere to sd tree standeth neere to sd heap of stones sd bounds are neer the foot of the pine hils

The bounds between the lotts of land belonging to benjamon Warren & James Barnebe are as followeth begining att a heape of stones on the banck nere the River and soe Ranig to a heape of stones in the lane neere where James Barnebes house formerly stood & from thence Rainging on a straite line as the lotts Run to a heape of stons standing att the southeast end of A swampe and from sd heape of stones Rainging as the lotts Run to the head of sd lotts and there bounded with a white oake tree Marked and A heape of stones by sd tree

Att A towne Meeting held at plimouth on the 19th of Aprill 1693 at this meeting The Committie that was Chosen by the Inhabitants of sd Towne to sell some lands in Comonage belonging to the towne of plimouth to defray the Towns Charges Relating to Clarkes Island sd Committie brought in theire account of lands they had sould of sd towns Comon for the End Aforesd and sd account was Redd in said Towne Meeting and after they delivered the overplush of the money to the select men for the towns use and the Towne Approved of theire account and allowed of and Confirmed what they had done therein

At A town Meeting held at plymouth february 12$^{th}$ 169$\frac{2}{3}$ The Inhabitants of sd Towne voated that the Selectmen of sd towne should Indeavour to get A scoolmaster to teach Children to Reade and write & the Inhabitants will take Care to defray the Charge therof att this towne meeting Isaac Cushman William Shurtlif Nathaniel Southworth and Baruck Jordan were Chosen to serve on the Grand Jury att the Superior Court att plimouth in this Instant february & John dotey John Sturtevant Joseph Bartlett James Warren John Mordow John Churchill Ephraim Coole and John Morton these to serve at sd Cort on the petty Jury and Samuell Lucas Ephraim Morton Jonathan barnes Nathaniel holmes and John foster to serve at the Country Cort at March nex after this date

[8.] Wheras We the Select men of the Town of plimouth Whose Names are under written have Received orders from the inhabitants of sd town at the Town Meeting held att plimouth March 13$^{th}$ 169$\frac{2}{3}$ to make such orders in sd towns behalfe for the preservation of the Timber on sd Towns Comons or to Improve it soe as it may be most beneficiall for sd Town

1 In pursuance of sd Towns order We do Agree and order as followeth that from henceforward Noe oak Timber of Any sort Cordwood or bark Cutt on said Towns Comons shall be transported out of sd Town on forfiture of all such Timber Wood or Bark soe Cutt or transported for the us of sd town or ye value of the same from the persons soe Cuting or transporting

2 Wee agree and order that all spruce or pine boards or planck that shall be Cutt of the timber on said Towns Comons and be transported out of said town by any person or persons all such person or persons so doing shall pay to the select or their order for the use of said town one shilling threpence pr thousand for boards or planck soe transported and If any person shall presume to transport any such boards or planck out of sd

town before Account be given and sattisfaction made to the Selectmen or their order for the use of sd town shall forfitt twenty shillings for every thousand soe transported

3 we agree and order that if any person or persons shall make and transport any Ceder Claboards or shingle of timber gotten on said towns Comons shall pay or Cause to be paid to the Selectmen or their order three half pence pr thousand for shingle & 6 pence pr thousand for Claboards and whosoever shall presume to transport or Cause to be transported any shingle or Claboards soe goten before Account be given and sattisfaction made to the Select Men of sd town or their order shall forfitt 12 pence pr thousand for shingle and five shillings pr thousand for Clabords for the use of the said Town

4 wee agree and order that all tarr that is made of knots picked on the Comons of sd town and transported out of said town the owner of said tarr shall pay one peny pr barrell to the select men or their order for the use of the town and whoseever shall presume to transport any such tarr soe made before account be given and the sum be paid to the select men or their order shall forfitt 12 pence pr barrell for the use of the town

5 we agree and order that henceforth Noe Ceder bolts or ffenceing stuff that is Cutt on sd towns Comons shall be transported out of sd town on penalty of forfiting all such bolts & fenceing stuff for the use of the town or the vallue of it

March 22 169$\frac{2}{3}$

    Isaac Cushman
    Nathaniel South
    William Shurtlif
    John Stirtevant
    Thomas ffaunce
The Select men for the town of plimouth

Memorandom

The abovesd orders on the day of the date therof Being publickly Redd before the Justices of the County of plimouth in sessions were approved and allowed by said Justices

    Attests Samuel Sprague Clerk

New plimouth January 26$^{th}$ 169$\frac{3}{4}$ Then Measured twenty five acres of land formerly Granted unto left: Ephraim Morton by the Inhabitants of the Towne of plimouth lying upon A plaine

Comonly Caled and known by the name of [1] Warrens Welss plaine and is bounded as followeth begining at A Red oake tree marked on 4 sides standing on the southerly side of A Cart way that leadeth downe to Josiah phinneyes and from sd tree Rainging southwest and by west one hundred pole and there bounded with A black oake tree marked on 4 sides standing on the brow of a hill on the westerly end of Warrens welles swamp and thence Rainging southeast and by south forty pole and there bounded with a Clumpe of maple bushes and A stake stuck into the Ground neere the brook and bounded by sd brook and thence Rainging Northeast and by East one hundred pole and there bound with A black oake tree marked on 4 sides Measured and bounded on the day and yeare Above Written pr me Thomas ffaunce Surveyor to the Town of plimouth

Ep$^m$ Morton

[9.] New plimouth January 26 169 3/4

Then measured Ten Acrees of land formerly Granted unto Thomas ffaunce by the Inhabitants of the Towne of plimouth upon Warrens wells plaine and is bounded as followeth begining at A black oake tree marked on 4 sides which is the southeast corner bound of leften: Mortons land at the Easterly End of sd land and Raingeth southwest and by west four pole and Adjoynins to left mortons land and is bounded at the head with two black oakes grow out of one stumpe sd trees are marked on 4 sides and thence Rainging south East and by south 20 pole and there bounded with a black oake tree marked on 4 sides and thence Rainging North East and by east four score pole to A forked black oake tree marked on 4 sides Measured and bounded on the day and yeare Above Written pr me Thomas ffaunce Surveyor to the Towne of plimouth and with the helpe of Nathaniel Morton & Thomas Morton

Tho: Faunce

The bounds of James Barnebes lott at the Eale River

---

[1] Warren's Wells was sometimes called Wallen's Wells, "Wells" means "springs," and Wallen is an obsolete word meaning "boiling." There was a "Wallens Wells" near Austerfield, the birthplace of Gov. Bradford.

**James Barnaby** — on the southerly side therof begining at the foot of sd lott and bounded with A heape of stones and from thence Rainging as the lotts Run to a Red oake tree & a heape of stones standing neere the half mile End; and Rainging still on a straite Corse to the head of sd lott and there bounded with A Red oake sapling marked on 4 sides

**Geo: Morton** — february 14th 169¾ Then measured unto George Morton 45 acrees of land lying on A plaine on the southerly side of the Eale River 30 acrees of which was formerly Granted unto left Ephraim Morton and by him given unto ye sd George Morton as by his will doth appear the other 15 acrees was Granted unto him the said George Morton by the Inhabitants of the Town as pr town Record doth ape sd land is bounded as followeth begining at a white oake tree Marked on 4 sides and thence Rainging south southwest six score pole to A Red oake tree Marked on 4 sides and thence Rainging South South East 60 pole to a black oake tre marked on 4 sides and thence Rainging Northnortheast 6 score pole and ther bounded with A white oake tree on 4 sides marked Surveyed measured and bounded on the day and yeare Above Ritten pr me Thomas ffaunce Surveyor to the Towne of plimouth

**Nath¹ Harlow** — ffebruary 14th 169¾ Then Measured unto Nathaniel harlow 15 acrees of land formerly Granted unto Serjant William harlow by the Inhabitants of the Towne lying on that plaine where left Mortons land lyeth and Adjoyneth to it and is bounded as followeth begining at George Mortons southeast Corner bound which is A white oake tree marked on 4 sides and from thence Rainging south southeast 50 pole and ther bound with A white oake tree Marked on 4 sides and from thence Rainging South southwest 40 pole and there bounded with A white sapling marked on 4 sides & from sd bound Rainging Nornorwest 50 pole and there bounded with A white oake tree marked on 4 sides standing on the side Rainge of George Mortons land Above mentioned Measured and bounded on the day and yeare above Mentioned

pr mee Thomas ffaunce
Surveyor to the Towne of plimouth

plimouth March 19th 169¾

Lucas & Ring

Then Reconed with Samuel lucas and Eleazar Ring the Cunstables of sd towne in the year 1692 of Rates Committed to them to gather in sd yeare and there is still due to the Towne from sd Cunstables 02=05=00 which is sumthing doutfull whether it will be gotten of those that were to pay it. The account was taken by the select men of the Town the day and year above Mentioned

[10.] At a towne Meeting held att plimouth March 10$^{th}$ 169$\frac{3}{4}$ by the Inhabitants of sd towne at this meeting they voated that Thomas ffaunce should still continew in the place & office of their towne Clerk for this present yeare att this Meeting the Inhabitants made Choyce of towne officers for the yeare ensuing which are as followeth for the Select men were Chosen Isaac Cushman William Shurtlef and Thomas ffaunce for Cunstables Were Chosen Giles Rickard Junior & John ffoster The ffence vewers were John dotey George Bonam Junior & James Warren The persons Chosen to se to the due observation of the law Relating to horses are Thomas & Benoney Lucas The Surveyors Chosen are John Gray William Ring Jonathan Shaw Junior & Nathaniel Morton

At this Meeting Isaac Cushman in the balf of him self and severall other of the proprietors of Jones River Meaddows Requested liberty of the towne for the Conveniencey of fencing their meaddows there to sett their fences straite though it tuck in som points of upland which Request was granted to them by said towne

John Stirtevant refuceth to serve the Towne in the service

At a town meeting held at plimouth on the 30 of Aprill 1694 by the inhabitants therof at this meeting John Sturtevant was Chosen by the Major part of the voters ther present to serve for and Represent them in the Grat and General Court ap * to begun and held at bostorn on the thirth of May one thousand six hundred ninty 4

At this Meeting Elkanah Cushman Nathaniel Wood &

Samuel Harlow were Chosen to the office of [1] Tithing men for this present yeare

At this Meeting George Bonam senior in the behalf of himself and several other of the propriators of the meadows at the South meaddows Requested liberty of the town for the Convenience of the fenceing their meaddows there to sett their fence straite although it took in some points of upland that are Common which Request was Granted to them by said town

att this meeting the Town declared themselves to be against Warning town meetings by set papers up for that end but doe Expect warning from the Cunstables by word of mouth when Ever there shall be ocasion for town meetings

At A town Meeting held at plimouth on the 14th day of May 1694 the Towne made Choyce of William Shurtlif to serve for and Represent them in the General Court at boston on the 30 of May 1694

At this Towne Meeting the Inhabitants of sd towne mad Choice of Isaac Cushman Thomas ffaunce and James Warren to be A Committee to settle Matters of differance betwe persons Respecting theire bounds or Rainges between them as there May be ocasion for their helpe *

At this Town Meting the Towne Granted unto Isaac Ring flifty acrees of land lying on the Westward side of a brook

---

[1] After the union of the Colonies a law was passed by the General Court of Massachusetts, in 1692, requiring tithing men to be chosen in every town, and their duties were specified as follows:—

"All and every person and persons whatever shall on the Lord's day carefully apply themselves to duties of religion and piety publicly and privately, and no tradesman, artificer, laborer or other person whatever shall upon the land or otherwise do or exercise any labor business or work of their ordinary callings, nor engage in any game, sport, play, or recreation on the Lord's day, or any part thereof (works of necessity and charity only excepted) upon penalty that every person so offending shall forfeit five shillings.

No traveller, drover, horse courser, wagoner, butcher, higler (poultry dealer, Ed..) or any of their servants shall travel on that day or any part thereof except by some adversity they were belated and forced to lodge in the woods, wilderness or highways the night before and in such case to travel no further than the next inn or place of shelter upon the penalty of twenty shillings.

No vintner, innholder or other person keeping any public house of entertainment shall encourage or suffer any of the inhabitants of the respective towns where they dwell or others not being strangers or lodgers in such houses to abide or remain in their houses, yards, orchards or fields drinking or idly spending their time on Saturday night after the sun is set or on the Lord's day, or the evening following.

All and every justice of the peace, constable and tithing man are required to take care, that this act in all the particulars thereof, be duly observed, as also to restrain all persons from swimming in the water and unnecessary and unreasonable walking in the streets or fields."

In 1698 their powers were extended to the inspection of licensed houses and the preservation of good order during the week as on the Lord's day, and the Selectmen were required to provide them with a black staff two feet in length, tipped at one end with brass.

Comonly Caled and Known by the name of Wesatuckit brook; which sd brook Runeth down by the sd Isaac Rings Now dweling house sd fifty acres of land with all and singular the proffitts priviledges and appurtenances therunto belongin or any wise appertaining is granted unto the above named Isaac Ring to him and his heires and assignes for ever

The bounds of the fifty acres of land granted by the Towne of plimouth unto Isaac Ring is as followeth the south East Corner thereof is bounded with A gore of the sd Isaac Rings meaddows and from thence Rainging Norwest thirty and four rod to a white oake tree marked with a heape of stones by it and from thence Rainging southwest to a white oake tree Marked with a heape of stones by it and from thence Rainging southeast to a Rock by the meadow sid    Surveyed and measured by
Isaac Cushman Survor

[11.] *James & Benj.ª Warren* — An agrement Made between James Warren and Benjamin Warren both of plimouth; on the first day of May 1694 with Referance to the settlement of the bounds betwen theire meaddows and uplands at the beach head bounds betwen the sd James Warrens upland and the sd Benjamen Warrens Meaddow there is as followeth begining at a heape of stones & a stake nere the sand bank & from thence Rainging to the southward to a stake and a heap of stones standing at the Edge of the meddow and from thence Rainging westwards to a stake and A heape of stones by it standing neere the River and from thence uppon a straite Corse down to the River

*John Barrows* — The bounds of John Barrows Meaddow Given to him by his Grandfather George Bonam Senior lying at the south meddows att the ffalls is as followeth bounded with A maple Tree at the South Corner leaning over the River and from thence to A pine tree Marked and from thence to A spruce tree marked which is the bounds of the land as well as of the meaddow

The 9$^{th}$ of Aprill 1684 Then laid out to John Barrows at the south meaddows ten acrees of upland Against his Meddow on the Norwest side of the Rever ye southerly bounds is A spruce tree standing neere the Meadow and on the Norwest Corner

Rainging to a pine tree Marked and bounded and soe up the meadow to a Red oake tree marked neere the meadow and his northerly bounds is a Red oake tree marked on 4 sides all fformer Cart wayes allowed to mens meadows surveyed and measured on the day and yeare Above Written pr me Isaac Cushman one of the surveyors of the town of plimouth

On the 9th of Aprill 1694 laid out to George Bonam 10 acrees of upland at the south meadows that is to say 5 acrees on the Easterly side of his meadows & 5 acrees on the westerly side of his meaddows The Easterly land bounded lying to the Eastward of the 'way that goeth to the Ceder bridge the southerly bound marke is A grate stone neer the bridge and soe Easterly to A grate oake tree Marked on 4 sides & northerly to A pine tree marked westerly to a pine tre marked on 4 sides 5 Acrees Bounded beginning at A Red oake tree the bounds betwen Jonathan Barnes and him Runing downe by his meaddows to A white oake that is betwen Nathaniel Wood and he to A pine tree Marked on the wester side or Corner and soe to A pine tree at the Norwest End or Corner both of them Marked on 4 sides All Cart wayes Allowed to mens meadows Measured and bounded on the day and yeare above written pr me Isaac Cushman surveyor to the town of plimouth

On the 9th of Aprill 1694 then laid out to nathaniel Wood ten Acrees of upland Against his Meaddows at the south Meadows the bounds at the Northeast end is A pine tree that is betwen him and Robert Barrows and soe Runeth down alonge the meaddows side and is bounded at the southerly Corner with A pine tree Marked on four sids and towards the Norwest Corner A pine tree marked on 4 sides Al Cart wayes allowed to mens Meadows Measured and bound pr me Isaac Cushman surveyor

On the 9th of Aprill 1694 laid out to William Ringe 10 acres of upland neere his meadows at the south Meadows & is bounded as followeth begining att A white oake tree which is bounded betwen George Morton and he and soe along his meaddows southerly to a Red oake tree Marked neere the Meaddows and soe westerly to A grate pine tree marked and at the norwest Corner to A pine tree marked on 4 sides al formen Cart wayes allowed to mens meadows Measured and bounded pr me Isaac Cushman surveyor

[12.] On the 9th of Aprill 1694 Then laid out to Jonathan Barnes at the south meadows 10 acres of upland on the southwest syde of his meadow and is bounded as followeth begining nere Barnes bridge soe Called and bounded with a Red oake tree Marked on 4 sides and soe upward alonge by the afore sd barnses meadow towards the North and bounded with A Red oake tree Marked on 4 sides by the meadow and from that to the southwest Corner to a Red oake tree Marked on 4 sides and soe southerly to a pine tree marked on 4 sides all old Cart wayes to mens meadows allowed Measured and bounded for Isaac Cushman surveyors

On the 9$^{th}$ of Aprill 1694 On the day and yeare above Mentioned Then laid out to Abram Jackson senior at the south meadows 10 acrees of Med Adjoyning to his meadows there on the southerly side of that meadow Comonly Caled polopoda Cove and bounded with a pine tree standing neere the meadow and soe toward the norwest to a white oake tree marked & soe towards the southwesterly marked with A pine tree Marked on 4 sides.

And the other tenn acrees of upland laid out to the sd [1] Abram Jackson upon the account of secratary Mortons Interest these said ten acrees of land above said is laid out on the northeast side of his meadow & is bounded as followeth at the south end with A pine tree marked; the westerly bounded with a Red oake tree nere the meadows betwen Eliazar Ringe and him Rainging Northerly to a Red oake sapling Marked & soe Rainging Easterly to a Rock All former Carts wayes allowed on to mens meadows Measured and boundid pr Isaac Cushman surveyor

At a towne meeting held at plimouth on the 30$^{th}$ day of July 1694

The assessors then Chosen to make the provence Rate were Isaac Cushman William Shurtlef and Thomas ffaunce

At A Town Meeting held at plimouth december 17$^{th}$ 1694 at this Meeting a small [2] Tract of land was Granted to George bonam senior lying on the souther side of the Town brook Adjoyning to his fuling Mill being an acree or thereabouts be it more or less sd land is Granted to him th sd George Bonam and to his heires for Ever sd land is bounded as followeth up streame bounded next the Grist Mill with a bush and A heape of stones by it neere the brook side and from sid bound up the banke to a stone sett into the Ground and from thence to an other stone set

---

[1] Abraham Jackson married Remember, daughter of Nathaniel Morton, the Secretary of Plymouth Colony.
[2] This acre of land extended from what is now called Robinson Street to the Brook.

in to the Ground neere to the Rainge of lands belonging to the heires of Elkanah Watson late of plimouth deceased and soe along that Rainge till it Cometh to a stone set into the Ground and from sd bound to Extend downwards towards the sd town brook on the Easterly syde of A gutter that leadeth towards sd brook and soe to the Taile of the sd fulling Mill

[13.] September 1692

The bounds of the Easterly end of Jones river Meaddows was settled by Isaac Cushman surveyor of the town of plimouth which is as followeth Mer Joseph Bradfords meadow on the Easterly side is bounded by the brook the bounds betwen Mer Joseph Bradford and John Gray on the south side of the Meadow is a Red oake tree standing on a side of a hill Neere the Meaddow Marked on 4 sides & soe Runing over the meadow to the aforesd brook on the Northerly side; on Northeast side of sd brook to an ash pole standing Neere the Brook Marked on 4 sides.

The bounds betwen John Grey & Samuel ffuller on the south side of the meaddow is a Red oak tree standing on the side of a hill Neere the meaddow Marked on 4 sides and soe Rainging over to the North side of ye Meadow to a white oake tree standing by the Meaddow side Marked on 4 sides and all the swampe that doth fall within this line from those two fore mentioned bounds belong to John Grey to make up his lot of meadow The bounds betwen Samuel ffuller and Caleb Cook on the South side of the meaddow is a white oak Sapling standing on the side of a hill Neere the Meaddow Marked on 4 sides and so Runing over to the Northside of the Meaddow to a Red oake tree Marked on 4 sides and all the swampe that doth fall within this line from those two fore mentioned bounds belong to Samuel ffuller to make up his lot of Meadow The bounds betwen Caleb Cook and Major William Bradford on the south side of the Meaddow is a Red oake tree standing on the side of a hill Neere the Meaddow Marked on 4 sides & so Runing over to the North side of the meadow to a white oake tree standing by the meaddow side Marked on 4 sides and all the swamp that doth fall within this line from these two fore mentioned bounds belonge to Caleb Cook to make up his lot of meadow The bounds betwen Major william Bradford and Isaac Cushman on the south side of the meadow is a Red oake tree staning on the side of a hill A good distance from the Meaddow Marked on 4 sides and soe

Runing over to the North side of the Meadow to A Red oake tree that is the bound betwen John Gray and Jacob Cook which is Marked 4 sides The bounds betwen Eliazar Cushman and Isaac Cushman on the south side of the Meaddow is a Walnut tree standing on the side of a hill by a hole of Water and soe Runing over the Meaddow till it Cometh to a lettle Iland or hummuck of land to a white oake tree Marked on 4 sides that was the bounds betwen Isaac Cushman & John Grey of John Greys uper lot of Meaddow

Settled by Isaac Cushman Survey<br>to the Town of plimouth

The bounds of the 3 acrees of land that Richard Cooper bought of Joseph Dunham are as foloth (viz) on the northeast Corner with a heape of stones at the head of the widdo sarah woods lot & from thence Runing westerly to a Red oak sappling & a heape of stones and from thence southerly to a black oake tree & a heape of stones & from thence Easterly to a Red oake tree & a grat stone sett an End & from thence Rainging Northerly upon a straite line to ye first bounds at ye head of the widow sarah woods lot;

[14.] New plimouth ffebruary 5$^{th}$ 169$\frac{4}{5}$

A Record of a Road or highWay laid out by the select men of the town of plimouth whose names are under Written for the Conveniencey of the neighborhood at Monoment ponds sd high Way is bounded as ffolloweth up the lane towards the ponds through the lands of Robert bartlet and benjamen Warren to the head of sd lane as the fence is now sett and from the head of sd lane to Run as their lotts Raing up leaveing ten foott of Each lot above Expressed throughout the length of sd lotts for the high way abovesd and above the head of lane is bounded as ffolloweth bounded upon Benjamen Warren's land with a walnut tree & A heape of stones by it and on Robert bartlets land opposate agans the sd walnut tree is a heape of stones sd bounds are nere to Robert bartlets barne and from sd bounds up to the half mile bounds of sd lotts and there bounded with a walnut tree on Each side and a heape of stones by them twenty foott of land long betwen sd boundereys and from thence up to the head of the lotts abovesd and there bounded with a Red oake tree standing on Roberts side and a heape of stones on benjamens

*Road to Monument ponds.* side and from sd bounds up along the path to sd ponds as the path Now goeth untill it Cometh To Thomas Clarks and from sd Thomas Clarks up along the lane to Samuel Riders house and then up by Samuel Riders house along till it Cometh to the Beaver dam path and up that path till it Cometh where the path terns out to Joseph Bartlets house and at the Turne of the path bounded with a Red oake tree on the Northward side and a heape of stones on the southward side and soe up the path till it Cometh to the Brook by sd Joseph Bartlets house

Bounded on the day & yeare above<br/>Mentioned by Isaac Cushman<br/>William Shurtliff<br/>Thomas ffaunce

At a towne Meeting held at plimouth March $6^{th}$ $1694/5$ at this Meeting liberty Was Granted to Caleb Cook and John Gray to fence their land at Rockenook downe to low water Mark upon Condition that Joseph Howland may have free passage through theire lands out of Rockey Nook up to the highway

At this Meeting The Town Granted to Thomas Lazel six acrees of land on the southerly side of his land at Colchester, upon Condition that the said Lazel leave a sufficient Road for the Neighbours to pas through his land there where the way Now goeth up towards Wenatuxet Meadows

at this Meeting The Towne gave liberty to ockanutas to sel a tract of land unto Jonathan Morey Junior lying upon the Clifts towards Sandwich which sd land he saith he bought of old Skepeunk

At this Meting A tract of land was granted to Isaac Cushman lying on the Northward sid of Thomas Lazell and on the northward sid by the way that goeth to Colchester swamp and on the westward sid by the land formerly granted unto Mer Thomas Cushman

[15.] Att a Town Meeting held at plimouth on the $29^{th}$ day of March 1695 ffor the Choyce of Towne officers for sd yeare which are as followeth The Select Men for sd yeare are

Joseph Bartlet senior<br/>John Waterman<br/>John Mordo

The Towne Clerke is Thomas ffaunce
The assessors for to make the Rats are
Joseph Bartlet senior
John Waterman
John Sturtevant
The Cunstables are Caleb Cooke and James Warren The surveyors for the high waies are
Left John Bryant
Elkanah Cushman
Nathaniel Wood
Josiah flinney
William Harlow
Jonathan Shaw Junior

At this Meeting the Town made Choyce of Major Bradford Left John Bradford Isaac Cushman William Shurtlef John Nelson & Thomas ffaunce A Comitty to Consider of and draw up such argements as may be of use to defend the Towns Right on the North sid of the Towne

Att A Towne Meeting held at plimouth on the 6[th] of May 1695 Mer John Bradford was Chosen Representative to act for sd towne and in their behalfe at the grat & Generall Cort at bostern voted that the Select men Shall take Spedy and efectuall Care for the Reparation of the Meting house and have liberty to make a Rate on the Inhabitants for to defray the Charge therof

At this meting the town granted unto Mer Nathaniel Thomas Junior the boggey land on the North side of the [1] Town brook from the fuling Mill to extend downe streame soe low as noe wais to prejudice the Comfortable passage of people throug sd town brook at the usuall way of going over; with Carts and horses as also liberty to sett the fulling Mill lower down upon the streame provided ye sd Nathaniel Thomas doth not hender the Alwives going up the brook by his sd mill at the seasons of their going up voted that there should be a town Meting on the 2[d] Mundday of June Next Ensuing for to se whether the towne Can Agree as to a division of sd towns Comons

[16.] At a Town Meeting held at plimouth on the tenth of June 1695 The towne Made Choyce of Major Bradford Lefton; Mory Isaac Cushman Will Shurtlif Joseph Bartlet William Clarke

---

[1] The Fulling Mill stood on the North side of Town Brook South of what is now called Mill Lane.

James Warren John Nelson Nathaniel Southworth John Mordo &
Thomas ffaunce to be a Comittie to give in their Reaseins why
the Remote Inhabitants of plimouth should not have their petition
granted them

And whereas there was divers orders made and agreed on
by the select men of the towne in the yeare $1693\frac{2}{3}$ for to prevent
the grate stroy of timber on the towns Comons and said orders
were allowed on by ye Justices in sessions then sitting at this
meeting the towne made choyce of persons to se these laws put in
Execution the persons Chosen are Capt Joseph Howland
Nathaniel Southworth John doty Elkanah Cushman M$^r$ Will:
Clarke John Mordo William Shurtlef and Joseph Bartlet senior

The bounds of the Meaddow of Mer Joseph Bradford
att Wenatuxet in the Township of plimouth is as followeth on the
southestward end with the bounds of Captain Thomas Southworth
deceased And att the Northwest End one the Northerly Corner
with a pine stump & a heape of stones by it and thence Rainging
Westward to a stake and a heape of stones by it and all the
meaddow that lyeth on both sides of [1] Whetstones vinyard brook
until an other brook Meeteth with sd brook is to belonge to sd lott

The bounds of the Meddow of John Cook at Wenatuxet
in the Township of plimouth which is as followeth That the
bounds of the sd Cooks Meaddow on the southeastward End is
bounded with the bounds of sd bradfords Meadow and att the
Northwestward End of sd Cooks Meadow att the Northward
Corner is A white oake Marked standing by a swampe which is
the bounds betwext sd Cooks and John dunhams meadow All
which bounds are Renued by Isaac Cushman surveyor To sd
Towne on the 27$^{th}$ of June 1695.

At A Towne Meeting held at plimouth february 5$^{th}$ $1695\frac{5}{6}$
An acount of Charges to be leaved by Rate on the Inhabitants of
the Towne for the defraying Towne Charges which was allowed
of at sd meeting which is as follows

| | |
|---|---|
| To John Bradford | 05—14—08 |
| for the seting the Grate Guns on Carriges | 06—00—00 |
| for the Cunstables Wages for gathering the Rates | 00—15—00 |

---

[1] This is Weston's vineyard brook probably named after Edward Weston who lived in that neighborhood.

| | |
|---|---|
| to James Warren 3 shillings to Josiah phiney | |
| for Keeping nan Ramsden | 01—05—00 |
| for Joseph Bartlet for Keeping Nan Ramsden | 06—00—00 |
| for Care for nan Ramsden | 01—10—00 |
| To Thomas Clarke for service on the Grand Jurey | 00—12—06 |
| To Elkanah Cushman | 00—15—00 |
| To Mer Bartlet | 01—15—00 |
| To John Sturtevant | 00—15—00 |
| To Mer John Mordo | 06—02—00 |

[17.] The bounds of the Meadows of Capt: Thomas Southworth deceased At Wenatuxet being formerly laid out by leftenant Ephraim Morton and Now Renewed which are as followeth on the northward side of the River at the Eastward Corner bounded with a white oake tree marked on 4 sides and thence Runing southward Crossing the River to a grate white oake tree Marked on 4 sides and at the westward Corner on the southward side of the River with a stake standing neere the upland and so Runing Northward Crossing sd River to a small white oake Marked on 4 sides May the 28th 1695

pr Isaac Cushman<br>Surveyor for the towne<br>of plimouth

Whereas the Court Granted unto [1] Mer John darbe deceased in ye yeare of our lord 1637 three acrees of land at Munks Hill in the towneship of plimouth Therefore the land Granted to sd darbe is laid out Neere to sd place and is bounded as followeth at the Northwest Corner with a white oak with a heape of stones by it sd tree is marked on 4 sides standing on the southward side of the highway that goeth from Nicks Rock to Lakingham and thence Runeth westward twelve score pole along sd way to a pine tree Marked on 4 sides with a heape of stons by it and thence Runing forty Rod to a pine tree Marked on four sides and thence Runing Eastward twelve score Rod to a pine tree Marked on 4 sides with a heape of stones by it and thence

---

[1] This is John Derby from whose family Derby or Darby Pond derives its name.

Rainging Northward forty pole to the boundery first named Measured and bounded on this 12th of June 1695

pr Isaac Cushman surveior to the<br>Towne of plimouth

May 28th 1695 laid out to Thomas Lazel six acrees of land on the southward side of Coulchester Brook and Joyneth to the land of the said Lazell and is bounded as ffolloweth on the Eastward Corner with a white oake tree marked on four sides standing by a Rock thence Rainging southward twelve Rood to a Red oak Marked on 4 sides and thence Runing Westward Eighty Rod to a Red oak tree Marked on 4 sides and thence Rainging Northward twelve Rod to a Chrocched Red oake standing nere to the said brook and Marked on 4 sides with sufficent allowance for a highway for the neighborhood

Measured and bounded by<br>Isaac Cushman surveior<br>To the towne of plimouth on the day<br>and year above Rit

[18.] Att a towne Meeting held at plimouth on the 15th of July 1695

upon Notice given at sd Meeting That Mer John Wodsworth and Mer Samuel Sprague were to Come to Run a dividing line betwen the sd towne and oure Remote Inhabitants on the westermost part of sd towne The Towne Made Choyce of Major Bradford left John Bradford Ephraim Morton John dotey and James Warren to meet these Gentlemen & to Request them Not to Run aney line in our township untill the Generall Cort are more thoroughly Enformed of our Circumstances with Refferance to our lands in that part of our towneship but if those Gentlemen se Canse still to Goe on in Runing sd line then to oppose them in their proceedings therein

at said Meeting abovesd John Nelson Giles Rickard Junior & John ffoster were Chosen to be tithing men for this present yeare

At said meeting William Shurtlef was Chosen Towne Treasurer

At a towne Meeting held at plimouth on the 29th of July 1695 at this Meeting the Inhabitants of sd towne Made Choyce of Major Bradford John Bradford Ephraim Morton John dotey and James Warren together with the towne Clerk to draw up and present to the Generall Court the towns Reasons why they did Reques the Gentlemen to forbeare Runing the devideing line at the present

At this Meeting William Shurtlif was Chose Comisioner to act with the Rators in making ye provence Rate Also at this Meeting M$^{er}$ William Clarke Isaac Cushman & Ephraim Morton were Chosen to make the Rate for the minister and for the defraying of all other towne Charges

At a towne Meeting held at plimouth on the 2$^d$ of September 1695 ordered that the Rators should make a Rate of 85 pound for the maintenance of the Ministry for the present yeare M$^{er}$ Cotton Considering the grat Charges lying on the Inhabitants of said Towne Consents thereunto

At this Meeting M$^{er}$ John Mordo John dotey Giles Rickard John Stirtevant and William Ring were Chose to serve on the pety Jury at the County Cort

At a towne meeting held at plimouth on the 16$^{th}$ of december 1695 at sd Meeting it was voated by the Inhabitants of sd towne that the Justiceses of the County should be Informed of sd townes Request that ye Road over Jones River might be where travelors doe Now usally pass & doe Request and appoint M$^{er}$ John Bradford and John Nelson to acquaint sd Justices with sd townes desire

The Jurors Chosen to serve at the County Court were Eleazar Churchill John Churchill John Rickard Ephraim Coole Samuel Lucas John Carver & John Churchill

at sd Meeting Left John Bradford doth Engage to said towne that in Case the County Court doe allow of the Turning the Road over Jones Rever That the Towne shall Not be Charged with the purchase of the way that may goe through aney mans land by the Turning sd way At sd meeting John Rickard was Granted the land on which his Whorfe now standeth and liberty to whorfe in breadth and length against his own ware hous leaveing sufficent Roome for Carts Convenintly to pass along the shore

[19.] Att the Towne Meeting last Mentioned The Towne Granted to William Shurtlef and Ephraim Coole to Each of them 30 foott of land square under the hill Northward from M$^{er}$ bartlets warehouse by the waterside with liberty to buld a Narrow

PLYMOUTH RECORDS.   241

whorfe from sd land into the sea alowing Convenient Rome for Carts to pass along the shore

Att a Towne Meeting held att plimouth on the second of March 169$\frac{5}{8}$ ffor the Choyce of Towne officers for said yeare as also for the Choyce of Jurors to serve at the Grand assise are William Shurtlif Ephraim Morton Samuel Rider Nathaniel Morton and John dotey At this meeting Thomas faunce was Chosen to be Town Clerk The persons to serve on the pety Jurey at sd Court are John Nelson Leftan Bryant Nathaniel Southworth M$^{er}$ John Mordo & Elkanath Cushman and for the quarter sessions the grand Jurors are George Morton William Ring Eleasar Ring and John ffoster and the Jurors of Tryals are M$^{er}$ William Clarke John Waterman Nathaniel Holmes John ffoster Samuel Stirtevant & Robert Bartlet The Surveyors for the high wayes are Nathaniel holmes Joseph Bartlet Junior Abram Jacson Samuel Bradford and Eliazar Jacson The Select Men are M$^{er}$ William Clarke John Ricord Junor & Thomas ffaunce The Cunstables are Josiah finney & Nathaniel Jacson William Shurtlif Chosen towne Treasurror Joshua pratt Eliazar Cushman & Jonathan Shaw Junior Chosen to be Tithing Men

At this Meeting it was ordered and agreed upon by the Inhabitants of the Towne that Every householder should kill 12 black birds and bring theire heads to persons appointed by the Towne to Receive the Tale betwen the Middle of Aprill & The last of May next Ensuing & those that Neglect to kill theire proportion as above sd shall pay a fine of 3 shillings for the use of the town to be leaveyed upon them in their Rates The Men appointed to Beceive the Tale of the birds are deacon Thomas Clarke Benjamen Warren William Shurtlif John Waterman John Gray Jonathan Shaw Junior

October 17$^{th}$ 1696 Then laid out and bounded unto William Shurtlif and Ephram Coole the land granted by the Town in this page above Mentioned; Northward from M$^{er}$ Bartlets hous A Considerable distance and there bounded out to William Shurtlif 30 fott of land in breadth on the front next the sea; where its bounded with two stakes drove into the ground and is to Extend in length from sd stakes 30 foot up towards the banck and leaveing of ten foott of Comon there is staked out to Ephraim Coole 30 foot of land still Northward from the sd William Shirtlifs land before mentioned and to Extend as afore

16

sd in length 30 ffott upwards from the sea towards the banck; surveyed and bounded out on the day and yeare herein last above mentioned pr Me Thomas ffaunce surveyor to the town of plimouth

[20.] This Inderture Made the 19th of March 169⅘ betwen John Gray and Caleb Cook on the one party & Capt Joseph Howland of the other party all of the towne of plimouth in New England Witneseth That whereas the Inhabitants of sd towne of plimouth att a Towne meeting held at plimouth on the 6th of March 169⅘ Granted liberty to us ye said Gray and Cooke to Run our fences at the foot of our lots downe to low water Marke upon Condition that the sd Capt Howland have liberty of free passage through our lands through Gates or barrs from his house att Rockenoock up to the Comon Roade upon which Consideration we the abovesd gray and Cooke have upon the day and yeare above Mentioned agreed upon and bounded oute A way from the sd Capt Howland through our lands up to the Comon Roade of Twenty foot in breadth The bounds thereof are as foloweth Regining at the sd howlands house & bounded on sd Cooks land on Each side sd way with a heape of stones and soe along sd way on sd Cooks land to a Red oake tree and a heape of stones on the south side thereof opposite to sd tree and from thence Rainging to a Rock on the one side and a heape of stones on the other on the southerly syde of sd Rock and soe to a walnut Tree and a heape of stones on the south side opposite against it and from thence to a white oake tree and a heape of stones on the Eastward side and soe to the End of the birch swampe and there bounded with a Rock on Each side of the way and stones laid about them and from thence to two Rocks more and heaps of stones about them and soe to a white oake Tree and a heap of stones on the south side opposite to sd tree and soe Right from sd Rock to a heape of stones in sd grayes land on the Northerly side of a white Rock and soe to an other Rock and a heape of stones on the south side of sd Rock and soe to the Top of a hill and there bounded with a heape of stones on Each side of sd way and from thence to the Comon Road and there bounded with a heape of stones on Each side of sd way Memorandom it is to be understood that this way thus bounded oute as aforesd is twenty foot in breadth through the whole length and the sd Capt Howland is to make by this Agrement and Maintaine the fence

from the bound tree betwen sd Cooke and Howland downe to low
water Marke and to Maintaine a Cart Gate on sd allowed way
before his owne dore and another upon sd way betwen sd grayes
land and Caleb Cooks and said Capt Ho vland both Engadge to
keepe within the boundereyes herin above Mentioned and agreed
upon to be for his Convenient Egres & Regress from his own
land to the Comon Road and the sd Caleb Cook is to make and
Maintaine A sufficent fence from high water Marke in the Rainge
betwen sd Cook and Gray down into the sea & att the Roade the
sd John Gray is from time to time to maintaine a Cart gate on
sd way from sd Capt Howland and the sd John Gray is to make
and Maintaine the out side fence into the sea and where Either
the said Cooke or Gray shall see it will be for their Conveniencey
they have liberty att their own Charge to set up Gates upon sd
way and the sd Capt Howland doth promise for him selfe his
heires or assignes that they haveing free pass along sd way above
Expresed will for Ever quitt all Claim of wais formerly laid oute
for sd Howland by the water side through the sd Grayes and
Cooks land And In Witnes of our Joyent Concorrance and
Agreement as to the settling and bounding out sd way and as to
observation of the particulars above Expresed we the sd Capt
Joseph Howland John Gray and Caleb Cook doe by These presents
bind ourselves our heires Executors and assignes for Ever as
Witnes our hands and seales on the day and yeare first above
written

                                                                     Joseph Howlands seale O
     signed sealed and declared    John Grayes    seale O
     to be our Joyent agreement In   Caleb Cooks    seale O
     presence of
        Benjamen Lumbert
        Abiall Shurtlif

[21.] The bounds of ye lands of severall of the Neighboures
on the south side of the Towne of plimouth as they were ordered
by the Court to be laid out & Bounded by Capt Southworth &
George Watson as followeth The bounds Betwen the lands of Left
Ephraim Morton and the lands of Thomas Morton are as
ffolloweth viz: it begins att the Eastermost Corner of a stone
wall below and soe Raingeth up into the woods on a southwest
line half A point southerly twelve score pole more or less unto a
black oake tree Marked with E M on the Northerly side & with
T M on the southerly side On the 25$^{th}$ of March 1696 the Rainge

betwen the lots above Mentioned was Run by Thomas ffaunce Giles Rickard Junior Nathiel Morton and Samel Cornish and is settled as ffolloweth viz begining below where the two stone wales mete and from thence Rainging up on the southerly side of the stone wall southwest half A point southerly bounded with severall heapes of stones in sd Rainge betwixt the foot bound and the head of the field and att the head of the field Neere the Corner of the old head ditch is a heape of stones and from said heape of stones Rainging up still on the same point and bounded by severall Rainge trees Marked and soe Extendeth up to the black oake tree above mentioned to be the Raingen bounds betwen sd lots

The bounds betwen the lands or lots between Nathaniel Morton and the Children of Josiah Morton late of plimouth deceased are as followeth viz bounded below with a heape of stones Neere the fence and soe Rainging southwest half a poynt southerly up into the woods bounded with severall heapes of stones in said Rainge soe far as the head of the fields and then bounded by severall Bainge trees untill it Cometh to the head of the lots and there bounded with A white oake sapling and a heape of stones which is the head bound betwen said lotts

The bounds betwen the lots of Nathaniel and Thomas Morton are as followeth viz bounded below Nere the seaside with A heape of stones and from thence Raingeth southwest halfe a point southerly up into the woods and bounded with severall heapes of stones in sd Rainge soe farr as the head of the feilds and from thence bounded by severall Rainge trees Marked: up to the heads of said lots and there bounded with a stake and a heape of stones

The Bounds betwen The lots of George Morton and Thomas Mortons lot are as followeth vis : its Agreed upon by said George Morton & the said Thomas Morton that the brook shall be the bounds between theire lots from A flat Rock with a heap of stones on it at the head of the brook and soe downe sd brook to the fot of their sd lands and att the head of said brook to Extend from sd flat Rock Neere two poli southeasterly to A heape of stones upon the hill side and from sd heape of stones to Range southwest half a point southerly up into the woods and bounded with severall heapes of stones in sd Rainge belowe and up in the woods with severall Rainge trees Marked ; up to the head of sd lotts and the Corner bound betwen said lotts is A Red oake sapling Marked on 4 sides and A heape of stones by sd sapling

[**22.**] The bounds betwen the lots of George Morton and Joseph Churchill are as followeth viz: bounded Neere the foot of sd lotts with a walnut tree on the southerly or southeasterly Corner of the sd Joseph Churchils stone wall by his orchard sd tree is marked on fouer sides and A heape of stones by sd tree and Raingeth from sd tree southwest half a point southerly up into the woods and bounded by severall Rainge trees marked; in sd Rainge and at the head of said Joseph Churchill lot next to wobery feilds is bounds with a forked Red oake tree marked on foure sides with a heape of stones by sd tree which is the bound between the sd Mortons lots and the said Churchils lot soe far as the said Churchils lot Raingeth with said Mortons lotts

The lots above Mentioned were Rainged bounded and in breadth Measured on the 25th and 26th dayes of March 1696 by Thomas ffaunce surveyore To the Towne of Plimouth

Each lott specifyed in page 21 & 22 are twenty pole in breadth to one single lott

At a Town Meeting Held at plimouth June 29th 1696 at sd Meeting it was ordered by the Town That the [1] uper society should have the schoolmaster the Next quortor & the 3d quortor to Remove to the Eelerever & the 4th quorter to Remove Noo further Northward in sd Town for settlement to keepe scoole Then John Greyes

At sd Meeting The Towne voted that five pounds should be allowed towards the payment for the Care of Mr hunters Wife Now under the doctors hands and also the Towne Agreed with John Nelson To Keep Nan Ramsden one yeare for five pounds & to furnish her at the Expiration of sd yeare with Cloathing as good as Now shee hath and whereas John Churchill senior late of plimouth deceased has a grant of land at ponds of fifty Acres & that grant Now faling to John Churchill and he haveing often solicited The Town for liberty to Remove sd grant to some other place; upon which at this Meeting The Town granted liberty to the sd John Church to throw up his grant at the ponds and to take up his fifty Acres at the uper sosiety where it may be least prejudiciall to aney perticular

[1] The Church in Plympton, then a part of Plymouth, was organized in 1696, and was often called the Upper Society.

[**23.**] At A town Meeting held att plimouth September 14th 1696 Not Relinquishing the Towns Just Right according to law to all theire Inhabitants paying their Rates as formerly The Conclusion & voate of the Town at this Meeting was that they would pay to Mer Cotton their Minister for this present yeare 1696 begining the 30th day of May last past the ffull sum of seaventy five pounds in silver money and the sd Mer Cotton Rests Contented with the sd sum for this present yeare it was also then voted that said sum be duely and seasonably paid the one halfe in october Next the other halfe att or before the first day of March next Ensuing At this Meeting the town Agreed upon the Raising of Moneys for the defraying the town Charges which is as followeth Inprimis for

|  |  |
|---|---|
| the scoolemaster | 33—00. 00 |
| John Bradford | 01—12. 00 |
| To Samuel dunham for sweping the meeting hous | 01—10. 00 |
| To [1] ffrench doctor fo Care of Hunters wife | 05—00—00 |
| To John Nelson for keeping Nan Ramsden on year | 05—00—00 |
| To Nathaniel Southworth for service att Cort | 03—12—00 |
| To John Nelson for service for the Town | 01—00—00 |

Grant to Holmes & Morton  At this town Meeting The Town granted unto Nathaniel Holmes and to Nathaniel Morton forty foot of land square betwen the land of Nathaniel Harlow and wenensly harbor by the shore side

At A town Meeting held at plimouth december 2rd 1696 they then Chose John Morton John Churchill James Barneb John doty Jun : John Coole and John Barnes to serve on the petty Jury at the quorter sessions in december 1696

Att A towne Meting held at plimouth on the first of March 1696 the Towne made Choice of Nathaniel Southworth John Nelson John doty senor William Shurtlef and Lef: Jonathan Mory to serve on the Grand Jury at the Grand Asize on the 2 tuseday in March and Epraime Morton Left John Bryant John Stirtevant Elkanah Cushman and Ephraime Cole to serve on the Jury of tryals att sd Court

---

[1] The French Doctor was Francis LeBaron.

Att sd Meting the towne made Choice of Samuel Rider James Warren Samuel Stirtevant and Nathaniel Morton to serve on the Grand Jurey for the yeare Insuing and also made Choice of John Morton Eliazur Churchell Jonathan Shaw and Joseph ffaunce to serve on the Jury at tryals on the 3$^{rd}$ tuseday of this Instant March

Att sd Meting An Indian Called Ralph Jones desired leave of the Towne to sell so much of his Intrest of lands in the towneship as will fech him 6 or 7 pounds which was Granted him and appointed Leftenant Jonathan Mory to purchase It of him

[24.] At sd towne Meting James Nutes desired leave of the towne to make sale of his 50 Akers of land which he hath lying at saltwater pond which he had of the towne In low land about half way pond the towne Granted liberty to Jonathan Mory Junior to purchase sd land of sd Nutes

Att a towne Meting held at plimouth the 8$^{th}$ of March 1696 for the Choice of towne officers for sd yeare the select men for sd yeare are M$^{er}$ Nathaniel thomas Jun; Ephraime Morton and thomas ffaunce The Cunstables are William Ring & benjamen Warren; Thomas ffaunce Towne Clerke; the Towne Treassurer William Shurtlef; surveyors for the High Wayes are Samuel Bradford Joseph Bartlet Jun; Robert Ransom sen Giles Rickard and John Bryant Jun; John doty senior Elknah Cushman & James Warren are Chosen fence Vewers M$^{er}$ Joseph Bartlet John doty and Benjamin Warren they are appointed by the towne to determine and settle the bounds of the land granted by the Towne Unto M$^{r}$ Nathaniel Morton late of plimouth deseaced what they shall Judge to bee a Meete Competency for the use of the Naiborhood according to the Towne Grant; Att sd Meting Left; Morey and M$^{er}$ Nathaniel Thomas Jun: are granted by the towne the Right of purchase of tenn Acres of land lying att the Herring pond Called [1] sandwedg Hering pond which Is the land of Will wapnut Indian deseaced Att sd meting The order Relating to the Killing of black Birds was Againe Renewed and those that have not killed their proportion of Black birds the last yeare are hereby ordered to make up theire full number of birds for the yeare Insuing and to make up theire Number of wt was wanting

---

[1] What is now known as Herring Pond was called Sandwich Herring Pond to distinguish it from what was called Herring Pond on the Eel River.

of their douzen the last year or 6 Crows in the Rome of 12 blackbirds for Each house holder and this to be done betwen the 8th of March 1697 and the last of october next Ensuing and bring their account of the birds heads as abovesd unto the persons appointed to Receive the Heads the last yeare.

Saml Harlow   At sd Meeting the Towne granted to Samuel Harlow the swampy land by the highway Joyning to his spring & soe downwards towards the *

At a towne Meting held at plimouth december 2d 1696 The town granted to John Morton & Samuell Lucas to each of them 30 foot of land square lying by the water side betwen Mer bartlets Ware house & William Shirtlifs land leaving a suficent Cart way on ye shore

[25.] March 11 169$\frac{6}{7}$ Measured and bounded out unto Mer John Mordo [1] A persell of land which sd Mordo Bought of Major Bradford over the streete to the westward of Ephraim Cooles shopp and begining at the Corner of the streete Against sd Cooles shop and therr bounded with a stone sett into the Ground and from sd stone to Extend Norwestward allong the streete six pole and there bounded with A heape of stones and thence Rainging southwestward 6 pole and there bounded with a heap of stones and from thence Rainging Eastward to the laine side and there bounded with a heape of stones a lettle above sd Mordows shopp and from thence Rainging downe sd lane 6 pole to the boundary first above Named Bounded out as abovesd on the day and yeare above Mentioned pr Thomas ffaunce
        Surveyor to the Towne
        of Plimouth

At A Towne Meeting Held at Plimouth on the tenth of May 1697 The Inhabitants of the Towne Made Choyce of James Warren to be theire Representative.

At sd Meeting 30 acrees of land was Granted unto James Warren and Benjamin Warren That is to say 15 acres Apeece to Each of them at the [2] drinking Place soe Called in the Towneship of Plimouth on Consideration of the Charge and trouble they have

---

[1] This lot was on the corner of Main Street and Town Square, and was sold to John Murdock by Major William Bradford, son of the Governor. The blacksmith's shop of Ephraim Cole was on the corner of Main and Leyden streets, and may now be seen in the rear of the express office of Harvey W. Weston.

[2] The drinking place is between the new Rocky Hill road and the shore.

ben att in the defence of their Right unto a sedg ffiatt yt they bought of the Agents of sd Towne liing at the Eeal River

At sd Meeting the Towne Granted unto John dotey senior A Confirmation of Six Acres of land which the sd dotey had bought of his Mother with his other lands which he could not as yet find a Record for on Consideration that John Cobb and John Holmes Consented thereunto sd land lyeth Above the Comon Road way on the southerly side of his own land and soe to Run up in length with his other lands

At this Meeting The Town Made Choyce of M$^{er}$ Isaac Cushman James Warren and Thomas ffaunce and Impowered them to settle aney difference that might Arise in Rainges of land : that Mite Arise in sd towne betwen one Neighbour and an other as there may be ocasion for their helpe therein The sd persons Were alike Chosen by the Towne to see that the Towns Comons be not Intruded on Either by our own Inhabitants or others'

At a towne meeting on the 10$^{th}$ of May the Inhabitants then Chose M$^{er}$ William Shirtlif to be Improved with M$^{er}$ Isaac Cushman James Warren and Thomas ffaunce : for what ocasion there may be for their helpe and Improvement in aney perticklors herein above Mentioned and it was alike voated by the Inhabitants then mett that what they or aney three of them should doe as to the settling of Rainges betwen one Neibour and an other and to defend the towns Interest from being Intruded on shal be of full force and vertue

[26.] New Plimouth May 11$^{th}$ 1697

Then laid out and bounded unto James & Benjamin Warren 30 Acrees of land which was Granted them by the Towne at Manoment high land Neere the drinking Place soe Called sd land is bounded as ffolloweth begining at the banck next the sea and there bounded With A Rock and a heape of stones on sd Rock and soe Rainging along the banck East North East six score pole to A Rock and A heape of stones on sd Rock & from sd Rock to Extend down to the sea sd Rock is a lettle to the Northward of A small swampe and from thence Rainging South South East fforty Pole and there bounded with a heape of stones there being A smal Red oake on Each sid sd heape Marked on 4 sids and from thence Rainging West southwest six score pole to another heape of stones and from thence Rainging Nor Norwest to the Roock herein first Mentioned and from thence on a straite line to the sea Surveyed and Measured on the day and yeare Above Mentioned by Mee Thomas ffaunce Surveyor To the Towne of plimouth

June 18th 1674

Measured and bounded unto abraham Jacson 30 Acrees of Land lying att the hering Ware att Monponsett brooke att the Northwest Corner Is a white oake marked from Itt the line Extends East or E northerly to the brooke leaving the poynt Common from the sd oake the line Runs S ½ westerly nearest to a Red oake then ½ Easterly to a white oake and so to the brooke then as the brooke Runeth till It meets with the East line that Coms from the first white oake breadth 60 pole length 80 pole

Att a towne Metting Held att plimouth June the 7th 1697 Att sd meting the Town voated that the Towne Treasuror should Take Acount of Mr Joseph Bartlet what he laid out About the Careges of the greatt guns and what Remains to Compleat the work the sd Treasuror Is hereby ordered to Agree with a workman to flinish and to pay It out to the Towne stocke

[**27.**] July 2d 1694

Laid out to Benoney Lucas by Isaac Cushman at a place Comonly Caled the south Meadows in the township of plimouth 24 acrees of upland and is bounded as ffolloweth on the Eastward Corner with A white oake Marked on 4 sides thence Runing Northward to a Red oake Marked on fouer sides and thence Runing Westward to a white oake tree marked on 4 sides and thence Runing southward to a pine tree Marked on 4 sides thence Runing Eastward to two Red oaks Marked on fouer sids and thence Runing Northward to the white oake first Mentioned and lyeth on the westward side of the seder bridg and ten acrees of sd land belongeth to the Meadow of William Harlow deceased which Meadow lyeth in the uper south Meadows ten Acres more of sd land belongeth to John Morton and four acres of sd land was granted by the towne to sd Lucas it is to be understood that there is sufficent lowance for a cart way for the Neighbours to fetch hay through sd land

Laid out to John Barrows ten Acrees of upland at a place Comonly Caled the southmeadows In the township of plimouth on the southerly side of sd Meadow and is bounded as ffolloweth five acres of sd land lyeth on the westerly sd of A bridg Comonly Caled Andrew Rings bridg and at the Eastward Corner Is bounded with a white live oake and thence Runing westward to a pine tree marked on foure sides and thence Runing Northward to a pine tree Marked on fouer sides which Is the bound of Robert Barrows meadow and bounded with a swamp on the Eastward side five acrees more lying on the Eastward side of sd bridge and Is bounded at the westward Corner with a Red oake Marked and thence Runing southward to A stone set into the ground thence Runing Eastward to a Red oak Marked and thence Runing Northward to a Red oake marked July the second 1694

By Me Isaac Cushman
Surveior

Mr Little called

At a towne Meeting held at plimouth November 15th 1697 the Inhabitants then preasent Gave Mer Ephraim Lettle a call to preach to them for the winter season in order to a probation of him for further Improvement of him: if the sd Little & the Inhabitants do mutually agree & the Inhabitants did vote to allow to sd Little for his labours in the ministre after the Rate of sixty pound per yeare

[28.] The 4 acrees of Meadow belonging to Samuel Harlow in the lower south meaddows over lease Recorded being Judged to fall into Middleboro purchas that is on the westward side of the River the sd harlow took up all the sd 4 acres on the East side of the River begining at Nathaniel Mortons bound tre in his Record Mentioned and soe Rainging down the meadow and soe Round the poynt of upland unto a place where the River Cometh Close to the upland and there bounded with a pine tre Marked on 4 sids and all the Meadow lying on the East side of the River from Nath: Mortons bounds down to sd pine tre is laid out to Samuel harlow for 4 acres   Measured and bounded on the tenth d₁y of May 1698         by Thomas ffaunce Surveyor
to the Towne of plimouth

The bounds between Baruck Jordans Meaddows at the South Meadows and an Acree of Meaddow that George Bonham bought of Nathaniel Morton is a Rainge of staks Rainging across the Meaddow and on the other side the Raing betwen Nathaniel Howland and the sd bonhams acree is a Raing of stacks Rainging across the meaddow

The bounds of Nathaniel Harlows 2 acres of Meaddow lying betwen an acree of Meadow belonging to George Bonam and William Ring is a Rainge of Staks Rainging a Cross the Meaddow

Whereas there was Granted to M$^{er}$ John Reynor then teacher of plimouth now deceased one hundred acrees of land in the yeare 1640 by the Honowered Court of plimouth Neere to a place Comonly Caled Jones River Meadow and whereas Capt Joseph Howland hath ben sence Improved by the Heires of the sd M$^{er}$ John Reignor to lay out act and doe upon sd land as though they themselves were there present

Therefore is laid out to the sd Capt Joseph Howland on theire behalf the hundred acrees of land on the Eastward side of Jones River Meaddows in the township of plimouth in New England & is bounded as followeth on the westward Corner with a small White oake Marked on 4 sides thence Rainging southeast one hundred Rodds to a Red oake Marked standing on the Northeast side of the way that goeth to Jones River Meaddow thence Runing North East Eight score Rodd to a Red oake tre Marked standing Neere to a place Comonly Caled hylly plaine grate hill and thence Runing Northwest one hundred Rodds to a white oake marked on 4 sides as the Rest of the bounds are & standing on the Northeast side of a swamp thence Runing southwest Eigh scoore Rodds to the bounds first Mentioned August 16 1697 By me IsaaC Cushman surveyor To the Towne of plimouth

[**29.**] July 24$^{th}$ 1697

Then measured and bounded unto Nathaniell Morton foure acers of meadow at the south meadows formerly granted to Left Ephraim Morton deceased from the boundereyes of Tinkhams meadow downe the River and bounded on the west side with a great pine tree marked on 4 sides 2 pine trees standing on the southwest side of sd tree surveighed and measured on the day and yeare above write

By me Thomas Thomas ffaunce Survaier to the Towne of plimouth July 24 1697

se the
alteration
of these
bounds in page
28 and
the Reason
of it

Sam¹
Harlow

Measured and bounded unto Samuel Harlow foure acrees of Meadow at the lower south meadow which was formerly granted unto sergant william Harlow late of plimouth deceased begining at Nathaniell Mortons boundareyes of His said meadow and so Rainging downe the River forty pole and bounded on. the Eastward side of the River with a spruce tree Marked on 4 sides and on the westerly side of sd River bounded with a swamp white oake Marked on foure sides standing a little within the meadow surveighed and measured By me Thomas ffaunce surveiyor to the Town of plimouth

July 24 1697

Measured and bounded unto Nathaniell Morton ten acrees of upland at the Southmeadows In the Township of plimouth six of which sd ten Acrees Is layed out in barnses Neck so Called and bounded by the land of georg bonham on the southerly side and on the Northerly side nex to abraham Jacson with a stake and a stone set into the ground nere the Coasway in the Cove and the uplands to Extend home to the meadow so far as the sd Mortons Meadow goeth and from sd stone and stake Ranging Northeastward 52 pole to another stake and stone set into the ground and from thence to Raing home to the Eastermost boundereyes of georg bonhams land and the other foure acrees Is layed out on the south side of the River and lyeth adjoyning to the sd georg bonhams land and bounded by It and on Each Corner bounded with a pine tree Marked on 4 sides

Surveighed and Measured by Mee Thomas ffaunce
Surveyher to the Towne of plimouth

[30.] Layed out to John Churchill fifty acres of land In the Township of plimouth and Is bounded as followeth sixteen Acres of sd land lyeth on the Westward side of William bonys land and Is bounded as followeth on the Northwest Corner with a Red oake Marked on foure sides thence Runeth westward forty Rod to a white oake Marked on foure sides standing by the swamp Commonly Called the Coasway swamp and thence Runing southward sixty Rod to a White oake Marked on foure sides and standing on an Island In the swamp and thence Runing Eastward

forty Rod to a White oake which Is the southwest Corner bound
of sd boneys land and thence Runing Northward 60 Rod to the
bounds first Mentioned More fiften acres on the south End of the
land of sd boneys and bounded As followeth at the westward
Corner with a white oake and thence Runing Eastward 60 Rod to
a spruce tree Marked and thence Runing Northward forty Rod
to a Red oake Marked on fouer sides thence Runing westward
sixty Rod to a white oake Marked thence Runing southward forty
Rod to the first bounds Mentioned and with a suffishant allowance
for the highway to goe to Meting And further Is Allowed to the
first sixten Acres a little Garden spot at the louer end of It on
the westward side of William bonys land More layed out to John
Churchil on the westward End of Isaac King and John bryants
land betwen that and Turkey swamp Nineten Acres of land and
Is bounded as followeth at the southwest Corner with a Red oake
Marked on 4 sides and thence Runing Eastward Nere 80 Rod
to a White oake Marked on fouer sides and thence Runing Northward to a small white oake Marked on fouer sides and thence
Runing westward to a Red oake Marked on fouer sides and thence
Runing southward to the bounds first Mentioned which land
iyeth diamond square by Isaac Cushman surveigher to the Towne
of plimouth March 30 1697

Memorandom this was layed out upon the Acount of a
grant at Manoment ponds formerly granted to John Churchel
deceased

[31.] At a towne Meting held at plimouth on the 13$^{th}$ of
september 1697 for the Choyce of Jurrors to serve at the County
Court the persons Chosen were M$^{er}$ William Clarke Abraham
Jacson sen John doty seni : Nathaniel Holmes and deacon Thomas
Clarke at sd Meeting M$^{er}$ William Shurtlef & M$^{er}$ Nathaniel
Thomas were Chosen by the Towne to treate with Middlebery
Agents Respecting the Rainge between the towne and Major
Churches & M$^{er}$ John Tomsons purchas and to make Report
thereof To the Towne

At a towne Meeting held at plimouth october 5$^{th}$ 1697 the
Inhabitants then Mett did voat to Contrebute Every sabbath day
to Carry on the worship of god Amongst them

March 30$^{th}$ 1697 laid out to samuel stirtevant twenty
Acrees of land by virtue of a grant to the Widdow Stirtevant

Now the wife of John bass of Brentree; which the towne granted to her in her Widowhood sd twenty acrees of land lyeth att Monponsett and on the westward side of the Meadow of Samuel Stirtevant Joyning to sd Meadow and is bounded as followeth on the south East Corner with a white oake Marked on 4 sides standing by the Meadow side and is the bound of the Meadow and thence Runing westward to a small Red oak Marked standing by A lettle swamp thence Runing Northward to a Red oake Marked on 4 sides which is the bounds of Adam Wrights and thence Runing Eastward to a white oake Marked standing by the Meadow side which is the other Corner bound of sd Meadow with sufficent allowance for a highway for the Neighbours to goe to Meeting

surveyed and Measured by Isaac Cushman
Surveyor

Att a towne Metting held at plimouth october 11 1697 The Inhabitants then Voatted to allow unto M$^{er}$ Cotton for his labhours in the Minestry on third of a yeare 25 pounds Which Is to be Raised by Rate on the Inhabitants of this society More six pounds for the Repairing of the Meting house six pound for the Representative to M$^{er}$ bartlet 12 shillings To Thomas ffaunce one pound 11 shiling for keeping John andros to M$^{er}$ Thomas for Cloathing for Nan Ramsden 12s 3d to John Rickard for Cloathing for John andros 10 shilings six pounds for the keping Nan Ramsden this present yeare to Samuell dounham one pound five shillings to Samuell stirtevant 5s To Ephraime Morton 2 shillings

[**32.**] Att a towne Meting held at plimouth december ye 6$^{th}$ 1697 for the Choice of Juniors to serve att the Court of Quarter seshons the persons Chosen were Eliazer Churchell John Churchell Samuell lucas John barnes James barnabe & benjamin soule

Att sd Meting the Towne Impowerid Le$^{ivt}$ Jonathan Morey James Warren & Samuell lucas to Run the Rang and settle boundereyes betwen sepecan and plimouth in wt yet Remains to be Run and settled

Att a towne Metting held at plimouth on the 13 of June 1698 John bradford Was then Chosen by the towne to Joyne With James Warren & Samuell Lucas to Run & settle the Rang abovsd in the Rome of Jonathan Mory because of his absence

Att a towne Metting at plimouth the 8 of March 169$\frac{6}{7}$ M^er Joseph bartlet senior John doty senior and benjamin Warren were apoynted by the towne to sette the differance betwen them and Nathaniell Harlow & we provided as followeth we set up a stake and a heap of stones at the Northeast end of sd land Close to the bay and from thence southerly on a straight line to a heap of stones before the ware house dore and from thence on a straight line to a Rock and a heap of stones on sd Rock and from sd Rock on a straight line westerly to another picked Rock & so Runing westerly to high Water Mark ; March 11 169$\frac{6}{7}$

John doty senior
Joseph bartlet sen :
benjamin Warren
signed in presence of
Thomas ffaunce
John bradford J^r

In testemony of My Consent to the settlement of the boundereyes above Mentioned I the sd Nathaniel Harlow have here unto set My hand and seale
Nathaniell Harlow

Att a towne Metting held at plimouth on the 4^th of March 1698 for the Choice of towne officers the selectmen Chosen are
William Shurtlef
John Rickard Jun &
John Mordo ;

the Towne Clerk Chosen was Thomas ffaunce

The Cunstables Chosen Were Benjamin Eaton & Abiall Shurtlef

The surveighers for the high Wayes Were Samuel ffuller John Morton John Clark John bryant Jun Ephraime Tilson & Eliazer Morton

The Tything Men Chosen are M^er Nathaniell Thomas & John Rickard Sen :

The fence Vewers Chosen are John Bradford
Jonathan Shaw Sen :
& Robert bartlet
William Shirtlef Chosen Town Treasurer

[33.] At sd Metting the towne Made Choyce of Grand Juriors for the Supperior Court Which are as followeth M^er Nathaniell Thomas John Stirtevant William Shirtlef & John dotey ;

the petty Jury for the grand assise are Nathaniell Southworth M^er Joseph bartlet Nathaniell Clarke Ephraime Cole Samuel Lucas & John foster ;

The grand Jury for the yeare are Giles Rickard Junior Thomas Clarke Sen Elknah Cushman & Joseph Bartlet Jun
The petty Jury for the County Court are Eliaser Churchill Eliazer Ring Jonathan Shaw Sen John Morton Nathaniell Wood Samuel fuller
Att sd Metting the Towne granted to georg Shaw 12 acres of land adjoyning to the land he liveth on att the south End of lakenham pond

Thomas
holmes
his fifty
aces
Recorded

Plimouth April 28 1705. Then forty acres of land was laid out to Thomas holmes that Was granted to his grandfather holmes in the year 1641 & ten acrees of land it being part of his 20 acre lot became Due to him by a settlemen of the propriety of the Comon land in plimouth sd 50 : accres of land was laid out at a place Caled four mile brook in the Township of plimouth aforesd & bounded on the west Corner with a white oak tree marked nere the brook & from sd tre the line to Extend South East : 67 : pole to a maple marked on 4 sids Neere a pond & then thre pole on the same point into ye swampe & then the line to Extend North East an hundred pole to a Red oak Marked & then the line to Extend southwest & by south to the brook and then bounded to sd Meadow & Meddowish ground to the bounds first mentioned leaving a way through sd land wher the way now is to Lakenham

James Warren } surv
Nathaniel Morton

[34.] New plimouth

This agreement Made the twenty fift day of Jaunary 169$\frac{4}{5}$ betwen John Nelson John dotey senior and Samuell Lucas all of them Inhabitants of the Towne of plimouth in the County of plimouth in the province of the Massachusetts bay in New England as followeth Namely the said John Nelson John dotey senior and Samuell Lucas doe by these presents declare that they are fully firmly and Joyntly agreed betwixt themselves for themselves Mutyaly and for there heirs and Assignes for Ever Concerning A Certaine persell of land Comonly Caled and knowne by the Name of the Gurnett being and scittuate Within the

Township of plimouth aforsd; that the said land at said Gurnett being surveighed and divided by Jacob Thompson of Midlebery in the County aforesd on the $22^d$ & $23^d$ dayes of this Instant January the first and second lots in sd divisin acordin as It Is Written by said surveyer are and shall be the proper lotts of said samuell Lucas and that the third lot Is and shall be the proper lott of said John doty and that the fourth lott Is and shall be the proper lott of John Nelson; furthermore said Nelson dotey and Lucas doe hereby firmly agree With and for themselves theire heires and assignes for Ever and that Each of them shall have free Egresse and Regreese through all the said lots with Carts and Cattle provided always thay be Carefull to shut up bars also said partyes doe all agree as abovesd that wt water there Is upon aney of said lots It shall be free for the use and benefitt of Each of said proprietors there heirs and assignes for Ever for the full Confirmation of This agreement above Writen in all particulors of It said Nelson doty and Lucas have sett to there hands and seals the day and yeare above Written;

Signed sealed and declared to be the agreement of the three partiys abovenamed in presence of
    John Cotton
    John Mordo

John Nelson   O
John dotey sen  O
Samuell Lucas  O

    Att a towne Metting held at plimouth aprill ye $11^{th}$ 1698 the Inhabitants of said towne did very unanimosly agree to give $M^{er}$ Ephrame Litle[1] a Call to setle in said towne to Carrey on the Worship of god as ther Minister of sd towne and did apoynt William Shirtlef John Rickard John Mordo Nathaniell Thomas & Thomas ffaunce to signifie the desire of said Inhabitants to sd $M^{er}$ Little as also It was voated at sd Metting to alow to sd $M^{er}$ Litle 60 pound for his sallery for the yeare insueing

[35.] New Plimouth May $11^{th}$ 1698

    Laid out to Abraham Jacson 10 acres of upland at the south meadows adjoyning to his land that buts hom to his Meaddow at the Cove at the head of Barnses Neck begining at sd Jacsons bound mark $w^{th}$ a forked Red oake and Raiageth from sd oake down along the Med 40 pole and there bounded with a

---

[1] Rev. John Cotton left Plymouth in 1697, and died in Charleston, South Carolina, in 1699. Rev. Ephraim Little of Marshfield, a graduate at Harvard in 1695, was his successor.

small white oake tree Marked on 4 sides and from thence Rainging Norward 40 pole to a Red oake tre Marked on 4 sids and thence Rainging Eastward across to the sd Jacsons boundery of his other land and bounded by it; with alowance ic. the fencing of the Meadow upon the upland and for A Cart way Either through gats or barrs through sd land to the Meadows lying against sd land

A Record of the Renewal of the boundaryes of M$^{er}$ Nathaniel Mortons lott of Meadow in the lower south Meaddow bounded on the Northerly end att the East side with a smal white oake tre Marked on 4 sides and on the northerly End on the west side with a grat pine tree Marke the River turning in at that place Nere to the upland and soe Rainging down the meaddow to a white oake sapling standing a lettle to ye Northward of a cartway that Coms out of amy Willisses Meaddow sd sapling being marked on 4 sids; standeth by the edge of the meadow and thence Rainging acros the meadow to the mouth of the Cove and there bounded with a grate pine tre Marked on 4 sids and from sd tree athort the mouth of the Cove to an other pine tree marked is to be understood to divide betwen the Med lying on the River and the Meaddow in the Cove

plimouth May 11$^{th}$ 1698 laid out unto abraham Jacson in the New Mead 6 acrees of Meadow begining at a grat pine tre Marked on 4 sids and thence Rainging southeast & by south aCross the Meaddow 40 pole to a stake Neere to the Iland and thence Rainging North East and by North 24 pole to an other stake and from sd stake 40 pole to the upland & there bounded with a stake by the Meaddow side and a pine tree Marked on 4 sids being on the shore.

May 11$^{th}$ 1698 then laid out to William Harlow upon Jonathan prats Right 6 acrees of Meaddow Joyning to abram Jacson six acrees above Mentioned on the Northerly sid there of and Raingeth from Jacsons boundarey on the shore 40 pole down along Jacsons Raing to his bound stak and from thence on a straite Raing 34 pole to a stake standing in the Meadow about 4 pole from the point of an Iland in sd meadow and from sd stake Rainging to a point of upland on the North side and acros that point to the Northerly part of it and there bounded with a pine tree Marked on 4 sids and from thence Rainging to abraham

Jacsons Corner bound next sd Harlow which is a pine tre standing on the upland

[36.] May 11th 1698 then laid out to George Morton 4 acres of Meaddow formerly granted to Samuel dunham in the New Meadow soe Called which is laid out adjoyning to William harlows 6 acres in Record mentioned begining at the stake standing in the Meadow about two pole from the upland at the Island in sd harlows Record Mentioned and soe Rainging aCross the pint of upland into the Cove and aCross the Cove to a pine tre Marked and from sd tree Extending farther Northward to the botom of an other Cove and thence Rainging Northwestward to another pine tree Marked on 4 sides and from thence on a straite line to William Harlows Corner bounderey in his Record Mentioned all these meaddows and lands of Jacsons harlows and Mortons last Entered on Record were Measured and bounded by Thomas ffaunce Surveyor
    to the towne of plimouth

New plimouth May 11th 1698 then laid out to Richard Cooper 10 acres of land at the South Meaddows at the southwest side of the Cove upon benijah pratts Right and sd land is bounded by William Rings land and soe Rainging from sd Wil^m Rings Corner bound which is a Red oake standing som distance from the meadow and so Rainging 40 pole SouthEasterly and there bounded with a stake standing about 4 pole from the Meadow nere 2 pines growing by the Meadow side and thence Rainging west and by south 42 pole to a pine tree Marked on 4 sids and from thence Rainging Norwest & by North 40 pole to William Rings head Corner bound being a stooping pine tree Alowance is made for all to have fre pasag to theire Meadow through sd land Either through gats or barrs at all times Surveyed and Measured per Thomas ffaunce surveyor
    to the Towne of plimouth

At a towne Meeting held at plimouth May the 10th 1698 for the Choyce of A Representative the first Choyce fell on Ephraim Morton but he making his Refusal of sd service for sd towne they then proced to a new Choyce which fell on Jonathan Mory Senior

[**37.**] New plimouth Aprill 17th 1698

 Measured and bounded unto Ephraim Morton twenty Eight Acres of land lying in the township of plimouth on a plaine above Lettle Towne Comonly Caled Lout pond plaine which sd land the said Ephraim Morton bought of severall persons as per deeds under theire hands and seals doth and May Appeare sd land is bounded as follows begining at a white oake sapling & a heape of stones by it sd tre being Marked on 4 sides and from thence Rainging southeast and by East 72 pole To an other White oake sapling Marked on 4 sides and from sd tree Rainging southwest and by south 66 pole to a young Red oake sapling standing in a valy Marked on 4 sides and a heape of stons about it and thence Rainging Norwest and by West 72 pole to a white oake sapling standing on the North East side of a hill a lettle to the Eastward of lout pond being Marked on 4 sides and a heape of stones by sd tree and from sd tree on a strait line to the white oake tree first above Mentioned Measured and bounded as above Mentioned pr Thomas ffaunce Surveyor to the Towne of plimouth

    January 28 169$\frac{4}{5}$

 An acount of the lots of upland upon the [1] Gurneett

 1 The first lot being about seaven acres and a quarter lyeth on the Southerly End of the said Gurnet and the Northerly side of the said lot Is bounded from a heap of stones from at the Westerly End Thereof Next the Marsh to a small hornbeam tre Marked at the East End Next the sea which tree hath a heap of stones about It;

 2 The second lot being about six acres and $\frac{3}{4}$ Is bounded on the southerly side thereof by the first lot and on the Northerly side thereof It is bounded from a soft forked Wood tree Marked standing Next the Marsh to a Walnut tree Marked With a heap of stones About It standing at the Easterly End Next the sea;

 3 The third lot being about six acrees and three quarters Is bounded on the southerly side thereof by the second lot and on the Northerly side thereof from a Cedar tree Marked standing at the Westerly end Next the Marsh to a Walnut tre Marked With a heap of stones about It at the Easterly End Next the sea

---

[1] The description of these lots is interesting on account of the information it gives concerning the character of the trees growing on the Gurnet. The "soft forked wood tree," mentioned in the description of the second lot, means a " forked soft wood tree,"—perhaps a poplar tree.

[38.]

4 The fourth lot being about six acres and three quarters Is bounded on the southerly side Thereof by the Third lot and on the Northerly side Thereof It Is bounded from a Cedar tree Marked at The Westerly End Next the Marsh To a heap of stones Att the Easterly End Next the sea;

pr Jacob Tomson<br>Surveigher

Att a towne Meting held at plimouth on the 13<sup>th</sup> of June 1698 The Towne voated that all Nessesary Charges that shall A Rise Relating to The setteling of the Townes bounds As Also in defending the Towns Write within theire township from The Intreusion of strangers shall be borne by The Inhabitants of The Towne The persons Chosen and Impowered in sd Work Rendring an Acount To the Towne of theire Reasonable Charges Therein

Att sd Meting The Juriors Chosen to serve at The County Court Were John Waterman Nathaniell Thomas John pratt & frances Cooke

New plimouth July 13<sup>th</sup> 1698

Then Measured and staked out to John Rickard 30 foot of land Each Way or square for nerly granted to said John Rickard by the Inhabitants of the Towne of plimouth Where his Warehouse Now standeth below the hill by the Water side and begining at the Warehouse Corner Next the sea side and so Ranging allong the shore Towards M<sup>er</sup> Nath<sup>l</sup> Thomas his Ware house 30 foott and there bounded with a stake and from thence Rainging up towards the upland or hill 30 foot and there bounded with a stake and from thence Ranging to another stake set or drove into the ground standing 30 foot from the lower corner of sd Warehouse dore

pr Thomas ffaunce surveigher<br>To the towne of plimouth.

[39.] on the day and yeare afore mentioned then Measured and bounded out to sd John Ricard 20 fott of land which sd Rickard bought of Robert Ransom late of plimouth deceased & adjoyneth Nere sd Rickards Ware house aforesd which land Was formerly granted to sd Robert Ransom by the Inhabitants of the Towne of plimouth as pr Towne Record dot<sup>a</sup> & May appeare sd land Is 21 foott in length and there bounded with a stake

Which stands about a foott to the south of the Ware house that stands on sd land and sd land It something Interferes on sd Rickards land aforesd It Is laid out 21 foot square and bounded With staks next the hill and from sd stakes to Extend the length of sd Ware house

pr Thomas ffaunce surveyor to the<br>Towne of plimouth.

New plimouth July 13 1698

Then Measured and bounded unto M$^{er}$ Nath$^1$ Thomas thirty foot of land squar below the hill by the Watter side Where his Ware house nowe standeth which sd land Was formerly granted by the Inhabitants of the Towne of plimouth unto John Murdo as per towne Record doth and May apeare and soe begining at the southermost corner of sd Na$^{th}$ Thomas his Ware house and so Measured 30 foott square and staked it out and there Is Remaining betwen M$^{er}$ Rickards bounds and M$^{er}$ Thomas his Ware house 17 foot in breadth of common land

pr Thomas ffaunce surveyor<br>To the Towne of plimouth

Att a towe Metting held att plimouth august 6$^{th}$ 1698

The Towne voatted that the Common Meadows lying upon sampsons brook towards Rochester and sampsons pond in ye Township of plimouth Which sd Meadows the agents of plimouth aforesd have lett out to sundry persons shall stand good for this present yeare

Att sd Meetting the towne voated that With Referance to the Contest bettwen giles Rickard & Jonathan barnes With Referance to a former grant about a percell of Meadow at the south Meadows in the Township of plimouth, that the said giles Rickard shall have 2 acres next to the Meadow formerly the Meadow of Josiah Cooke & then the said barnes to have 4 acres & then ye said Rickard to have two acres More of Meadow or Meadowish land

[40.] Att sd Metting M$^{er}$ Joseph bartlett Engaged to ffinish & Compleatt the setting the greatt guns upon Carraiges With Iron Work and all other Things suttable for said Work by the last of october Next Ensueing this date for three pound ten shillings the town also Improved the sd M$^{er}$ bartlett to agree with a Workman for ye Repareation of the Metting house

[1] Att a towne Metting held att plimouth September 10th 1698 for the Choice of Juriors to serve at the County Court Which Were John Stirtevant Nathaniell Morton Benim soule & Eliazer Cushman ;

Att a towne Metting held att plimouth on the 3d day of october 1698 The town voated to allowe to M$^{er}$ Ephraime Little their present Minister fifty five pounds towards the building of an house and one Acree of land that Is to say: one half acre Neare about the pound If It be there to be had upon the towne Commons & the other half acree as Neare the abovesd place as Can be Conveniently had provided that the sd Little Continew some Considerable Terme of years Not less than ten in the Work of the Ministrey in sd town then sd land and Money abovementioned to him the sd Little & to belong to him & his heirs for Ever And in Case the sd Little should decease in the Work of the Ministry in sd town before sd terme of years be Ended then the sd land & Money to belong to sd Littles heirs for Ever ;

Att sd Metting the towne agreed unto the Makeing of a Rate for the defraying of town Charges & Is as followeth

|  | £ | s | d |
|---|---|---|---|
| viz for the Representative ten pounds | 10 | 00 | 00 |
| for keeping John Andros one yeare | 10 | 00 | 00 |
| for the Constables fifteen shillings | 00 | 15 | 00 |
| for the towns Agents for running the line betweeen sipecan & plimouth | 01 | 13 | 00 |
| for James Warren for obtaining Records from Court | 00 | 06 | 00 |
| to the select Men for making Rates fifty shill | 02 | 10 | 00 |

[41.] Att the town Metting last Mentioned M$^{er}$ Nath$^{ll}$ Thomas James Warren & samuel stirtevant Were Chosen & a,͡ ͡ynted a Committy In the towns behalf To take an account of the late Cunstables selectmen & town treasurer of What Moneys are in theire hands

Nath
Thomas

---

[1] At this time there were three Courts established by the Province Laws—"The General Sessions of the Peace," held by the justices of the peace of each county, and "Inferior Court of Common Pleas," which was also a County Court, and the "Superior Court of Judicature," which was a Province Court. Besides these Courts, justices of the peace had judicial power "in all manner of debts, trespasses and other matters not exceeding forty shillings in value, wherein the title of land was not concerned."

belonging to the sd town; Att sd Metting the town granted to M$^{er}$ Nath$^{ll}$ Thomas Jr to Whorfe from the southerly side of his owne Whorfe to the southerly side of M$^{er}$ bartlets If he shall give him libberty to Joine thereunto   Att sd Metting the town granted to James Warren 30 foot square Each Way of land With liberty to Whorfe downe into the sea or bay against sd land as May be Convenient & to take sd land aney Where by the shore side betwen the lands formerly laid out to Ephraim Cole & the New stretts End so Called provided he take sd land below high Water Mark so as to leave a sufficient Cart way betwen sd land and the hill or bank & also Not to Come No Nearer towards the New streets End then shall be thought fitt by Men apointed to Judge What Roome May be thought Convenient to be left for publick use;

*James Warren*

Att sd Meting before Mentioned the Towne granted to John Churchill sen 30 foott of land square liing at Wellensly Nere Nathaniell Holmeses Ware house

*John Church*

Memorandom on the 4$^{th}$ of March 169$\frac{8}{9}$ Then was the Rainge Run and settled betwen Eliazar Churchill and Robert Bartlett both of plimouth of lands which sd bartlett bought of Nathaniel Harlow lying adjoyning to said Elizar Churchills land on which his house Now standeth & is bounded as followeth begining at the lower End of sd land Next the sea upon the banck and there bounded with A Rock and a heape of stons upon sd Rock Now the Midway betwen the foot boundery and the highway sd Rock lyeth across the Range and from thence to Extend to the fence Neere the highway and there bounded wth a heape of stons

[42.] Att a towne Metting held att plimouth December 19$^{th}$ 1698 for the Choce of Juriors to serve at the County Court december 20$^{th}$ 1698 Which Were John foster Ephraime Cole John Cole Eliazar Morton Nathaniel Jackson and Richard serves

Att sd Meting the town agreed with Abraham Jackson sen to Ring the bell & sweepe the Meting house & to see to the keepping the doores & Windowes of sd house shutt for one yeare & are to allow to sd Jackson one pound ten shillings for his sallery for one yeare Att sd Metting voated that Eight pounds should be Raised to be added to the Charges before mentioned at a towne Metting held at plimouth october 3 1698 as also one pound ten shill to Sam dounham for his service in keeping the Metting house & Ringing the bell

   Att a town Meeting held at plimouth March ye 6$^{th}$ 169$\frac{8}{9}$ for The Choice of town oficers The select Men Chosen are William Shirtlef James Warren & John Waterman The Cunstables Chosen James barnaby & frances Cooke The grandjuriors Chosen for the yeare Were Caleb Lorein Jonathan Shaw Junior Eleazer Ring & Joseph faunce The surveighers for the high Wayes Chosen Were Nathaniell holmes Will harlow John gray John pratt & Richard Cooper, The Tithing Men Chosen are deacon Nath Wood & John foster The fence veiuers Chosen Were John dotey sen & samuell harlow The grandjuriors Chosen for the Sup$^{or}$ Court in March 169$\frac{8}{9}$ Were Ephrame Morton James Warren Nath Warren Samuell Stirtevant & Lev John bryant The pety Jury for the Superior Court are Nath Southworth John Waterman Nath Morton benjamin Warren & John Rider The pety Jury for the County Court are Will Ring Robert bartlett Ephrame Cole & Sam fuller

   Att sd meting the towne granted to John barnes 30 foot front of land betwen the towne pond in the township of plimouth and the Cart Way that goes downe by barnsses Ware house & soe to Extend towards the Town pond and to his heirs for Ever

   At sd Meting the towne granted to Thomas ffaunce all that poynt of land lieing between the Ele River and the 20 acres of upland formerly given to James barnabe from the Cart way that goeth out of blackmurs feild athwart the Ele River to barnabes westward corner bound on the Northerly End and so Ranging down and bounded by his Rai ge to the double brooks and soe downe the double brooks home to the sd River Leaveing a suffiishant way through sd land to the River Through gates or bars for Ever

[**43.**] At the sd Town Meeting March 6$^{th}$ 169$\frac{8}{9}$ The towne granted to Nathaniel Warren 50 fot frunt of land below [1] Coles Hill soe Caled by the shore side and soe to Run down from High Water Marke in to the sea to whorf out soe farr as may be Convenient

---

[1] This is the first mention of Cole's Hill in either the Plymouth Colony or Town Records.

the sd Warren alwayes leaveing A sufficent way for Carts to pass along the shore between the banck & the sd land to be taken upp

Att sd Meeting the town Granted to Abiall shurtlif 30 futt of land square below sd Coles hill by the shore side he leaveing also a sufficent Cart way betwen the banck and sd land

March 5$^{th}$ 169$\frac{8}{9}$ Then laid out to Nathaniel Holmes and Nathaniel Morton the forty foot of land formerly granted to them by the town of plimouth at Welleusle wher their Ware house Now standeth sd land is bounded at Each Corner with heaps of stons and leaveing ten fut of Comon land

Then bounded out to John Churchill thirty foot of land next to Nathaniel Holmes above sd which sd land is bounded out by four heaps of stons.  surveyed and bounded pr me

Thomas ffaunce surveyor.

Att a towne Meeting at plimouth Aprill tenth 1699

1 The Inhabitants voated that the present select Men of sd Town doe in some Convenient time Run the line betwen plimouth and Middlebery Towneships and are herby appointed as agents or trustees for and in behalf of the town with full power to agree with the agents of other towns and settle boundarys and In sd Town's behalf to defend what land fals within sd Town's line from any that shall make Intrusion upon it.

2 voted That the select men are to Rent oute the Meadows lying in Comonage for the use and benifitt of the town for this yere

3 voted That the select men are to be the assessors to make the Rats for this yeare.

4 voted That M$^{er}$ William Clarke haveing as was alledged fermerly a grant of forty acrees of land on the southerly side of the eale River and the Record Not to be found of the grand but only of the bounds The Inhabitants therfor herby grant a Confirmaty of sd land formerly laid out to sd Clark

6 voted To Joseph Bartlet Juner ffiftene acres of land lying on the Easterly side of Mer bartlets brook at Manement ponds for thre pounds To be paid for the use of the Towne by said Joseph Bartlet or his order.

[44.] voted That what Interest of swampy or Medoish ground was formerly granted to Benijah pratt late of plimouth deceased shall be taken up by his sons at the Horse Neck soe Caled at the south Cuntery in plimouth Townshíp.

voted & granted to John Rider forty foot of land to Run up from his barne towards the highway and then to Run square of against his house for his Convenience of building

Granted to Eliazar dunham 60 foot of land square on the North side of the way leading to Lakenham on the hill side above followels medow

Granted to John dotey fifty foot of land square betwen the [1] grate gutter & the half acre of land laid out to $M^{er}$ Little on the uper sid of the way Nere the pound.

The bounds betwen Robert bartlets Meadow & swamp Lying on the southerly side of the Elereiver & the Land of Ephraime Morton begining at sd Mortons landing place so Called at the head of the Meadows and there bounded with a stake & a Clump of brush by the River side and from thence East Northerly to a Red oake sapling sproutting out of a stump & from thence Rainging Northerly to a White oake sapling Marked on 4 sides standing on the Easterly side of sd swampy ground and soe down to the River and ther bounded with a stone sett in to the Ground.

New plimouth Aprill $7^{th}$ 1699

Then measured and bounded to $M^{er}$ Ephraime Litle Junior half an Acre of Land formerly granted unto him by the Inhabitants of the Town of plimouth att Th head of The [2] New street soe Called begining at a ditch and There bounded with a stake & so Running North Westward 8 pole and There bounded With another stake & so Running up the hil side from the sd stakes That standeth Neare The Common Road that Leadeth out of town ten poles in Length and there bounded with another stake & then running southeastward 8 poles & there bounded with another stake & from thence Extending to the stake first mentioned    Measured and bounded on
the day and yeare first above Written
per Mee Thomas ffaunce surveier to the Town
of plimouth

[45.] Memorandom Whereas $M^{er}$ John doone had a grant of one hundred Acrees of Land at Joans River in the yeare 1637 & haveing sold sd land to Govener bradford and now in the posesion of Joseph Bradford & the boundarys of sd land being lost;

---

[1] The "grate gutter" was what is now Court Square.

[2] This half acre lot included the two estates opposite the head of New or North Street, owned and occupied by William P. Stoddard and the heirs of Mrs. Isaac L. Hedge.   Mr. Little sold the lot in 1709 to Isaac Lothrop, who built the Lothrop house, which was taken down about the year 1830.

Nesesitats a new surveighing and Measuring Therfor Measured and bounded out sd land to sd bradford on the 23$^d$ of May 1699 & is bounded as followeth bound att the fot of sd lott by Joans River and begining where the brook Cometh into Jons River Comonly Caled The trout brook and is bounded by sd brook & Raingeth up along sd brook 2 hundred pole in length & bounded at the head with three Maple trees standing all together in one Clump which sd Maples are all Marked on 4 sides & stand prety neere to sd brook & from sd trees Rainging west and by North Nerest foure score pole and there bounded with A Red oake sapling Marked on 4 sids standing Neere a valley that leads to [1] Causon's pond so Caled & from sd sappling Rainging down towards the River 6 score pole to a white oak marked About four score pole in bredth from the Abovesd brook & from sd oake to Raing on a strait Corse to A stake and a heape of stons A little to southward of the sawmill & soe to Extend to the River

Measured and bounded on the day<br>and year above written pr me<br>Thomas ffaunce survier

At a town Meeting held at plimouth on the 10$^{th}$ of May 1699

The Inhabitants Made Choyce of Mer Nathaniel Thomas Junior for to serve as theire Representative at the Grat and Generall Cort on the 31 day of May & at the severall adjornments of it

New plimouth May 27$^{th}$ 1699

Then Measured & staked out To John Morton and to Samuel Lucas 30 foot front of land square to Each of them along the shore by the shore side to the Northward of Joseph Bartlets Ware house betwen that and William shurtliffs warehouse There being 12 foot of Comon left betwen Every lott & free Egres and Regress for Carts along shore as ocasion may be Measured and bounded out on the day and year above Written pr Thomas ffaunce surveior To the town of plimouth.

---

[1] Causons pond is probably the pond known as Crosman's Pond. It has been supposed in recent years that the name Causon was the result of a vulgarised evolution from the name Crosman, and this supposition was reinforced by a story that a man by the name of Crosman was once drowned in the pond. It is probable, however, that Causon is correct, and that Crosman, as laid down on recent maps, is wrong.

[46.] At a Town Meeting held at plimouth July 31 1699 voted that the select men should take Care to provide A scoole Master for the town with all Conveniant sped & should settle him as Neere the senter of the Towne as may be with Conveniency & that Every scollar that Coms to wrigh or syfer or to lern latten shall pay 3 pence pr weke if to Read only then to pay 3 half pence per weke to be paid by their Masters or parents & what shall Remain due to sd scole to be Levied by Rate on the whole Inhabitants in there Just and Equal proportion

And for to prevent further strey of the Comons The Inhabitants thought meete to make Choyce of A Comitty to Endeavour to draw up som Method or Rule to propose to the Town in order to a division of sd towns Comons sd Comity are

     Lef : Bradford
     Joseph Bartlet sen
     M$^{e}$ Nathaniel Thomas
     John Waterman
     & James Warren.

and its further ordered and voted by the Inhabitants of the Town that Noe Cordwood, oake timber or planck shall be Cut on sd Comons to be transported out of sd towne untill sd Comitie have prepared some Method & propos to the towne as abovesd on forfiture of sd timber or the valew of it for the use of sd Towne & have Made Choyce of Joseph Bartlett John doty & Caleb Cook as Agents or trustees of sd town to se this order be duely & truly performed & to Mak seisyur of aney wood or timber that shall be soe brought down to be transported out of sd town as abovsd

At sd Meting A spot of land was granted to M$^{er}$ Little and Caleb Loren to the Eastward of the Road Neer New strete and by the fence side which was somtime M$^{er}$ Nath : Clarks fence : to dig a well Not to Exceed 5 foot into the lane from sd fence

At sd Meeting Liberty was granted to Ephraim Cole to set up a pew behind the North dore in the Meting house

Whereas sundry of the Inhabitants of The Town of plimouth haveing Takein in Certaine Tracts of Common Lands To The prejudace of sundry Neibhours whereupon the Inhabitants of sd Town Att a town Metting held at plimouth on the 15$^{th}$ day of May 1699 Made Choice of William Shirtleif John Doty sen James Warren & Thomas faunce to be agents for & trustes in the behalf of said town to defend the sd Commons

from particular Intrustions & In the Town's Behalf to Warne
aney of sd Inhabitants that have Made aney Incloser of sd
towns Commons to Remove theire fences of said Comons and
upon Theire Neglecting or Refussing in Convenient time soe to
doe the agents or trustees above Mentioned are hereby Impowred
by sd Inhabitants To Remove all such fences found upon sd Towns
Commons or sue such persons so Neglecting or Refusing to
Remove Theire fences of sd Commons upon Warning given Them
by sd Agents Its Further voated by sd Inhabbitants that aney
three of sd fouer Agents agreeing In setlement of The Ranges
betwen The Towns Commons & particular persons Rights shall
be and Remain good

[47.] November 16th 1699

Then laid outt to John dotty sen six acres of land
granted to him by the town liing on the southerly side of his
owne land above the Common Rhode Way and bounded as
followth, below Next the Rhoad with a Red oake sapling Marked
on 4 sides and Runneth up in length with his lots & at the half
mile End It Is bounded With a White oake sapling standing on
the North side of the Cart Way Nere sd Way

    Measured and bounded The day
    above Written
    per Mee Tho : ffaunce surveigher

November ye 16 : 1699

Wheras old M^er John holmes had a grant of ten acres of
land att The head of his land above the Common Rhoad Way
betwen The sd Way and James hursts land now in the posseshon
of John Cob and Whereas Thay have by Their Anchient Claime
and Common Estimation of Neibhours held this strip of land
betwen the abovesd Way and the land of The abovesd Cobb and
the six acres of land laid outt to John doty above Mentioned
Therefore The sd strip of land Is laid outt to the sd holmses
heirs for ten acres be It more or less and Is bounded as ffolloweth
by the Road at The southerly End With a White oake bush and
a stone sett into the ground and soe Ranging up to sd Cobs
bounds Which Is a Red oak sapling and att The Northwest End
bounded Next the Road With a Red oake sapling Which Is John
dotys Corner bound of his acres above recorded and so to Run
up in Length with John dotys land and there bounded With a

White oake sapling Marked on 4 sides standing on the southerly side of the Way opposite against dotys Corner bound at the head Which sd White oake Is a side Rang of sd Cobs Land, Alwayes provided that the sd holmeses heirs Leave a Way for Carts and Cattle to pass Through sd land up to ye Commons att the head Thereof ass theire May be ocation for the Neibhours to pass Through to the Commons

       Measured and bounded The day
       above Written per Mee Tho : Faunce
         surveigher
November 17th 1699

 Then Measured & bounded out unto George Morton ten Acrees of land att a place Comonly Caled & Known by the Name of the high Ridg & is bounded as followeth begining at the Norwest Corner of ye swamp below sd Redg & there bounded with A stake and a heap of stons About it & thence Rainging West southwest 40 pole to a Red oake sapling Marked on 4 sides & a heape of stones by it and thence Ranging south southeast 40 pole to a grate white oake tree and a heap of stones by sd tree said tree being Marked on 4 sides and thence Rainging East Northeast 40 pole to the swamp below the Ridg & there bounded with a grat Red oake tree Marked on 4 sides & soe bounded by the above named swamp till it Cometh to the stak & stons above mentioned

      Measured and bounded per Thomas ffaunce
       surveyor to the town of plimouth

 At a Town Meeting held at plimouth october 19th 1699 The following bill of Charge was alowed of by the Inhabitants to be leavied by Rate on sd Inhabitants which is as foloweth Imprimis for ye

|  | £ | s | d |
|---|---|---|---|
| Representative | 12 | 00 | 00 |
| for Keeping John Andrew | 10 | 00 | 00 |
| for glasing the Meeting house | 02 | 11 | 06 |
| To abraham Jacson for Keeping the Meeting house & Ringing | 01 | 14 | 00 |
| To John Bradford for service at bostorn for the Town | 01 | 10 | 00 |
| To the Comitty for Taking account of the select men | 00 | 09 | 00 |
| To the select men for Atending to give the acount | 00 | 05 | 00 |

|   |   £ | s | d |
|---|---|---|---|
| To the present select men for Making Rates | 02 | 00 | 00 |

In Referance to a former order Made by a Comitty Chosen by sd Inhabitants for that End bearing date March 13$^{th}$ 169$\frac{2}{3}$ for the preventing the strey of timber on the Town's Comons which were allowed by the Justesses acording to law viz that henceforth noe spruce or pine timber or boards made of Either of them shall be Caried or transported out of the town upon forfiture of sd timber or boards or ye vallue of them for the use of the Town and if any person or persons shall bring down aney boards or timber in order to transport outt of the town he or thay shall be Liable to Make It appeare that thay have Cutt sd timber upon theire owne Lands or out of some other township on forfiture of sd timber or boards As abovesd, Its further voatted that the same obligation shall be upon Coardwood Ceder or oake timber for the partyes that briug It to transport away out of the town such persons so bringing sd Wood or timber shall be Liable to prove as abovsd that thay have Cutt sd Wood on theire owne Land or otherwise to pay The dutyes on shingle Claboard or Railes by the former orders sett upon them and these orders to take place Within a month after the date hereof and henceforth noe more Timber to be Cutt to be transported out of the town and that the mouths time spessefied is only to Transport what Is Already Cutt, The town apointed Leut Mory & Lev briant John doty sen benjamin Warren Elknah Cushman and Caleb Lorein to have the Inspection of these orders.

[49.] Att a towne Metting held at plimouth December ye 11$^{th}$ 1699

The Juriors Chosen att sd Meting were John Morton Eliazer Churchell John Churchell Ephraime Cole Nathaniel Jackson and John barnes

Att sd Meetting the towne voatted to Let out a sertaine branch of a Ceder swamp Lying about The head of Wonquonquany unto shuball smith at Sandwidg for three years for forty shillings per yeare, Also the select men are Impowered to Lett outt a small Ceder swamp Liing neare Roches for lhree years provided he pay five pound downe upon his takeing of the Lease for the use of the towne : Its further voatted att sd Met that with Refferance to the settlement of the bounds between plimouth and Midleborough the town voatted to stand to the proposition Made by the Agents of

Midlebereh viz to Chose Capt basseett Cap$^t$ Edson & Capt Chittengton to Run the line and settle the bounds betweu sd plimouth and Midleberough acording to oure Court grant of township.

Att a town Meetting held att plimouth february 26$^{th}$ 1700 The Grandjuriors Chosen for the yeare Were William Ring Thomas Lorein Benjamim Eatton Jun & Georg Shaw

The petty Jury Chosen to serve att the County Court the fifth of March Were Capt Warren M$^{er}$ Mordo John ffoster and William harlow;

Att sd Metting The town voatted to Alow the sum of ten pounds to Mistris Cotton upon the Acount of Arears Due from the Town to her Latte Husband M$^{er}$ John Cotton deceased and thatt upon the payment of The Money she give a General Acquittance To the Town;

Att the Metting abovesd The town doe order Thatt with Refferance to all former grants of Lands within the Township shall have Nott yett ben Laid out and bounded That thay shall be Laid out within 3 months after this Datte

[50.] And with Refferance to aney grants of Lands within the township That shall be hereafter Made Thatt the persons to whome It Is granted shall have theire Land Laid outt within three Months after It Is granted or Else forfeitt theire grant, And Thatt No Records of bounds of Land shall be Recorded by the Clerk of the Town but it Comes from under the hands of 2 of the surveighers of the Town and for that End the Town Made Choice of James Warren & Will Shurtlif to be surveighers for the Town for the Measureing of Lands as ocation shall be

Att a town Metting held att plimouth March 18$^{th}$ 1700 The Select Men Chosen Were William Shirtlef James Warren & John Mordo; The Cunstables Chosen Were Richard seers & Benjamin sole; The surveighers Chosen for the High Wayes Were Samuell Stirtevant samuel ffuller Isaac Lathrop Ebenaser holmes & Ben Praat; William Shirtlef Chosen Town Treasurer

The Town Mad Choice of a Committy To settle how far Each surveigher shall Mend and surveigh; Which is Capt Bradford William Shirtlef Ephrame Morton John briant & John praat; The Tithing Men Chosen were John Dyer Eliazar Morton & William Churchell Att sd Meetting The Town granted to samuell ffuller Libberty to Exchange The hundred acres of Land formerly granted to M^rs Bridgett ffuller att her Meadow at Lakenham & to take Itt up att the Indian pond plaine

Att sd Metting Ten acres of Land Is granted to Nicolas May at Manomet ponds Ten acres Is granted to Samuell Cornish at or Neare the sam place

Att sd Metting Samuell Rider protests against the grants

[51.] Att sd Meeting The Gran Juriors Chosen to serve att The superior Court were James Warren Nathaniell Southworth & Nathaniell Morton The petty Juriors Chosen to serve att sd Court were William shirtlef Ephraime Morton John Mordo Samuel Stirttevant John Stirtevant & John Carver

Att sd Meetting The town grantted to Isaac Lathrop A peice of Land att the gutter by The Corner of John Wattsons ffence to sett a house on sd Land to be 50 ffoott ffront.

Att sd Meetting The town voated to seett up a pound on the Towns Charge

Plimouth Aprill 3 1700

The Land granted to Isaac Lathrop by the Town of plimouth Is Bounded as ffolloweth : on the Easterly Corner of John Watsons ffence with a stake seett in the ground and from thence Extending 80 foott Westerly by The sd Watsons ffence to a stone seett unto The ground and from thence Southerly ffifty foott to a stone seett into the ground and from thence Easterly 80 fott to a stone set in the ground nere the high way and from thence fiftty foott to ye bounds first mentioned

Measured and bounded The day and year first mention^d per James Warren & William Shirtlef surveyer of ye Town of plimouth

Att A Town Meeting held at blimonth on the 13^th of May 1700 Nathaniel Warren was Chosen Representative ; The Juriors Chosen to serve at the County Court in June were Benjamen Warren John Bradford Junor John Watson & Thomas Shirtlif ; At sd Meeting The Inhabitants Then Mett voated that the select men should be the assessors for the yere Ensuing att sd Meeting The Town voted to Raise the sum of 63 pound for to defray publick Charges in sd town (viz)

|  | £ | s | d |
|---|---|---|---|
| To the scool Master | 33 | 00 | 00 |
| & for M^er Cottons Arrears 10 00 00 | | | |
| & for the Asembly man | 10 | 00 | 00 |
| & for the pore 10 00 00 & this sums to be Rated for on the Inhabitants & paid in by the last of September Next after this date | | | |

[52.] At the Meting last Mentioned A former grant of 10 acrees of land to Giles Rickard was Confirmed Lying at the south Meadows against his meadow

Att sd Meeting The Town granted to Elisha Holmes & Manasses Morton fifty foott frunt of Land along the Road Above John Riders land in the Comon ty Lyeth betwen sd Riders land & the Road that is to say to each of them fifty foot frunt A peece & to Extend in length down towards the sea till Coming with 12 or 14 foot of sd Riders land; provided sd holmes & morton build or Cause to be builded dweling housing upon sd spotts of land within two years after this date or otherwise to Return to the Town againe Att sd Meting Liberty was granted to Nathaniel Warren to fence in A pece of Comons betwen the Town brook and barrows land for 7 years provided at the End of sd time he Remove his fence and leave it to the towne.

April 24 1700 The Meadow Granted To Giles Rickard & Samuel dunham at A place Caled southers Marsh is bounded as followeth from the Northermost beaver dam southerly all the meadow lying upon sd brook To the bounds of Will: Rings Meadow is laid out to samuel dunham

    Surveyed and bounded per William Shurtlif
    & James Warren surveyors

May 9^th 1700  The Meadow Granted to Giles Rickard at south Meadows is bounded as followeth the first two acrees are on the southwest by M^er Jonathan barnes Meadow & is in length 26 poole and a half and Runs over at Each end West Norwest to pine trees Marked at Each Corner

      Wm Shurtlif
      James Warren sur:

May 9th 1700   The 4 acres of Meadow Granted to Jonathan barnes at the south meadows is as followeth southwest by Giles Rickards & Runs up the River or brook from Giles Rickards one hundred Rood 80 Rood is six Rood Wide and Twenty Rod is Eight Rood wide & at the uper End two pine Trees Marked on Each side upon the upland

per Wm Shurtlif & James Warren surv ;

The 4 acres of Meadow & Meadowish land laid out at south Meadows To Giles Rickard by vertue of A grant is as followeth from the aforesd barnses Meadow it Raingeth Eighty Rood up the brook towards swan hold & is betwen Eight or Nine Rood in bredth & at the head two pine trees Marked on the upland Rainging west norwest & East south East Wm Shurtlif & James Warren surveyors

Att a town Metting held at plimouth May 13th 1700 The Towne granted to Ephrame Tilson a Certain Cove of Meadow being an acre and a half or there abouts liing on the Easterly side of The south Meadow brook

[53.] May 9 1700 The ten acres of upland granted to Giles Rickard at south Meadows Is bounded as ffolloweth, viz It Lieth on the southeast side of his Meadow a stake stuck in the ground on the southwest Corner Neare a Run of Watter that goeth into the Meadow and from sd stake Runeth 32 Rod East and by south to a stake Neare the Way that goeth to south Meadows and from thence to a nother stake 50 Rod North and by East to a pine tree Marked and from sd tree 32 Rod West and by North to a stake sett by the Meadow side and from sd stake 50 pole southwest & by West & the Meadow to be the Westerly bounds till it Comes to the stake first mentioned per Wm Shirtlef & James Warren survighors

May 9th 1700

The Meadow granted to Daniel Dounham on south Meadow brooke is bounded as followeth thirty six Rod to the Westward of south Meadow brook to two pine trees Marked one on the North side and another on ye south side Liing on horse Neck brook per William Shirtlef & James Warren surveyers

May 9th 1700

The Meadow granted to Benijah praatt att horse Neck brook is bounded as ffolloweth on the Easterly End of Daniel Dounhams Meadow and soe Extendeth up to a stake stuck in the ground where ye upland Comes Neare to ye brook on the Westerly side and a pine Tree on the Easterly side Marked

p$^r$ William Shirtlef and James Warren surveyers

The twenty acres of Land formerly granted to Deacon Dounham is Laid out and bounded as followeth, att Wenham, viz, bounded Northerly by The Way aboutt six or seven Rood that Cometh from thence to Towne & from Thence the brook and way or Rhoad that goeth to south Meaddows to be the other bound one Each side East & West till it Come down to a Red oake tree Marked by a swamp and from sd tree to Extend Westerly to the brook to a Maple tree Marked p$^r$ William Shirtlef & James Warren

surveiers

plimouth Aprill 2$^d$ 1700

The Land granted to John Rider is bounded as followeth on the southeast Corner with a stone sett into the ground by sd Riders fence, from sd stone Northwesterly to a Nother stone set into the ground, from thence on a straite Line Nere the southeasterly Corner of sd Riders house to a stake sett into the ground Nere the southeasterly Corner of sd house about 6 ffoott from sd house, from sd stake East Northerly to sd Riders other Land

pr William Shirtlef and James Warren<br>surveyers To The Town of plimouth

March 28 1700

Whereas Elder Thomas Cushman deceased gave unto his three sons Thomas Isaac & Elknah 12 acres of Meadow at Winattuxett Liing between the Meadow of John dounham formerly deceased and the Meadow of M$^{er}$ John howland deceased, The sd Thomas Isaac & Elknah have agreed that ye sd Thomas is to take the uper and Next the sd dounhams Meadow & the sd Elknah Is to Take in Midle next to the sd Thomas and the sd Isaac Takes his at the lower end next the sd howlands Meadow, and The bounds of division are as ffolloweth That the bound on the Northerly side of The River betwen The sd Thomas and Elknah Is a White oak Marked, The bounds on the southerly side is a pine tree Marked on 4 sides and the bounds between the sd Elknah and Isaac on the Northerly side of the River is a Maple tre Marked on 4 sides and on the southerly side of a pine tree Marked on fouer sides

       Thomas Cushman
       Isaac Cushman
       Elknah Cushman

Bartlet 5   The eight Acres of Meadow Granted to Joseph bartlet att a town Meeting held at plimouth on the 14$^{th}$ of July 1667 at the south Meadow River is bounded as ffolloweth from Samuel Eedys bounds down the River to A pine Tree Marked on the North East side of the River & from sd tree to Run south-west and by west to an other tree Marked on the south west side of the River All the Meadow on both sides the River with the above mentioned bounds
     William Shurtlif & James Warren
      surviors to the Towne of plimouth

Coombs 1   The six acres of Meadow Granted to frances Combs at south meadow River At a town Meeting held at plimouth on the 14$^{th}$ of July 1667 is bounded as followeth on the Eastward side of the River A lettle below John Bensons it Runs 26 pole by the

This shold have ben first Entered

River to a stake stuck in the Meadow Neere a Run of water & from sd stake 28 pole about East & by south to an other stake stuck in the Meadow & soe Running to the upland the same Corse to A yong Red oake sappling Marked & the upland to be the Northerly & Easterly bound together with an other acre lying up sd River Above John Bensons
     survyed & bounded per
     Will: Shurtlif James Warren
     surveyors To the town

Aprill 22 1710

 Then ye 4 acrees of meadow Granted by ye Town of plimouth on ye 31 of August 1702 To Nathaniel holmes senior and Joseph faunce at ye Ceder swamp on southers Marsh brook & bounded on the North end with a spruce tree marked & then to Extend Northwesterly to a maple it being ye bound of Robert barrows Meadow & then by sd meadow a

Nathallen holmes & Joseph ffaunce their medow

Cross ye brook to A Crooked Maple Marked on 4 sides and then to Extend 44 pole southwest 7 Lc- grees westerly to a Crooked Maple standing in the brook Marked on 4 sides & then 14 pole southeast 7 Degrees southerly to ye bounds of ye Ceder swampe & then to Extend soe as to take in all ye Meadow Ground to ye bound first mentioned

James Warren }
Nath. Morton } surveiors

hugh Cole

[55.] 2 The Ten acres of Meadow granted to hugh Cole att a town Meeting held at plimouth July 14 1667 liing at south Meadow River is bounded as ffolloweth on the Northerly side by francis Combses Meadow and Easterly With a pine tree standing on the upland on the Northerly side of sd Meadow and from sd tree to run southerly by a Little Neck of upland to two pine trees Marked on the southerly side growing both out of one Root which is the Eastward bounds of sampsons brook and from sd bounds all The Meadow down the River on both sides Within our bounds to a pine tree Marked on 4 sides where the River Comes Nere the upland and from sd tree to Run over the River south south west to another pine tree Marked and soe on the same Course till It Come to Rochester bounds

surveyed and bounded By William Shurtlef and James Warren Surveyers to ye town

John Cole 3

The six acres of Meadow granted to John Cole Liing on South Meadow Biver att a town Metting held at plimouth July 14 1667 is bounded as followeth Itt Lieth on The southwest side of the River in a Body of Meadow below Willesses and Is bounded Westerly by sepecan Line: 53 Rood in Length and is Eighteen Rod in breadth and at The Eastward Corner stakes stuck into the Meadow

surveyed and bounded By Will Shurtlef & James Warren surveyors to The Town

Sam Eddy 4    The Meadow grantted to Samuell Edey on south Meadow River att a Town Meeting held at plimouth July 14 1667 is bounded as ffolloweth from the aforesd hugh Coles bounds att the Meadow Liing Down the River to a great pine tree Marked on the Northeast side of the River and from thence to Run southwest and by south to the Northeastermost part of John Coles bounds

    surveyed and bounded By Will Shurtlef & James Warren surveyers to ye town

John 6  The five acres of Meadow granted to John ffallafallowell well at south Meadow River att a town Metting held at plimouth July 14 1667 is bounded as ffolloweth Att The Meadow below Joseph Bartlets bounded down the River till It Come to sepecan bounds That Lieth on sd River

    surveyed and bounded By William Shurtlef and James Warren surveyers to the town of plimouth

[56.] plimouth June ye 8[th] 1700

  The Land granted to Manasses Morton and Elisha holmes Att a town Meetting held att plimouth May 13[th] 1700 and Is bounded as followeth that Is to say Mannasseth Mortons partt on the southwesterly Corner with a stone sett in the ground Nere The high way and from sd stone Running Northeasterly to a stone sett into the ground 14 ffoott from John Riders Land and from sd stone Running fifty foott westerly To another stone seett into the ground and from sd stone Running southerly To another stone sett into the ground Nere the high way and from sd stone fifty foot to the stons Last Mentioned.

  Elisha holmeses part Is bounded as followeth that Is to say on the Easterly side With Mannasseh Mortons Land and from Manasseth Mortons southwest Corner bound Running Northwesterly fifty foott to a stone sett in the ground Nere the high way and from sd stone Running Northeasterly to a stone seett into the ground about 14 foott from sd Riders Land and from sd stone Running Easterly to Manasseth Mortons Northwest Corner bound

    Surveyed and Bounded By William Shirtlef and James Warren surveyers to The Town of plimouth

The bounds of Nicolas Mayes Land Granted him by the town above Manoment ponds is as followeth on the North East side bounded by samuell Cornishes Lands from the Red oake Tree Marked standing by the path thatt Goeth to the herring pond To Extend west and by north fifty pole to a grate Rock & from thence to Extend south and by west 32 pole to a Red oake tree Marked on : 4 : sides & from thence to Extend East : and : by south fifty pole to a Red oake bush standing neer the aforesd path & from thence to Extend 32 pole North & by East Till it meteth with the bounds first Mentioned

Measured & bounded on the 26<sup>th</sup> of Aprill 1700<br>pr James Warren<br>William Shurtlif surveyors

The bounds of Samuell Cornishes Land granted to him by ye Town above Maneoment ponds is bounded as followeth viz on the southeast Corner With a Red oake Tree Marked on 4 sides standing by a Run of Watter and from Thence to Extend East and by south 40 pole To another marked Red oake Tree standing by The way y<sup>t</sup> goes to the herin pond and from Thence to Run North & by East 38 pole to a Red oake sapling Marked and from ye bounds first mentioned to Run 42 pole to a White oak Tree marked on 4 sides North and be East and from sd White oake To Run on a straite Line till It Comes to ye Red oake sapling.

Measured and bound on ye 26 of Aprill 1700<br>per James Warren & William Shurtlef surveyers

[**57.**] Att a town Metting held at plimouth September 14 1700 for The Choice of Juriors To serve att The County Court Lieu<sup>tt</sup> Southworth John Watterman Nathaniell Morton & Adam Wright

Att sd Metting Lieu<sup>tt</sup> Southworth & John Mortton Were Apoynted by ye Town To Vew The Land Desired by Cap<sup>t</sup> Warren & to Make Report Thereof to The town

Att sd Metting Liberty Was Granted To Elknah Cushman Benjamin Bartlett & others To sett up a pew up in ye old Gallery

Att sd Metting John Rickard John Churchill Jacob Cook Together With The Rest y<sup>t</sup> had formerly an Intrest In a seatte Liberty Is granted Them To Raise sd seate higher If They see Cause provided Thay Raise ye hindermost seats in Like proporttion To Theirs.

Att a town Metting Held at plimouth Decem<sup>br</sup> 16 1700 For The Choice of Juriors To serve att The Quartter sessions on 17

Iust int The persons Chosen at sd Metting are John Mortton John Churchell Ephrame Cole Eliazer Ring Thomas Mortton & Stephen Barnabe

Att sd Metting Capt Bradford Was Chosen To Answer ye Towns presentment for want of a pound.

At sd Metting Eliazer Dounham Is agreed With By ye Inhabitants of The town To Ring The Bell & sweep the Metting house & To Keep The Dores and Casements Carefully shutt for one yeare from The Datte Last above mentioned & The town Is to aLow to sd Dounham for sd service sd year Thirty shillings

Att sd Metting Cap$^t$ Bradford Capt$^t$ Warren Lei$^{tt}$ Southworth Elknah Cushman & Samuell Sterttevant were appointed a Committy To Draw up some Method To propose to The town The next town Metting in order to The Division of The Comons Which Is to be on The first Munday in January next.

[58.] Att a Town Meeting held at plimouth January 20$^{th}$ 17$\frac{00}{01}$ at sd meting a leter was Red to the Inhabitants signed by the agents of Medlebery Relating to some Controversey betwen the purchasers of the south purchis soe Caled lying partly within the township of plimouth & Midlebery wherein sd agents moved for Agents to treat them in order to a Complyance if it mite be or to sserve it in a Cort of law The Ihabitants of plimouth doe apprehend themselves to be the Rightful propriators of the land in Controversey and Chose Left Jonathan Mony Left William Shurtlif and deacon John Waterman to be their agents to prosecute the mater in a Corse of Law if put upon it and the Inhabitants voted to stand by them therin and to defray the Charge that shall aRise therupon

The hundred acrees of land Granted to samuell ffuller at a town Meeting held at plimouth ye 18$^{th}$ of March 17$\frac{00}{01}$ att the Indian pond in the Lew of A hundred acres formerly Granted to M$^{rs}$ brigget fuller at dotyes plaine Neere dotyes Meadow is Bounded as followeth on the Northwest Corner w$^{th}$ A White oake tree Marked which is the Corner bounds of Jacob Cooks Land & from sd tree to Extend Northeast and by East half a pint Easterly till it Cometh down to the Indian pond & from thence to Extend 136 pole southeast and by south half a pint southerly till it Cometh to two White oake trees standing together Marked a lettle to the southard of the aforsd pond & the pond to be the East side bounds as far as it Extends & from Thence to Extend 108 pole southwest

and by west half a pint westerly to two trees Marked and from thence to Extend on a straite line to the bounds first Mentioned if it doth not Infring on Jacob Cooks land
      laid out and bounded July 1700
      per James Warren & Will Shurtlif
        surveyors to the Town.

 plimouth January 16$^{th}$ 1700 We being desired by Joseph alden & Josep Haward to Renew & settle ye bounds of the peace of land granted by the select men of the Town of plimouth to John dunham [1] on the 15$^{th}$ of february 1658 doe Renew & settle them as ffolloweth as they were formerly Reputed to be settled That is to say a white oake tree on the westerly Corner nere ye head of the little pond & from sd tree southeasterly by a Rainge of trees to an other pond Caled ffresh lake neere an old Wolf trapp and soe bounded southerly by fresh lake and Northerly by the sd little pond till it Cometh to the Northeastermost End of sd pond to a grate pine tree Marked & from thence southeasterly by an old sawpitt & from thence to a white oake bush & so on a straite Corse to a birch bush Marked on 4 sides standing by the brook that Cometh out of fresh lake.
     per William Shurtlif & James Warren
       surveyors To the Town

[59.] September 1641
  The 8 acres of Meadow granted to John dunham senior at swan hold is bounded as followeth with a black oak tree standing on the west side of the Meadow Marked on 4 sides and from sd tree Extending East 60 pole to a white oake stake set in the Meadow & from thence to Extend North 22 pole to a pine stake stuck in the Meadow and from sd stake to Extend West 60 pole to a pine tree standing Neere the Meadow Marked on 4 sids & from sd tree to Extend south 22 pole to the bounds first Mentioned
     per William Shirtlif James Warren
  The 4 acrees of Meadow granted to daniel dunham on the 14$^{th}$ of July 1667 at south meadow brook is bounded as ffolloweth on the southwest Corner with a white pine tree standing on the East side of the south meadow brook and from thence Running Westerly aCross sd brook to 3 maples growing out of one Root &

---

[1] The ten acres granted to John Dunham are included in the Plymouth park at Billington Sea. In ancient deeds the land between the two ponds is called Dunhams Neck.

soe up the brook to two pine trees Marked on Each side the brook a letle above where hors Neck brook Cometh into south meadow brook that hath not ben laid out to any particular within sd bounds surveyd and Mea. by us the 17$^{th}$ of January 1700 per William Shurtlif & James Warren surveyors to the Town Whereas The bounds of the forty Akrees of Land formerly granted unto M$^{er}$ William Clarke on the southerly side of the Eale River by the town of plimouth being lost are Renewed as followeth (viz) bounded by the Eale River with A black birch tree Marked on 4 sides standing Neere the sd River on the southerly side of the path that goeth over the River about 25 foot of from Thomas fances fence there ; & thence Rainging south East & by south Easterly forty six Rood to a stake set into the ground 12 foot Easterly from A white oake tre Marked on 4 sides & from thence to Extend southwest by A Raing of Marked trees Eight score Roods till it Cometh to two Red oaks Marked with A heape of stones at the Roots & from thence to Extend 36 Rods till it Cometh to the River where a White oake tree is marked on 4 sides & soe the River to be the bounds till it Cometh to the black birch tree first Mentioned ;

Measured and bounded on the 21$^{st}$ day of June 1701 per James Warren and William Shurtliff Surveiors to the Town

[60.] For Choice of Town officers

Att a Town Meetting Held att plimouth March ye 3$^{d}$ Ano 1701 Thomas faunce Chosen Town Clerk for the yeare Ensueing

The Sellect Men Chosen Were Cap$^{tt}$ Bradford M$^{er}$ Nath Mortton and Leit William Shurtlef ; The Cunstables Chosen Were Isaac Lathrop & Jonathan Shaw Jun ; The surveiors for ye high Wayes are M$^{er}$ Joseph bartlett Dea John Watterman John pratt Nathaniell Holmes & James Winslow ; The Tithing Men Chosen Were Richard seeres James Barnabe & Isaac King, The Grand Jury for The yeare Ensueing are samuell harlow John Bryantt & John Dyer, The fence veuers Chosen Were Elknah Cushman Benjamin Warren and William Ring. John Dyer Chosen To be sealler of Weights & Measures

Att sd The grandjuriors Chosen To serve att The Superior Court Were Samuel Rider M$^{er}$ Joseph bartlett & John stirtevant; The petty Jury Chosen to serve att sd Courtt Were John doty sen samuell Lucas Eliazor Cushman & benjamin Warren The Juriors Chosen To serve att The County Court are Leivtt Southworth Robert bartlett John foster & Thomas howland

Att sd Metting Cap$^{tt}$ Warren & Leivt Shirtlef Were Chosen agents to Run the Line betwen plimouth and sandwidg;

At sd Metting It was voated That the persons be trusted with The oversight of the Commons To see Thay bent Entruded upon Doe further prosecute The Matter Relating to John Grayes Claime of Land att Rockey Nook

Att sd Metting John Morton had Libberty from sd town to build a seat up in the North Gallery in the Metting house under The window

[61.] At A Town Meting held at plimouth on the 19$^{th}$ of May 1701 Capten James Warren Was Chosen Representative to serve sd town in the General Cort at bostorn this present yeare At sd Meting Adam Wright Chosen to serve on the grand Jury for this present yeare, The Juror for Tryals Are Benjamin Soule

At sd Meeting The Town voated that M$^{er}$ Little should have all the Contrebut That is Contrebuted on the Acownt of the Maintanance of the Minest for this present yeare in sd town & the use of the 20 pounds in banck belonging to sd town for one yeare: from the date abovesd he ye sd M$^{er}$ Little Giveing in securety to sd town to Respond sd Money at the Expiration of sd yeare

At sd Meting Capt John Bradford was Chosen to be helpfull defend the towns Wright from being Intruded on: with Capt Warren & Left Shurtlef in the Roome of John doty latly deceased & aney two of them Agreing shal be Accounted valed

At sd Meeting it was voted by the Town That noe person should fence hence forward Any part of the Towns Comons with out leave from the Town & whosoever shal presum soe to do shal be proseeded with and prosecuted Acording to law by the agents of sd Town

At sd Meeting 20 foot of Land Is granted To James Warren & 20 foot to Nathaniell Warren on The Northward side of There Whorf below Coles hill so Called and soe downward Into The sea

Att sd Metting M$^{er}$ Mordo had Liberty from The Town to Wharfe a Cross from his one Wharf To M$^{er}$ bartlets Whorf

Att sd Metting The Like Liberty Is granted To M$^{er}$ John Rickard To Wharf from his one Wharf To M$^{er}$ Thomases Wharfe

Att sd Metting Is Granted unto John ffoster That spot of Land already fenced in about his shop below The bank

Att sd Meeting Leut Shirtlef is granted Liberty to purchas 50 or a hundred acres of Land upon The Towns Commons of said Town for 2s. an acre to him & his heirs for Ever att The Westward of barnses bridg at The south Meadows

At sd Meeting liberty is granted to John Stirtevant To fence ACross some pints of upland on the Towns Comons for the more Convenient fenceing his Meadow at doties Meadow

[62.] At sd Meeting Nathaniel Thomas & Leften Jonathan Morey was granted Liberty To purchas of the Indians Land within the bounds of the town Towards Sandwedg hereng pond on the Eastward to the quantety of one hundred acres

[1] At sd Meeting the Town voted yt with Referance to the 4 spots of land in Controversey betwen Major Bradford & the Town (viz) that part he sold to John Dier & the spot of land where the old Meeting house stood & the spot of land sold to Nathaniel howland Neere M$^{er}$ Littles house and the spot of land lately fenced in by Ephraim Cole Att the second brook by the widow Nelsons : The Town doe herby quitt their Clame to sd lands

Sam$^{l}$ Harlow

At sd Meeting Samuel harlow is Granted the swampy land at the southeast of his own land whereon his house Now standeth

At sd Meeting Granted to John Eaverson 6 acres of land Next his own land where he Now liveth

At sd Meting the Town granted to Benijah pratt 2 Acrees of Meadow Next his own Meadow upon hors Neck

---

[1] The land sold to John Dyer was sold by Major William Bradford in 1698, and is described in the deed as running on the street northeasterly "as far as the northeasterly corner of the old storehouse which formerly stood on the lot." It was the lot on the south side of Leyden Street, opposite the Universalist Meeting-house, on which the house with a brick end stands. Whether the old storehouse referred to was one of the very early structures is left to conjecture.

The " spot of land on which the old Meetting-house stood," was the upper part of the Odd Fellows' lot in Town Square. This land was sold by Major William Bradford to John Murdock in 1698.

Att sd Meeting Liberty is Granted to the Rickards that have Meadow at Annasnapet to fence A Cross from pints of Comons for the more Convenient fencing theire Meadows there Att sd Meeting The Town gave Liberty to the surveyors of the Town to sell a persel of swampe unto peter Thomson that lyeth Neere & Convenient for him of Comons belonging To the Town which was done and bounded out to him the sd peter Tomson which bounds are as followeth A Maple tree on the East side of the land he now liveeth on standing in a swompe & soe Cross sd swompe 16 Rood southeast & by East to A white oake tree marked on the East side of the swomp & from sd tree southwest and by south 50 Rood to the brook and then the brook to be the bounds to the head of the brook

James Warren &<br>William Shurtlif<br>surveiors

New plimouth october 7<sup>th</sup> 1701 Then laid out to Thomas ffannce 10 Acres of land at the south Meadow soe Caled by vertu of Right therto by vertu of an Ancient Grant of meadow at sd south meadows & sd land is bounded as ffolloweth (viz) begining at a grate Red oak tree standing neer the Meadows which is the Corner bounds of a lott of land Now in the posesion of George bonam & Jacob Cooke & from sd Tree to Extend 40 pole southeast to a small Red oake Marked which is the head bounderays of sd Bonman & Cooks lott abovesd & from thence to Extend 44 pole southwest to A small pine tree Marked on 4 sides & from thence to Extend Norwest 40 pole to a grat pine tree Marked on 4 sids & A Red oake sappling by it & soe bounded by the Meadow to the bounds first Mentioned

surveied & Bounded per<br>James Warren<br>William Shurtliff<br>Surveiors

[63.] The bounds of the land which William Shurtlif bought of the Inhabitants of plimouth At A town Meeting held at plimouth May 19<sup>th</sup> 1701 Lying at south meadow ; for two shilling p$^{er}$ Acree as p$^r$ Town Record doth & may Apere sd land Lyeth on the Northwest side of the south meadow brook or River Against A place that is Caled the fals & on the Northwest

Grant
to Wm.
Shurtleff

Corner bounded w<sup>th</sup> A grat Rock by beaver dam brook & there is 2 or 3 small White oak trees Marked on the North side of the Rock by the brook & from thence to Extend Nere East Northeast one hundred Thirty two pole it Runeth by the brook About 20 or 30 pole to A grate Whitewood tree Marked & from thence by marked trees till it Cometh to a grate pine Tree standing alone which is marked on 4 sids & from thence to Extend six score Rod or More south southeast till it Cometh to a Red oake Tree Marked w<sup>th</sup> A hepe of stons at the Roote & soe down to a grate Rock thence by the side of the Meadow that was granted by the town to the Ministrey & from sd Rock to Extend one hundred thirty two pole Nere west southwest bounded by the Meadow & River & the Lands formerly granted to Anthony snow & now Claimed by John Barrows & att the Extent of the hundred thirty two Rods to Run Neer Norwest on A straite line six score Rod till it meeteth with the bounds first mentioned. This land was Laid out by us who have herunto subscribed on the 22<sup>d</sup> day of May one thousand seaven hundred & one

      James Warren
      William Shurtleff
       surveyors

Jurors

At A Town Meting held at plimouth on the 28<sup>th</sup> of May 1701 The Jurors Chosen to serve at the County Court att September Next are John Mordo Abiall Shurtlif John doty Stephen Bryant & Ebenazur Cobb voted that Aney two of the select men shall Attend the Cort to Answer the Towns presentment for Want of A scoolmaster

Voted That with Referance to the petition of the uper society for A township its Refered to further Agitation at the Next Town Meeting

Voted That A scoolmaster shall be hired for the yeare by the select men

At this Meeting A Comitte was Chosen to take account of the late select Not as yet Reconed with & the Town treasurer of what Moneys belonging to the Town in their hands The Comitte are Capt Bradford Left: Jonathan Morey & Samuel Stirtevant

[64.] At sd Meting Nathaniel Warren was Chosen to gather the Money that is due from perticular persons Relating to the scooling there Children the last year

At sd Meeting The town voted to sell A persell of Meadow Neere unto Will: Elless for to defraying publeck Charge & gave power to the select men to sell it for the Ends aforsd

Voted that the first Monday in october Next to be a Town Meeting

Swing Bridge   At sd Meeting The Town granted Liberty to Richard seers to Make A swing bredg over the town pond Creek

At sd Meeting Totman had liberty to bring his family into the town

At [1] sd Meting George Morton Ephraim Morton

---

[1] It does not appear with certainty that the work of making a stream was done at this time. No further reference to the matter is found in the records until October 28, 1771, when the Town voted "to choose a committee to consider about making a way for herrings from South Pond into Eel River, and accordingly made choice of Thomas Foster, Esq., Lemuel Jackson. Ichabod Holmes, Stephen Sampson and William Watson, Esq., a committee for that purpose, they to view the place and report to the town what they think best to be done in said affair at the next March meeting."

On the 16th of March, 1772, the committee reported and another committee was chosen "to take into consideration the matter of the land through which the brook may run, whose property it is, and to examine the laws of the Province respecting alewives and the brook through which they do or may run, and to examine the records and all matters and things respecting said way." The committee chosen for this purpose consisted of "John Cotton, Esq., Thomas Foster, Esq., Deacon John Torrey, Mr. Stephen Sampson and Mr. Jeremiah Howes."

On the 13th of April, 1772, the report of the committee chosen October 28, 1771, was read as follows:

"The committee appointed by the town at their meeting in October, 1771, to take a view of South Pond and the passage from thence to the Brook that leads from Finneys meadows into Eel River, and report their opinion whether there may not a convenient passage or brook be made to run from said Pond into Eel River for the alewives to pass up said Eel River into said South Pond to cast their spawn; the major part of said committee have attended that service, and a number of people being desirous of making a trial offered their services to labor part of a day upon free cost, and did stop the water, and dug a passage thirty or forty rods long, and on opening a passage found a very considerable brook run down, quite large enough for alewives, and are informed a very considerable brook runs ever since, though we do not apprehend that what is dug already is sufficient, yet your committee are of opinion that a sufficient passage may be made with not more than thirty pounds cost to make a sufficient brook for the alewives to pass and go up out of Eel River into said Pond to cast their spawn."

"And further, your committee, on the best information, find that numbers of alewives annually come up the Eel River, and doubtless if there was a good passage dug would go up the said River and Brook into said Pond to cast their spawn, and we are of the mind that there is the greatest probability, if the affair be well managed, the Brook would soon be very profitable to the town."

On the 15th of March, 1773, it was voted by the town "to choose a committee of three men to clear the passage for alewives from Eel River to South Pond; also to carry up in hogsheads one cartload of alewives, the first that come in the town brook this year, and put them into said South Pond; and Thomas Foster, Esq., Deacon John Torrey and Mr. William Warren were chosen."

The above extracts are interesting in view of the disputed point as to whether the South Pond Water course is natural or artificial. A fair inference to be drawn from them is that before the year 1701 there was no outlet from South Pond, and that in that year one was dug which, proving insufficient, was reopened in 1773.

Nathaniel Morton Josiah ffinney Benjamin Warren Ebenazur holmes & Thomas ffaunce Requested of the Town that in Case they Can Make A stream from the grate south pond soe Caled into the brook that Runeth through finneys Medows into the Eale River in order to the leting up alwives into sd pond that the town would grant them the privilidg of two or three pole breadth on Each side of sd strem; of land down along sd strem soe far as the town Comons goeth; which sd Request was granted to them & to stop the pond when it needs

*voted to allow these men Liberty to make a Herring brook from South pond*

At sd Meting the select men or any two of them are Apinted to lay out A highway from the sandy hill to Lakenham & from sandwedg Rooade A Mile & a half over dubble brooks towards Agawam

*Ways*

At A Town Meeting held at plimouth october 6[th] 1701 At sd Meeting the Town Granted unto Left: William Shurtlif all the Meadow or Meadoish Ground Lying upon Samsons brook on both sydes therof betwen the Meadow of Josiah ffinney there & the Meadow laid out to hugh Colle & all the Comon Meadow betwen hugh Cooles & the bridg Above William Ellises for 18 pound in silver To be Expended for the defraying Town Charges At sd Meeting it voated That the surveiors have liberty to leave of the Comons in laying out of land where they Judg it Nessesary for Convenience for men to Come to their lands that they bent penned up voted that the land sold by abraham Jacson to Nathaniel Warren lying on both sides the way to Lakenham sd Warren hath Liberty to take it all on the left hand of said way together

*Grant to Will[m] Shurtleff*

*Nathaniel Warrens grant*

At sd Meeting The town granted to Left: Bryant & frances Cooke A persell of land that lyeth Adjoyning to their land att Billentons holes soe Caled About 15 or 16 acrees & leave it to the judgment of the surveiors of the Towne as to the worth of it & sd Money to be Improved for the defraying publick Charges of sd Town.

[65.] September 22 1701

Wee being desired To Renew The bounds of The forty acrees of land That was formerly Granted and Laid out To John Dounham senior of plimouth Betwen Colchester and Winatuxett The bounds are as ffolloweth on the Northwest Corner with a horn beam tree and a Red oak standing By Colchester Brook Both Marked and from thence Eight score Rod south and by West by divers Marked trees Till itt Comes to a greatt Maple Tree standing in a swamp Marked on 4 sides Which is The south west Corner bounds and from Thence 40 pole East and By south to a beach and horn Beam Tree Both Marked Which is The southeast Corner bound and from Thence To Extend North and by East Eight score Rod By Marked Trees till itt Comes to a horn beam tree Marked and from Thence Down to The Brook aforesd and Then to Run 40 pole Down the brook till it Meets With The bounds first Mentioned There was Allowance to The Lott above Mentioned for a Road or high Way 40 foot Wide Where itt now is laid out By us The Day above Mentioned

James Warren & William Shirtlef<br>Surveighors

*John Donham*

The Two ten Acrees of or Lotts of Land laid out to John Watson At popes Neck by vertue of Meadow his Grandfather had ther at the south Meadows are both in A Twenty acree lott & Joyning to his Meadow it is bounded as followeth (viz) on the southwest Corner with a Red oake tree standing by the Meadow & from thence to Extend 40 pole Northeast & by North to A pine Tree Marked on 4 sides & from thence to Extend Eighty pole Norwest & by west to an other pine Tree Marked on 4 sides with stones at the Roote of it & from thence to Extend forty poole southwest & by south to an other pine tree Marked and soe down to the Meadow & ther the Meadow to be the bounds on the southwest side

James Warren<br>William Shurtlif<br>Surveyors

*John Watson*

[66.] Att a Towne Metting Held at plimouth December 8 1701 Juriors Chose To serve att The quarter seshions In sd December are John Morton Ephraime Cole John Churchell Eliazer Ring Thomas Morton & Stephen Barnabe : Att sd Metting It was orddered That The Town Clerk should Enter upon Town Record That Leuft Shirtlef hath paid the sum of Twenty Eight pounds for The sd towns use That Was Due from sd Shirtlef To sd Town For The hundred Acres of land sold by ye Town To sd Shirtlef Liing Att The south Meadows Betwen Beaver Damm Brook and Sothe Meadow River on The North side of sd River and For The Meadow or Meadowish Ground Liing upon sampsons Brook and The south Meadow River Which was sold unto sd shirtlef as upon Town Record doth and May appeare

The propriators of The Meadows of Saquash vis Georg Morton Claiming The one half in deale of all the Meadow or Meadowish ground belonging to Saquaish And Nath Morton & The heirs of Josiah Morton deceas[d] & Thomas Morton Claiming the other half of sd Meadow upon sd [1]Island & being all Meett Together upon Saquash as Abovesd on the 2d[d] of July 1701 Haveing all agreed to Make a division of sd Meadowish Ground into 2 parts or shares & to Cast Lots Who shall have Each part or ½ as Abovesd upon Which we The persons above named vis Georg Morton Nathaniel Morton Deceas[d] & Thomas Morton Haveing agreed and fixed boundereys in order to a Divission of sd Meadow as followeth Begining at The beach that leadeth to the stage point so Called We fixed a stak and a heap of stones and from Thence Rainging North Eastward By a Rang of stakes aCross The Meadow to a greatt pine Tree standing upon the beach Marked on 4 sides And Wee doe hereby Agree that all The Meadowish ground that falleth on either side of The Dividing Raing above Mentioned shall belong to and be Acounted his or their proper Interest Acordding as These Lots should fall upon Which The Lots Were given forth and the Southeasterly Lott fell to Georg Morton & the other Lott To The above named Nath[n] Morton Thomas Morton and the heirs of Josiah Morton and it is hereby To be understod that all the Meadowish ground that fals Within the Rang of Either lots To the utmost Extent Thereof shall belong to the Lots in wich it fails In Testimony of our Joynt Concurance Hereunto We The above-

---

[1] Saquish is laid down as an Island on the map of Champlain, made in 1605, and it so remained until the passage between it and the Gurnet filled up at some time during the latter half of the last century.

named Have Hereunto sett our hands on the day and yeare first above mentioned

         Georg Mortton
         Nath Mortton
         Thomas Mortton

[67.] Plimouth December ye 13 ano 1701

 The 8 acres of land sold by M$^r$ Edward gray of plimouth deceased To John Rickard liing betwen the first and second [2] Brook at The North end of The town of plimouth is Laid out by us The subscribers and bounded as followeth That is to say that one the Northeasterly Corner with a heap of stones about 6 pole to The Northeast of Deacon Woods barn and from the sd heap of stones southwest and by west 12 pole $\frac{1}{2}$ to a heap of stones on the North side of The Cart Way that goes to Atwoods swamp soe Cald and from thence 32 pole Northwest and by North to another heap of stones & from thence 12 pole $\frac{1}{2}$ Northeast and by est to a heap of stones below The Country Road and from thence 32 pole southeast and by south to the bounds first Mentioned Allowing 45 foott in breadth for the Kings high way Through sd lott Where the Way now is

        per William Shirtlef
         & James Warren
           Surveyers

 Att A Town Meting held at plimouth on the 9$^{th}$ of february 170$\frac{1}{2}$ for the Choyce of Grand Jurors for the year Ensuing & for Jurors of Tryals at the Next quarter sesions of the peace in March next The Grad Jurrors were John Churchell Samuel Stirtevant Ephraim Cole & John doty The Jurors for tryals above Named are Caleb loren Elish Bradford ffrances Cooke & John holmes

 At this Meeting it was voted and Agred upon by the Inhabitants That every ffreeholder That hath ben soe for six years last past That hath not had 30 ackers of land Granted to them by the Inhabitants of the Town within 20 years last past shall have 30 acrees of land laid forth to them out of the Comons belonging to sd Town (by the persons hereafter Named that are the Towns Comitty or Trustees to act in ye Affare) or soe much land as to

---
[2] This land lay on both sides of Court Street, including the Samoset House lot and the Burns' lot and others.

Make it up 30 acrees with what they have already had Granted to them sience sd Tirme of years & its further voted That all Town born Children now Inhabitants in sd Town that have been Rated towards defray publick Charg in sd Town for 14 years last past shall have 30 acres apece of land laid out to them out of sd towns Comons as abovesd & that None shall Take up aney Meadow ground or sedor swamps by vertue of this Grant and it further voted that every man May take up his share abovesd as ner to his one land as may be: and noe man shall take up sd land aganst an other Mans land until the owner of sd land doth Refuseth it & if two men doe pitch on one pece of land the Comitty have hereby power to determin whose it shall be and it was agred on at sd Meeting that Monday the 16$^{th}$ of this Instant february shall be a town Meeting for to Consider what farther to doe about the seder swamps

   The Comitte or trustees Chosen by the Inhabitants at sd Meeting to lay out Each propriators lott are as followeth (viz)

         Capt John Bradford
         Capt James Warren
         Left Shurtlif
         Left Nath: Southworth
         Insign Nath: Morton
         & Samuel Stirtevant

[68.] Att the Town Meeting last mentioned the Town voted that the spot of land formerly Granted unto Elisha holmes lying by manases Mortons house above John Riders by the highway upon Conditions shall belong to sd holmes free and Clere to him & his heires and assignes for Ever.

 These are to give Notice that the land that did formerly belong to John flinney senior and to Robert flinney senior betwen princes bottom and deepe Water is disposed of to Samuel King Junior being in quantytie 12 Acrees and is laid out by George Bonam & Andrew Ring & lyeth upon sd depe Water swampe bounded with A stake upon A hill at the southwest Corner & Runeth Norwest 38 pole to A small Red oake by the Cart way at the northermost bound from thence to A small Red oke at the Northeast Corner upon 5 sides Marked a little above princes bottom and Runeth along to A small pine upon the side hill soe Crosing the Cartway that Cometh from deep water and that Cart way is to be a bound & it Runeth along on the west side of a litle Round swomp & to A small white oake by deepe water swompe March 11th 168¾

At A Town Meeting held at plimouth on the 16th of March 170½ for the Choyce of Jurrors for the superior Cort The Grand Jurors were deacon John Waterman Nathaniel Morton & Benjamin sole The Jurors for tryols were John Stirtevant Thomas Loring John ffoster Benjamin Warren & Benjamin Eeaton The select men are Capt John Bradford John Rickard Jun & Samuel Stirtevant The Cunstables John pratt & Thomas Howland Tho : ffaunce Chos Town Clerk & sworn The surveyors for the highwayes are Ebenazer holmes Samuel harlow Elisha Bradford Edmond Tilson & Benjomen Eaton Junior The fence vewers are Caleb Loring Eliazar Cushman & Benjamen Warren

Mile & half voted

At This Meeting It was voted that A mile and [1]half from the Water side up into the woods from John Cobbs to Joseph Churchils land shall lye Comon for the use of the Town That the select men of this Town shall make the several assesments that fals within the Town for this present year.

That forty Acrees of land be laid forth out of the Town Comons for the use of ye Ministrey perpetually & that there shall be noe wood Cutt on sd land for 10 yers from this date.

Voted that Thirty Acrees of [2]land be laid out for the use of the Ministrey in the uper society & A Convenien for a burieng place & Traing place as Neere the meeting house there as may be Convenient Voted Granted att sd Meeting unto Mer Ephraim Little our present Minister & unto Thomas ffaunce to Each of them thirty acres of land A piece

[69.] The Inlargment of land Granted to Mer John Atwood by the Court of Assistants on the 2d of october 1637 At [3]plain-

---

[1] This tract of land, a mile and a half square, was bounded by a line beginning at the shore, near the mouth of Eel Creek, and extending southwesterly to a point forty rods easterly of Triangle Pond, now marked by a pile of stones near the road; thence running southeasterly across the highway near the foot of Sparrow's Hill, over Little Pond to Lout Pond, and so on to a point in Rider's orchard, so called, and marked by a white oak tree, and thence northeasterly to the harbor, crossing the Sandwich road and Warren Avenue a little south of Jabez Corner.

[2] The upper Society was the Society in what is now the town of Plympton and was incorporated in 1695. The first meeting-house of this Society, built before 1698, stood on the southerly end of Plympton Green, opposite the old lane which leads easterly by the house of Wm. S. Soule and the thirty acres of land referred to in the text included the Green and the Burial Ground.

[3] Plaindealing was what is now called Seaside. Its meaning is a Plain by the sea, as the Town of Deal, on the English Channel.

dealing is bounded as ffolloweth (viz) on the southeast Corner with A pine Tree Marked on fouer sides standing by a Red swompe & from thence to extend fouer scoore poole Northwest till it Cometh to two pine Trees Marked with A heape of stones at the Roots & from thence to Extend Eight scoore Rods southwest till it Cometh to another pine tree Marked on fouer sides with a heape of stones at the Roote & from thence to Extend fouer score Rood southeast till it Comes to two Red oakes sapplings Marked & from thence to Extend Eight scoore Rood Northeast till it Cometh to the bounds first Mentioned This was Laid out by us whose Names are hereunto subscribed on the 2$^d$ of March 170$\frac{1}{2}$

         James Warren
         William Shurtlif
          Surveyors

  Memorandom on the 11$^{th}$ of March 170$\frac{1}{2}$ A Renuall of the bounds of land betwen William Harlow & Elisha Holmes at manoment pint soe Caled is as followeth (viz) Its agreed upon by both parties above mentioned that the sd harlows Northermost bounds of his land on which his house now standeth on or he liveth upon shall Com hom to said holmes southermost bounds next to sd harlow & the bounds are as followeth (viz) from a heap of stones Rainging Northeast and by North Nerest to a Remarkable Rock upon the high Ground & from thence to A heape of stones upon the banck by A Red oake bush Marked This settlement of the Raing of the land betwen the parties above mentioned was made and Concluded upon by us the sd Will: harlow & Elisha holmes to be a finall settlement of ye Raing betwen us as Witness our hands on the day and year Above Mentioned

Signed In presence of
Nathaniel holmes Jun      William harlow
& John ffaunce        Elisha holmes

[70.] New plimouth

 *Memorandom* March ye 16 1702 Then a devision of lands Made Betwen Ephraime Tilson & Edmund Tilson his son Both of plimouth in New England; of Lands Thatt Was in partnership Betwen Them is As followeth viz; The Garden spott on Which There houses Now standeth on The Westerly part is To belong To The sd Edmund From a heap of stones by The high Way nere about The Middle of The length of sd spot; and from thence Across To a White oak sapling Marked standing by The swamp And Wee have Devidded The field Where The barnes standeth as followeth from A heap of stones by the high Way & soe to a swamp on the southarly side to A heap of stones and soe all the land from sd bounds To The high Way To belong to The sd Edmund Att the Easterly End Alsoe The land at The Neck soe Called Wee have devided as ffolloweth begining Att a small White oak sapling Marked standing nere lands Bellonging To Sam[ll] Watterman att The Easterly End, and from Thence To A Bluesh Rock nere the midle of The field and from thence Northwesterly To A White oak Marked standing by The neck swamp soe Called And The Westerly part to bellong to Edmund and the fourten acres of land that Was Robert Ransoms is to belong to Edmund sd land Lieth on the neck in the Northeast side of The land Above Mentioned And for The lands yett undevided liing in partnership betwen us shall in Convenient time be Equally Devided betwen us both : And In Testimony That this shall stand good unto us and our heirs for Ever Wee The partys Above Mentioned have hereunto sett our hands on the day and yeare first above Written

signed in presence of  
us Wittnesses  
Jonathan Shaw  
Nathaniell dounham

Ephraime Tilson  
Edmund Tilson

  The Fifty foot of Land square That Was granted unto John doty senior Att a Town Metting held at plimouth Apriell 10 1699 was laid out & Bounded as ffolloweth on the Northerly End of M[er] Littles Garden his house stands on & on the Westward side of the highway & is flifty foot square and at Each Corner a stake drove into the Ground This was laid out on the 12[th] of July 1701 by

James Warren &  
William Shurtlif  
Surveyors

[**71.**] At A Town Meeting held at plimouth on the 15[th] of May 1702 Capt James Warren was Chosen Representative Nathaniel Morton was Chosen select Man in John Rickards Roome he Refusing to serve the town in that office Jurours Chosen for the quarter sesions in June Next are M[er] Joseph Bartlext serjant Rickard Samuel harlow & John Watson

  At sd Meeting 20 acrees of land was granted unto Nicolas May Neere to his own land at Manoment ponds At sd Meeting Liberty was Granted unto John Stirtevant to take up 30

Acrees of land at Monponset of the hundred Acrees of land formerly Granted unto M{er} Atword at doties Meadow.

At sd Meeting 30 Ackors of land was Granted unto Ephraim Bradford on the North side of blackwater in Case he pay or Cause to be paid fouer pounds for the Towns use for sd land

*Grant to Nath[l] Morton and Thomas Morton to drown swamp at Warrens Wells*

At sd Meeting liberty was Granted unto Nathaniel Morton & Thomas Morton to make a stopage on Warrens wels Brook to drownd A persel of Swompe belonging to sd Mortons there upon sd Brook as also the Conveniant upland Neere the place of daming or stoping sd Brook & the scirts of swompy Ground that may be drond by sd dam.

*Ebenezer holmes land*

Wee being desired To settle bounds att The head of the Land That Was formerly granted to Mr Thomas Southworth and now in posseshon of Ebenezer holmes are setled as followeth—viz—With Two Red oaks Marked on 4 sides standing by The Ele River and from thence To Extend Northwest ½ poynt Westerly by Marked Trees so far Till Itt meet With his Southmost Line or Rainge

August 6th Jame{s} Warren

1702 William Shirtlef

*Samuel dunhams land to Abraham Jackson & from him*

The bounds of the 30 acrees of land formerly Granted to Samuel dunham at or Neere Warrens Wells & sold by him to abraham Jacson & by sd Jacson to M{er} William Clarke the bounds being lost Were Renewed & bounded as ffolloweth by us whoo have hereunto subscribed on the 6th of August 1702 (viz) with A white oake tree on the Northerly Corner standing in Ebenezar holmes Rainge & from thence to Extend about 92 pole southwest and by west 2 degrees Westerly to a Red oake standing Neere Warrens Wels brook & then by Warrens Wels brook to Eeale River brook & then bounded down the Eeale River brook Easterly till it Cometh to Ebenezer holmes Corner bounds which was 2 Red oaks and then bounded by Ebenezer holmes to Wm Clark — land Northwest half a pint Westerly About 60 Rod till it Comes to the bounds first Mentioned

James Warren<br>William Shurtlif<br>Surveyors

[72.] The bounds of the 30 Acrees of land formerly Granted to Joseph dunham & sold by him to M$^{er}$ William Clarke the bounds being lost or not known are Renewed by us Whose Names are hereunto subscribed on the 6$^{th}$ of August 1702 Nere warrens wells (viz) with a white oake sappling on the East Corner which was Josiah ffinneys Corner bounds and stands in the Rainge of Ebenazar holmes land & from thence doth Extend Northwest half a pint Westerly 53 pole to A Red oake tree Marked on 4 sids & from thence to Run southwest 2 degrees Westerly about 92 pole to a Red oak tree marked on 4 sides standing by Warrens Wells brook & then bounded by the sd brook 53 pole till it Cometh to Josiah ffinneys land & bounded by the aforesd ffinneys land till it Cometh to the bounds first Mentioned

*Joseph dunhams land to W$^{m}$ Clark*

James Warren<br>Will : Shurtliff<br>Surveyors

The 58 Acrees of land Granted to William barnes by the town of plimouth At senter hill for three pounds & ten shillings in money was Laid out the 25 of ffebruary 170⅔ and bounded as followeth on the southeast Corner with A pine tree Marked on 4 sides with A heape of stones About it & from thence to Extend west and south by A Marshie pond 80 pole to another pine tree Marked on 4 sids & then to Extend North and by west one hundred pole to A pine tree Marked on 4 sids with A heape of stones About it & then to Extend East and by North About one hundred & twelve pole to A Rock and soe down to the sea & then bounded by the sea southerly till it Cometh to the bounds first Mentioned

*William Barns his land*

John Bradford<br>William Shurtlif<br>Nath : Morton Com$^t$

The 3 pound and ten shillings in money was paid by Will: barns to Major John Bradford & Insign Nathaniel Morton select men of the town of plimouth for the use of sd Town on the first of March 170$\frac{2}{3}$.

[**73.**] At A Town Meeting held at plimouth August 31 1702 Jacob Cooke Will: harlow Joseph holmes senior & Jonathan Bryant were Chosen to serve in a Jury of Trials on the third Tusday of September next Ensuing this date M$^{er}$ Nath: Thomas Chosen Modderator for sd meeting With Refferance To the defraying Town Charges for sd yeare it was voted by the Inhabitants therr Mett To sell from out scirts of Comon lands belonging to sd town Not to Exceed 30 pounds worth Those that did then appere to by sd land were then Entered in town Meeting which are as followeth (viz) Captain Warren & Ephraim Morton senior they both put in for 6 pounds worth A pease Will: Shurtlif for som land adjoyning to his own land at the south Meadows Samuel Lucas for som land betwen Jacob Tomsons lands & his at Monponset about 30 acrees M$^{er}$ Joseph Bartlet 6 pounds worth on the Easterly side of Island pond soe Called & James Clark 6 pounds worth at the same pond & John Bryant 20 ackors at his own land & John Rickard Junior A slip of land and meadowish Ground betwen his own land & Winatuxet River and annasnapet brook Also William Barns hath liberty to purchas of the Towns Agents 50 acrees of land at the senter hill soe Caled & Capt John Bradford Left Jonathan Mory and Ensign Nathaniel Morton are Chosen & appointed The Towns Agents or Trustees To vew the severall spotts of land above Mentioned & to set A prise on Each spot of land what Each byor shall give pe acre for what shall be laid forth to them by vertue of the act of the Town Above mentioned & any two of them have power to act & the money to be Imploued for the defray The Town

Agents to view & set prise on Land

Indian

Charges as abovesd At sd Meeting Ralph Jones an Indian hath liberty from the town to sell som of his land neere sandwedg bounds & have Apointed Capt Warren and Left Jonoth : Morey to purchas it of him for the Towns use.

Abraham Jacksons 20 acrees

At this Meeting 20 acrees of land is Granted to abraham Jacson at the 4 Mile brook soe Caled Next to his sons land there.

Joseph Faunce

At sd Meting it was Granted to Joseph ffaunce all the Comon land Joyning to his own land at the High Redg & betwen Baruck Jordans John Churchels Eliazar Churchells & Deacon Georg Mortons lotts there

Joseph Churchel

Also at sd Meeting Ten acrees of land was Granted to Joseph Churchel to Mack up his old Addition of land to his lott

Widow Patience Holmes

Granted to the Widdow patience holmes half an Acree of land Neere to deacon Woods land on the Westerly side of the Roade or an acree on the west side of the Road to Lakenham Neere where Jonathan pratt formerly lived

Granted to John Bradford Junior a persel of land betwen his own land & Samuell Bradfords land not Exceeding 20 acrees

[74.] At this Meeting upon Complaint Made to the town of the grat damage likly to accrew the harbour by the cutting down the pine trees at the beach The Inhabitants doe therefor voate that henceforth Noe pine trees shall be felled on sd beach on forfiture of 5 shillings pr tree to be Recoverable of those yt soe doe & that Noe Man shall set aney fire on sd beach on forfiture of 5 shillings per time for the towns use

Nath[1] Holmes

At the sd Meeting the Inhabitants Granted to Nathaniel holmes senior & Joseph ffaunce four acrees of Meadow Next to Robert Barrows at the sedar swompe

Will : Church[ll]

Like wise William Churchell is Granted 5 or 6 acrees of swompy land on the westerly side of a swompe Neere Joseph Kings

Eleazer Prat

Eliazare prat is Granted liberty to Enjoy the 30 acres of land that was laid out to him by the towns Comity under a suppossition of his then Right therto ;

but being found to the Conterary the town ordered him to hold sd land & that yt should be his share till other yong men of his Age & standing had a like proportion

At sd Meeting it was voated that M$^{er}$ Joseph Bartlet shall herby have power to Gather in the Arrears of what moneyes is yet unpaid Relating to the scoole in [1] M$^{er}$ hales Tim by vertue of an act of the town then made

sedge
in ye Town
pond granted
to ye Ministry

At sd Meeting it was voated by the Town That Nathaniel Southworth should be ReImbursed the money he paid to M$^{er}$ Cottons sons Relating to the pew in the Meeting house & it was further voated at this Meeting that all the [2] sedg that Grows on the Comon flats About the Town pond is henceforth Reserved for the use of the Ministrey of this lower sosiety perpetually Never to be allienanated from that use for Ever it is to be understood that sedg that shall yearly Grow thereon

At sd Meeting The town Granted A sertain swompe known by the Name of Litle Meadows swompe unto sunderey of the Neighbours (viz) deacon Thomas Clarke Left Jonathan Morey Jonathan Mory Junior William harlow Samuel Cornish James Clarke Juner John Clarke Joseph Silvester humphrey Turner Samuel Rider Joseph Bartlett Juner Elnathan Bartlett Benjamin Bartlett John May the sd swompe is Granted to those Above Named or soe Maney of them as will take the trouble of drounding sd swompe & they are to drown sd swomp within 2 yeares after this date & then to belong to them and their heires for Ever

[75.] plimouth october 7$^{th}$ 1701

The ten Acrees of land laid out to Jonathan Shaw at the south Meadows by vertue of Meadow

---

[1] Moses Hale taught school in Plymouth a year or more. He was the son of John Hale of Newbury, and graduated at Harvard in 1699.

[2] This sedge grew on flats on both sides of the Town Pond and now flowed by it. The flats on the north side were leased by the Precinct in 1795 to William Hall Jackson for nine hundred and ninety-nine years, at an annual rent of six bushels of corn, and those on the south side, in 1788, to Stephen Churchill for the same period, at an annual rent of four bushels. Until the death of Rev. James Kendall, the pastor of the First Church, rent was regularly paid to the pastor, by the grantees of the original lessees.

Jonathan Shaw

he had there of his Grandfather George Wattson it is bounded as ffolloweth (viz) on the Westward syde of poopes Neck soe Called with A bunch of swompe White oakes Marked & from thence to extend East till it Cometh to two swompe White oakes Marked on the East side of the aforesd Neeck & soe all the upland from the fore Mentioned southerly bounds in sd Neck only leaveing sufficant way for Carting hay through Gates or barrs when sd land shall be fenced

James Warren
William Shurtlif
Surveyors to sd town

Plimouth

Shirtlef William

Wee Who have hereunto subscribed being Chosen by The Town of plimouth To prise a Certaine Trackt of Land The town aforesd granted unto William Shirtlef of plimouth and is bounded as followeth viz all The land in the Neck Betwen beaver Dam Brook so Caled and The South Meadows Which sd town has Nott bin formerly granted or disposed of Itt Is to Extend from pollapoda Cove To Beaver Dam pond and then bounded by The brok that Runs out of The Beaver Dam pond or swomp Till Itt Comes To the South Meadows and Then bounded up The South Meadows by sd Meadowe Till Itt Comes To The pollapod Cove abovesd; all The Land Within The bound abovesd Which Is Towns Commons Wee have prised and vallued att 8 pounds and awarded The sd William Shirtlef To pay unto The town of plimouth or Theire order The full Sum of 8 pounds That Then the land Within the bounds abovsd to be his and his heirs for Ever This 14th day of october 1702 pr John bradford
& Nath[ll] Morton

At A Town Meeting held at plimouth on the 7[th] of december 1702 the Town of plimouth Granted unto William Shurtlif of the town aforesd for Eight pounds in Money A sertaine Neck of land which lyeth betwen beaver dam brook & the south Meadows & is bounded as followeth (viz) it Extends from pollopody Cove to beaver dam pond & then bounded by the pond & swomp Neere southwest till it Cometh to beaver dam brook soe Called & then bounded by sd brook southwesterly till it Cometh to the south

Meadows aforsd & then bounded up the Meadows by sd Meadows till it Cometh to pollopody Cove first Mentioned All the lands within the bounds abovesd upon the Consideration above mentioned was Granted unto the sd William Shurtlif & his heires & assignes for Ever Excepting only what the Town had formerly mad A grant of to aney particular persons before this Grant which sd sum of money above mentioned was paid by sd Will Shurtlif to the select men for the Towns use March first $170\tfrac{2}{3}$

[76.] Att a Town Metting held att plimouth december $7^{th}$ 1702 The Juriors Chosen To serve att The County Courtt are John Mortton Eliazar Ring & Thomas Mortton

Att sd Metting Itt Was voatted That The 8 pounds That William Shertlef paid for Lands Thatt he bought of The town shall Go Towards paying The County Ratte.

Att sd Metting a Certaine swamp or Meadowish Ground about Swan hold so Called Beying above The Way Thatt is Now of use Goeing over Swan hold Brook Was Grantted unto Sundry of The Neibhours Thereabouts (viz) Joseph Dounham John pratt $Nath^{ll}$ dounham Micajah dounham Beniiah pratt Jeduthan Robins Eliazer pratt Joseph pratt Joseph Dounham sen & Abiall Shirtlef With Libertty of Makeing stoppidg upon sd brook for The drowning sd Land

Att sd Metting Itt Was Granted That Edmund Western shall have fifty acres of Land Laid outt To him upon Winattuxett neck so Called against his own Meadow Ther in Case he Rellinqish aney Right or prettence of Rightt unto The percell of Land Thatt Was Grantted and Laid forth for The use of The personage in the upper sosiety

James Warren

At A Meeting of the propriators & Inhabitants of plimouth on the 31 of August 1702 Then liberty was Grantted by the Town to James Warren senior for to buy 6 pounds worth of their Comon lands at A place Caled Clampudden plaine in the township aforesd to be prised to him by men Appointed for that purpose & since the sd Warren being desirous to have the grant of sd land at A place Called duble brooks in the Township Aforesd Neere to his own land it being more Convenient for him To Grattify him in that matter At a metg of sd propriators & Inhabitants of the Town of plimouth on the $7^{th}$ day of december 1702 The Town granted to him the sd James Warren for six pounds in money w$^{ch}$ sd 6 pounds the sd Warren hath already paid to the select men for the use of the town 30 Acrees of land on the west side of the aforesd brook Nere unto and to be laid out with the 30 acres of land Granted to him by the Town At the Generall grant on the 9$^{th}$ of ffebruary last past

Att A Meeting of the Inhabitants & propriators of the Town of plimouth on the 7$^{th}$ of december 1702 Then the town Granted to Ephraim Morton senior one 110 Acrees of land at A place Called Clampudden plain for & in Consideration of six pounds which the sd Ephraim Morton hath already paid unto the select men of the Town for the towns use

[**77.**] The 6 acres of upland Granted unto John Eaverson by The Town of plimouth is bounded as followeth (viz) att The South-East Corner With a stake and a heap of stones and from thence 24 pole East To another stake and a heap of stones and from thence 40 pole North to a pine Tree Marked on 4 sides and so Down To his Meadow and from Thence 24 pole by The Meadow Westerly until Itt Comes unto His other Lands and his Land To bee The West bounds That he had of Stephen Bryant Sen This Was Laid outt By us The 23$^{rd}$ of September 1701

pr James Warren<br>William Shirtlef<br>Surveighers

Att a Town Metting held att plimouth february 1$^{st}$ 170$\frac{2}{3}$ The Grandjury Chosen for The yeare Were Calleb Lorein John foster Samuell fuller & John Clark ; The Juriors Chosen To Serve att The County Courtt Were John Mordo Abiall Shirtlef Josiah finey & Ebenazer Holmes

Att sd Metting The Town voatted to pay [1] Mr Dyer six Acres of Meadow in pollopoda Cove Next To Will Rings Meadow

At sd Metting Itt was voatted Thatt The Land veued and sett outt To Mr bartlett James Clark & John Rickard shall be Recorded upon Town Record acording To The Metes & bounds Thereof Granted unto Adam Right 3 acres of Meadow on Colchester brook If Itt be There to be had The Town Grantted unto Josiah finey Liberty To Run The Same poynt of Compas upon The

---

[1] John Dyer followed Moses Hale as Teacher and succeeded Thomas Faunce in the office of Town Clerk in 1723.

Southerly Side of his Land on Which he now Liveth as he doth upon The Northerly side of sd Land provided There be Common There To be had and dont Infringe upon aney partickular Mans Right
Att sd Metting The town Granted unto Samuel Sonett Indian 200 acrees of Land Where he now Lives

[78.] The Land Granted unto Joseph bartlett sen by The town adjoyning to his other Lands at Mannomett ponds is Laid out and bounded as followeth begining att The south End of The fresh pond so Called & There bounded with a pine Tree Marked on 4 sides and from Thence To Run on a straight Line to a stake and a heap of stones about Itt at a place Called Churches Landing by the saltwater and from Thence Northward by the Watter side untill Itt Comes unto his other Lands and Then againe begining on The Northwest side of The fresh pond att a Little brook thatt issueth out of the pond and so allong The brook and swamp to a Red oak tree Marked on 2 sides and from thence athwort a small poynt of upland to a pine Tree Marked and so allong The swamp to another pine tree Marked and from the pine Tree West north west to a ditch and aLong The ditch to an arme of The maine brook and so down The maine brook till Itt Meets With his other Lands
John bradford
Nath[ll] Morton

ffebruary 10$^{th}$ 170$\frac{2}{3}$ then ye 28 acrees of land Granted to John Bryant was laid out & bounded as ffolloweth (viz) with a small Red oak tree Marked on 4 sids which was peter Tomsons Northwest Corner bound of his 30 acre lott & from thence to Extend East half a pint southerly 28 pole to A pine tree Marked on 4 sids & from thence to Extend south half A pint Westerly to the land that was formerly John Cobbs & ther bounded by the west side of sd Cobbs land as ffarr as that goeth & then to A stake stuck into the Ground 165 pole distant from the pine tree before Mentioned & from sd stake to Extend west half a pint Northerly 28 pole to A pine tree Marked on 4 sids & from thence to Extend North half A pint Easterly by the Easterly side of the aforesd peter Tomsons land 165 pole till it Cometh to the bounds first Mentioned The 5 pole in length over Measur was allowed for the highway that goeth through sd land to bridgwater & also A way to lay through sd land to A hering ware
James Warren

March The first 1702 The above Named John bryant paid unto The Sellect Men of The Town for The use of sd Town Two pound fiften shillings for sd Land above mentioned

[79.] At A Town Meeting held at plimouth on the first day of March 170$\frac{2}{3}$ for the Choyce of Representatives & Town officers The select Men Were Major John Bradford Samuel Stirtevant & Nath: Morton, The Cunstables Chose at sd metting were John Barnes & Elisha Bradford, Thomas ffaunce Chosen Town Clerk Jacob Cooke & Eliazar Ring were Chosen Tithing Men The Grand Jury Chose to serve at the Superior Court are Left Nath: Southworth Left Jonathan Morey Elkath Cushman Eliazar Cushman & Samuel Lucas The Jurors for Tryals are M$^{er}$ Joseph Bartlet deacon Wood Benoney Lucas Richard Seeres & Eliazar Morton, The Surveyors for the highwayes are John Morton Josiah ffinney James Howland Thomas Shirtlif Benoney Shaw & James Clarke Junior

At sd Meting it was voted That Capt James Warren and Left Mory should sell the Indians land (viz) Ralph Jones soo much of his sd land as may pay for his Cure & the Town promiseth to give purchas Grant to thos that ye sd Warren & Mory shall sell it to for sd Indians use.

At sd Meeting Nathaniell Thomas proposed to the town to Make A Trough for the herings to goo through his mill dam into his mill pond & soe to keep his dam up at the season of the fishes going up which sd Mosion being Made the Town Aproved thereof & voted That in Case the sd Nathaniel Thomas Make a throwfare for the fish abovesed that he shall keep up his mill dam at all seasons & doe herby forbid & prohibbitt any person from Taking or Killing aney alwives below sd Thomasses mill dam down stream to the sea on forfiture of 5 shillings a pec for aney that shall offend in this kind that soe the fish mite be preserved if it mite be that they mite not be beaten out of the brook And doe Appointd an Request

*Town officers*

*Liberty to sell Indian Land*

*Alewives not to be*

| | |
|---|---|
| taken below the Mill | John dyer John foster & Richard seeres to have Inspection of this affaire and to forewarn persons of Trespasing on ye particulars above mentioned and to prosecute aney that shall offend in that kind the forfiture to be one half to the persons apointed to have the Inspection of this affare & the other half to the poore of the Town |

At sd Meeting liberty was Granted to the Neighbours on the southerly End of the Town to fence from the southeast End of billentons sea down to finney meadow soe Called to prevent their Cattle going to the boggs

At sd Meeting the Inhabitants granted to Eliaz Ring 10 acres of land Joyning to his land Neere frances Cooks

| | |
|---|---|
| a Confirmation of Land to Ephraim Cole | At sd meeting the town voted that Ephraim Cole hath A Confirmation of his Grand father Cols land on the southeast sid of Atwoods swomp which is Comonly known by the name of Cools feild & to be bounded out by the surveyors of the Town According to the Raings of the old fence about sd land |

[80.] At A Town meeting held at plimouth March 15<sup>th</sup> 170⅔

| | |
|---|---|
| Joseph Churchell & Eleazer Churchell agent | At sd meeting Capt James Warren was Chosen Representative to serve the Town At the General Court Now siting at Boston  At sd meeting the Town granted to Joseph Churchill & Eliazar Churchill that their land at the south ponds shall extend home to & be bounded by the pond on the southwest side of sd land |
| Bradford Major | At sd meeting liberty is Granted to Major John Bradford to milk the pine Trees upon the Towns Comons from the head of blackwater to ——— Meadow & from duxbery bounds to Jones River & hath liberty to Imploy straingers lately Com from the westward upon sd Comons within sd limits upon Condition the sd Bradford doth give in bonds to the selectmen of the town to secure the town from Aney Charge yt may fall on sd town Respe sd persons & doo also Instruct Aney of said Inhabitants in what scill sd strainger hath in Milking the pines soe far as they are Capable of Instructing any |

| | |
|---|---|
| Sturtevant samuel Warren benjamin | in that Art At sd Meeting Samuel Sturtevant and benjamin Warren were Chosen & Aded to Major bradford Capt Warren & Liften William Shurtlif with what they were betrusted with Relating to the Comons of sd Town that they be not Intruderd on by aney particulars & that Aney 3 of the 5 persons May legaly act tnerin |
| Shaw Benoney | At sd Meeting About 3 quortors of An Acre of land be it more or less was Granted to Benoney Shaw Lying upon the south East side of his 40 Acree Lott to Extend hom to the brook & soo bounded by the brook home. |
| Cole Ephraim | The Acree of land Granted to Ephraim Cole at the Town Meeting held At plimouth ——— was laid out on the west side of the way that goeth to Nelsons brook[1] and bounded as ffolloweth to Extend from John Rickards land Northerly 4 pole in breadth & 40 pole in length at the 2 Northermost Corners with heaps of stones the length lyeth Neere southwest and Northeast it was laid out the same day the sd Rickards land was laid out by us     James Warren |
| |                 Will Shurtlif surveyors |
| Reed pond Holmes Thomas | The Reed pond[2] Granted to John holmes of plimouth deceased on the 13th of october 1667 was bounded the 17th of Aprill 1702 as followeth (viz) with A stake where John Nelsons Raing Cometh to the forsd pond & from sd stake to Extend southeast by two heapes of stones Neere the southeasterly End of the pond & then More Easterly to an other heape of stones Nere the Creek that Isueth out of sd pond & soe down to a heape of stones by A Rock & then the other part of the pond bounded by the beach Northerly & the aforesd holmes other land     James Warren |
| |                 William Shurtlif |
| |                     Surveyors |

[81.] New plimouth october 7th 1701

    The 10 Acrees of land laid out to George Bonam Junior belonging To Meadow his father had in ye lower

---

[1] Nelsons Brook is Cold Spring Brook.

[2] Reed Pond was an overflow of Cold Spring Brook near the point crossed by the Railroad.

Bonam
George

south Meadows is Bounded as ffolloweth (viz) on the Easterly End by the land or ffarme he now liveth on 40 pole & from his Eastermost bounds 32 pole Northeast & by East to A pine tree Marked on 4 sides & from thence to Extend 40 pole to A pine tree Marked standing by the Way that Cometh from thence to Town & then by the Road or way 32 pole Southwest & by west to the bounds first mentioned & 2 Acrees More by his house betwen the way and the Meadow

James Warren
William Shurtlif
Surveyors

The half Acre of land Granted to the Widow patience holmes by the Town of plimouth was laid out on the Westward side of ye Way Towards the first brook on the 26 of Aprill 1703 it is in length About 10 pole Northwest & Southeast & in Wedth about 8 pole Northeast & Southwest & at Each Corner A stake drove in the ground About A Rod & a half from the land deacon Nathaniell Wood had of The Town Aforesd

Widow
patience
Holmes

James Warren
Will Shurtlif
Surveyors

Att a Town Metting Held att plimouth Aprill ye 26<sup>th</sup> 1703 Mr Nathaniell Thomas Was Chosen Representative att sd Metting Capt James Warren was Chosen Comishener

Know all men by these presents That we Samuel barrows and John Tincom both of the Town of Middlebery in the County of plimouth in New England being Joynt parteners in A Certain parcell of Meadow lying and being upon both sides of the River Called the south Meadow River in the Township of plimouth in the County aforesd which sd parcell of meadow is bounded up streame by the meadow yt was formerly William harlows & Down stream it is bounded by the Meadow of Nathaniel Morton Whereof we have Now by mutuall Agreement Divided sd percell of meadow Equally betwen us haveing Respect to quallity as well as to the quantety as followeth (viz) Namely We pitched A Raing of staks ACross sd meadow and we doe by these presence Mutualy agree that all yt part of sd parsell of meadow lieth up streame from sd Raing of stakes shall belong unto sd Samuel Barrows and his heires and assignes for Ever And all the part of sd parsel of Meadow which lyeth Down strem from sd Raing of stakes shall belong unto sd John Tinckom and to his heires and assignes for Ever Now the aforsd Rainge of stakes thus sett and the Division thus made we Doe mutualy agree shal stand and Remaine as a full settlement us and our heires and assignes for Ever In Witnes Wherof we the aforsd Samuel Barows and John Tinkom have herunto sett our hands and seales this 28 Day of March one Thousand seaven hundred and Nine

Signed and sealed
in the presence of
Ephram Wood
Isaac howland

Samuel Barrows sel ()
John Tinkom ()

[82.] Att ye Town Metting Last Mentioned The Inhabitants of plimouth voatted Thatt all ye Seder Swamp Throughout ye township shall Bee Divided and Laid out Acording To ye Directions following Thatt Is To Say yt all old propriators and other Inhabitants of ye age of 21 years yt are Free holders and house Keepers Born Within ye Town shall have Each of y$^m$ a full share Also ye other of The Inhabitants Viz Male Children which Were born in ye Town and Doe Reside Now in Itt who have Arived unto ye Age of 21 years shall have Each of y$^m$ half A share: And That all such Other Inhabitants That Doe Sucksed aney of ye Ancient propriators To have a full share Unles Such Ancient Inhabitant have A Son Come in upon his Wright and yt Noe person To have More Then a Single Share Though he May have More old propriators Rights Then one And yt The Children of such persons Who are Dead and Would by this Voate have had a right had he bin Liveing viz: Such Children Who are under The Age of 21 years shall have ye Right yt Was Their fathers That Is To say a full Right and That No person upon aney prettence whatsoever shall have Aney share Exept They Reside Now in ye Town Except The Children under Age afore Mentioned And Such persons who have in ye Town a Farm Containing An 100 Acres of Tillage Leased out With A Tennant upon Itt Though himself Nott Now Residing in ye Town To have a full share Also ye Town made Choice of Leiut Jacob Tomson To be Theire Surveigher To Lay out The Ceder swamps in sd Town acording To ye Method abovementioned Att sd Metting Major John Bradford and John Stirtevant Were Chosen and Apoynted by ye sd Inhabitants Their

## PLYMOUTH RECORDS. 313

Agents or Trustes To Assist Leut Tomson in Laying out sd swamps and To se ye orders of ye Town Relating To Aney Trespas Done upon The Ceder Timber in sd swamps Duly Executted and To prosecute aney yt shall ofend in ye breach of sd Towns orders Respecting The Swamp and Timber

Itt is further voatted by ye Inhabittants yt If aney of ye Inhabitants Shall Cut aney Seder Timber from ye Dates Last Mentioned To ye first of august Next in aney of the Seder Swamp Within ye Township shall forfeitt Their Shares in sd swamp and aney other yt shall presume To Cutt aney Seder Timber in sd swamp yt Is not a propriator Shall forfeit 20 Shillings per Tree and yt Those Swamps To be Laid out betwen This and The first of August Next Itt Was Voatted also yt There shall be 5 shares Laid out in one Lott and yt ye persons Laying out sd swamp shall have Respeckt To Equalise sd Shares both in quantity and quallity as nere as may be and yt Every propriator shall bear ye Charg of Laying outt his one Lott or share

[83.] At A Town Meeting held att plimouth on the 24th of May 1703 for the Choyce of Jurors which were Samuul Waterman ffrances Cook Thomas Holmes & Edmond Tilson

Att this Meeting it was voted by the Inhabitants that ye Laying out of ye Ceder Swomps shall be suspended until the next winter & that none of the Inhabitants shall Cutt aney Green Ceder trees in aney of the Ceder Swomps untill sd swomps be devided if the Town procced to a division of sd swomps on forfiture of 20 shillings per tree & Chose & appointed Major John Bradford John Stirtevant francis Cook Benjamin Warren & Bennejah pratt to have Inspection of this affair those last mentioned were added to those Chose by the town at a town Meeting on the 16th of ffebruary 169½ for the like service

M<sup>er</sup> Isaac Cushman Benjamin Soule

At sd Meeting a certain Tract of land lying Neere to lands belonging to M<sup>er</sup> Isaac Cushman & Benjamin Soule where they Now live if it Exceed Not 18 acres is granted unto sd Cushman & Soule on Condition that they ye sd Cushman & Sole allow of a suficiant Roade to be laid out by the select men of the Town through their other lands for the use of the Neighbours there & Travilors as they may have ocasion The Road through the sd souls land is alReady laid out as on town Record doth Appeare

| | |
|---|---|
| Jacob Cooke | Jacob Cooke is Granted all the Comon land lying without the bounds formerly sett by Capt Thomas Southworth unto M$^{er}$ Joseph Bradfords 100 acres of land at Jons River & within the bounds ser·ce sett by Tho: ffaunce for five pounds in Money |
| At this Meting May 24 1703 ——— sheepe pastor | It was voated by the Inhabitants of the Town That all the Comon land¹ yt lyeth within A mile & half upon A square Every way distant from the head of Cobbs Meadow soe Caled ; which 'sd Meadow lyeth betwen Munks hill and annasnappet shall ly for A perpetuall Comon for Ever Excepting only meadows swomps & swompy Ground or land & whereas sundry of the Inhabitants of sd town have subscribed to an agrement to have their sheepe keept in A General fflock on the sd perpetuall Comons & to build a house for a shepard to dwell in & liberty for the sheapard for the time being to brok up fence & Improve 20 Acrees of land for the Generall benifit of the owners of the sd flock on Aney part of the aforsd Comons also aney other freeholder of the town hath liberty to Joyn with those who have already subscribed aney time within 3 years from the date herof Next & to have the like priviledg w$^{th}$ them he or they paying their proportion of the Charge for the shepards wages house folds etc Acording to the number of sheepe they shall have keept in sd flock also aney other free holder of sd town who shall se cause to put their sheepe in the Generall flock at any time herafter shall have liberty & an Equall share in sd house folds (etc) & privilidg of Comonage provd he or they pay to those who are the first undertakers the [84.] Charge of this present year for the first yeare their sheepe go in the Generall flock after the sam Rate p$^r$ head as the first undertakers pay for this pres- |

---

¹ The head of Cobb's meadow is at the easterly end of a grassy meadow now owned by Albert Benson a short distance south of the road leading from Parting Ways to Plympton. The sheep pasture extended a mile and a half each way from this point, including a lot of three miles square. A part of it was within the present bounds of Plympton, Kingston and Carver. On its southerly side it extended across the Carver road and nearly over to the South Meadow road. One of the wood lots within the bounds is still called the "Shepherd's Tent lot." It was finally abandoned as a sheep pasture, and in 1784 the town voted to sell it. The towns of Plympton and Kingston, which had been incorporated in 1707 and 1726 respectively, put in claims for a share, but it was finally decided that they had no interest in it, and the whole was sold in lots at various times by the town of Plymouth.

ent year for the shepards wages house folds (etc) also
yt noe person what soever shall have more sheepe go
in the sd flock at aney time hearfter then proportionall
with other subscribers according to the number he or
they put in the first yeare & alsoe yt Noo person may
have herafter aney sheepe goo on sd perpetuall Comons other then such as shall Joyn w$^{th}$ the first undertakers their heires or assigns or pay pro Rate for their
sheepe as aforsd provided and its ye In tent of this
voate that the first undertakers or those yt are Con-
serned in sd flock the first 3 years shall build a shepards house & shepe folds & also fold their flock of
shepe the first 3 years somers on sd perpetuail Comons for the benifit of the Generall acording to Each
mans propo : in order to bring sd Commons to gras

Harlow
Will:
Senior his
Ten acree
Lott

The 10 Acrees of land Granted to William
harlow senior deceased By vertue of his haveing
Meadow at the lower south Meadows was laid out
at the south Meadows by pollopody Cove & is
bounded as followeth with A white oak bush on
the southwest Corner which was the Corner bounds
of George Mortons 10 acre lott & from thence to
Extend Northwest half a pint Northerly 28 pole
to a pine bush Marked & from thence to Extend
Neere Northeast 52 Rod till it Cometh against the
head of the Cove abovesd & then Easterly down
to the Cove & then southwest 32 Rod by the Cove
to a white oak bush which was abraham Jacsons
Corner bounds & ther bounded by the sd Jacsons
and George Mortons land Neere southwest till it
Comes to the bounds first Mentioned leaveing A
way to goe to the Meadows By us the 3$^d$ of
Aprill 1702        James Warren
                Will : Shurtliff surveiors

John
Brad$^d$
Jun Lott

The 20 Acres of Land Granted To John Bradford Junior ye 31 of august 1702 Was Laid outt
on ye Southwest Side of Jonses River ye 23 of
September 1702 and bounded as followeth viz on
ye Northerly Corner w$^{th}$ a Red oak Standing by ye
River and from Thence To Extend south and by
East about 18 pole by ye Land yt Capt John

# 316 PLYMOUTH RECORDS.

Bradford bought of ye Town To a pine Tree Marked on 4 sides standing in ye Raing of ye aforesd Land and from Thence To Extend Southeast by East Till Itt Comes To Sam[ll] bradfords Land Till Itt Comes to Jonses River and Then Neare Northeast Till Itt Comes To ye bounds first Mentioned

James Warren &<br>William Shirtleff<br>Surveyers

[85.] Att a Town Metting held att plimouth September 12[th] 1703 Att sd Metting ye Juriors Chosen Were Caleb Lorein Benj Eaton James barnabe & John Watson

Att sd Metting Itt was voated by ye Inhabittants of ye Town To allow unto [1] Mr Ephraime Little our present Minester sixty pounds for his Sallery for This present yeare Which is To Commence from ye 15[th] of May Last past and w[ch] hath since sd Term bin Contrebutted To goe Towards sd sum and Whatt fals shortt of 60 pounds by Way of Contrebution To be forthwith Levied by Rate upon ye Inhabittants of this Lower Sosiaty & ye Inhabittants To be Notified by ye Cunstable What Each Mans proporttion is of sd sum—And ye Town Doe further Voate To Keep up Theire Weekly Contrebutton & Each Inhabittant Contrebutting is To Mark his money Which he shall Contrebute— Which shall be substractted out of his Rate att ye Close of ye yeare ;

The Town further Voatte yt all Moneys Contrebuted unmarked shall be Acounted Strangers Money and shall be Allowed To Their Minester over and above 60 pounds ye sd Sum To be paid in money or provishions at money price

Att sd Metting Itt Was Voatted To Make a Rate Towards ye Defraying Town Charges To be paid by ye first of december Next Ensueing ye Date abovsd The Town Charges are as followeth

|  | £ | s | d |
|---|---|---|---|
| for ye Scole Master | 13 | 00 | 00 |
| To M[r] Nath[ll] Thomas Representative | 12 | 00 | 00 |

---

[1] Rev. Ephraim Little of Marshfield, a graduate at Harvard in 1695, was settled over the First Church in 1699, and continued in the ministry until his death November 23, 1723.

|   | £ | s | d |
|---|---|---|---|
| for ye Releif of ye pore | 5 | 00 | 00 |
| for Ringing ye bell | 1 | 10 | 00 |

To Mʳ Mordo for a Lather[1] and Lock

Att sd Metting William Shirtlef and Nath Thomas Were apointed and Desired To prosecute John Cole for Trespasing upon ye Towns Intrest of Sedg ground viz ye Town pond given by ye Inhabitants for ye use of ye Minestrey

Voatted yt Capt Warren & Leiut Shirtlef shall vew a persel of Land Desired by Deacon Wood and To Make a Reportt thereof To The Town in order To a Grant from ye Town to him

Abiel Shurtleff — Granted to Abiall Shirtlef 20 Acres of Land Nere about ye South Meadow on Consideration of Sum Loss Sustained by him With Refferance To a bargaine Made With ye Selleck Men about building a bridg over Jonses River

Granted To Deacon Tho: Clark and Will harlow a slip of Common Liing betwen There Lotts att Mannoment ponds To Each of Them a like proportion Granted

Tho: Doty — To Tho. Doty on ye westward of his fathers Land To Extend To a Slow for ye Conveniencc of water not to Exced a Quarter of an acre

[86.] There is seaven Acrees of Meadow laid out for Robert Ransom at the south meadows on both sides the River Caled the south meadow River bounded as followeth on the East Corner a Maple tree marked & on the North Corner a spruce tree marked & from thence Runing 30 Rood down the River to a small white oake marked & from thence Crossing the River Eastward to A black oake Marked More of upland laid out for Joshia & Robert Ransom on the Eastward side of the River 10 Acrees of upland bounded as followeth on the Northward Corner with A pine tree marked from

Robert Ransom — thence Runing Eastward 40 Rod to a small Red oake marked from thence Runing southward 40 Rood to a pine tree marked standing in A swompe & from thence Rainging Northward 40 pole to A black oake tree marked which is southward Corner bounds of the Meadow laid out for Robert Ransom May 27 pr

Isaac Cushman surveior

---

[1] A Latch.

May 24 1703

At a Town meeting held at plimouth on the 24th of May 1703 at sd meeting M<sup>er</sup> William Shurtlef Made A motion to the Town to Exchainge some part of his meadow at the high pines[1] soe Caled with the Town for the upland and meadow at the southmeadows belonging to the Town there for the use of the minestrey upon sd motion the Town Made Choyce of Capt Warren and Nathaniell Morton for their Agents or trustees to agree with sd Shurtlif as to an Exchainge of sd lands & to Make Report therof to the Town in order to the Towns Confirmation therof & Wheras M<sup>er</sup> William Shurtlif hath passed a deede to sd Agents of som part of his sd meadow acording to his Agrement with sd Agents or trustees Therfore

December 15th 1703

at a town meting held at plimouth on the 15th of december 1703 the Town Granted unto M<sup>er</sup> William Shurtlif abovesd both the upland & meadow land at sd south meadows that was belonging to the Ministrey & Now Exchainged to him & his heires & assignes for Ever

At sd Meeting Ephraim Coole Richard Seers Thomas Holmes & Nathaniel Howland were Chosen to serve on the Jury

december 15 1703

At sd Meting Information being given that there was strey of wood upon the lott of land laid out for the use of the Ministree Therupon the Inhabitants Made Choyce of William Ring & Isaac Lothrop to have Inspection of sd land that the wood bent destroyed & they are Invested herby with full power from sd town to prossecut aney that shall trespas theron according as the law dyrects

Att a Town Metting held att plimouth on ye first of March 170¾ For the Choice of Town officers for the yeare Insueing viz Thomas faunce Chosen Town Clerk. The Selleckt Men Chosen Were Major John bradford Samuell Stirtevant & Nath<sup>ll</sup> Morton The Cunstables Chosen Were Thomas Shirtlef and John Watson—The Grandjuriors for ye yeare Were Ephraime Morton sen John Dyer Eliazer Ring and John holmes Juriors for Tryals att ye Inferior Court Chosen are John Churchel Benj: Warren Thomas Morton & Calleb Lorein: The Tything Men

---

[1] "High-pines" is a place on Salt-house, or Duxbury Beach, where pine trees of considerable size once grew, as they did on Plymouth Beach.

Chosen are James barnabe & sam[ll] Bryant: The surveyhers for ye high Wayes Chosen Were Deacon Clark Benj: Warren Thomas howland Calleb Cook John bryant & benijah pratt ---- The Grand Juriors for ye Supperior Court Chosen are Sam[ll] Stirtevant Nath[ll] Morton & Abiall Shirtlef The petty Juriors att sd Courtt Chosen were Leu[t] Shurtlef Deacon Clark John Mordo John Stirtevant & Eliazer Churchel

[87.] At sd Metting Last Mentioned Itt Was voatted by ye Inhabitants That there Should be a Grammer Scole Master provided for ye use of ye Town for ye yeare Ensueing Which shall be Settled in the Senter of ye Town & Capt Warren Nath[ll] Thomas & Mr Mordow are appoynted by The Town To procure one voatted That There shall be a Rate Made upon ye Inhabitants of The Town To Defray ye Charge Thereof

school 170¾ in ye Center of ye Town

Att sd Metting An Antient Grantt of Meadow To Edward Dotty att Rockey Neck brook Is Confirmed unto Sam[ll] Dotty being 6 acres If Itt be There To be had and Nott to Exced six acres

[88.] Att sd Metting The Agents of the purchassers of ye South purchase in ye Township of Midlebery moved To ye Inhabitants of ye Town of plimouth To Chuse Three Agents or Trustees To Give yu A Treatty in order To A Complyance With Refferance To ye Differance yt hath a River Relatting To ye Tittle of Lands betwen ye sd Inhabittants of plimouth and ye purchassers of sd Tracks upon Which Considerattion ye Town made Choice or Major John Bradford Capt Warren and Leu[t] W[m] Shirtlef as Theire Agents or Trustes in Theire behalf & Doe herby Invest Them With full power To Agree w[th] ye Agents of sd purchase & putt a Fineall Isue unto ye Matter of Differance: & w[ht] Thay Doe one ye Towns behalf Respeckting ye Differance shall stand Good and Remaine in full force and vertue

At A Town Meeting held at plimouth on the 22[d] of May 1704 for the Choyce of a Representative & other Conserns as followeth (viz) Capt James Warren was Chose Representative for the yeare The Jurors Chose to serve at the County Court on the 20[th] of June were Robert Bartlet Will: harlow Eben Cobb & Ben: Soule

At sd Meeting it was Agreed upon & voted by the Inhabtants That ye select men should make a Rate of 30 pounds upon the Inhabitants of this lower society for the ministers sallery for one half year Comencing from the 15<sup>th</sup> of this Instant May to be gathered in by the middle of october Next & when sd half year is Expired then to Make A Rate for ye whole year yt soe the whole sallerey for ye yeare Relating to the mantenance of Ministrey may fall within the Compos of one Cunstabls time in Every yeare & to Keepe Contrebution afoot in the Congregation & to be Regulated acording to former Town order

Cedar Swamp

Att sd Metting Itt was voatted yt all The Cedar Swamp Within ye Township shall be Devided acording To former Town Ackt and yt There shall be no Sedar Timber felled upon sd Towns Commons from this date To ye first of Aprill Next Ensueing on penalty of Ten shillings per Tree for Every default & Samuel Stirtevant & George Bonam are Apinted to be helpfull to the surveyor in deviding sd swomps & the persons hereafter Named Are desired & apointed to have Inspection of sd swomps to se the Towns order herin above Mentioned Respecting the Sedar Timber duely Executed The persons are Major Bradford Left Shurtlif Samuel Stirtevant John Stirtevant Caleb Loring Elkanah Cushman & George bonam & none of sd Comitie May Cut aney sedar timber on forfitur of 20 shillings per tree

Joseph Churchels Grant

At sd Meeting A small Goore of land lately Taken in by Joseph Churchell on the Northerly side of his lott is granted to sd Joseph Churchill yt is to say all yt lieth within the fence lately set up by him up to the Comon Roade Way

[89.] Att sd Metting Last Mentioned Samuel King Junior

Samll King Grant

had Liberty Granted him by ye Town To heave up his 30 Acre Lot Lately Laid outt and To Take Itt up Nere Mr Cushmans Land

Att sd Metting Granted To John Gray a Small Goare of Land Liing on ye Northward of his 30 acre Lott and The head of ye Land he bought of benjamin Eatton and home to ye Line Lattely Run by Leiu<sup>tt</sup> Thompson This Grantted in Case Itt may

## PLYMOUTH RECORDS. 321

prove a peaceable Complyance betwen him and ye Rest of ye Neibhours Respeckting Theire Rainges of Their old lots

Adam Rights Grant
Att sd Metting Adam Right had Grantted him Ten acres of Land Which is Granted in Consideration of ye Rhoad Laterly Laid Through his Land by ye Seleck men for ye use of ye Neibhourhood

Jacob Michels Grant
Att sd Metting ye Town Grantted To Jacob Michell 20 Acrees of Land Liing Neare To Major bradfords Land Att Jonses River voatted To Repair ye Metting hous and Request Mr Nath[ll] Thomas To See Itt Done & To Returne his acount To ye Town in order To pay Major John bradford and Nath[ll] Morton are Chosen surveighers for ye Town for Measureing Land

Nicolias Mayes 20 Acre Loott
May ye 15[th] 1704—Then Laid outt To Nicolas May 20 Acres of Land formerly Grantted by ye Town and bounded as followeth begining att a Red oak Tree on ye Easterly side of ye Rhoad That Leadeth To ye hering pond at Mannoment ponds so Northerly To Sam[ll] Cornishes Land Easterly 24 pole To a Red oak Tree marked on 4 sides & from Thence Extending South & by West 90 pole and There bounded with a Red oake Marked on 4 sides and from Thence To Extend West and by North 28 pole To a Red oak Marked on 4 sides on ye southerly side of ye aforesd path and from Thence To Extend North and by East something more Easterly 90 Rod to ye bounds first mentioned Which is 15 acres of ye 20 above mentioned : The other 5 acrees was Laid out att ye same time and bounded as followeth begining att a Red oak Tree Which is ye West Corner bound of ye said Cornishes other Land and from Thence To Extend Southerly by Joseph holmsses Land Till Itt Cometh To his southeast Corner bound w[ch] is a heap of stones by a Swamp and so bounded by ye Swamp South Southeast To a Red oak Tree and a heap of stones on ye side of a hill nere sd Swamp and from Thence To Extend Nerest Northeast Till Itt Comes To ye Southeast Corner bound of his other land

surveighed and Measured on ye Day and yeare above written by

James Warren
& Thomas Faunce
Surveighers

[90.] On the 11th of June 1696 Then Measured and bounded unto John Nelson helkiah Tincom & Isaac Tincom 8 acrees of Meadow which was formerly Granted unto William Nelson & Ephraim Tincom both late of plimouth deceased at the lower south meadow at a place Comonly Caled the duble brooks Next adjoyning to the meadow belonging to Benjamin harlow & begining att his Corner bound on the North side of the brook & soe Rainging down sd Meadow southwest and by south Neerest 32 pole to a pine tree marked & from sd tree Raing accross the Meadow 40 pole to a Rock on A point of upland & from sd Red oake Marked standing About 5 pole from sd Rock & from thence Rainging Northeast and by North to a point of upland and there bounded with a pine tree & from thence Rainging Norwest & by west to the bound tree first mentioned.

John Nelson helkiah Tincom Isaac Tincom their lots of meadow

Measured and bounded on the day & yeare above Mentioned p$^r$ Thomas ffaunce Survyor to the Town

Aprill ye 15 1704

James Clark Jun his Loott

Twenty six Acrees of Land Laid out and Bounded To James Clark Junior Which ye Town Granted him Liberty To buy of ye Towns Commons of those men which ye Town had apoynted To Sell Land—20 Acrees Ling at a pond Called Island pond and bounded As followeth—With a Red oak Tree w$^{ch}$ Was ye West Corner bound of his 30 Acree Loott and from Thence To Run West Northwest 23 pole To a pine Tree Marked on 4 Sides And from Thence Raingeth Northwest and by west 40 pole and There bounded With a Red oake Marked Standing nere his other Land and so Joyning to The other Six Acrees Laid out on ye Northwest Side of beaver Dam Swamp & bounded As followe$^{th}$ viz on ye North Corner With a Red oak Marked on 4 Sides and Raingeth East South East 22 pole To a pine Tree

PLYMOUTH RECORDS. 323

Marked Standing in ye Swamp side and from Thence To Extend Southward allong ye Swamp 56 pole and There bounded With a pine Tree Marked and from Thence Raingeth West Northwest 22 pole To a Red oake Tree Marked And from Thence Northward by a Raing of Trees Marked To ye bounds first Mentioned Measured and bounded ye day and year abovsd by

       John Bradford
       & Nath[ll] Morton
        Surveighers

[91.]  The 10 Acrees of Land Granted To Adam Wright by
Adam   ye Town of plimouth Upon ye Acount of his
Wrights   Allowing land for a way from Lakenham To ye
10 Acrees  Mettinghouse in ye uper Sosiaty is bounded as followeth on the 27[th] of June 1704 on the North east Corner with A Maple Tree marked on 4 sids & from thence to Extend west about 27 pole to a small Maple Marked on 4 sides standing by Colchester brook & from sd Maple to Extend south 60 pole to two Red oaks Growing both out of one Roote Marked on 4 sides & from thence to Extend North 60 pole till it Cometh to the bounds first mentioned This land was laid out in A spruce swompe betwen Colchester brook & George Samsons att Wenatuxett  John Bradford
           James Warren
           William Shurtlef
           Surveyors

Town    At a Town Meeting held at plimouth on the 21 of
Meting  August 1704 for the Choyce of Jurrors to serve at the quorter sessions in september Next Which were as followeth ffrancis Adams Samuel Cornish Giles Rickard Jonathan Bryant

At sd Meeting The following Account of Charges was Taken in open town meting & voted to be Rated for upon the Inhabitants of the Town which is as followeth

| | |
|---|---|
| Imprimis for the scoole Master | 22—00—00 |
| Item for the assembly man | 12—00—00 |
| Item for Nathaniel Morton | 01—16—00 |
| Item for Major Bradford | 00—15—00 |

| | |
|---|---|
| Item for Samuel Stirtevant | 00—08—00 |
| Item for Making Rates for the year 1703 & for 1704 | 01—00—00 |
| Item for the Releif of the poore | 05—00—00 |
| Item To Thomas Howland for keeping Will : yong a strainger | 02—00—00 |
| Item for the Reparation of the Meeting house only forty shillings is to be allowed to the uper sosiaty out of sd 8 pounds | 08—00—00 |
| Item for the Cunstables Sallerey for two years past & this present year | 02—05—00 |
| Item for benjamin Warren | 00—06—00 |
| Item for John pratt & Thomas howland | 00—06—00 |
| Item for the New Sosiaty | 00—10—00 |

[92.] The bounds of the 6 acrees of Meadow of Joseph Churchill & the 6 acres of George Mortons & the 6 acres yt was John Tilsons at the South meadows was Renewed & settled on the 19[th] of July 1704 & bounded as followeth (viz) Joseph Churchels East bounds is a white oake stake stuck in ye Ground on the southeast of the meadows & from sd stake to Extend Nere North Northwest half a pint Westerly to a white oake tree Marked on 4 sides standing by Watsons Cove which is the Raing betwen Ransoms and the aforsd Churchels Meadow & from sd white oak tree to Extend southwesterly by the upland 20 pole to an other white oak tree Marked on 4 sides & from thence to Extend Neere Southeast and by south 3 degrees southerly across the Meadow to a stake stuck in the ground standing on the west side of a little Cove about 14 poole from the bounds first mentioned all betwen the bounds first Mentioned is Joseph Churchils

*Joseph Churchill bounds*

*George Mortons Meadow*

George Mortons is bounded on the East side by the aforesd Joseph Churchels & is on the Norwest End 30 pole in wedth from Churchils white oake tree to an other white oake tree Marked on 4 sides

Towards popes point & from sd white oake tree to Extend Neere south southeast across the meadow to a Red oake stake & from sd stake by the upland till it Cometh to the aforesd Churchels meadow

<small>John Tilsons Now Edmo Tilsons</small>
John Tilsons Now in the posession of Edmond Tilson was bounded on the Easterly side by the aforesd George Morton & down the Meadow till it Cometh to deacon Nathaniel Woods which is a white oak tree on the Northwest side of the Meadow & from sd white oake tree which was the sd Woods bounds on a straite line to a pine tre on the southeast side of the Meaddow all betwen the sd mortons and the sd Woods from upland to upland was laid out to the sd Tilson To which bounds they the above mentioned Churchill Morton & Tilson Consented & agreed which was Renewed & settled the day above Mentioned by me
William Shurtlif<br>Surveyor

<small>Rings Ten acre Loott</small>
The 10 acres of land Granted to Eliazar Ring by the Inhabitants of plimouth At a town meeting held at plimouth on the first of March $1703\frac{2}{3}$ was laid out on the $27^{th}$ of June 1704 & bounded as followeth (viz) 5 acres thereof next his other land at Jones meadow & bounded on the west Corner with a small white oake marked on 4 sides & from thence to Extend 30 pole East North East to a Red oake tree marked on 4 sides & then Extending south southeast 20 pole to a birch tree marked in a swompe & there bounded by the swomp southerly to his other lands & then bounded by his other lands to the bounds first mentioned The other 5 acres was laid out at a place Called bradford's bridg & bounded at the west Corner with a white oake tree marked on 4 sides & then Extending southeast 16 pole to a maple standing by A swompe marked on 4 sds & then bounded southwesterly by the swompe & brok as it turneth Glebing West North * till it Coms to the bounds first mentioned
John Bradford<br>James Warren<br>Surveyors

At A Town Meeting held at plimouth on the 11th of desember 1704 for the Choyce of Jurrors & other Town buisnes the Jurrors Chosen are Stephen Barneb Joseph Holmes senior Thomas holmes & ffrancis Cooke

Ceder Swamp

At this meeting The Town granted to Left : William Shurtlif & Ephraim Coole Liberty to whorfe down below their land under Coals hill soe Caled down into the sea soe farr as may be Conveniant for them At this meeting the Agents of the Town yt were improved in laying out or surveing the seder swamps in order to a division of ym Gave the town an account yt they had survyd ym & a vote being Cald for to know the towns mind whether they would Chouse a Comittie to take notice of the Clamors or propriators their was objecttion made by some which ocasioned much Discorse at last this voat pased yt is to say yt a Comity should be Chosen to Consider of som Method to propose to the town against the next town meeting wch is to be on ye 18th instant in order to their more peaceable agrement about the settlement of division of sd swomps there was 2 things proposed for sd Comity to Consult which would be most sattisfactor Eith to devide m into Neighbourhoods or to leas them out for yeers the Comitty are Major Bradford Capt Warren Left Shurtlif Ensign Morton Samuel Stirtevant Caleb Loring & Benjamin Warren or aney five of ym to act

[93.]

P 83-4 is page 83 & 84

Whearas the Town of plimouth at A Town Meeting held att plimouth on the 24 of May 1703 did Grant A pasell of land for a sheepe pasture That is to say three miles square from the head of Cobbs meadow A mile & a half Every way to such of the Inhabitants of sd Town as shall undertake to keepe sheepe theron or on sd land & build on it & endeavour to bring it to Grass & to such other of sd Town as shall Joyne with the first undertakers to keepe sheepe on sd land paying the first undertakers for such sheepe as they shall keep thus in the Generall flock per head as the first undertakers paid pr head for keeping their sheepe the first yeare with the charge of building sheapards housing & sheepe folds (etc) & wheras the men here

under named with the number of sheepe Each hath
signed & paid for hath ben at Grate Charge in building on sd land & keeping sheepe there the 2 last sum-
mers To bring sd land to Grass on the 26 day of december 1704 the town being Mett together voted yt
sd land abovesd shall be & Remaine to the men herafter Named According to the Number of sheepe they
have signed for & to such others as shall Joyne with
them pursuant to sd town act for the uses aforesd &
said land is by these presents Granted to them &
their heires & assignes for Ever for the uses aforesd

| | |
|---|---|
| James Warren | 40 sheepe |
| Nathaniel Thomas | 40 shepe |
| M$^{er}$ Ephraim Little | 20 shepe |
| John Watson | 20 shepe |
| Thomas Howland | 20 shepe |
| John Holmes | 24 shepe |
| John barns | 20 shepe |
| Isaac Lathrop | 20 shepe |
| Thomas Holmes | 20 sheepe |
| | 224 |
| Josiah ffinney | 20 shepe |
| Ebenazar Cobb | 20 sheepe |
| Abiall Shurtlef | 20 shepe |
| William Barns | 20 sheepe |
| John ffoster | 20 sheepe |
| The widow labaron | 12 sheepe |
| Samuel Lucas | 20 sheepe |
| | 178 |

Cooke
ffrances
his land he
Bought of
ye Town

The land yt ffrances Cook had A grant of att
Billentons hooles to buy of the Town upon Ap-
prizement was laid out & bounded on ye 26$^{th}$ of
May 1702 as ffolloweth (viz) with A Redoake tree
standing on ye North side of the way on the southwest Corner & from thence to Extend North half
a point westerly to A pine tree Marked & then to
Run North seaven degrees Easterly to A white oak
tree Marked & from thence to Run Neere North
East to another white oake tree marked on the

North side of A brook & then to Run Northeast & by East to an other white oak Tree marked standing on A hill on the south side of the aforesd brook & from thence to Extend southeast & by south till it Coms to the Rooad or way yt Goeth to Monponsett & then bounded by ye way till it Cometh to the bounds first Mentioned The land was prised at fforty shillings

James Warren<br>John Bradford<br>William Shurtlif<br>Surveyors

Barnes John his Grant of 30 foot of land Recorded bound

The 30 foot of land Granted to John Barnes at A Town Meetin held at plimouth on the 6$^{th}$ of March 169$\frac{8}{9}$ was laid out by us the subscribers on the 20$^{th}$ of March 170$\frac{4}{5}$ and bounded as ffolloweth (viz) by A Rock on the Northeast Corner next to barnses Crek[1] & from sd Rock to Extend southwest 30 ffot to A stake sett in the Marsh neere the upland About high water marke & from sd stake to Extend North Norwest half A point Westerly to a stake sett in the bank Neere the town pond & ffrom thence Northeast 20 foot to A stake att the point Neere sd barnes Crek & from thence south southeast half A poin Easterly to the bounds first mentioned

James Warren<br>Nathaniel Morton

[94.] At a Town Meeting held at plimouth on the 26$^{th}$ of ffebruary 170$\frac{4}{5}$ for the Choyce of Jurors which are as ffolloweth for the Grand Jury for the year Ensuing are

William Ring<br>Elisha Bradford<br>Samuel Waterman<br>& Ebenazar holmes

The Jurors Chosen to serve on the Jury of tryals at the County Court in March Next Ensuing this date are John ffoster John Churchill hunfrey Turner & Thomas Howland

---

[1] Barnes' Creek was a small brook, draining what is now called Dublin, and crossing Water Street into the rope-walk pond. It is now filled up, and a drain into the harbor was made some years ago which imperfectly supplies its place.

The land belonging to Thomas Lettes

The 20 Acrees of land fformerly Granted unto Thomas Lettice of plimouth at dotyes Meadows & laid out The bounds being lost or not known wee have Renewed or new settled as ffolloweth (viz) With A pine tree on the Northeast Corner Neere to the sd Lettices Meadow Next to Annasnapet & from sd tree to Extend Northwest about half a pint Westerly 56 pole to a white oake bush marked & from thence to Extend southwest About half a pint southerly 55 pole to a stake & then to Run southeast 66 pole to a stake neere or in the meadow yt was John dunhams which stake bears nere Northeast & by North from the pine tree first mentioned This Was laid out by William Shurtlif & Nathaniel Morton Surveyors for the Town

Nathaniel holmes his 10 acres Granted by the Town

September the 16$^{th}$ 1710 laid out by us ye subscribers To Nathaniel holmes ye son of John holmes Ten Acres of land at ye head of ye land of Samuel Nelson pursuant to a Grant of the Town of plimouth at a meeting held september 15 1710 and is bounded as ffolloweth (viz) with A bunch of small Red oake saplings with a heape of stones about them standing nere the uper End of Atwoods swomp & in the Rainge of the sd Nelsons land and thence Morth Northwest 69 pole to a bunch of small Red oake saplings with a heape of stones About them and thence West Southwest 2 Degrees southerly 41 pole to A stake with stons about it standing on ye East side of the path & from thence 37 pole south southeast to a stake standing on leavill Ground and from thence East Northest to ye bounds first Mentioned Nathaniel Thomas Thomas Dyer

Nathaniel holmeses

At a Town Meeting held at plimouth on the 2$^{d}$ of March 170$\frac{10}{11}$ for and in Consideration of the sum of Twenty shillings by Nathaniel

two acres
he bought
of the Town

holmes son of John holmes of plimouth unto John Watson Town Treasurror for ye use of sd Town well and truly paid the Town have Granted bargained & sold unto him the sd Nathaniel holmes and to his heires and assignes for Ever two acres of land and laid out by us the subscribers Adjoining to ye 10 acres of land Granted to him some time before at ye head of Samuel Nelsons land and is bounded as followeth (viz) with a bunch of small Red oak saplings with stons about them being ye Northerly Corner bounds of the above sd 10 acres and thence North Norwest 15 pole to ye way and thence southwesterly as ye way lise to a stake with stones about it it being ye Westerly Corner bound of ye aforsd 10 acres & thence by ye Rainge of the aforsd 10 acres to ye bounds first mentioned

James Warren    Nathaniel Thomas

10 acrees
of land
belonging to
Deacon Morton

The 10 acrees of land granted to GeorGe Morton by vertue of his haveing Meadow at ye uper South Meadows Was laid out and bounded as foloweth (viz) With a pine tree Marked on 4 sides Which Was abraham Jacksons southwest Corner bounds & from thence to Extend 20 Rod Neere southwest to small white oak bush marked & from thence to Extend Neere southeast to a Grat Pine tree marked standing neere William Rings & soe Down to William Rings Northest Corner Bounds & then Bounded by ye Meadow to ye aforsd Jacksons land & Then by sd abraham Jackson seniors land to the Bounds first mentioned leaveing a Way through sd land

September 28 1701

James Warren  }
William Shurtlif } surveiors

[**95.**] Know all Men by these presents That We Nathaniel
Nathaniel Morton & Thomas Morton both of plimouth
& Thomas in New England in the County of plimouth
Mortons aforesd That Whereas there hath ben or was
Release to A Controversey lately betwen George Morton
their brother of plimouth aforesd & the aforesd Nathaniel
George Morton Morton & Thomas Morton Concerning a
persell of salt Marsh Ground at Sagaquash
in plimouth aforesd & that the aforesd nath :
morton & Thomas Morton hath and doth lay
Claime unto a persell or part of salt marsh
ground that is in the posesion of the aforesd
George Morton & was by a former division
bounded out to ye sd George Morton as is
hereafter mentioned (viz) from a stake &
heape of stones standing on the beach against
the Cove to Extend Neere Northeast on a
straite line across the sd Marsh to a pine tree
marked on 4 sides which is ye dividing line
betwen ye sd George Morton & Thomas &
Nathaniel Morton for the Ending of which
Controversary abovesd Wee the sd Nathaniel
Morton & Thomas Morton Good Causes
moveing us thereunto have Remised Released
& for Ever quitt Claime & by thes presence
doe for us our heires Execators & administrators Remise Release and for Ever quitt
Claim unto George Morton of plimouth
aforesd his heires Execators & Administrators
All our Right title & Interest unto all ye salt
marsh Ground & sedg Ground yt lyeth
Eastward of the Cross line or bounds aforesd
& yt was fformerly in the posesion of the
aforesd George Morton with all the appurtenances & privilidges thereunto belonging or in
aney wayes appurtaining to him the sd George
Morton his heires & assignes for Ever & for
the True performance herof we the above
Named Nathaniel Morton & Thomas Morton
have herunto sett our hands & seals This

ffifteenth day desember 1703
signed sealed & delivered in the
presence  William Shurtlif
           Ephraim Morton
                Nathaniel Morton & a seal ()
                Thomas Morton & a seal   ()
Memorandom yt on the 15<sup>th</sup> day of desember 1703 then the above Named Nathaniel Morton & Thomas Morton personally appeared before me the subscriber one of her M$^{at}$ Justices of the peace for the County of plimouth & Acknowledg this above written Instrument to be their act & deede
                                              James Warren

[96.] Know all Men by these presents That I Ephraim Morton son of George Morton of plimouth in ye County of plimouth in New England Wheras there is & may be Ground of Controversey betwen George Morton senior of plimouth & Ephraim Morton son of ye sd George Morton aforsd Concerning the land wheron they now live in plimouth Aforesd doe Agree & settle the dividing line betwen them as ffolloweth (viz) from the bay or beach To Run the same Rainge as the fence of the sd Ephraim Morton now standeth to A heape of stons at the head of the aforesed feild and from thence to Extend southwest half a point southerly by divers marked Trees till it Coms to a Red oake tree marked on 4 sids standing at the head of ye aforesd Ephraim Mortons land on which he now liveth in plimouth all the land lying southerly of the bounds aforesd the aforesd Ephraim Morton have Remised, Released & for Ever Absolutely quitt Claimed unto my father George Morton of plimouth Aforesd to all the lands southerly of the bounds aforesd with all my Right Tittle & Interest unto ye land aforesd with all the appurtenances & privilidges thereunto belonging or in any wise appurtaining unto my father George Morton aforesd his heires Executors & Administrators firmely and Absolutely to Remise Release & quitt Claim to all the lands southerly of the bounds aforesd to my father George Morton his heires and assignes for Ever In Witnes whereof I have herunto sett my hand and seale this 15 day of desember 1703.
                                           Ephraim Morton
Signed sealed in
the presence of
Thomas Morton
William Shurtlif

Memorandon that on the 15th day of desember 1703 Then the above Named Ephraim Morton parsonably appered before me the subscriber one of her Ma^tis Justices of the peace for the County of plimouth & acknoledged the above written Instrument to be his Act and deed.

James Warren

[97.] At A Town meeting held at plimouth on the 12th of March 170⅔ for the Choyce of Town officers which were Chosen at sd meeting as ffolloweth (viz) The select men Chosen at sd meeting were Leften: William Shurtlif Nathaniel Morton & Caleb Loring The Cunstables ffrances Adams John Bradford Junior & Isaac King; for the Town voated to Chose 3 Cunstabls for this present yeare The Tithing men Are James Barneb Jonathan Shaw Giles Rickard & Isaac Cushman Jun: Isaac Lathrop Chosen sealer of Leather yt is Taned within sd Town Capt dyer Chosen pound Keeper Surveyors for the high Wayes Chosen are Mer Joseph Bartlet Capt dyer Mer John Stirtevant ffrances Cooke & John pratt ffence vewers Chosen are Benjamin Warren Ebenazar Cobb & Benjamin Sole it was also voted That the select men now Chosen should make all the assesments in sd Town for this present year

Grand Jurrors Chosen To serve at sd Court Are Samuel Startevant John Stirtevant Benjamin Warren Ephraim Cole & Thomas Morton

At this Meeting it was voated That Every house Keeper should kill half a dusen of black birds betwixt this date & the middle of May next Ensuing this date & if aney man kill more Then his half dusen shall be allowed a peney pr head to such person or persons by the Town Treasurer & Every person Neglecting to kill his half dusen of birds as abovesd shall pay two shillings to the Towns use to be Aded to his Town Rate & Gathered by the Cunstable for the Town use & have Chosen Men to Receive the birds heds which men are Benjamin Warren John Gray & Samuel ffuller

At sd Meeting it was voted That from & after the last day of october next 1705 Noe swine of aney age or sort What soe Ever shall Run on the Comons or at liberty but be keept up in styes or in ye Inclosurs belonging to their owners on penalty of the forfiting of Every such swine found at liberty as aforesd the one half Towards the Maintanance of the scoole keept in sd Town & the other half To such person or persons as shall be appointed by sd

Town to take up the same & That in the month of March annually there be 3 or more meet persons Chosen by sd Town aney or all of them haveing power to take up any swine found Runing at large as foresd & uyon the oath of two Witneses before a Justis of the peace That such swine were found Runing at large out of an Inclosur or stye as aforesd haveing obtained a surtifficate from such Justice of ye peace that such swine were by the oath of Two wittnesses found at large as aforesd Then such persons appointed as aforesd May sell such swine or Keepe them for his own use Rendering the one half of their vallew To the select men of sd Town for the use of the scoole as aforesd

Shurtlif
Abiall

Ten of the 20 acres of land granted unto Abiall Shurtlif by the Inhabitants of plimouth was laid out at Samsons pond on the 19[th] of April 1705 & bounded as ffolloweth with A spruce tree marked on 4 sids standing by Samsons pond & from sd Tree to Extend 43 Northwest to a pine tree marked on 4 sides & from thence to Extend Northeast 35 pole to another pine Tree marked on 4 sids & then to Extend 52 pole south A little Easterly to A white oake tree marked on 4 sids & then to Run south southeast to ye aforesd pond and then bounded by the pond to the bounds first mentioned leaving a way or alowing a way through sd land where it now goeth

James Warren
William Shurtlif
Surveyors

[98.]

William
Barnes
the way
Recorded

Ways

plimouth March ye 20[th] 170$\frac{4}{5}$ We the subscribers being Appointed by the Town of pļimouth at the Request of William Barns to vew A way yt was formerly laid out on the Northwest side of the 8 acres of land ye lot of his fathers which land lyeth neere little Town A little above the brick kill sd way on the North side of sd land being very unconvenient both for sd barns & for the Neighbours yt have most ocasion for it Therefore in the Roome & stead of sd way on the North side & from Comon land on the Northeast of sd land we laid out a way on the East side of sd land betwen sd land & John Watsons land &

bounded sd barnses land on the East side as followeth that is to say a heape of stons on a small hill nere the brick kill on the west side of them & soe Northward to the fence & from sd heap of stones the Rainge to Extend south & by west 7 degrees Westerly to a heape of stones 9 pole Westward from John Watsons land leaveing the way there 9 pole wide & from sd heap of stons to an other heape of stons by a stumpe at the uper End of sd land being 6 pole distant from sd Watsons land the line to Run straite towards the way 9 pole at the lowest End & 6 pole at the uper End  James Warren
          Nathaniel Morton

May 21
1705
Asembly
man Chosen

 At A Town Metting held at plimouth on the 21st of May 1705 at sd Meeting The Inhabitants of sd Town made Choyce of Major John Bradford as their Representative To serve for & Represent them in the Grate & Generall Court To be holden at boston on the 30 of this Instant May & the several adjoinments thereof throughout ye yeare

Jurors
Chosen

 At sd meeting Eliazar Cushman John Watson Ephraim Morton son of Ephraim Morton senior & Job Cushman were Chosen to serve on the Jury of Tryals at the County Court in June next

Comittie
Chosen

 At sd meeting The Inhabitants Made Choyce of M$^{er}$ Nathaniel Thomas Junior & Benjamin Warren as Their Agents or trustees to act for them & in their behalf to Require money due to the Town : of Samuel pratt & Isak howland both of middlebery for their Improvement of lands there some years past belonging to sd Town of plimouth for the use of the Ministree of plimouth successively & upon their Refusall or neglect to make sattisfaction to sd Comittie or agents of sd Town as aforesd Then to prosecute sd pratt & howland in A Course of law & the sd Inhabitants doe hereby Invest their sd Agents or trustees above named With full power soe to doe

Jurors Chosen

At A Town meeting held at plimouth on y 10<sup>th</sup> of September 1705 the Jurors then Chosen were Abiall Shurtlif Josiah ffiney Samuel Lucas & James Clark Junior & for the settling a scoolmaster & agreing on Town Charges it was voted to be adjorned untill Mundday ye 17<sup>th</sup> of this Instant september because but few people did apeare to attend this meeting by Reason Maney of the Inhabitants wer at see & others through unavoidabl ocasions wer hendred

ERRATA.

In the foot note on page 106 "Saquash" should be "Saquish."
In the second foot note on page 179 "Clampudder" should be "Clampudden."
In the foot note on page 202 the date "1651" should be "1691."
In the foot note on page 237 "Edward" should be "Edmund."

# INDEX.

| | Page. |
|---|---|
| Acconutus, | 41, 60, 172, 235 |
| Adams, Francis, | 323, 333 |
| Agawam, 84, 86, 112, 124, 140, 157, | 171, 291 |
| Alarm, | 17, 18 |
| Alden, | 1 |
| Alden, Joseph, | 284 |
| Alkarmus, Field, 84, 97, 115, 116, 125, | 127, 152 |
| Ancient Inhabitants, | 312 |
| Andrew, John, - | 94, 103, 213, 272 |
| Andrew Ring's Bridge, | 251 |
| Andrew's Bridge, | 79 |
| Andros, | 192 |
| Andros, John, | 255, 264 |
| Annasnapet, | 288, 314, 329 |
| Arms, | 14 |
| Armstrong, Gregory, | 17 |
| Arthur's Swamp, | 178 |
| Assembly, | 204, 323, 335 |
| Assessors, | 151, 232, 236, 275 |
| Atkins, Honoris, | 21, 33, 37, 67 |
| Atkins, Thomas, | 6 |
| Atkinson, Thomas, | 4 |
| Atwood, Ann, | 37, 68 |
| " John, | 7, 134, 168, 296 |
| " Mr., | 2, 11, 14, 208 |
| " Nathaniel, | 149, 170, 181 |
| Atwood's Swamp, | 294, 329 |
| Austerfield, | 226 |
| Awampocke, | 93 |
| Bacon, Nathaniel, | 45 |
| Baker, William, | 8 |
| Bandeleroes, | 14 |
| Bangs, Edward, | 16 |
| Bark, | 105, 142, 144, 224 |
| Barnaby, James, 127, 137, 220, 223, 226, 246, 255, 266, 285, 316, 319, 333 | |
| Barnaby, Stephen, | 283, 293, 326 |
| Barnes' Bridge, | 232, 287 |
| " Creek, | 328 |
| Barnes, Goodman, | 34 |
| " John, 13, 14, 15, 22, 30, 36, 48, 50, 68, 77, 84, 101, 102, 183, 193, 211, 255, 266, 273, 308, 327, 328 | |
| Barnes, Jonathan, 97, 101, 118, 141, 148, 151, 180, 181, 187, 189, 190, 201, 216, 223, 224, 231, 263, 276, 277 | |

| | Page. |
|---|---|
| Barnes, Mr., | 44 |
| " Neck, | 258 |
| " William, 183, 300, 301, 327, | 334 |
| Barnstable, | 213 |
| Barrow or Barrows, John, 102, 119, 142, 149, 176, 177, 181, 230, 251, 289 | |
| Barrow or Barrows, Robert, 91, 112, 149, 175, 181, 231, 251, 279, 302 | |
| Barrow or Barrows, Samuel, 311, 312 | |
| Bartlett, Benjamin, 32, 125, 211, 282, | 303 |
| Bartlett, Elnathan, | 211, 303 |
| " Joseph, 49, 51, 55, 80, 89, 93, 97, 100, 102, 114, 118, 119, 136, 146, 154, 161, 169, 170, 171, 172, 174, 176, 180, 182, 189, 193, 200, 204, 211, 213, 214, 224, 235, 236, 237, 238, 241, 247, 250, 257, 263, 267, 269, 270, 279 281, 285, 298, 301, 303, 307, 308, 333 | |
| Bartlett, Mr., | 238, 255, 306 |
| Bartlett, Robert, 18, 22, 25, 28, 32, 33, 37, 41, 43, 54, 59, 61, 62, 67, 89, 160, 195, 210, 213, 222, 223, 234, 241, 256, 265, 266, 268, 286, 319 | |
| Baruck Jordan's Meadow, | 251 |
| Bassett, Capt., | 274 |
| Beach, | 302 |
| Beach Head, | 230 |
| Beacon, | 18 |
| Beaver Dam Brook, | 75, 96, 293, 304 |
| Beaver Dam Path, | 235 |
| Beaver Dam Swamp, | 322 |
| Bell, 161, 188, 190, 265, 266, 283, 317 | |
| Bellows, | 45 |
| Benson, John, | 215, 279 |
| Bible, | 141 |
| Billington, Francis, 4, 9, 12, 16, 21, 24, 33, 37, 40, 43, 47, 57, 66, 83, 86, 87, 100 | |
| Billington Sea, | 384, 309 |
| Billington Holes, | 155, 162, 291, 327 |
| Billington's Tree, | 94 |
| Bills of estates, | 117 |
| Blackbirds, | 131, 164, 241, 247, 333 |
| Black, Myles, | 114 |
| Blackwater, | 309 |
| Boards, | 114, 273 |
| Bogles Cropp, | 222 |
| Bolts, | 114, 172, 225 |

22

338

INDEX.

Bonney, Wm., . . . 253, 254
Bonum, George. 22, 25, 36, 41, 44, 46,
 50, 52, 62, 74, 75, 76, 80, 81, 82, 88, 90,
 96, 101, 111, 121, 122, 125, 128, 131,
 135, 136, 138, 140, 144, 148, 152, 163,
 167, 168, 172, 176, 177, 181, 182, 184,
 187, 188, 189, 190, 193, 194, 201, 202,
 207, 208, 209, 210, 213, 228, 229, 230,
 232, 251, 252, 253, 288, 295, 310, 311
Bosworth, Jonathan, 54, 81, 102, 104
Bounds of land, . . . 249
Bradford, Alice, . . . 36, 68
 " Capt., 49, 50, 59, 77, 94, 113,
 125, 126, 134, 139, 140, 274, 283, 285,
 . . . . 289
Bradford, Elisha, . 264, 296, 308
 " Ephraim, . . . 299
 " House, . . . 201
 " John, 27, 114, 149, 171, 176,
 177, 180, 184, 186, 189, 191, 193, 195,
 198, 200, 201, 202, 203, 204, 213, 214,
 236, 239, 240, 246, 255, 256, 272, 275,
 286, 295, 296, 300, 301, 302, 307, 308,
 309, 312, 313, 315, 318, 319, 321, 323,
 . . . 325, 328, 333, 335
Bradford, Joseph, 102, 110, 148, 180,
 . . 188, 192, 233, 237, 268, 314
Bradford, Lef, . . . 270
 " Major, 287, 309, 310, 321,
 . . . . 323, 326
Bradford, Mr., 8, 14, 17, 18, 19, 21, 25,
 . . 29, 44, 145, 149, 151, 161
Bradford, Samuel, 180, 211, 225, 247,
 . . . . 316
Bradford, Wm., 36, 92, 95, 100, 124,
 130, 131, 148, 163, 167, 171, 174, 176,
 177, 180, 183, 184, 186, 194, 233, 236,
 . . . . 239, 248
Bradford's Bridge, . . 325
Bradford's Marsh, . . . 87
Braintree, . . . . 255
Bread, . . . . . 15
Breakheart Hill, . . . 97
Brewster, Jonathan, . . 2
Brick, . . . . 11, 15
Brick Kiln,| . . . 334, 335
Bridgewater, . . 95, 133, 307
Bridgewater Path, 76, 162, 176, 177, 178
Brinsme, Mr., . . . 77
Broken Wharf, . . . 16
Browne, John, . . . 25
Browne, Mr., . . . . 2
Browne, William, 21, 25, 34, 37, 65, 100
Bryant, John, 149, 155, 161, 173, 174,
 175, 181, 217, 236, 241, 246, 247, 254,
 . 256, 274, 285, 307, 308, 319
Bryant, Jonathan, . 27, 216, 301, 323
 " Lt., . . . 273, 291
 " Samuel, . . . 27
 " Stephen, 2, 4, 21, 39, 40, 44,
 49, 50, 52, 62, 79, 80, 105, 111, 112, 125,
 126, 130, 133, 147, 148, 155, 161, 174,
 . 181, 182, 188, 210, 266, 289, 306
Bull, . . . . . 8, 13
Bullets, . . . . . 18
Burial Ground, . . . 296
Butler, Thomas, . . 56, 62

Callivers, . . . . 14
Calves, . . . . . 5
Captain's Hill, . . . 18
Carbines, . . . . 14
Carver, . . . . . 314
Carver, John, . . 183, 240, 275
Cattle, 3, 4, 5, 7, 8, 9, 12, 13, 18, 19, 20,
 25, 27, 28, 29, 30, 55, 56, 89, 99, 116,
 . . . 133, 158, 163, 211, 216
Causon's Pond, . . . 269
Caussetan, . . . . 97
Cedar Bridge, . . . 50, 80, 231
Cedar Swamps, . . 312, 313, 326
Cedar Timber, . . . 313
Cedar Trees, . . . 43, 313
Champlains Map, . . . 293
Charter, . . . . 202
Chauncey, Mr., . . . 6
Children, . . . . 295
Chimneys, . . . . 59
Chittengton, Capt., . . 274
Church, Richard, 17, 18, 28, 46, 52, 139
Church's Landing, . . 307
Churchill, Eleazer, 123, 181, 185, 240,
 247, 255, 257, 265, 273, 302, 309, 319
Churchill, Elkanah, . . 217
Churchill, John, 22, 25, 34, 37, 51, 69,
 76, 85, 110, 183, 224, 240, 246, 253, 254,
 255, 265, 267, 273, 282, 283, 293, 294,
 . . . . 302, 318, 328
Churchill, Joseph, 102, 123, 141, 149,
 . 159, 181, 245, 296, 302, 296, 309, 324
Churchill, Stephen, . . 303
Churchill, William, . 183, 274, 302
Clampudden Plain, . . 305, 306
Clam Pudding Pond, . . 179
Clam's Island Meadow, . 198, 199
Clapboards, . . . 225, 273
Clark, Abigail, . . . 2, 13
 " Deacon, . . . 319
 " George, . . 16, 86, 87
 " James, 92, 93, 94, 95, 98, 100,
 102, 119, 148, 165, 182, 183, 215, 216,
 . 301, 303, 306, 308, 322, 336
Clark, John, . . 256, 303, 306
 " Josias, . . . 18
 " Nathaniel, . . 256, 270
 " Thomas, 6, 8, 11, 16, 20, 22, 24,
 25, 28, 30, 31, 32, 33, 36, 38, 62, 63, 101,
 102, 149, 182, 183, 201, 206, 207, 218,
 . 223, 235, 238, 254, 257, 305, 317
Clark, William, 43, 60, 71, 73, 82, 83,
 85, 86, 87, 88, 90, 91, 92, 94, 101, 105,
 110, 111, 115, 116, 117, 118, 124, 125,
 126, 130, 131, 139, 140, 143, 145, 146,
 147, 148, 151, 155, 157, 161, 164, 167,
 168, 169, 170, 174, 182, 189, 196, 219,
 236, 257, 240, 241, 254, 267, 285, 299,
 . . . . 300,
Clark's Island, 7, 29, 30, 47, 53, 99, 156,
 158, 163, 172, 192, 193, 197, 198, 224
Cliff, . . . . . 85
Cobb, Ebenezer, . 289, 319, 327, 333
 " Eleazer, . . . 216
 " John, 48, 72, 74, 101, 137, 146,
 148, 181, 210, 218, 219, 220, 221, 249,
 . . . . 271, 296, 307

# INDEX. 339

Cobb's Meadows, . . 314, 326
Colchester, 51, 53, 54, 61, 104, 121, 139,
. . . . 202, 235, 292
Colchester Brook, 140, 193, 239, 292,
. . . . . 306
Colchester Swamp, . . 197, 235
Cold Spring Brook, . . . 310
Cole, Ephraim, 183, 204, 224, 240, 241,
246, 256, 265, 266, 270, 283, 287, 293,
. . 294, 309, 310, 318, 326, 333
Cole, Hugh, 19, 33, 45, 51, 73, 82, 84,
. . 86, 88, 89, 90, 102, 280, 281, 291
Cole, James, 14, 16, 19, 21, 25, 26, 34,
37, 49, 67, 80, 101, 118, 139, 148, 157,
. . . . 168, 176, 183, 188
Cole, John, 48, 89, 115, 183, 246, 265,
. . . . . 280, 317
Cole's Hill, . . 266, 267, 286, 326
Cole's Shop, . . . . 248
Colony Laws, . . . . 123
Combe or Combs, Francis, 39, 40, 49,
76, 77, 86, 87, 89, 93, 102, 143, 212, 216,
. . . . . 279, 280
Combe or Combs, Mr., . . . 16
Commissioner, . 195, 205, 240, 311
Commonage, . . 197, 224, 267
Common Lands, . . . . 301
Common Meadows, . . . 263
Commons, 34, 41, 47, 72, 84, 105, 118,
142, 144, 156, 158, 170, 197, 223, 224,
225, 237, 249, 270, 271, 273, 283, 286,
287, 288, 291, 294, 304, 305, 309, 310,
. . . . . 314, 317
Constable, 28, 31, 47, 78, 111, 112, 113,
132, 145, 147, 150, 151, 155, 156, 161,
164, 170, 173, 174, 176, 184, 185, 189,
193, 195, 196, 201, 204, 205, 223, 228,
229, 236, 239, 241, 247, 256, 264, 266,
. . 284, 285, 296, 308, 318, 324, 333
Cooke, Caleb, 26, 149, 180, 185, 205,
. . 233, 235, 236, 242, 243, 270, 319
Cooke, Francis, 2, 17, 21, 24, 33, 36, 66,
180, 208, 210, 262, 266, 291, 294, 309,
. . . . . 326, 327, 333
Cooke, Jacob, 21, 24, 28, 37, 46, 54, 68,
83, 100, 105, 133, 135, 149, 167, 180,
187, 188, 195, 207, 234, 282, 283, 284,
. . . . 288, 301, 308, 313, 314
Cooke, John, 11, 12, 16, 17, 21, 24, 28,
29, 30, 31, 32, 42, 43, 45, 46, 66, 73, 86,
. . . . . 87, 206, 237
Cooke, Josias, . . . . 1, 14
" Wm., . . . . . 41
Cooper, Richard, . 223, 234, 260, 266
Cordwood, . . . 224, 270, 273
Corn Mill, . 122, 123, 167, 168, 171
Cornish, Samuel, 244, 275, 282, 303, 321,
. . . . . . 323
Cotton, Joanna or Mrs., 145, 165, 274
" John, 91, 100, 105, 144, 148,
180, 183, 219, 220, 258, 274, 290, 291
Cotton, Mr., 87, 98, 111, 136, 145, 158,
. 165, 167, 205, 240, 246, 255, 276
Council of War, . . . 15, 145
County Court, 188, 189, 200, 204, 224,
240, 254, 257, 262, 264, 265, 266, 282,
. . 286, 289, 305, 306, 319, 328, 335

County Justices, . . . 240
County Rate, . . . . 305
Court of Assistants, . . . 296
Court Street, . . . . 294
Cows, . . 5, 8, 13, 19, 23, 27, 28, 29
Crane Brook, . . . 89, 208
Crosman's Pond, . . . 269
Crow, Mrs., . . . . 175
" William, 44, 47, 48, 49, 50, 58,
71, 75, 83, 87, 90, 91, 92, 97, 99, 100,
101, 104, 105, 106, 110, 111, 112, 113,
115, 117, 118, 120, 122, 123, 124, 126,
128, 129, 131, 132, 134, 135, 136, 137,
138, 139, 144, 145, 146, 147, 148, 150,
151, 152, 153, 155, 157, 159, 161, 162,
163, 164, 165, 170, 171, 173, 175, 192,
. . . . . . 219
Crows, . . . . 164, 248
Crow's Bounds, . . . 187
Curtis, Francis, . 132, 159, 161, 210
Cushing, John, . . . . 215
Cushman, Eleazer, 182, 234, 241, 264,
. . . 286, 296, 308, 335
Cushman, Elkanah, 149, 180, 187, 188,
191, 204, 223, 228, 236, 238, 241, 246,
247, 257, 273, 278, 279, 282, 283, 285,
. . . . . . 308
Cushman, Isaac, 147, 149, 173, 176,
180, 183, 185, 186, 187, 188, 189, 193,
195, 198, 200, 201, 203, 231, 232, 233,
235, 236, 237, 238, 239, 240, 249, 250,
251, 252, 254, 255, 278, 279, 313, 317,
. . . . . . 333
Cushman, Job, . . . . 335
" Mr., . . . . 62
" Thomas, 14, 15, 16, 19, 22,
25, 28, 36, 39, 77, 81, 89, 95, 100, 102,
105, 110, 118, 119, 125, 131, 132, 139,
148, 149, 170, 172, 175, 180, 186, 192,
193, 195, 205, 206, 208, 209, 210, 235,
. . . . . 278, 279
Cutbert, Samuel, . . 21, 24, 34

Darby, John, . . . . 238
Deal, . . . . . 296
Deane, Stephen, . . . 140
Deep Water, . . . 140, 295
Deep Water Swamp, . . 184, 295
Deputies, 111, 132, 147, 150, 151, 164,
. 170, 173, 174, 184, 185, 203, 204
Dexter, Thomas, . . . 212
Dogs, . . . . . 99
Done, John, . . . 15, 17, 268
" Mr., . . . 11, 16, 18, 19
Doten or Dotey, Edward, 16, 21, 37, 66,
79, 91, 94, 99, 102, 106, 118, 120, 121,
122, 133, 149, 162, 207, 208, 219, 220,
. . . . . . 319
Doten or Dotey, Isaac, . . 214
" " John, 44, 79, 95, 102,
133, 149, 185, 190, 197, 201, 204, 206,
214, 224, 228, 237, 238, 239, 241, 246,
249, 256, 257, 266, 268, 270, 271, 273,
. . . . 286, 289, 294, 298
Doten or Dotey, Samuel, . . 319
" " Thomas, 99, 116, 152,
. . . . . 153, 317

# INDEX.

Doten's Field, . . . . 177
Dotey, Goodman, . . . 34
Dotie's Meadow, 49, 55, 61, 80, 88, 139,
. . . . 283, 287, 329
Dotie's Plain, . . . 100, 283
Dotie's Pond, . . 47, 82, 186, 209
Double Brook. 127, 130, 137, 175, 191,
. . . . 199, 220, 221, 266
Double Brooks. . . 291, 305, 322
Drew, John, . . . 102, 149, 181
Drinking Place, . . . . 249
Drumheads, . . . . . 14
Dunham, Daniel, 89, 102, 117, 127, 141,
. . . . 156, 277, 278, 284
Dunham, Eleazer, . 182, 268, 283
" Goodman, . . . 16
" John, 1, 2, 3, 4, 4, 15, 18, 19,
20, 22, 23, 24, 25, 27, 28, 29, 30, 31, 32,
33, 34, 36, 37, 46, 48, 50, 51, 57, 58, 59,
60, 61, 66, 68, 81, 82, 99, 100, 161, 127,
146, 163, 188, 206, 208, 209, 216, 237,
. . . . 278, 284, 292, 329
Dunham, Jonathan, 26, 37, 40, 44, 48,
. . . . . . 57, 66
Dunham, Joseph, 48, 50, 53, 61, 80, 102,
. . 118, 145, 181, 206, 234, 300, 305
" Micajah, . . . 305
Dunham, Nathaniel, . 298, 305
" Samuel, 22, 25, 36, 49, 50 53,
67, 80, 82, 106, 111, 112, 113, 115, 122,
136, 141, 148, 149, 161, 181, 182, 188,
190, 207, 208, 209, 246, 260, 276, 299
Dunham, Thomas, 105, 115, 121, 152
Dunham's Neck, . . . . 284
Duxbury, . . . . 18, 309
Dyer, Capt., . . . . . 333
" John, . 274, 285, 287, 369, 318
" Mr., . . . . . 306
" Thomas, . . . . 329
Eaton, Benjamin, 12, 33, 47, 86, 87,
101, 148, 152. 153, 181, 256, 274, 296,
. . . . . . . 316

Eddy, Samuel, 4, 19, 20, 22, 25, 27, 28,
36, 63, 89, 101, 127, 138, 157, 279, 281
Edson, Capt., . . . . 274
Eel Creek, . . . . . 296
Eel River, 3, 11, 18, 42, 43, 55, 60, 72,
79, 89, 126, 127, 130, 133, 137, 139, 160,
191, 197, 198, 207, 218, 227, 249, 266,
. . . . . . 285, 290
Eel River Bridge, 28, 71, 85, 90, 174,
. . . . . . 175, 179
Eel River Brook, . . 123, 299
Eel River Swamp, . . . 179
Ellis, Mordecai, . . . . 147
Ellis, William, . . . . 290
Everson, John, 105, 106, 112, 287, 306
" Martha, . . . . 112
" Richard, . . . 105
Excise, . . . . . . 82
Extravagant Persons, . . 143

Fallowell, Gabriel, 12, 14, 21, 25, 37,
. . . 41, 48, 62, 64, 79, 101, 208
Fallowell, John, 89, 102, 117, 132, 143,
. . . . . . . 281

Fallowell, Wm., . . . . 16
Faunce, John, 22, 37, 42, 68, 218, 297,
. . . . . . . 298
Faunce, Joseph, 149, 152, 153, 181, 204,
. . . . 247, 266, 279, 302
Faunce, Patience, . . . 37, 42
" Thomas, 102, 149, 165, 171,
173, 174, 182, 183, 191, 195, 198, 199,
201, 202, 203, 204, 205, 209, 211, 217,
218, 219, 220, 222, 223, 225, 226, 227,
228, 229, 232, 234, 236, 237, 241, 242,
244, 245, 247, 248, 249, 250, 251, 252,
253, 255, 256, 258, 260, 261, 262, 263,
266, 267, 268, 269, 270, 272, 285, 288,
. . 291, 296, 306, 308, 314, 318, 322
Fence Viewers, 225, 247, 256, 266, 285,
. . . . . . . 333
Fences, . . . . . 5, 271
Fencing Stuff, . . . . 225
Finney, John, 9, 14, 16, 22, 28, 209, 295
Finney, Josiah, 196, 197, 226, 236, 238,
241, 290, 291, 300, 306, 308, 327, 336
Finney, Robert, 16, 18, 22, 25, 30, 34,
37, 42, 45, 47, 48, 53, 54, 59, 61, 67, 71,
73, 77, 78, 79, 82, 83, 84, 85, 87, 101,
106, 110, 111, 125, 133, 146, 148, 182,
. . . . 196, 197, 209, 295
Finney's Meadows, . . 291, 309
Firewood, . 34, 77, 156, 158, 167
First Brook, . . . 177, 184, 311
First Fire, . . . . . 83
First Parish, . . . . 303
Fish Ware, . . . . . 132
Fishing Stage, . . . 98, 106
Fort, . . . . . . 162
Fort Hill, . . . . . 11
Fortifications, . . . 9, 16, 146
Foster, John, 183, 204, 205, 224, 228,
239, 241, 256, 265, 266, 274, 286, 287,
. . . 296, 306, 309, 327, 328
Foster, Richard, . 26, 33, 37, 69, 103
" Thomas, . . . . 290
Four Mile Brook, . 59, 96, 257, 302
Fowling Pieces, . . . . 14
Freeholders, . . . . 312
French Doctor, . . . . 246
Fresh Lake, . 140, 166, 189, 284
Fresh Pond, . . . . . 307
Fuller, Bridget, . 166, 275, 283
" Mathew, . . . . 14
" Mr., . . . 16, 17, 208
" Mrs., . . . . 1, 48
" Samuel, 26, 100, 130, 135, 142,
148, 166, 181, 192, 223, 233, 256, 257,
. . . . 266, 274, 283, 306, 333
Fulling Mill, 122, 138, 144, 232, 233, 236

Galhouse Hill, . . . . 18
Gallows Lane, . . . . 84
Gardner, Samuel, . 102, 149, 174, 182
General Court, 228, 229, 236, 269, 286,
. . . . . . 309, 335
Gibbs, Mr., . . . . . 211
Giles' Holes, . . . . 219
Glace, James, . . . . 22
Glasse, James, . . . 34, 37
Goats, . . . . . . 5

# INDEX. 341

Golder, Goodman, . . . 208
Goulder, Francis, . . 18, 22, 24
Grand Assize, . . . . 241, 246
Grand Jury, 28, 111, 132, 147, 151, 165, 170, 173, 174, 183, 185, 195, 201, 204, 205, 215, 223, 224, 228, 246, 247, 256, 266, 274, 275, 285, 286, 294, 296, 306, 308, 318, 319, 333
Graves, . . . . . 32, 35
Gray, Edward, 21, 24, 37, 45, 47, 48, 49, 50, 59, 62, 66, 73, 74, 83, 87, 90, 91, 97, 100, 110, 114, 117, 118, 123, 124, 125, 128, 129, 135, 136, 139, 143, 146, 147, 148, 151, 154, 155, 156, 158, 163, 165, 167, 168, 194, 294
Gray, John, 149, 174, 178, 181, 185, 187, 189, 197, 201, 204, 213, 228, 233, 234, 235, 241, 260, 286, 333
Gray, Thomas, . . . . 33
Great Guns, . . 237, 250, 263
Great Gutter, . . . . 268
Great Meadow, . . . . 208
Great South Pond, . . . 123
Greme, Mr., . . . . 15
Greenes, John, . . . . 7
Green, Joseph, . . . . 33
" William, . . 172, 173
Green's Harbor, . . . . 6
Grist Mill, . . . . 232
Groome, John, . . . . 17
" Mr., . . . . 17
Guns, . . . . . 44, 150
Gurnet, 53, 90, 95, 195, 257, 261, 293
Gutt, . . . . . . 97

Hale, Moses, . . . 303, 306
Hale, Mr., . . . . 303
Half Way End, . . . 219, 227
Half Way Hill, . . . . 210
Half Way Pond, . . . . 160
Half Way Pond River, . . 171
Hallet, Mr., . . . . 4, 9
Hanbury, Mr., . 13, 14, 15, 16, 17
Harlow, Benjamin, . . . 322
" Nathaniel, 204, 210, 227, 246, 252, 265
Harlow, Samuel, 149, 181, 201, 203, 204, 229, 248, 251, 253, 266, 285, 287, 296, 298
Harlow, Wm. 22, 26, 32, 33, 36, 41, 44, 47, 48, 51, 58 67, 73, 76, 78, 80, 82, 83, 84, 86, 88, 91, 97, 98, 99, 101, 105, 107, 110, 111, 112, 113, 115, 118, 122, 124, 125, 126, 131, 132, 134, 136, 139, 145, 147, 148, 150, 151, 152, 153, 157, 165, 168, 170, 172, 174, 176, 180, 181, 182, 183, 184, 185, 190, 193, 195, 197, 198, 201, 202, 203, 204, 213, 227, 236, 250, 253, 259, 260, 266, 274, 297, 301, 303, 311, 315, 317 319
Harmon, John, 23, 49, 50, 80, 168, 173, 194
Hathaway, Arthur, . 26, 36, 68
Haward, Heywood or Hayward, John, 19, 21, 23, 24, 27, 28, 29, 34, 37, 38, 68, 89
Haward, Joseph, . . . 284

Haward's Swamp, . . 220, 221
Hedge, Mrs. I. L., . . . 268
Heifers, . . . . . 116
Herrings, 5, 6, 7, 52, 53, 59, 60, 98, 114, 131, 139, 171, 172, 236, 290, 308
Herring Brook, . . . . 291
Herring Pond, . . 160, 191, 321
Herring Ware, . . 3, 17, 159
Hewes, Thomas, . 99, 127, 153, 186
Hickes, Ephraim, . . . 208
" Margaret, . . . 37
" Mrs., . . . . 64
" Samuel, 13, 24, 33, 37, 64, 203
Higgins, Richard, . . . 16
High Pines, . . . . 318
High Ridge, . . 187, 272, 302
Highways, 72, 152, 177, 178, 179, 180, 196, 234, 240
Hill, Thomas, . . . . 4
Hinckley, . . . . . 45
Hobshole, . . . . . 33
Hodkinson, Mrs. . . . 4
Hodges, Nicholas, . . . 33
Hoggkins, William, . . . 20
Hogkins, William, . . . 24
Hogs, . . . . 89, 90, 99
Holman, Edward, . 22, 24, 101
Holmes, Ebenezer, 183, 214, 216, 274, 291, 296, 299, 300, 306
Holmes, Elisha, . 276, 281, 295, 297
" Ichabod, . . . 290
" John, 4, 19, 34, 91, 102, 148, 181, 190, 208, 249, 271, 294, 310, 318, 327, 329, 330
Holmes, Joseph, . 214, 301, 321, 326
" Mr., . . . . 20, 21
" Nathaniel, 125, 149, 170, 181, 183, 204, 224, 241, 246, 254, 265, 266, 267, 279, 280, 285, 297, 302, 329, 330
Holmes, Patience, . . . 302, 311
" Thomas, 257, 310, 313, 318, 326, 327
Holmes, William, . . . 2
Hopkins, Mr., . . . 14, 16
Hornbeam Tree, . . . 261
Horses, 71, 89, 99, 100, 116, 117, 133
Horseneck, . . 267, 277, 278, 287
Hoskins, Samuel, . . . 217
" William, 9, 33, 100, 103, 104, 165, 168, 170? 185, 194
Housekeepers, . . . 312, 333
Howes, Jeremiah, . . . 230
Howland, Capt. . . . . 243
" Henry, . . . 4
" Isaac, . . . 312, 335
" Jabez, 83, 102, 118, 127, 129, 131, 132, 138, 144, 146, 150
Howland, James, . . . 308
Howland, John, 7, 19, 31, 32, 36 39, 41, 73, 82, 100, 105, 129, 206, 278
Howland, Joseph, 80, 87, 91, 95, 96, 102, 104, 114, 115, 119, 123, 134, 135, 139, 146, 147, 148, 150, 151, 162, 170, 174, 180, 189, 190, 193, 194, 202, 235, 237, 242
Howland, Lieut., 153, 173, 176, 177, 183, 188

# INDEX.

Howland, Mr., 17, 21, 22, 24, 28, 29, 46, 48, 62, 123, 142, 206
Howland, Nathaniel, . 287, 318
" Thomas, 286, 296, 319, 324, 327, 328
Hunter's, John, wife, . . 245
Hunting House Brook, . . 178
Hurst, James, 10, 21, 36, 38, 70, 206, 208, 271
Hylly Plain Great Hill, . . 252

Idle Persons, . . 82, 84, 138
Indian Bridge, . . 132, 159
Indian Brook, . . . 38, 76, 80
Indian Land, . . 107, 287, 308
Indian Pond, . . . 94, 96, 210
Indian Pond Plain, . . . 275
Indians, . . 15, 94, 145, 170, 173
Inferior Court, . . . . 318
Island Pond, . . . 301, 322

Jabez Corner, . . . 85, 296
Jackson, Abraham, 44, 45, 48, 53, 61, 94, 98, 102, 127, 132, 148, 151, 162, 165, 180, 181, 188, 189, 204, 206, 210, 232, 241, 250, 253, 254, 258, 259, 265, 272, 291, 299, 302, 315, 330
Jackson, Eleanor, . . . 241
" Lemuel, . . . 290
" Nathaniel, . 241, 265, 273
" Wm. Hall, . . 303
Jenkins, John, . . . . 16
Jenney, John, . 6, 7, 8, 11, 13, 14, 16
" Mrs., . . . 37, 65
" Samuel, . 159, 165, 168
Joanes or Jones, Ralph, 21, 247, 302, 308
Johns' Pond, . . . . 169
Jones River, 3, 16, 17, 26, 39, 42, 45, 49, 76, 83, 89, 97, 105, 115, 132, 133, 137, 142, 155, 159, 208, 240, 309, 314, 315, 316, 321
Jones River Bridge, 16, 174, 178, 183, 317
Jones River Meadow, 62, 135, 172, 187, 209, 228, 233, 252
Jones River Pond, . . . 142
Jones' Meadow, . . . 335
Jourdaine, Baruck, 149, 176, 180, 181, 201, 224, 302
Jourdaine, John, 22, 24, 37, 48, 54, 60, 61, 68, 72, 79, 91, 101, 112, 127, 128, 132, 148
Jury, 189, 199, 201, 204, 206, 223, 224, 240, 241, 246, 254, 255, 257, 262, 264, 265, 273, 274, 275, 282, 286, 298, 301, 305, 306, 308, 313, 316, 318, 319, 323, 335, 336

Keith, John, . . . . 26
Kempton, Manassah, 11, 14, 16, 17, 18, 19, 22, 24, 28, 29, 31, 32, 33, 36, 69
Kennedy, Alexander, - 125, 126, 137
King, Goodman, . . . 209
" Isaac, - 201, 210, 254, 285, 333
" Joseph, . . . 210, 302
" Samuel, 21, 24, 37, 49, 50, 67, 79,
80, 81, 94, 100, 111, 120, 126, 133, 148, 166, 181, 183, 217, 295
Kingston, . . . . . 314
Knowles, Richard, . . . 14
Knowles' Meadow, . . . 196
Lakenham, 47, 49, 51, 61, 73, 75, 95, 98, 100, 120, 191, 238, 268, 275, 291, 323
Lakenham Brook, . . . 178
Lakenham Pond, . . . 61, 257
Land Grants, . . . . 274
Latham, Robert, . 80, 128, 146, 194
Latham's Cartway, . . . 133
Lather or Lacher, . . . 317
Lazell, Thomas, . 182, 202, 235, 239
LeBaron, Francis, . . . 246
" Widow, . . . . 327
Lee, Mr., 16, 17, 21, 24, 37, 208, 209
Lee, Robert, . . . . 66
Lettice, Thomas, 4, 8, 18, 21, 33, 37, 49, 64, 74, 101, 118, 148, 208, 329
Little Brook, . . . . 157
Little, Ephraim, 26, 251, 258, 267, 268, 296, 298, 316, 327
Little Pond, . . . 284, 296
Little, Thomas, 22, 23, 24, 28, 38, 76, 83, 207
Little Town, . 61, 125, 153, 261, 334
Little Town Valley, . . . 124
Little's Meadows, . . . 303
Lobdell, Isaac, . . 149, 185
Lock, . . . . . 317
Looms, . . . . . 117
Lord's Day, . . . . 171
Loring Caleb, 266, 270, 273, 273, 294, 296, 306, 316, 318, 326, 333
Loring, Thomas, . . 274, 296
Lothrop, Isaac, 274, 275, 285, 318, 327, 333
Lout Pond, . . 125, 140, 189, 296
Lout Pond Plain, . . . 261
Lower Society, . . . . 316
Lucas, Benoni, . 182, 215, 250, 308
" John, . 111, 120, 121, 132
" Samuel, 182, 205, 210, 224, 240, 248, 255, 256, 257, 269, 286, 301, 308, 327, 336
Lucas, Thomas, . 26, 101, 118, 140
Lumbert, Benjamin, . . . 243

Mahuchett Brook, . . . 185
Male children, . . . 312
Manomet High Land, . . 249
" Point, . . 51, 297
" Ponds, 38, 43, 47, 50, 51, 82, 93, 94, 95, 98, 100, 103, 138, 161, 203, 234, 235, 254, 267, 275, 282, 298, 307, 317, 321
Mares, . . . . . 116
Marshfield, . . . . 18
Martin's Vinyard, . . . 91
Matchlock, . . . 14, 44
May, Edward, . . 115, 120, 122
May, John, . . . . 303
May, Nicholas, . 275, 282, 298, 321
Meadows, . . . . 35
Messengers, . . . . 11

# INDEX. 343

Meeting-house, 46, 52, 71, 143, 155, 161, 168, 169, 171, 173, 188, 205, 236 255, 263, 265, 266, 272, 283, 286, 287, 324
Michell, Jacob, . . 78, 90, 217, 321
" Thomas, . . . 121
Middleboro, or Middlebery, 184, 214, 251, 267, 273, 311, 319, 335
Middleboro Agents, . . 254
Middleboro Bounds, . . . 178
Mile and a Half, . . . 296
Mile Rock, . . . 177
Military Companies, . . 214, 215
Military Officers, . 118, 214, 215
Milking Trees, . . . 309
Mill, . . . 41, 53, 98, 309
Mill Brook, . . 127, 129, 139, 172
Minister's Call, . . . 251
Minister's Cattle . . . 164
Minister's House, 45, 47, 52, 54, 58, 72, . 78, 87, 111, 112, 136, 144, 145,
Minister's Lot, . . . 53
Minister's Salary, 106, 113, 115, 123, 124, 126, 141, 146, 150, 154, 157, 160, 161, 164, 165, 166, 171, 175, 190, 191, 195, 205, 206, 240, 246, 251, 255, 264, . . . 286, 316
Ministry, . . . . 303
Ministry Land 289, 291, 296, 318, 335
Mitchell Experience, . . . 1
Moderator, . . . 161, 301
Mohutchett, . . . . 165
Monponsett, 121, 125, 126, 132, 133, 167, . 175, 177, 191, 205, 255, 299, 301
Monponsett Brook, . . 135, 250
Monponsett Meadow, . 122, 142
Monponsett Pond, 59, 89, 92, 94, 122, . . 129, 130, 136, 137, 142
Monument, . . . . 207
Mordow, Mordo, or Murdock, John, or Mr., 199, 204, 206, 215, 223, 224, 235, 237, 238, 240, 241, 248, 256, 258, 263, 274, 275, 287, 289, 306, 317, 319
Mordow's Shop, . . . 248
Morey, Jonathan, 49, 76, 79, 88, 94, 102, 143, 149, 154, 155, 156, 180, 182, 217, 246, 247, 255, 260, 268, 283, 287, . . 289, 301, 302, 303, 308
Morey, Lieut., . . 205, 273, 308
Morton, Deacon, . . . 330
Morton, Eleazer, . 256, 265, 274, 308
" Ensign, . . . 326
" Ephraim, 22, 25, 33, 36, 44, 45, 46, 47, 48, 49, 50, 52, 53, 54, 59, 72, 73, 77, 78, 79, 84, 96, 101, 104, 110, 130 139, 148, 149, 150, 160, 163, 174, 175, 180, 182, 184, 189, 190, 191, 197, 199, 203, 204, 205, 224, 225, 226, 227, 238, 239, 240, 241, 243, 246, 247, 252, 255, 260, 261, 266, 274, 275, 290, 301, 306, . . . 318, 332, 333, 335
Morton, George, 85, 111, 132, 147, 149, 160, 180, 181, 187, 227, 231, 241, 244, 245, 260, 272, 290, 293, 294, 302, 315, . . 324, 325, 330, 331, 332
Morton, John, 2, 16, 21, 25, 33, 36, 49, 50, 52, 68, 71, 73, 74, 77, 79, 83, 86, 88, 101, 115, 122, 128, 157, 161, 182, 207,

208, 214, 224, 246, 247, 248, 250, 256, 257, 269, 273, 282, 283, 286, 293, 305, . . . . 308
Morton, Josiah, . 182, 195, 244
" Josias, . . 102, 293
" Lieut., 57, 58, 80, 82, 83, 86, 90, 91, 92, 98, 105, 106, 107, 111, 112, 115, 116, 118, 122, 123, 124, 125, 132, 136, 139, 143, 145, 146, 147, 150, 151, 152, 153, 157, 161, 162, 163, 165, 167, 168, 169, 170, 171, 173, 174, 176, 177, 184, 185, 186, 190, 193, 199, 201, 204, 226,
Morton, Manasses, . 276, 281, 295
" Nathaniel, 2, 16, 22, 25 32, 33, 37, 38, 44, 47, 49, 51, 53, 54, 59, 69, 73, 75, 76, 77, 80, 84, 86, 91, 97, 101, 102, 106, 107, 110, 113, 116, 123, 125, 127, 139, 140, 141, 148, 151, 160, 163, 166, 170, 182, 208, 211, 212, 215, 216, 226, 228, 241, 244, 246, 247, 251, 252, 253, 257, 259, 264, 266, 267, 275, 280, 282, 285, 291, 293, 294, 295, 296, 298, 299, 300, 301, 304, 307, 308, 311, 318 319, 321, 323, 328, 329, 332, 333, 335
Morton, Thomas, 25, 33, 37, 42, 44, 69, 101, 148, 182, 196, 212, 214, 217, 226, 243, 244, 283, 293, 299, 305, 318, 331, . . . . 332, 333
Morton, Secretary, . . . 232
Moses, John, . . 21, 25, 101, 148
Mount Hope, . . . 168
Munk's Hill, . . . 238, 314
Musket, . . . . 14, 44
Mylam, Samuel, . . . 94, 103

Nahuckett Brook, . 103, 120, 137
Nan Ramsden, . 238, 245, 246, 255
Naponsett Ponds, . . . 115
Nelson, John, 182, 204, 206, 219, 220, 221, 223, 236, 237, 239, 240, 241, 245, . . . 246, 257, 310, 322
Nelson, Samuel, . . . 329, 330
Nelson, Widow, . . . 287
Nelson, William, 3, 14, 19, 21, 23, 25, 27, 28, 29, 33, 36, 62, 70, 80, 89, 101, . . 134, 137, 155, 208, 322
Nelson's Brook, . . . 310
New Mill, . . . 171
New Society, . . . 324
New Street, . . 172, 177, 268
New Street End, . . 186, 265
Nick's Rock, . . . 238
North Street, . . . 268
Nutes, James, . . . 247

Oath of Fidelity, . . . 210
Odizar Bush, . . . 199
Old Prison, . . . 147
Ordinance, . . 11, 146, 147
Ordinaries, . . . 188
Oxen, . . . . 7, 8

Paddock, Robert, . 13, 14, 208
Paddy, Mr., 11, 13, 14, 15, 16, 21, 25, 28, . . . 31, 35, 69
Paddy, Wm., 7, 8, 14, 19, 23, 27, 29, . . 206, 207, 209

# INDEX.

Pallasadoes, . . . . 146
Parting Ways, . . . . 314
Pearce, Abraham, . . . 16
Pew, . . . 270, 282, 303
Phillip, . . . . . 73
Pimkin Bridge, . . . 178
Pine Boards, . . . . 224
Pine Knots, . . . . 119
Pine Trees, . . 302, 309
Plain Dealing, . . 16, 46, 296
Plank, . . . . 224, 270
Plymouth Park, . . . . 284
Plympton, . . . 296, 314
Polapoda Cove, 232, 304, 305, 306, 315
Pontus Meadow, . . 133, 159
Pontus, Wm., . 1, 3, 5, 7, 19, 27
Poor of Plymouth, . . . 3
Pope, Thomas, 2, 14, 22, 25, 36, 48, 65,
. . . . 75, 79, 93, 96, 101
Pope's Neck, . . . . 304
Pope's Point, . . . . 325
Pottle, . . . . . . 13
Pound, . . 133, 186, 268, 275, 283
Pound-keeper, . . . . 333
Pratt, Benajah, 41, 57, 61, 80, 82, 89,
101, 111, 133, 141, 144, 151, 159, 267,
. . . 287, 305, 313, 319
Pratt, Benjamin, . 33, 209, 274, 278
" Eleazer, . . . 302, 305
" John, 182, 186, 201, 204, 209, 266,
. . 274, 285, 296, 305, 324 333
Pratt, Jonathan, 61, 102, 149, 173, 182,
. . . 189, 195, 259, 302
Pratt, Joseph, . . . . 305
" Joshua, 4, 9, 13, 19, 20 22, 26, 27,
. . 63, 149, 181, 207, 208, 241
Pratt, Phineas, . . . . 17
" Samuel, . . . . 335
Prince, Mr., 11, 13, 14, 15, 16, 17, 18,
. . . . . . 19, 72
Prince Thomas, 2, 6, 8, 14, 83, 96, 100,
. . . . . 110, 124
Prince's Bottom, . . 140, 184
Province Courts, . . . 264
Province Rate, . . . . 232
Public Charges, . . . 8, 275
Punckateesett, . . 35, 46, 62, 73

Quarter Sessions, 223, 241, 246, 255,
. . . 282, 293, 294, 298, 323

Rails, . . . . . . 273
Ramsden, Daniel, . . 100, 178
Ramsden, Joseph, . . 21, 24, 65
Ransom, John, . . . . 317
" Robert, 56, 61, 81, 96, 102, 175,
182, 186, 187, 191, 195, 205, 247, 262,
. . . . . 298, 317
Ratable Goods, . . . . 116
Raters, 16, 28, 31, 32, 71, 82, 88, 92, 106,
112, 113, 115, 116, 122, 124, 126, 145,
151, 153, 157, 161, 165, 168, 171, 183,
. . . . 198 202, 240
Rates, 6, 8, 17, 19, 22, 31, 35, 45, 72, 88,
91, 92, 106, 112, 115, 125, 138, 139, 145,
147, 150, 151, 153, 161, 168, 184, 190,
191, 193, 201, 205, 228, 236, 237, 240,

. . . . 255, 272, 311, 324
Rating, . . . 116, 117, 122
Rayner, John, . . . . 41
Records of Lands, . . . 193
Reed Pond, . . . . 91, 310
Regiments, . . . . 214
Rehoboth, . . . . . 39
Relief of Poor, . . . 317, 324
Representatives, 206, 228, 229, 236, 248,
260, 264, 269, 272, 275, 286, 298, 308,
. . . 309, 311, 316, 319, 335
Reyboth, Hill, . . . . 185
Reyner, John, . . . . 252
" Mr., . . 13, 36, 59, 70
Rhode Island, . . . . 35, 46
Rickard, Giles, 25, 26, 31, 33, 36, 59, 61,
62, 63, 64, 73, 74, 77, 78, 84, 88, 89, 101,
117, 122, 127, 128, 129, 141, 144, 148,
152, 153, 181, 182, 188, 205, 207, 228,
239, 240, 244, 247, 257, 263, 276, 277,
. . . . . . 323, 333
Rickard, John, 26, 32, 34, 37, 49, 61, 64,
101, 140, 175, 176, 181, 182, 184, 186,
188, 240, 241, 255, 256, 258, 262, 282,
. 287, 294, 296, 298, 301, 306, 310
Rickard, Widow, . . . . 188
Rickett, Giles, . . 2, 12, 16, 22
Ring, Andrew, 17, 21, 25, 28, 33, 37, 45,
50, 62, 64, 101, 111, 132, 141, 144, 148,
151, 152, 155, 157, 173, 181, 184, 207,
. . . . . . 208, 295
Ring, Eleazar, 205, 228, 232, 241, 257,
266, 283, 293, 305, 308, 309, 318, 325
Ring, Isaac, . . . . 229
Ring, Samuel, . . . . 33
Ring, William, 175, 176, 228, 231, 240,
241, 247, 252, 260, 266, 274, 276, 285,
. . . . 306, 318, 330
Risse, Peter, . . . 120, 133
Robbins, Jeduthan, . . . 305
Roches, . . . . . 273
Rochester, . . . . 215, 263
Rocky Neck Brook, . . . 319
Rocky Nook, 42, 57, 58, 86, 123, 125,
. . . . 235, 242, 286
Rosse, John, . . . . 119
Ryder, or Rider, John, 266, 268, 276,
. . . . 278, 281, 295
Ryder, Samuel, 51, 82, 95, 102, 118,
138, 143, 148, 155, 182, 185, 235, 241,
. . . . 275, 285, 303

Saconnett Lands, . . . 152
Saffin, John, . . . . 111
Sagaquash—Sagaquish, or Saquish, 33,
. . . 106, 186, 197, 331
Salaries, . . . . . 117
Salt, . . . . . 6, 13
Salt House Beach, . . . 89
Salt Water Pond, . 154, 180, 247
Sampson's Country, . . 48, 61
Sampson's Pond, . . . 48
Sampson, Stephen, . . . 290
Samson, George, . . . 210
Samson's Brook, . 263, 291, 293
Samson's Pond, . . 215, 234

# INDEX. 345

| | Page. |
|---|---|
| Sandwich, 49, 53, 56, 61, 80, 83, 88, 154, | 221, 235, 286 |
| Sandwich Herring Pond, | 91, 287 |
| Sandwich Line, | 176 |
| Sandwich Road, | 221 |
| Sandwich Street, | 84 |
| Sandy Hill, | 291 |
| Saquash, | 293 |
| Savory, Anthony, | 9 |
| Savory or Savery, Samuel, | 216 |
| Savory, Thomas, 9, 19, 20, 22, 25, 27, | |
| 28, 37, 48, 59, 96, 101, 169 | |
| Scales and Weights, | 190 |
| School, 124, 141, 245, 303, 333, 334 | |
| Schoolmaster, 115, 224, 245, 246, 270, | |
| 276, 289, 316, 319, 323, 336 | |
| School Rate, | 319 |
| Scituate, | 155 |
| Sealer of Leather, | 333 |
| Sealer of Weights, | 193 |
| Sears, Richard, 265, 274, 285, 308, 309, | |
| | 318 |
| Second Brook, | 177, 287, 294 |
| Sedge Flats, | 303 |
| Sedge Ground, | 317, |
| Selectmen, 75, 82, 83, 106, 111, 124, 125, | |
| 132, 138, 140, 143, 147, 151, 165, 170, | |
| 173, 174, 176, 185, 189, 195, 201, 204, | |
| 205, 223, 228, 235, 241, 247, 256, 264, | |
| 266, 274, 274, 275, 296, 298, 308 | |
| Senter Hill, | 300 |
| Sepecan, 30, 32, 45, 77, 100, 114, 116, | |
| 124, 136, 140, 163, 264 | |
| Sepecan Bounds, | 255 |
| Servant, | 153 |
| Seven, Men, | 30, 31, 32 |
| Shaw, Benoni, | 308, 310 |
| " George, | 257, 274 |
| " Goodman, | 33 |
| " James, | 26, 37, 66 |
| " John, 4, 9, 16, 21, 24, 36, 39, 67 | |
| " Jonathan, 47, 49, 51, 56, 61, 79, | |
| 81, 95, 102, 132, 148, 174, 180, 182, 183, | |
| 185, 191, 195, 197, 201, 204, 205, 228, | |
| 236, 241, 247, 256, 257, 266, 285, 298, | |
| 303, 333 | |
| Shaw's Brook, | 134 |
| Sheep, | 99, 117, 326, 327 |
| Sheep Pasture, | 314, 315 |
| Shepherd's Tent Lot, | 314 |
| Sherive, Thomas, | 21, 34 |
| Shifting Cove, | 41 |
| Shingle, | 59, 114, 172, 225, |
| Shingle Brook, 43, 160, 191, 192, 194 | |
| Shoes, | 13 |
| Shirtleff, or Shirtley, Abiall, 243, 256, | |
| 267, 289, 305, 306, 317, 319, 327, 334, | |
| | 336 |
| Shurtleff, Elizabeth, | 63 |
| " Lt., 286, 287, 293, 295, 317, | |
| | 319, 326 |
| Shurtleff, Thomas, | 275, 308, 318 |
| Shurtleff, or Shirtley, William, 33, 38, | |
| 62, 63, 174, 180, 188, 195, 204, 205, 216, | |
| 223, 224, 225, 228, 229, 232, 235, 236, | |
| 237, 239, 240, 241, 246, 247, 248, 249, | |
| 254, 256, 258, 266, 269, 270, 274, 275, | |

| | Page. |
|---|---|
| 276, 277, 278, 279, 280, 281, 282, 283, | |
| 284, 285, 288, 289, 291, 292, 294, 297. | |
| 298, 299, 300, 301, 304, 305, 306, 310, | |
| 311, 315, 316, 317, 318, 319, 323, 325, | |
| 326, 328, 329, 330, 332, 333, 334 | |
| Skepeunk, | 235 |
| Single Men, | 117 |
| Smalev, John, | 18 |
| Smelt Brook 115, 121, 135, 142, 143, 178 | |
| Smith, or Smyth, John, 13, 18, 21, 22, | |
| 23, 25, 26, 27, 29, 33, 36, 37, 53, 64, 101 | |
| Smith, or Smythe, Mr., | 9 |
| " Mrs., | 9 |
| Smith, Nehemiah, | 2 |
| " Ralph, | 4 |
| " Richard, | 22, 23 |
| " Shuball, | 273 |
| Snaphance, | 14 |
| Snow, Anthony, | 16, 289 |
| " Nicholas, | 16 |
| Soldiers, | 145, 146 |
| Sonett, Samuel, | 307 |
| Soule, Benim, | 264 |
| " Benjamin, 274, 286, 296, 313, 319, | |
| | 333 |
| Soule, George, | 1, 4 |
| " John, | 185 |
| South Country, | 80, 207 |
| South Meadow, 45, 61, 79, 70, 86, 91, 96, | |
| 133, 207, 208, 229, 231, 232, 250, 251, | |
| 253, 258, 259, 260, 263, 276, 277, 278, | |
| 288, 293, 301, 304, 311, 315, 317, 318, | |
| | 324 |
| South Meadow Brook, 89, 277, 284, 285 | |
| South Meadow River, 279, 280, 311, 317 | |
| South Pond, | 291 |
| South Ponds, | 309 |
| South Purchase, | 319 |
| South Pundar, | 319 |
| Souther's Marsh, | 59, 175, 207 |
| Souther's Marsh Brook, | 276, 279 |
| Southworth, Capt., 45, 52, 59, 70, 72, | |
| 73, 77, 78, 79, 82, 130, 243 | |
| Southworth, Lieut., 2, 25, 29, 34, 36, | |
| 42, 282, 283, 286 | |
| Southworth, Mr., | 44 |
| " Nathaniel, 102, 132, 147, | |
| 148, 170, 172, 176, 180, 181, 188, 193, | |
| 195, 200, 204, 214, 223, 224, 225, 237, | |
| 241, 246, 256, 266, 275, 295, 303, 308 | |
| Southworth, Thomas, 13, 14, 15, 16, 18, | |
| 21, 30, 74, 100, 110, 134, 186, 206, 209, | |
| 237, 238, 299, 314 | |
| Sowther, Nathaniel, 4, 14, 15, 16, 18 | |
| Sparrow, Richard, 10, 13, 14, 16, 21, 209 | |
| Sparrow's Hill, | 178, 296 |
| Sparrow's Plain, | 166 |
| Spooner, Wm., | 21, 24, 33, 36, 68 |
| Sprague, Samuel, | 225, 239 |
| Spring Hill, | 215 |
| Squirrel Rock, | 179 |
| Stockbridge, Charles, | 171, 172 |
| Standish, Alexander, | 162 |
| " Miles, | 14 |
| Steers, | 19 |
| Stoddard, Wm. P., | 168 |
| Strangers, | 99, 106, 169, 309 |

23

## 346 INDEX.

Stranger's Money, . . . 316
Strawberry Hill, . . . 177
Stray Sattle, . . . . 216
Sturtevant, John, 181, 188, 197, 201,
204, 206, 214, 223, 224, 225, 228, 236,
238, 240, 246, 256, 264, 275, 285, 287,
. . . 296, 298, 312, 313, 319, 333
Sturtevant, Joseph, . . . 223
Sturtevant, Samuel, 21, 24, 27, 33, 40,
49, 66, 72, 79, 89, 92, 100, 110, 136,
149, 175, 185, 194, 195, 205, 208, 241,
247, 254, 255, 264, 266, 274, 275, 283,
289, 294, 295, 296, 308, 310, 318, 319,
. . . . . . 324, 326, 333
Sturtevant, Widow, . . 132, 254
Superior Court, 224, 256, 266, 285, 296,
. . . . . . . 308, 314
Surveyors, 28, 46, 173, 200, 201, 228,
. . . . . . . . . 234
Surveyors of Highways, 83, 111, 132,
147, 151, 165, 170, 175, 176, 185, 189,
195, 204, 223, 236, 241, 247, 256, 266,
. . 274, 285, 296, 308, 319, 333
Summer Street, . . . . 215
Swan Hold, 50, 81, 82, 96, 127, 169,
. . . . . . . . . 305
Swan Hold Brook, . . . 305
Swine, . . 6, 34, 56, 117, 333, 334
Swing Bridge, . . . . 290
Swords, . . . . 44, 150
Sylvester, Joseph, . . . 303

Tantanega, . . . . 103
Tar, 43, 44, 48, 58, 78, 86, 118, 119, 225
Tar Pits, . . . . . 100
Taspequan's Pond, . . . . 80
Tatoson, . . . . . 116
Tayler, . . . . . 117
Thomas, Mr., . . . 18, 255
Thomas, Nathaniel, 214, 236, 247, 254,
256, 258, 262, 263, 264, 265, 269, 270,
287, 301, 308, 311, 316, 517, 319, 327,
. . . . . 329, 330, 331, 335
Thompson or Tomson, Jacob, 258, 261,
. . . . . . . 301, 312
Thompson, John, 21, 28, 46, 52, 184, 209
" Peter, . . . 288
Tilden, John, . . . . 1
Tilson, Edmond, 9, 18, 19, 22, 34, 37,
. . . 65, 223, 296, 297, 313, 325
Tilson, Ephraim, 97, 102, 103, 147, 149,
. 165, 182, 184, 256, 277, 297, 298
Tilson, Goodman, . . . . 20
" John, . . 119, 324, 325
Timber, 85, 86, 114, 142, 144, 172, 223,
. . . 224, 225, 227, 270, 273
Tincom, Helkiah or Elkiah, 182, 210
" John, . . . 311, 312
Tincome, or Tinkham, Ephraim, 21, 24,
33, 36, 47, 49, 64, 80, 128, 148, 151, 163,
. . . . . . 175, 208, 322
Tincome, Isaac, . . . . 322
Tinkham, Sgt., . . . 91, 112, 147
Tinkham's Meadow, . . . 252
Tithingmen, 229, 239, 241, 256, 266, 274,
. . . . . 285, 308, 318, 333
Tomson, Peter, . . . 307

Town Book, . . . . 193
Town Boundary, . . 177, 186, 262
Town Bridge, . . . . 177
Town Brook, . . . . 232, 236,
Town Charges, . 138, 246, 301, 336,
Town Clerk, 223, 228, 241, 247, 285,
. . . . . 296, 306, 308, 318
Town Council, . . . . 198
Town Debts, . . . . 163, 170
Town Meetings, 3, 5, 6, 7, 8, 11, 12, 13,
14, 15, 16, 17, 18, 19, 20, 21, 24, 28, 29,
31, 32, 33, 45, 46, 47, 48, 52, 55, 58, 59,
60, 70, 71, 77, 78, 83, 86, 87, 90, 91, 97,
99, 104, 105, 111, 112, 113, 114, 115,
116, 118, 122, 123, 124, 125, 126, 132,
136, 138, 139, 140, 141, 144, 146, 147,
150, 151, 153, 154, 155, 156, 157, 160,
162, 163, 164, 165, 166, 167, 168, 169,
170, 171, 172, 173, 174, 175, 176, 183,
184, 185, 186, 188, 189, 190, 191, 195,
197, 198, 200, 201, 202, 203, 204, 205,
206, 223, 224, 228, 232, 235, 236, 237,
239, 240, 245, 246, 247, 248, 249, 250,
251, 254, 255, 256, 260, 262, 263, 264,
265, 266, 267, 269, 270, 272, 273, 274,
275, 282, 283, 285, 286, 289, 291, 294,
296, 298, 301, 304, 305, 306, 308, 309,
311, 313, 316, 318, 323, 326, 328, 329,
. . . . . . 333, 335, 336
Town Pond, . . 266, 303, 317, 328
Town Pond Creek, . . . . 290
Town Records, . . . . 83, 162
Town Treasurer, 239, 241, 247, 256, 264,
. . . . . . . 274, 330
Town's Stock, . . . . 105
Township Line, . . . . 239
Townsmen, . 90, 105, 107, 108, 109
Tracy, Stephen, . . . . 1
Training Day, . . . . 139
Training Green, . . . . 179
Trees, . . . . . . 85
Triangle Pond, . . . . 296
Trout Brook, . . . . 269
Turkey Swamp, . . 49, 79, 80, 81
Turner, Humphrey, . . 303, 328

Upper Society, . 245, 289, 296, 323

Voters, . . . 100, 148, 180

Wadsworth, Christopher, . . 1
" John, . . . 239
Walck, Path, . . . . 183
Wallen, Ralph, . . . 4, 85
Wallen's Wells, . . . . 226
Wampocke, . . . . 41
War, . . . . . 11, 292
Warren, Benjamin, 183, 223, 230, 234,
241, 247, 248, 249, 256, 266, 273, 275,
285, 286, 291, 296, 310, 313, 318, 319,
. . . . . . 324, 326, 333, 335
Warren, Capt., 274, 282, 283, 286, 301,
. . 302, 310, 311, 318, 319, 326
Warren, Elizabeth, . 36, 161, 212
" James, 182, 189, 198, 200, 201,
204, 205, 213, 222, 224, 228, 229, 230,
236, 239, 247, 248, 249, 255, 257, 264,

# INDEX. 347

266, 270, 275, 276, 277, 278, 279, 280,
281, 282, 284, 285, 286, 288, 289, 292,
294, 297, 298, 299, 300, 304, 305, 306,
307, 308, 309, 310, 311, 315, 316, 319,
322, 323, 325, 327, 328, 330, 332, 333,
. . . . . . . 334, 335
Warren, Joseph, 18, 25, 36, 45, 49, 50,
51, 58, 59, 63, 77, 86, 87, 90, 91, 94,
100, 102, 106, 107, 110, 117, 119, 125,
132, 134, 136, 139, 140, 141, 143, 145,
146, 148, 150, 151, 157, 160, 162, 163,
169, 170, 171, 172, 173, 174, 176, 177,
180, 182, 183, 184, 185, 189, 190, 191,
193, 195, 198, 199, 200, 202, 203, 212,
. . . . . 213, 219, 221
Warren, Lieut., . . . 174
" Mrs., . . . 65, 212
" Nathaniel, 22, 25, 31, 33, 36,
41, 44, 45, 46, 48, 50, 53, 54, 59, 60, 64,
72, 73, 77, 78, 79, 82, 83, 84, 85, 86,
102, 161, 183, 212, 266, 275, 276, 286,
. . . 280, 292, 294, 235, 311
Warren, Sarah, . . . 161
" Widow, . . . 184
" Wm., . . . 290
Warren's Wells. . 50, 98, 123, 299
Warren's Wells Brook, . . 293
Warren's Wells Plain. . 173, 226
Washanest, . . . . 172
Washburn, John, . . . 217
Wast, Gate, . . . 114
Watch, . . . . . 15, 48
Watch-house, 11, 15, 16, 17, 146, 147,
. . . 159, 223, 262, 268, 270
Water Course, . . . . 290
Waterman, John, 112, 125, 127, 132,
133, 137, 182, 204, 235, 241, 275, 282,
. . . 283, 285, 296, 315
Watson, Elkanah, 165, 170, 173, 195,
. . . . . 198, 233
Watson, George, 13, 22, 25, 33, 37, 41,
41, 45, 47, 49, 51, 60, 61, 67, 75, 77, 79,
82, 84, 91, 95, 101, 107, 117, 118, 124,
. . 139, 148, 153, 181, 208, 243, 304
Watson, Goodman, . . 207, 208
" John, 275, 292, 298, 316, 318,
. . . . 327, 330, 334, 335
Watson, William, . . . 230
Watson's Cove, . . . . 324
Ways Laid Out, . . . 84
Weavers, . . . . . 117
Wecanucked, . . . . 103
Weekes, John, . . . . 1
Weights and Measures, . . 285
Well, . . . . . 270
Wellingsley, 16, 18, 33, 38, 84, 122, 124,
. . . . . 127, 179
Wellingsley Brook, 77, 153, 265, 267
Wenham, . . 205, 209, 215, 278

West Meddow, . . . 208
Weston, Edmund, . . . 305
Whales, . . . . 119, 200
Wharf, . 204, 240, 241, 265, 286, 287
Whetstones Vinyard, . . . 237
Whitney, Thomas, 22, 25, 34, 37, 48,
. . . . . 68, 101, 124
Whitten, Thomas, . . . 208
Willet, Capt., . . . . 25
" Mr., . . 20, 21, 23, 28
" Thomas, 4, 6, 8, 18, 29, 30, 31,
. . . . 55, 59, 69, 206, 207
William and Mary, . . 192
Williams, Thomas, . . . 18
Willis, Patience, . . . 158
" Richard, 11, 79, 80, 98, 102, 110,
. . . . . 123, 156, 158
Willis, Ruhamah, . . . 189
Winnatucksett, 31, 35, 38, 39, 50, 54,
57, 94, 95, 99, 110, 127, 133, 134, 136,
162, 191, 206, 237, 238, 278, 292, 303
Winnatucksett Brook, . . 133
Winnatucksett Meadows, 55, 104, 139,
. . . . . . 235
Winnatucksett River, 73, 135, 142, 301
Winslow, Edward, . . . 3
" Isaac, . . . 215
" James, . . 183, 285
" John, 6, 8, 11, 12, 17, 21, 31,
. . . . . 36, 83, 206
Winslow, Mr. . . . . 34
Winter, Christopher, . . 20, 24
" Goodman, . . . 33
Wolf, . . . . . 29, 160
Wolf-traps, . . 16, 31, 179, 284
Wolves, . . 30, 32, 154, 165
Wompatuck, Josiah, . . . 186
Wonquonqnany, . . . 273
Wood, . . . . . 85, 142
" Deacon, . 294, 302, 308, 317
" Ephraim, . . . 312
" Henry, 22, 25, 34, 48, 49, 52, 70,
. . . . 76, 79, 101, 208
Wood, John, 6, 13, 21, 25, 34, 37, 65,
. . 75, 95, 101, 117, 141, 157, 208
Wood, Nathaniel, 149, 152, 160, 174,
181, 184, 195, 223, 228, 231, 236, 257,
. . . . . . 266, 325
Wood, Sarah, . . . . 234
" Stephen, . . 17, 22, 208
Worship of God, . . . 254
Wright, Adam, . 282, 306, 321, 323
" Richard, 14, 21, 25, 33, 34, 36,
38, 39, 42, 43, 46, 49, 50, 54, 64, 95,
101, 111, 121, 128, 133, 135, 148, 172,
. . . . . . 181, 208

Young Men, . . . . 138
Young, Wm., . . . . 324

www.ingramcontent.com/pod-product-compliance
Lightning Source LLC
Chambersburg PA
CBHW072133220426
43664CB00013B/2228